T0385724

Advance Acclaim

The Norton Series on Interpersonal Neurobiology
Allan N. Schore, PhD, Series Editor
Daniel J. Siegel, MD, Founding Editor

The field of mental health is in a tremendously exciting period of growth and conceptual reorganization. Independent findings from a variety of scientific endeavors are converging in an interdisciplinary view of the mind and mental well-being. An interpersonal neurobiology of human development enables us to understand that the structure and function of the mind and brain are shaped by experiences, especially those involving emotional relationships.

The Norton Series on Interpersonal Neurobiology will provide cutting-edge, multidisciplinary views that further our understanding of the complex neurobiology of the human mind. By drawing on a wide range of traditionally independent fields of research—such as neurobiology, genetics, memory, attachment, complex systems, anthropology, and evolutionary psychology—these texts will offer mental health professionals a review and synthesis of scientific findings often inaccessible to clinicians. These books aim to advance our understanding of human experience by finding the unity of knowledge, or consilience, that emerges with the translation of findings from numerous domains of study into a common language and conceptual framework. The series will integrate the best of modern science with the healing art of psychotherapy.

The Emotional Foundations of Personality

A Neurobiological and Evolutionary Approach

Kenneth L. Davis and
Jaak Panksepp

Foreword by Mark Solms

W. W. NORTON & COMPANY

New York • London

For information about permission to reproduce selections
from this book, write to Permissions, W. W. Norton & Company, Inc.,
500 Fifth Avenue, New York, NY 10110

For information about special discounts for bulk purchases,
please contact W. W. Norton Special Sales at
specialsales@wwnorton.com or 800-233-4830

Manufacturing by Edwards Brothers Malloy
Production manager: Christine Critelli

ISBN: 978-0-393-71057-1

W. W. Norton & Company, Inc., 500 Fifth Avenue, New York, N.Y. 10110
www.wwnorton.com

W. W. Norton & Company Ltd., 15 Carlisle Street, London W1D 3BS

1 2 3 4 5 6 7 8 9 0

Contents

Preface and Acknowledgments

Jaak Panksepp needs to be the first words written in this book. He was the inspiration for the book. Indeed, it was his idea for me to write a book applying his years of affective neuroscience research to personality, an area that had interested him, but the ever-pressing demands on his time would not allow him the opportunity to do so on his own. He first suggested the idea at one of the "get away" seminars that Doug Watt had organized. Jaak and I had previously developed the Affective Neuroscience Personality Scales, but I would likely have never embarked on such an ambitious journey without Jaak's encouragement. As the project developed, it became a great privilege to write chapters and work with Jaak as we polished and reworked the content.

But let there be no mistake, Jaak is the central figure in this story, which really began with his insight as a gifted undergraduate psychology student that understanding emotions was the key to understanding people, both their personalities and their pathologies. As his career developed (research that spanned nearly 50 years), Jaak worked with many students and colleagues too numerous to mention to assemble what eventually amounted to a theoretical fortress of evidence (Jaak preferred to speak about evidence rather than proof) that human behavior was built upon a bedrock of emotions that had evolved over millions of years. Perhaps more than anyone else, Jaak Panksepp advanced the nearly 150-year-old Darwinian dictum that "The difference in mind between man and the higher animals, great as it is, certainly is one of degree and not of kind."

This son of Estonian immigrants to the United States became a tireless advocate that, like humans, other animals subjectively experience feelings and are psychologically motivated by them. Guided by their affective experiences, they are active players in their environments and not robotic automatons. His collective research documented supporting neurochemical and neuroanatomical emotional cross-species homologies, especially between humans and other mammals that led to many therapies and novel insights into the human condition.

In *Emotional Foundations*, we try to tell Jaak's story, for the first time, from a personality perspective and try to do it with less technical detail than his previous books. The story explores how affective neuroscience causal (not merely descriptive or correlational) research relates to human motivations and actions and thereby to consistently recognizable patterns of individual behavior, namely, our personalities. Our goal was to share an affective neuroscience personality narrative that would appeal to a broad audience, from those simply interested in exploring personality, to students who were looking for an approach to personality from a neuropsychology/evolutionary point of view, and to professionals—from personality theorists to psychiatrists, psychotherapists, and veterinarians—interested in reading a broad "Pankseppian" interpretation of personality issues.

Sadly, Jaak did not live to see the many hours of work he put into each chapter of our book actually reach print. However, thanks to Deborah Malmud and the staff at W. W. Norton, *Emotional Foundations* has been refined and formatted to their standards such that Deborah Malmud can now take credit for shepherding two Jaak Panksepp books through to the public including, of course, this last book-length project.

Jaak was my teacher. He became my intellectual anchor. Writing this book was like taking a multi-year seminar with him, almost like doing a postdoc. The remarkable breadth and depth of his knowledge revealed itself in every chapter. His awesome intellect was difficult to challenge. Yet, he never belittled my efforts, and I only remember a single time he criticized me and that was for "getting too far ahead of the data."

However, Jaak was not the only teacher who facilitated my personal journey. At Earlham College, Dr. Jerry Woolpy, known for his work socializing wolves, took me under his wing by nurturing my budding interest in cross-species studies, and he was responsible for identifying an opportunity to become one of John Paul Scott's students at Bowling Green State University. Dr. Scott was at the peak of his eminent career in comparative animal behavior and luckily took me on as his student and was able to offer personal and financial support through most of my graduate days. Dr. Bob Conner, who eventually became the chairman of the Bowling Green psychology department, was another of those generous intellects who somehow managed to work as hard as you did on whatever project needed his attention and served on my graduate committee. However, it was Jaak who took me on as his student after Dr. Scott retired and gave me my first real glimpse of affective neuroscience as he guided me through my dissertation on the "Opioid Control of Canine Social Behavior."

There are a few others whose support I would like to acknowledge. Anesa Miller, Jaak's wife, and a published poet and writer in her own right, often went beyond tolerating to even encouraging my visits to their home that on occasion dominated their weekends but which also were critical to my continuing education, as well as the rewriting and reorganizing of book chapters. Another Panksepp student, Larry Normansell, provided extensive support in developing the Affective Neuroscience Personality Scales. Dave Gilmore, a good friend, who also helped collect early ANPS data as well as providing support at various times during the writing process.

My children, Matt, Jennifer, and Megan have been consistently supportive and encouraging, even providing good suggestions from time to time. Yet, it is my wife, Nancy, more than anyone else who lived through the many years of writing and rewriting *Emotional Foundations*. Through what must have sometimes seemed endless, she remained supportive and encouraging, often reading my latest efforts and offering helpful comments.

Ken Davis
November 30, 2017

Foreword

Mark Solms

THE APPROACH TAKEN to personality in this book is revolutionary. It builds upon decades of careful research, not only concerning the development and application of the Affective Neuroscience Personality Scales themselves (work which is already being extended by scientists around the world, myself included), but also concerning the monumental program of neuroscientific research upon which the Scales were based. This program of research, itself revolutionary, was conducted by Jaak Panksepp and his students (among whom Ken Davis may be prominently counted). The research builds upon earlier work conducted by such pioneers as Walter Hess and Paul Maclean, starting in the 1920s already. In fact, their work can ultimately be traced all the way back to the seminal observations of Charles Darwin, who dared to suggest that we human beings are after all just another species of animal.

To say that the approach taken to personality in this book is revolutionary is not to say that it is wild or surprising. It is common-sensical and obvious. But this can only be said in retrospect, now that the work has been done. It required the insight of Ken Davis and Jaak Panksepp to see the yawning gap in this field, and then to fill it with the evidence for the new personality assessment instrument they provide in this book. With the book now published, however, it becomes obvious to the rest of us that this is the most sensible way (by far) to classify and measure the basic building blocks of the human personality.

When I say that theirs is the only sensible way to proceed, I must add that we could not have done so before now. The knowledge that was accumulated through the research program of Jaak Panksepp mentioned above was a necessary prerequisite, before Ken Davis and he could do the obvious regarding personality. What I mean is that it is obvious that the classification and measurement of personality must be predicated upon an identification of the "natural kinds" that constitute the actual building blocks of personality; but what are those "natural kinds?" The research upon which this book is based (research that was grounded in deep brain stimulation studies and pharmacological probes, which revealed the elementary emotional circuits of the mammalian brain, and then traced the same circuits—in the same structures, mediated by the same neurochemicals—in the human brain) provides us with nothing less than an answer to this fundamental question.

What could be more valuable for mental science than that?

It may be confidently predicted that the re-conceptualization of personality reported in this book will be followed by a revolution of equal importance (if not greater importance) in the classification and measurement of mental disorders. Just as the instruments that preceded the Affective Neuroscience Personality Scales relied upon taxonomies of personality that were generated by blind statistical measures of its superficial features (or worse, culturally and linguistically mediated self conceptions of those features), so too the classification and measurement of psychiatric *disorders* is embarrassingly arbitrary—grounded in and confounded by the history and conventions of the discipline, rather than empirically based understanding of how the emotional brain really works.

This book heralds a new era of personality research, but there is much more to come from the approach it adopts. It shows the promise of affective neuroscience for the psychiatry, psychology and psychotherapy of the future.

The Emotional Foundations
of Personality

Introduction

Personality and Basic Human Motivation: Prime Movers

But "feel" is a verb, and to say that what is felt is "a feeling" may be one of those deceptive common-sense suppositions inherent in the structure of language. . . . To feel is to do something. . . .

Feeling stands, in fact, in the midst of that vast biological field which lies between the lowliest organic activities and the rise of mind. . . . It is with the dawn of feeling that the domain of biology yields the less extensive, but still inestimably great domain of psychology.

—Susanne K. Langer, *Mind: An Essay on Human Feeling*

IN SEARCH OF FUNDAMENTAL
CAUSES OF PERSONALITY

WHY IS IT THAT each of us can be described by a set of traits that can almost be used as a behavioral fingerprint? The fascination with knowing personality profiles has spawned a multibillion dollar personality testing industry (*Economist*, 2013, citing Nik Kinley, a coauthor of *Talent Intelligence* [Kinley & Beh-Hur 2013]). But beyond just describing our behavior, why does one person consistently behave differently than another? What actually causes our behavior? What prods us out of a state of inertia toward any particular goal-directed activity? Moreover, what would we be like without some spark, some prod that could spur us to action—a primary mover that could motivate and guide our behavior?

One hint regarding our prime movers comes from research showing that damage to specific emotional brain structures, with such daunting names as the *medial forebrain bundle* (Clark, 1938; Teitelbaum &

Epstein, 1962; Coenen, Panksepp, Hurwitz, Urbach, & Mädler, 2012) and
the *periaqueductal gray* (Bailey & Davis, 1942, 1943; Depaulis & Bandler, 1991), results in a profound loss of motivation and a condition of
helplessness. Due to extreme self-neglect, including even lack of eating
and drinking, these subjects require intensive care to keep them alive.
It is significant that both of these brain structures are deeply embedded
in evolutionarily ancient parts of the brain intimately related to primary
process emotions and to motivations, because these two concepts overlap enormously.

That these brain structures are so deeply rooted in our evolutionary past suggests that Mother Nature (meaning the process of evolution) had to answer a basic motivation question early in the evolution
of animal life: What would move an animal to action? It is through better understanding of these primary ancestral motivations linked to our
ancestral origins that we can more fully appreciate why we feel and act
the way we do.

On safari in Africa, if one is fortunate enough to observe a pride of
lions, after the initial excitement of such an opportunity one is struck
by how inactive the lions are most of the day. One can watch them for
hours and see little else than adult lions swishing away flies and lion
cubs playing with each other. Is it possible that what one observes lions
doing (or not doing) most of the day until they head out for their nightly
hunt is the default mammalian state, and if it were not for homeostatic
motivations such as hunger and the primary emotions, we would likely
lack focused goal-oriented activity?

However, beyond just describing behavior, the essential question for
a discussion of personality is, What prods us to act in the ways we do?
Why do human babies and puppies try to climb out of their playpens
when all their physical and emotional needs seem to be generously provided through maternal care? What causes us to be so easily focused on
a crying baby? What makes children expend so much energy chasing
each other about with no apparent purpose?

SUBCORTICAL EMOTIONAL AFFECTIVE
SYSTEMS ARE CAUSAL MECHANISMS
UNDERLYING PERSONALITY

It is our position throughout this book that, without an understanding
of the psychobiological systems underpinning our feelings and actions,
our understanding of the motivations behind our behavior is limited
to obvious verbal pronouncements, and we may be restricted to just
describing behavior, as linked to environmental contingencies, rather
than explaining it. (Just describing rather than explaining it is what the
Anglo-American behaviorists tried to convince the rest of psychology

was quite enough; indeed, they at times argued that in their scheme the study of the brain was not really necessary.) For some purposes, regularly observing how caring a person is in his or her interactions toward other people may suffice, and even the observation of other animals may provide us with enough knowledge to reliably describe past behavior and perhaps predict future interactions. (In a sense this was the behaviorist perspective on what needed to be studied.) However, we are still left without an understanding about the *causal* mechanisms underlying this person's gentle interactions with others. It is our premise that all the emotional affective systems that evolution (or Mother Nature, to use the most common metaphor) constructed within the subcortical brain are the primary causal mechanisms underlying our personalities that consistently guide emotional and other motivated actions. In the colorful words of the epigraph's author, they are evolved affective designs for having "a psychical entity pushing a physical one around" (Langer, 1988, p. 4). Furthering our understanding of these prime movers will enable progress in psychology and psychiatry.

Affective neuroscience, the study of our *subcortical* affective Brain-Mind,[1] has begun to clarify these prime movers—what Freud called the id, his supposedly unconscious foundation for the conscious mind. Now we know that this subcortical terrain of mind is not deeply unconscious (Solms & Panksepp, 2012), but it is a primal mind that can make snap decisions to various life challenges almost instantaneously without the need for reflective thought. For example, imagine yourself on a lovely day peacefully hiking through the woods. Suddenly seeing a large snake just ahead of you would generate immediate fear in most people. It is likely that the closer the snake is to you at that moment, the more intense your alarm would be. If the danger is imminent, your subcortical brain will likely halt all your other activity and prompt you to immediately seek a safer distance, from which you may again become more reflective—at which point some would attempt to observe the snake more carefully and determine whether it is poisonous and how it behaves. That is, you will return to using your upper brain to cognitively evaluate what you are seeing.

The initial fear response is an example of a prediction, made largely by the subcortical brain, namely, that you are in danger—spotlighting an immediate survival issue. Your brain made this prediction automatically without any conscious analysis or effort on your part. As a result of this ancestral prediction, your brain concurrently created a fearful emotion and *motivated* a specific type of action. Regardless of how relaxed and pleasant you were feeling as you were enjoying your hike, this fearful event charged your whole being with strong emotion and set in place many bodily reactions, including the compelling urge to move away, to seek safety, without needing any intervening cognitive reflections.

This scenario is an example of an evolved response pattern—a prime mover—that helps us avoid physical harm to our bodies. This response pattern does not need to be learned. Somehow, all primates, indeed most mammals, not just humans, are instinctively afraid of snakes and have subcortical brains innately equipped to identify snakes as life-threatening dangers. From a personality perspective, once your brain has made the prediction that there is a dangerous snake in your path, it sets off a series of adaptive actions and feelings to ensure your safety and even survival. The feeling may temporally lag the action, prior to conditioning, but it is still an unconditioned flight response of our FEAR/Anxiety system (more on this below) that probably evolved as a mental heuristic, which can extend an anticipatory attitude in time and space. The brain mechanisms that generate such valenced feelings may constitute what behaviorists, without any perceived need for brain research, called reinforcements (Panksepp & Biven, 2012).

In any event, FEAR (the use of all caps indicates a formal name for an evolved emotional brain system) is an example of one of the *primary movers*, one of the evolved elements in the mammalian brain that can break our behavioral inertia and excite our entire being to action. As you walked along the path, you were probably not actively looking for snakes. However, your vigilant brain spied the animal and automatically set off a series of adaptive responses that included sparking you to action. Your action was not set off by conscious intention—it was instinctive and reflexive. And it also *felt* like something and hence can be used as a model for those "ancestral voices" that move us out of our resting state into active coherent behavior.

This example briefly illustrated the brain's FEAR system. A key part of this emotional system being aroused is the feeling of fear. Somehow, our subcortical brain has evolved a way for us to experience this feeling of fear as strongly aversive, even punishing, something to terminate as soon as possible. The FEAR emotion was not learned. In some manner that is yet to be fully understood, it is built in as part of our brain's intrinsic tools for living so that the primary feeling of fear itself never fundamentally changes over the course of our entire lives, even though it can come to be regulated in space, time, and intensity as it becomes associated with various life events. FEAR also never loses its capacity to provoke an urge to act, even though at less intense levels of arousal FEAR can motivate us to "freeze" in place.

The arousal of the FEAR system alters our thoughts and perceptions as well. After seeing a dangerous snake on the trail and being intensely frightened, we will likely become more cognitively attuned to spotting snakes. We may even spot a snake when there is no snake, just a tree branch on the trail that looks a little like a snake. Likewise, our minds may fill with thoughts about venomous snakes we have read about or heard about on television, some with venom that can kill in a very short time. We may recall vague memories about how to recognize the distinctive diamond-shaped head of most poisonous snakes. We may also make plans of what to do if actually bitten by a snake and vow to come better prepared if ever hiking this trail, or any potential snake habitat, again.

Many kinds of learning can be motivated by this system, but the important point is that FEAR is an example of a prime mover, one of the archetypal emotional brain systems that strongly shape our behavior and, for our purposes here, define aspects of our personality usually measured in humans by asking appropriate questions (i.e., personality tests).

Life is full of fear-provoking situations. Importantly for a discussion of personality, some of us are more sensitive than others to these fear-provoking events. Some would feel quite apprehensive about venturing into a forest in the first place. Few have the courage to attempt rock climbing up the steep side of El Capitan at Yosemite (the fifth ever "free ascent" was completed by Jorg Verhoeven in 2014). Indeed, some would intensely dislike walking through a strange part of town, especially at night, and especially alone. On the other hand, others of us are not so easily frightened and are much less likely to be inhibited by such challenges. It is these kinds of emotional differences that give rise to unique personalities by motivating and guiding our diverse action tendencies so consistently from day to day. These individual differences in the sensitivities of our emotional brain systems lead each of us to experience the world differently and therefore to respond differently, resulting in our recognizable individual personalities. To varying degrees, depending to a great extent on our inherited makeup, our emotions move us out of our resting state. They are the prime movers of personality.

PRIME MOVERS ALSO GUIDE LEARNING

Importantly, these instinctive emotional brain systems are not fixed and immutable. Again, using the FEAR system as an example, while the *feeling* of fear itself does not change, *what* we fear does change. Indeed, the FEAR system, like each of our brain's emotion systems, learns spontaneously without any conscious effort on our part. The feeling of fear can be psychologically very punishing; still, fear is an important part of how we learn to adapt to a changing world. Although we have no innate fear of knives, we quickly learn knives can cut our skin and injure our bodies, but we also learn to use such tools as we need to cut into things. And, of course, we naturally learn how dangerous knives can be in the hands of a menacing individual who wants to hurt us. We can also learn less fearful responses to snakes. We can learn how ecologically beneficial snakes are in the control of rodents, and we can learn how to pin a snake's head with a forked stick and handle it safely, and even "milk" the venom out of its fangs—a skill surely acquired more readily by those who begin life with a less arousable FEAR system. Such lack of fearfulness can be inherited, along with the variations in all the other basic emotions, as has been indicated by abundant selective breeding research in animals.

So, in addition to being our motivators and guides, emotions are also our teachers. There are other primary emotional affects, such as the pleasant, warm feelings we experience when we care for babies and help others in need. Collectively, the punishing and rewarding qualities of these primary emotional affects help us learn about the idiosyncrasies of the world. They are the rewards and punishments that help us adapt to an ever-changing environment. Without these pleasant and unpleasant *affects*—the learning-facilitating function of our primary emotions, we might be locked into acting as if we continued to live in the ecological niche our ancestors evolved in. We would function like fruit flies that instinctively fly toward the light regardless of whether that light is the sun or an ultraviolet insect trap. Unlike coyotes, we would be unable to learn to avoid killing and eating sheep in areas where farmers bait coyotes with dead sheep carcasses laced with nauseating chemicals. And, unlike the proverbial fox, we would never learn to take advantage of the fact that humans have also domesticated the chicken.

Our primal emotional strengths and weaknesses endow us with the foundation of our various human personalities, beginning with an inherited base, which is adapted in many ways as we mature and learn from life experiences. We experience our emotions at various affective levels, from subtle moods shifts to full-blown RAGE or PANIC reactions. They are always ready to move us to action, and it is these ancestral emotions, evolved over millions of years, that we must learn more about to better understand why we act and feel and generally experience the world as we do. These systems are the foundations of our personality structures, but a great deal of complexity is added by learning—to a point where we can assess human personalities by simply asking the right psychological assessment questions, rather than having to focus merely on large-scale bodily behaviors, vocalizations, and various autonomic responses of our sympathetic and parasympathetic nervous systems.

THE BASIC STUDY OF EMOTIONS

Jaak Panksepp, the second author, recognized early in his career that powerful emotional drivers such as desire, anger, fear, and feelings of loneliness were keys to understanding our personality differences and even the sources of some of our major psychopathologies, especially mania, excessive anger, anxiety disorders, and depression. As a result, in the mid-1960s he began his psychological research in the nascent specialty of physiological psychology, exploring the subcortical emotional systems embedded in the evolutionarily older parts of our brains—a field founded on the work of Walter Hess starting in the late 1920s, with Paul MacLean adding important observations a generation later, names we will revisit shortly. With the technical tools that were emerging to study the actual workings of the brain, especially deep brain stimulation (DBS), Panksepp began to study the mammalian brain and its evolved emotional systems.

Panksepp first described four distinct brain emotion systems, SEEK-ING (a generalized form of appetitive-exploratory-foraging desire), RAGE (anger), FEAR, and PANIC (aka separation distress), weaving them into one of the first global psychobiological theories of emotions (Panksepp, 1982). However, he shortly realized that there were at least three more of these blue ribbon systems: sexual LUST, maternal CARE, and juvenile PLAY. We believe that these subcortical brain emotion systems are the tools nature has evolved to move us to action and, with the possible exception of LUST, form the emotional drivers that lie at the foundation of our personalities and psychopathologies.

Early on, personality theorists including Sigmund Freud and Gordon Allport also realized there had to be biological mechanisms underlying our personalities and psychological imbalances—"neurophysiological brain causes" in the case of Freud and "psychophysiological systems" in the case of Allport. But, as impressive as their careers were, technology had not yet provided psychological researchers with the experimental tools for studying such brain intricacies. So, despite their interest in the biological explanations of personality, both Freud and Allport chose to pursue psychological analyses along with clinical therapeutic approaches to understanding human behavior.

A great many investigators laid the foundations for and have contributed to our slowly accelerating efforts to understand emotions and other feelings, which with modern human brain imaging (functional magnetic resonance imaging and positron emission tomography studies; see Chapter 16) has now reached a fever pitch. However, two pioneers, Walter Hess in the first third of the twentieth century and Paul MacLean in the second third, were especially eminent in advancing neuroscientific approaches to tease out parts of the emotional puzzles encapsulated in the subcortical regions of mammalian brains. Hess explored the technique of probing ancient areas deep in the center of the brain with DBS—tiny electric currents to reveal what areas were linked to specific emotional responses such as rage/anger. MacLean pursued an evolutionary approach to the "limbic" anatomy of the brain. He envisioned the brain to be a layered organ with more evolutionarily recent areas (neocortex) surrounding middle layers (the basal ganglia, or "limbic system," as he called it), layered on top of even more evolutionarily ancient areas (the upper brain stem, consisting of thalamus, hypothalamus, and mid-brain), which guided the actions of the lower brain stem and spinal cord.

The "limbic" approach to emotions, although not much used by modern neuroscientists, described areas in the human brain that could be traced to "lower" mammals, from monkeys and rats to even reptiles and fish. One could actually see the work of evolutionary changes within the brain, much more than any other bodily organ. There were newer mammalian structures (cortex) layered on top of old mammalian ones (limbic system), with reptilian foundations still evident as investigators studied all species they could lay their hands on.

There were also evolutionarily more recent areas of the cortex that were indeed unique to humans, and ever since the philosopher-psychologist William James wrote his remarkable *Principles of Psychology* in the late nineteenth century and speculated that feelings emerged from our higher neocortical brain regions, many psychologists (even some neuroscientists who should know better) have speculated that our emotional feelings arise from cortical activities—brain regions that are critical for our ability to think. But they are wrong, even as it is clear that those higher brain regions can regulate our behaviors and thinking in ways that most other animals cannot imagine.

Panksepp blended these clinical therapeutic and neuroscientific evolutionary traditions utilizing additional neuroscience tools such as precise pharmacological methods to continue picking the lock on what some called the "black box," a metaphor for the brain intended to suggest the futility of exploring the deeper biological causes of behavior hidden in the brain itself. Indeed, the neuroscience revolution had begun in the early twentieth century, and tantalizing questions could begin to be asked—even though all answers are provisional—questions that often suggested additional questions, many of which cannot yet be answered. In any event, many, many more generations of enthusiastic empirical brain investigators will undoubtedly be required to generate fully satisfactory answers to the secrets of human behavior and the various instinctive and learned drivers of our individual personalities.

However, in this volume we make the case that the primal brain processes that control our affective arousals, so important for constructing learning and memory, can provide a foundational understanding of our personalities. Thus, the seven *blue ribbon emotions* (Grade A evolutionary prizes all mammals inherit) ——illuminated by the work of Panksepp and his colleagues (perhaps excluding LUST from the list of seven) provide an experimentally verifiable theory of shared personality foundations in both humans and other animals: they are the prime movers of our interactions with our world that shape our personalities. Even the word *emotion* itself suggests such an approach. The etymological roots of emotion are "out" plus "move" or "to move out"—for our purposes, to move out of a resting state into diverse and coherent adaptive behaviors that, based on millions of years of evolution, have a high probability of dealing effectively with whatever life-challenging events we are facing. Emotions provide an affectively rich action readiness, along with thought and memory facilitation, that helps structure what kind of individual we become based on both heredity and individual life trajectories.

ENCAPSULATED AFFECTIVE
NEUROSCIENCE THEORY OF PERSONALITY

The affective neuroscience theory of personality proposes that we are born with various *endophenotypes*: primary emotional-affective personality profiles generated initially from our individual genomes. That is, our personalities arise through our endophenotypes, which are constructed from these primal emotional brain systems that provide our capacities not only to act but also to act consistently over time, without needing any conscious effort on our part, and that also promote affectively regulated patterns of learning and memory, allowing for diverse adaptations to life events.

Our primary emotions with their built-in affects and reaction tendencies can be thought of as birthright survival systems. In urgent survival situations, they move us to react in ways that have worked effectively for countless generations of ancestors. In less urgent situations they still bias our perceptions and actions, generate both constant and coherent streams of thoughts, and add value and meaning to our experiences through the positive and negative feelings they generate. Our primary emotions begin as *unconditional responses* (the behaviorist term for instincts) to stimuli arising from life-challenging circumstances, but they are continuously revamped as they control and guide learning, and hence memory formations and retrievals—brain mechanisms that also operate automatically, but in those cases completely unconsciously. In addition, emotional arousals always have feeling states associated with them, which may be the first form of consciousness that emerged on the face of the earth (Panksepp, 2007a, 2009), providing a solid foundation for all the rest (Panksepp, 2015; Solms & Panksepp, 2012).

Along with learning and memories, these emotional systems guide our behavior over a lifetime in ways that are sufficiently consistent that each of us can be accurately described by personality dimensions—our personal endophenotype. Our developing endophenotype is sufficiently complex that we are not completely predictable. Yet, there is a day-to-day sameness in our behavioral interchanges with the other humans, animals, objects, and circumstances we encounter that our endophenotypes provide: a modus operandi that is recognizable to those around us such that others will remark when we are "not being ourselves," "out of sorts," or "just acting," so to speak.

Why do we do anything at all, let alone in a consistent way that is recognizable to all who know us well? It is our primary-process psychobehavioral abilities, our prime movers, that arise from our subcortical brain's primary emotional action systems that move us out of our resting state into coherent behavior patterns, which if adequately understood could be seen as our endophenotype's optimal ways of trying to cope with life challenges, with further refinements being added by our learning mechanisms and thereby individual memories.

These blue ribbon emotions provide a window into our deeper, some may say "true," nature. We all experience the world through the lenses of these emotions. And understanding how strong or weak an influence each of these emotions has on our personal ways of feeling, thinking, and behaving is a good first step toward understanding ourselves. If we resolve to make needed adjustments in our lives, basing our efforts on an understanding of our deeper nature is likely to make our attempts more fruitful. In a sense, we are all survivors of the same evolutionary seas, cruising in similar boats, but in many different lakes, with slightly different patterns of affective winds in our sails. These winds are distinct personality dimensions, and a key that has been missing in personality theory is a credible cross-species neuroscientific foundation of those personality dimensions. That is why we developed the Affective Neuroscience Personality Scales and have written this book.

CHAPTER 1

The Mystery of
Human Personality

We need to be agnostics first and then there is some chance at arriving at a sensible system of belief.

—D. Elton Trueblood
20th-century American Quaker author and philosopher

As you read this book, you will be exposed to a view of human personality from a distinctly new vantage. If you are a seasoned student of personality, we hope you can briefly put aside your previous training in personality theory and suspend judgment for a while, for you may appreciate a novel approach to personality contained within these pages—one that arises from the study of the primal (evolved) emotional systems of mammalian brains rather than the diverse personality traits enshrined in the study of human languages. In any case, we hope you will find the present approach fresh and challenging, for here we focus on personality, perhaps for the first time, from the perspective of the actual neurobiologically ingrained emotional systems of mammalian brains (even though there are others who have *conceptually* initiated such endeavors—Robert Cloninger (2004), Richard DePue (1995), and Jeffrey Gray (1982) come easily to mind).

Of course, emotionality has traditionally been seen as the foundation of personality. That is, the classic view was based on the supposition that various presumed bodily forces (humors) that control our moods were the foundation of our temperaments. According to medieval scholars of personality, some people are *sanguine*, basically happy and easygoing, while others are *choleric*, easily irritated and willing to show their anger. Some are *phlegmatic*, slow, ponderous, and uninteresting (basically cold fish), and yet others are *melancholic*, chronically sad and depressed.

Various later approaches to personality were based on clinical experiences and insights, because many of the early personality theorists were therapists and psychiatrists (see examples in Chapter 5). Their patients were primarily people with serious behavioral and/or emotional problems, so it was natural for these early personality theorists to try to distinguish their patients on the basis of temperamental differences and to assign them to diagnostic categories. By the late nineteenth and early twentieth century, Emil Kraepelin (1856–1926) had compiled a taxonomy of psychological "diseases" based on medical diagnostics derived from distinct patterns of psychologically evident symptoms. One of the diagnoses Kraepelin is well known for is schizophrenia, which he originally labeled dementia praecox, or premature dementia or precocious madness, because it usually began in the late teens or early adulthood.[2]

If you are a therapist, physician, psychiatrist, or some other medical professional, we note that this book does not focus on using personality or personality tests to try to diagnose psychiatric problems or personality disorders, even though it may provide insights to understanding people with diverse mental problems. It is more about trying to explore the ancestral neural roots of personality, what personality means, and to gain a deeper appreciation for the individual differences that make each of us human beings on this planet not only unique but also inheritors of emotional ways of being in the world that are reflected in characteristic personalities. When extreme, such personality traits can be seen to reflect psychiatrically significant personality tendencies. As we describe in several chapters, neurogenetic findings are providing abundant support for ingrained emotional foundations for human and animal personalities. Such emerging knowledge will eventually change the way we understand human personalities as well as psychiatric disorders.

The science of psychiatry is experiencing a crisis of confidence in traditional psychiatric diagnostic categories, which was illustrated with the unveiling of the fifth edition of the *Diagnostic and Statistical Manual of Mental Disorders* (*DSM-V*; American Psychiatric Association, 2013). Many psychiatrists still believe that such diagnostic traditions, which arose from the way physicians learned to describe characteristic bodily disorders in the middle of the nineteenth century, are essential for progress in the field. This transformation toward a systematic classification of mental disorders, inspired by a coterie of physicians in Germany called the Berlin Biophysics Club, aimed to establish medicine on a solid scientific foundation. However, there is a growing consensus that this might not have been the best way to proceed with the diversity of mental disorders that psychiatrists currently deal with. Recognizing that we really have no good evidence for homogeneous types of brain problems that underlie many psychiatric diagnostic labels (including autism, depression, schizophrenia, and most especially personality disorders), many favor falling back on simply using consistent symptoms, namely, fundamental psychophysiological signs (the so-called endophenotypes) that may reflect the changing activities of distinct brain circuits, as a better way to approach human personality and psychiatric problems, in ways that can be scientifically linked to distinct brain systems.

Of course, the ongoing debate on the nature of human personality and the value of diagnostics in psychiatry is by no means resolved. Disagreements and debate are bound to remain with us for a long time, especially in psychiatry, because conceptual categories provide useful ways to standardize ways to prescribe increasingly large numbers of drugs that are becoming readily available to treat the various *DSM*-specified psychiatric categories. Regrettably, the range in medicinal effects varies enormously, and only a few have been developed by trying to model the relevant shifts in affective states in animals (for recent summaries, see Panksepp, Wright, Döbrössy, Schlaepfer, & Coenen, 2014; Panksepp & Yovell, 2014; Panksepp, 2015, 2016).

We do not delve into this active area of debate but note that the relationship between the psychiatric profession and pharmaceutical companies has solidified to such an extent that it would take a great deal of scientific data to change established practices. Robert Whitaker's frank critique and hard-hitting condemnation of this area of medicine (see Whitaker, 2010) has emerged from the recognition that many current mind medicines often precipitate mental/personality problems other than the ones clients started with. Indeed, medicinally induced shifts in the chemistries of mind can provoke strong "opponent processes" that gradually destabilize chemistries to such an extent that feelings of normality can no longer be achieved. We return to psychiatric issues toward the end of this book in Chapter 18. Our immediate goal is to focus on the normal variability of human personality arising from the diverse characteristics of our core emotional systems and to discuss how this knowledge can help us better understand ourselves.

It is hard to define what is psychologically normal. Obviously there are many cultural and other environmental variables that impact development, but neuroscientists are revealing that it is partly based on the emotional strengths and weaknesses we are born with—variation arising from the brain manifestations of one's genetic heritage, which are typically further shaped by individual experiences. As we describe in this book, this perspective has been amply affirmed through the identification of many genetic predispositions for diverse personality traits. But because every baby confronts the "booming, buzzing" confusions of its surrounding social world, to borrow William James's terms for newborn mental life, we also have to pay attention to how genes are influenced by environments. The concept of epigenesis captures the simple fact that environmentally induced influences on gene expression are as influential in the construction of stable personality as one's heredi-tary endowment of genes (see Chapter 15). The stability of these early influences, as expressed in the construction of basic brain circuits that control emotional feelings—more so than other affects, for example, bodily sensory and homeostatic ones—are the very bedrock of personal-ity development. These are what modern biological psychiatrists would call the endophenotypes of the mind—the natural affective processes that guide the individualized paths of learning and memory. Indeed, not all of the types of feelings we are born with, neither the sensory ones (sweet delights and dreadful disgusts) nor the bodily homeostatic urges experienced as hunger and thirst, are as influential as the emotional systems that exist inside our brains, conveying various basic affective feelings, the strengths and weaknesses of which constitute, we suggest, the most influential brain endophenotypes for personality development.

OUR THEORETICAL ORIENTATION

Each human being is unique. Our faces and voices easily identify us as individuals. We now know that each of us is endowed, by heredity, with our own unique genetic patterns. Even identical twins develop dif-ferences over their life-span, through epigenetic effects, as well as, of course, learning (Fraga et al., 2005). While it might initially be more obvious that our physical features are different, it is also true that each of our personalities is unique as well. However, one of the great puzzles in psychology has been how to explain the origin and development of rather stable personality similarities and differences seen across many individuals. Even though we know there are strong genetic influences on our individual traits and characteristics, the sciences of psychology and neuroscience have struggled to explain how those genetic differ-ences emerge into personality differences (Crews, Gillette, Miller-Crews, Gore, & Skinner, 2014; Weaver et al., 2014).

A partial explanation and one of the themes of this book is that our personalities are all different because of our underlying geneti-cally based as well as environmentally promoted emotional differences that lead each of us to perceive and react to the world differently. Our unique personalities are a reflection of how we individually experience and respond to the world. Because we cannot experience our environ-ments directly but must rely on our brains to interpret each life event, we all experience the world in our own unique ways. In a way, each of us lives in a different world because we each perceive the world some-what differently, although in the midst of abundant differences, there are also abiding traits we share with many others.

Of course, none of us perceives our world directly. Our perceptions of the world are constructed by the brain. For instance, vision arises from light waves entering our eyes. However, our eyes do not directly "see" images; we perceive only a narrow part of the electromagnetic spectrum that allows us to have vision. The light-sensitive receptors in our eyes are capable of detecting only points of light energy, like pixels on a computer screen. Some of these receptors, the cones, respond to different-frequency light waves, which create a primary experience of red, green, and blue colors. However, the eye itself does not have the capacity for identifying whole images. It is primarily our visual cortex—just under the skull at the back of our heads—that processes the ascending signals from the light receptors in our eyes, which through successive ascending neural refinements identifies subtler color differences, as well as features such as lines, motion, and eventually actual images. All perceptions—from color to objects—are created by brain functions that are experienced as representations of the world.

It requires yet another level of processing to give meaning to the images we eventually "see," and it is at this level that we begin interpreting and adding affectively experienced values to images. It is at this stage of interpreting and adding value when major individual differences begin to emerge that provide each of us with foundational pillars for our various unique personalities. It is when we try to make sense of our images that we all begin to "see" the world in our own personal way. It is at this point that our emotional personality differences begin to become more apparent. For example, when we see a baby, we are not all equally attracted to the little one; some of us feel more warm and nurturing toward babies (females usually more than males). When we see a stranger, we are not all equally suspicious of or friendly toward the stranger; some of us feel more wary and anxious toward strangers. These feelings have been the most mysterious aspects of psychology, with little agreement on how they should be discussed, conceptualized, or studied. Our perspective here is that it is within the intrinsic strengths and weaknesses of our emotional feelings that we will find the major primal forces for the development of personality differences.

As we add our affective feelings and values to life events, we simultaneously have different thoughts and memories, as well as different behavioral reactions. The fact that two people can stand side by side and yet perceive the same scene differently with different feelings, interpretations, thoughts, and actions is what adds uniqueness to our personalities. Try this exercise with a mix of friends who are willing to cooperate in a little experiment: Ask them to imagine a somewhat bedraggled person walking toward them at dusk in a lonely parking lot as they unlock their car after a long day at work. Give them some paper and ask them to write down their likely feelings and to provide a little more information about the person approaching them. Then ask your friends to share their notes with the group. If you are fortunate enough to have a variety of personalities participating in your little game, you may be amazed at the range of responses you hear. Some will likely be concerned about the health of the person or whether the person is lost or hungry. Others may express fear of the stranger, and still others may respond with some hostility toward the vagrant. In this case, perhaps you will see differences in care and kindness—flexible empathic urges on one hand and dogmatic authoritarian and punitive ones on the other. It is these differences of feelings, interpretation, thoughts, and reactions that provide windows into our basic personality differences.

THE AFFECTIVE FOUNDATIONS
OF PERSONALITY

A fuller explanation of our personality differences is that these feelings, perceptions, thoughts, and behavior reactions are all wrapped up and packaged (intimately integrated) as our various instinctive emotions. Each of the many primary emotions we have inherited is basically an evolutionarily adaptive action system with intrinsic *valences*—various positive and negative feelings—reflecting in part that all mammals are born with the capacity to express and experience a set of primal emotions. In his 1998 text *Affective Neuroscience*, Jaak Panksepp described seven of the primal emotional responses shared by all mammals, including humans. They are capitalized as SEEKING, RAGE, FEAR, LUST, CARE, PANIC, and PLAY, to highlight their primary-process inherited nature (although this does not mean that their typical activities are not modulated by living in the world–indeed, they guide a great deal of learning). Each emotion not only has its own characteristic feelings but also guides perceptual interpretations, thoughts, and behavioral reactions, both unlearned and learned. However, the strength and sensitivity of each brain emotion system, as well as the developmental learning it has guided, vary from individual to individual. So, there is substantial variation across different people in each of these basic emotion systems, part of it inherited and part of it learned. Such variations in each of these brain emotional responses promote different perceptions and reactions that map onto diverse higher-order traits and personality characteristics—from a broad and open friendliness to a narrow and obsessive neuroticism. In developing our ideas about human personality, we discarded LUST—our sexual urgencies—as perhaps a bit "too hot to handle": important but often so personal that people may avoid frankness in rating their other personality traits. In other words, inquiring about people's sexual interests may be just too personal, which may promote diminished frankness about other personality dimensions.

The following are brief examples of the six blue ribbon emotions we focused on in developing our new Affective Neuroscience Personality Scales (to be introduced shortly):

We all get curious and energized during new experiences, whether about new neighbors moving in next door or the excitement of buying a new car, especially our first one (all such activities entail SEEKING).

We are all frustrated when we do not get the job we want and perhaps more than a little irritated when family members do not do their share of the work (we can all get enRAGEd).

Most of us are afraid of snakes and bears and no doubt would be a bit anxious if we were lost in the woods or had to walk alone through a rundown neighborhood in a strange city. The capacity for FEARfulness is built into us.

Many of us would feel especially tenderhearted and CAREing toward baby animals and might be inclined to give a little money to a homeless beggar.

We all feel loneliness and psychological pain that comes with broken relationships, especially the death of a loved one, and a similar feeling of "separation distress" when we are socially marginalized or rejected; we call this feeling PANIC/Sadness.

We all enjoy having fun with our friends and laughing at a good joke, which are all related to ancestral PLAY urges that we still share with the other mammals.

While we humans do share emotional feelings illustrated by these six examples, all are not equally expressed in our individual personalities. That is, while we all enjoy having fun with friends, some of us are much more friendly than others and more inclined to seek out opportunities for social fun. While many of us, especially females, are prone to feel tenderness toward baby animals, few of us would be moved to actually take home a baby bird that had fallen out of its nest to try to save it. So, the strength of our inclinations and reactions associated with each of these six emotions can differ dramatically across individuals. It is the variation across these six powers of the BrainMind, with their different feelings, typically exhibited in distinct life circumstances, which have been developmentally well integrated with our perceptions, thoughts, and behavioral reactions, that help constitute our diverse, often unique personalities.

Stated another way, each of the above six basic emotions arise from our inherited cerebral tools for living—arising from ancient, highly evolved brain survival systems that color and guide our perceptions and diverse responses to life events. These six brain systems are automatically, continuously, and intimately involved in our interpretations of the life situations we encounter. Our various positive and negative affective feelings are "value indicators"—they are all ancient survival mechanisms genetically passed down through millions of generations, long before modern humans or Neanderthals walked the face of the earth, and they automatically and continuously monitor the world as we encounter it. When it comes to survival, Mother Nature (aka evolution) did not leave foundational survival issues to chance. What she did provide, with ever-increasing generosity to primates, reaching its pinnacle in our species, were higher brain tissues, namely, the most massive neocortical expansions (relative to body size), which allow us to become really smart (and all too often perplexed, indeed confused, about mental life, which is rich mixture of our affective and cognitive abilities).

It is becoming ever clearer that the lower emotional regions of the brain are very important in programming the higher reaches, namely, our various affective feeling systems govern learning processes, allowing each organism to develop cognitions that emerge in lockstep with its temperamental strengths and weaknesses. This often leads to many life situations when people simply do not understand their own motivations or the motivations of others. However, we leave this complex topic for a later time.

TOWARD A NEW PERSONALITY TEST

It is most significant that the above seven basic blue ribbon emotional brain systems are shared not only by all humans but also by all other mammals. So, your pet dogs and cats have these evolutionarily related brain emotional systems in common with humans—SEEKING, RAGE, FEAR, CARE, PANIC and PLAY. (Although, as mentioned, we focus only on six, we occasionally reflect on LUST in some later chapters.) Indeed, the subject of animal personalities is reviewed in Chapter 10. For now, we emphasize that the existence of these brain systems, which are affectively (albeit perhaps not cognitively) experienced by all animals that possess them, makes these animals *sentient*—creatures that experience themselves in the world. The direct evidence for the existence of experienced feelings in nonspeaking animals is the simple fact that whenever we artificially arouse those systems, as with electrical deep brain stimulation (DBS), both animals and humans experience those states. Humans can directly tell us about their feelings, while we must interrogate animals that cannot speak through their behavioral choices. They can inform us of their likes and dislikes by either voluntarily turning on brain stimulation, as for SEEKING, CARE, and PLAY systems (these evoked states are rewarding), or turning off brain stimulation, as for RAGE, FEAR, and PANIC (for overviews, see Panksepp, 1998a, 2005; Panksepp & Biven, 2012). Accordingly, we developed a new human personality inventory to monitor how these shared emotions are expressed as distinct dimensions of human temperaments—a test we call the Affective Neuroscience Personality Scales (ANPS), presented more fully in Chapter 2 (for latest versions, see Davis & Panksepp, 2011 and the appendix).

Panksepp and his students have extensively studied and provided formal scientific names for these six brain systems. They are written in all capital letters to give them some separation from vernacular usages—to indicate that their meanings are not identical with their lowercase equivalents. Thus, the formal scientific names for these brains systems are SEEK-ING, RAGE, FEAR, CARE, PANIC, and PLAY. We have so far learned about the fundamental evolved nature of these emotional systems more by studying animal brains than human ones. The first three emotion systems, SEEKING, RAGE, and FEAR, have very ancient origins, because they can be traced back to reptiles and even fish. The other three, CARE, PANIC, and PLAY, are more uniquely mammalian and give mammals their higher social abilities (for instance, the CARE/Nurturance system may be one of the main sources of empathy; for a discussion see Panksepp & Panksepp, 2013). All six have been repeatedly shown to be linked to distinct personality differences across cultures, with early ANPS translations into German, French, Italian, Norwegian, Spanish, Turkish, and various other languages. The seventh system, sexual LUST, bridges ancient socioerotic SEEKING urges and mammalian desires to CARE for young and for the young to PLAY with each other. Clearly some females and males are more LUSTy than others, and this could also be viewed as a personality dimension, but we chose not to include it in the ANPS—as mentioned above, we were concerned that many people would not wish to reveal this aspect of their personality to strangers and suspected that if it were included, negative affective responses to such personal questions might turn people off and thereby potentially affect their responses to some of the other emotional dimensions. It is also noteworthy that we are aware of no other personality inventory that currently includes sexuality as a personality factor (nor do they evaluate homeostatic affects like hunger and thirst, which LUST may be conceptually closer to than the other emotions, because it is also controlled by bodily states, such as hormone levels).

UNDERSTANDING EMOTIONAL PRIMES MAY BE ESSENTIAL FOR UNDERSTANDING THE NEUROSCIENCE OF PERSONALITY

Before we turn to personality testing, we briefly describe these fundamental emotional systems of the brain:

> The SEEKING system may have originally evolved as a general-purpose foraging system (a "seek and find" system) energizing the search for food and other resources needed for survival. With other life goals, the function of this all important system (which probably lies at the core of our feelings of "selfhood," a topic we return to in Chapter 17) was evolutionarily broadened to energize the exploration for resources in general.

The RAGE system responds when the loss of resources is threatened—for example, loss of food, family, or money—and prepares the body to fight to get them back if necessary. We also sometimes call it the RAGE/Anger system, as a reminder that these fundamental systems probably link up reasonably well to our vernacular use of traditional emotional labels.

The FEAR/Anxiety system identifies and predicts when dangers are imminent and prepares the body to either freeze or flee, depending on which response will be most adaptive.

The CARE/Nurturance system motivates and coordinates the caretaking and rearing of infants from the time they are totally dependent newborns throughout the long period of early childhood development (although, of course, the youngsters of others species are typically not called their children). However, the CARE system may also motivate social helping behaviors in general.

The PANIC/Sadness system is engaged, especially in youngsters, when they lose contact with their mothers—we assume this is the feeling of psychological distress/pain that all infant mammals and birds suddenly feel when they lose close contact with supportive others. It is often associated with crying in children separated from their parents, with the death of a loved one, and with social rejection in general. At times we have also called it the Grief system or the Sadness system, because many people don't understand the implications of PANIC—the extremely agitated state young animals exhibit when they are lost or even accidentally separated from parents for even very short periods of time.

The PLAY/Joy system motivates physical social-engagement (aka "rough-and-tumble") play in all young mammals and commonly provides an affectively positive developmental context for learning how to socially interact with others, which thereby facilitates social integration in general.

At their fundamental (primary-process) level, each of these six brain systems can be thought of as distinct instincts (unconditioned responses in behavioral parlance) consisting of highly integrated ways of being and acting in the world—survival systems that help engender and solidify abundant learning. They are all natural systems, meaning their basic brain structures and functions have been inherited and hence do not require individual learning (although the systems may be refined by being used). It has long been clear that we do not need to teach children to play or to feel panic when they have lost contact with their parents.

Of course, that does not mean that these instincts cannot be modified

by life experiences and that related behavior patterns cannot be modified through learning for adaptive integration with current environmental circumstances. Indeed, these six brain systems govern much of the
early learning that children spontaneously exhibit. For example, children
quickly learn which of their friends play nicely and are most friendly
toward them. They also learn that the dog that bit them was threatening
when it growled and to fear and avoid growling dogs in the future, especially if they were nipped at. In short, the fundamental affective guidance
provided by these six behavioral-emotional systems can be thought of
as ancestral tools for living that we are born with. They are genetically
provided "original equipment" that provide rapid, inborn (instinctual)
answers to life challenges—ways of behaving and feeling that promoted
survival of ancestral mammals many, many millions of years ago.

These six behavioral-emotional systems may be stronger or weaker in
different species, but all exist to some extent in all mammalian species.
They are essential for survival and, with learning, become ever more
deeply embedded in our personalities. They are action-oriented systems
that consistently bias our perceptions, thoughts, and actions; they are
elaborated in our lives as stable behavioral-feeling patterns that contribute substantially to the growth of our personalities. Most people do
not think of "motor" or "action-generating" systems as having any consciousness, but these systems have a feel to them that seems to be an
intrinsic part of their organization. As noted earlier, artificial activation
with electrical DBS in animals, just like natural activation in humans,
feels good and bad in various ways. In formal animal-behavioral terms,
these systems can be shown to be rewarding or punishing, and that is
the only scientific measures of affective feelings we have in nonspeaking
animals (Panksepp, 1998a). In this affective sense, all vertebrate species
are conscious—they experience themselves in the world. Of course, this
does not necessarily mean they are *aware* that they are experiencing—
that higher level of reflective consciousness is reserved for animals that
know they possess awareness (i.e., knowing one is experiencing), which
is much harder to study in other animals than whether they feel positive
or negative—good or bad in the vernacular.

THE NATURE OF THE PRIMAL
EMOTIONAL AFFECTS

This point is very important: *These six emotions engender feeling states
within the brain* (as does LUST), and these experiential characteristics
are especially important when we talk about personality. Each emotion
has an affective component that feels either good or bad. These *affects*,
or feelings, are either pleasant or aversive, even in other animals. They
help automatically inform animals, including humans, which internal

conditions of the brain are rewarding, and hence support survival, and which are punishing, signaling that survival may be in jeopardy. Again, the SEEKING, CARE, and PLAY emotions are experienced as desirable feelings (*rewarding affects*), whereas the FEAR, RAGE, and PANIC emotions are all experienced as aversive feelings *(punishing affects* to use behavioristic language).

On the positive side, the SEEKING system provides us with a very special euphoric "buzz" (we humans commonly call it enthusiasm) as we explore possibilities and anticipate desired outcomes. The CARE system infuses us with a "warm glow" as we support the lives of our children and help others overcome their problems. The CARE system, along with the PANIC/Sadness system, may be especially important for engendering our feelings of empathy and sympathy when bad things happen to nearby others, but especially to those that we love. The PLAY system fills us with "delight" as we have fun with our friends.

On the negative side, the RAGE/Anger system sparks feelings of "irritation" and directs us to "attack" whoever or whatever threatens us or our possessions. The FEAR system makes us anxious, indeed can grip us with "terror" when we sense that our life or well-being is in danger. The PANIC/Sadness system overwhelms us with "desperate helplessness," a painful distress (that can gradually become despair) we felt when as children we lost contact with our parents, or later in life when we lose (or are suddenly locked out of) a close, sustaining relationship.

The affective tone of our personal world—the world we individually perceptually live in at an affective level—is constructed by the positive or negative valence of these affects. In other words, it is among the pleasant or aversive qualities of these emotional feelings that we often find the value of our experiences. We positively value and are attracted to situations and experiences we associate with good feelings. We avoid and place negative values on situations and experiences that feel bad. Indeed, although many animal researchers are shy about even talking about the feelings of the animals they study (often just preferring to study learning and memory, where such concepts do not seem necessary), it seems likely that the various evolved feeling-generating systems (primal emotional affects) actually directly control many of the learning and memory processes of human and animal brains. This is a complex neurochemical story that we will not address here (but for a readable synopsis, see Panksepp & Biven, 2012, chap. 6).

IN SUM

It is surprising that no personality test has tried to represent all of these brain emotional systems explicitly and equally. As we describe in the chapters that follow, during the past century many personality tests were developed. Some did represent features such as anxiety and aggressiveness, and even curiosity (sometimes called "openness to experience"), but none focused on the whole package that we describe here. Partly this is because more recent personality tests typically started from a "top-down" perspective, from the many words and concepts we use to describe one another's temperaments. Within the complexity of words, scientists were more prone to use complex statistics to ferret out consistent patterns among the adjectives we use to describe one another. Perhaps because an understanding of the basic brain emotional systems requires cross-species neuroscience, no one has used the full riches of our emerging understanding of the basic emotional systems of our brains, so critically important for creating our feeling of selfhood, as one critical foundation pillar for personality theory.

The ANPS that we describe in this book attempts to do that, and in so doing it allows us to better connect our increasing understanding of the brain sources of basic human emotions to the kinds of knowledge (e.g., understanding the anatomies and chemistries of these systems) that can currently be achieved by studying the brains and behaviors of other animals. In a sense, our approach is much closer to the classical medieval approaches to personality, with their four major temperamental types—sanguine (PLAYful), choleric (RAGEful), melancholic (full of that PANICy psychic pain that we commonly call sadness), and phlegmatic (the coldness of temperaments that arises perhaps from too much anxiety engendered by excessive FEAR).

Why was SEEKING not represented? Perhaps because the ancients implicitly recognized it was a universal part of mental life itself (as encapsulated in the concept of *conatus*, the essential force or urge underlying human effort and striving; within the philosophy of Baruch Spinoza this was the psychological "force" in every living creature to preserve its own existence (for an excellent and readable overview, see Ravven, 2013), which in its most positive form becomes the very ground of "social joy" so magnificently represented in happy-sanguine temperaments. Why was CARE not represented? Perhaps because it was more highly feminine and simply accepted as something that women are skilled at, while males are not, for the temper of those times was governed so much more by men than during our more enlightened era. And, of course, everyone knew about LUST, but for a long time few wished to talk about it openly. Before we start summarizing where we have been as humans (and at time scientists) interested in human personality, during the past century and a half of scientific psychology, we will proceed in the next chapter to our own neoclassical view of human personality as represented in the Affective Neuroscience Personality Scales (ANPS).

CHAPTER 2

Affective Neuroscience Personality Scales and the Big Five

Delgado, Roberts, and Miller (1954) have shown that cats will learn to turn a wheel to avoid the unpleasant emotion of fear produced when certain parts of the brain [hypothalamus] are stimulated. The cats act as if the sensation or feelings produced by electrically stimulating the brain are real emotions. We may anticipate that this same demonstration will eventually be made with the emotion of anger.

—John Paul Scott, *Aggression*

IN THIS CHAPTER we introduce the major personality model for which there is the greatest agreement among personality psychologists, the Big Five, with discrete factors for Extraversion, Agreeableness, Conscientiousness, Emotional Stability, and Openness to Experience. And we contrast this model with our emotional-trait-focused Affective Neuroscience Personality Scales (ANPS). This new way of looking at personality is admittedly a radical departure from the history of the field, and before continuing with that complex history, we highlight why such a radical shift is needed in order to integrate our emerging understanding of the neural infrastructure of primal emotional feelings with our understanding of human personality.

The Big Five has emerged as perhaps the most scientific personality assessment model to this point, with no preconceptions about the underlying structure of mind. It was guided by the recognition that the language of personality should map well onto our linguistic use of adjectives to describe human traits. It let the chips fall in whatever way they would, based simply on allowing a statistical analysis of our language dictate what differences existed in our personalities. Clearly, our ANPS emerged from very different premises, namely, an understanding of the subcortical brain fundamentals of our emotional-affective natures. Pausing to consider these issues, before proceeding to the history of the field, we hope will help readers appreciate not only the dynamics of science in this contentious field but also possible lasting neurobiopsychological solutions. First, however, we backtrack a bit.

TOWARD A THEORY OF PERSONALITY FOCUSED ON PRIMAL EMOTIONAL AFFECT

As we describe in Chapter 15, there are significant connections between genetics and personality. In Chapter 3, we also summarize discussions by Darwin that animals exhibit emotional personalities similar to human personalities. In Chapters 4 and 5, we review how psychological and psychoanalytic pioneers at the beginning of the twentieth century engaged in active discussions about the relations between emotions and personality. But first, in this chapter we continue to make the case that modern affective neuroscience has, for the first time, provided a coherent, evidence-based view of mammalian minds as rooted in the value/survival-coding affective circuits situated at the very basement of the brain and mind. This kind of evidence makes a strong case that our personalities are firmly grounded in the ancestral roots of our biological bodies and brains. But what is it in our neurobiology that mediates the connections between our genes and our personality traits?

As introduced in Chapter 1, Jaak Panksepp has outlined a dynamic view of human behavior that integrates an advanced understanding of mammalian brain anatomy, brain chemistry, and the diverse emotions that can be aroused by direct electrical stimulation of isolated deep brain structures. His explicit view is that various basic emotional/affective action systems, grounded in a rich evolutionary past, remain laid out in very similar ways in very ancient brain regions (Panksepp, 1982, 1998a). The more traditional behaviorist label for these brain emotion-generating systems is *unconditional response systems*. These emotional-action survival networks (or simply emotional instincts) constitute the evolutionary foundation of the "mind," which is easier to talk about in many psychological terms (e.g., see Chapters 4 and 5) than to study neuroscientifically.

The main theme of this book is that these primary emotional processes are the links between our evolutionary heritage and our current major personality characteristics. These emotional systems support subjective affective experiences that motivate and guide our actions, control learning and memory, and promote diverse cognitive activities. They may constitute the underlying basis for our individual personality traits (Davis, Panksepp, & Normansell, 2003; Davis & Panksepp, 2011).

These are *primary* processes in that they do not need to be learned, although they control learning and reciprocally are refined by learning. That they have an evolutionary past is evident from the fact that all mammals share their instinctual-genetic foundations, and many of these primary processes are evident in birds and reptiles, perhaps even fish, although the degree of homology (genetic relatedness) remains ever more open as the degree of genetic relatedness diminishes. Still, it is the evolutionary relationship that we humans have especially with other mammals that has allowed for much of our current understanding of these emotional systems across species. Indeed, it is this same bodily relationship with mammals that has also allowed us to make giant strides in medical research and therapeutics based on working out details of underlying biological processes in animal models. This is also happening in psychiatry (Panksepp, 2005, 2016; Panksepp & Yovell, 2014).

As noted already, there is substantial evidence for six primary emotional systems, which are closely linked to personality traits. Humans experience these emotional systems as motivating affects and potent urges to behave in particular ways. Subjectively, we experience three of these affects as negatives or aversive feelings in our lives: RAGE/Anger, FEAR/Anxiety, and PANIC/Sadness. We also subjectively experience three of them as positive, desirable, or pleasant feelings: SEEKING/Enthusiasm, CARE/Nurturance, and PLAY/Social Joy. (We leave out consideration of LUST/Eroticism for now.) Each of these six systems is adapted to promote our survival and responds characteristically to specific environmental situations and emergencies. When highly aroused, each of the six evokes powerful negative or positive affective feelings, and these systems promote distinctive *instinctual* reactions. We know that they feel like *something* to other animals as well as to humans, because deep brain simulation (DBS) of each of these brain systems is rewarding or punishing to animals. Our key hypothesis here is that the strengths and weaknesses in these six brain emotional affective systems, whether genetically dictated or developmentally refined, are the very foundations for the emotional traits that constitute our personalities. This beckoned us to get into the complex (at times chaotic) field of human personality.

FROM PRIMAL EMOTIONAL AFFECTS
TO PERSONALITY DIMENSIONS

How can one measure the emotional strengths and weaknesses of people? How does one assess the activity in one's emotion systems? It cannot yet be done clearly or directly by any physiological measures, even though there are many linkages. So how might clinicians and researchers appraise the personality relevant urges and affective tendencies of their subjects? At present, it can be done only by asking the right questions. How might research physicians evaluate the underlying primary emotional strengths and weaknesses of their patients, some seeking help for their addictions, to get to know them nomothetically (the study of universals that we share with others), not just idiographically (focusing on individual differences), to refine a diagnosis, prognosis, and treatment plan? Psychiatrists and clinical psychologists can benefit from psychometric scales that attempt to directly assess individuals' emotional strengths and weaknesses. For instance, how might psychiatrists assess the extent to which addicts have experienced real changes in the emotional makeup during treatments for their addictions? No good tools yet existed. Thus, the first task we set for ourselves was to construct a psychological assessment tool that measured primal emotional traits. At first blush, one option seemed to be the Big Five personality model, which had emerged as a prominent factor-analytically derived model for parsing the human personality. Namely, it had revealed patterns of human personality based on assessment of a host of adjectives that had emerged in human language to describe temperamental differences among people. Furthermore, at present it is arguably the most widely accepted personality evaluation tool produced by psychological science.

BRIEF INTRODUCTION TO THE BIG FIVE, AKA THE FIVE-FACTOR MODEL

Unfortunately, the Big Five did not turn out to be a satisfactory model for assessing primary emotions. Why? Because it had no vision of the core emotional traits of human beings! Except for Emotional Stability, the Big Five did not deal directly with affects. Indeed, all negative (aversive) affects were lumped into the low pole of the Emotional Stability dimension, which is sometimes given the negative label *neuroticism*. From our perspective, there were no separate measures for the RAGE/Anger, FEAR, and PANIC/Sadness systems.

The Big Five is the subject of later chapters as well, but here we provide a brief background. The Big Five model is the culmination of many years of psychometric research. It is the direct outcome of a statistical method called factor analysis and asserts that human personality variation can be described with five traits usually named Extraversion, Agreeableness, Conscientiousness, Emotional Stability, and Openness to Experience.

There is an historical background that we do not focus on in this chapter, but there were many significant players. More than any other, it was Lewis Goldberg who brought the Big Five to its peak visibility (see Goldberg, 1990) by using factor analysis to place self-ratings of hundreds of English-language adjectives on the Big Five axes, including adjectives that seemed to "blend" more than one Big Five trait (Hofstee, de Raad, & Goldberg, 1992). He also provided researchers with a list of one hundred "marker" adjectives—twenty for each of the Big Five traits (Goldberg, 1992). Indeed, we used seventy of the clearest markers to measure the Big Five traits in our own personality research. Examples of these markers were "talkative" and "assertive" for Extraversion, "kind" and "helpful" for Agreeableness, "systematic" and "organized" for Conscientiousness, "irritable" and "moody" for low Emotional Stability, and "complex" and "imaginative" for Openness to Experience.

However, despite all of Goldberg's (and many other's) fine theory-free work, all of the negative emotionality in human behavior was simply lumped into a single trait: emotional stability. Even though fear, anger, and sadness are distinct feelings for all humans, and even though fear, anger, and sadness, in their psychiatric extremes, are each associated with different psychological problems, with different recommended treatments, the most widely accepted psychometric personality model only offered a single personality dimension that lumped all three of these unique and powerful emotions into a single psychological trait.

Because there were no satisfactory psychological tests, we decided to construct a tool to measure each of the six primary brain affects, which we call the Affective Neuroscience Personality Scales (ANPS). The ANPS was modeled after the State-Trait Personality Inventory (Spielberger, 1975, 1983) developed by Charles Spielberger (1927–2013). But the ANPS aimed to measure six emotional traits instead of Speilberger's three (anger, anxiety, and curiosity, although Spielberger created many additional variants). The ANPS was designed as a self-report instrument that would tap into the six major affective-emotional tendencies hypothesized to underlie our personalities. It would be the first psychological assessment that would position an individual in affective space, based on our emerging knowledge of cross-mammalian core (primal-evolved) emotional systems.

Tertiary Level of Emotion Processing

At this point, a brief explanation is in order about levels of emotion processing (addressed in more detail in Chapter 5) and what we were actually attempting to measure with this new assessment. In Chapter 1 we discussed primary-level affective processes. We also described primary emotions as supporting learning, which in Chapter 5 we will refer to as secondary-level processing. This secondary adaptive emotional learning is based on the primary-level affective processes, thereby helping refine our responses to life events and create new survival responses to meet the challenges of an ever-changing world. The idea that humans, indeed all mammals, exhibit this secondary capacity to automatically learn from our affective experiences and adapt our behaviors to the specific demands of our environments makes us much less reflexive and more dynamic/flexible beings with multiple ways to handle specific environments.

However, for humans—perhaps other animals as well, but especially humans, with our massive cerebral cortices and thereby capacity for speech—there is also a tertiary level of processing, based on thoughts and decision making, that is surely more complex than that found in any other species. (However, it may be that whales and dolphins—sea dwelling mammals—are exceptions.) This tertiary level is the level of cognitive processing or, more simply, just thinking. Because humans can talk about our experiences, including cognitive perceptions, thoughts, and memories, we are usually reporting our affective experiences to each other verbally, both in nonverbal tone and in semantic content. The importance of the primary, secondary, and tertiary levels is discussed in Chapter 5, but for now it is important to acknowledge that there are no clear scientific words to adequately describe what we feel at the primary level, and the data we sought to collect with our new assessment were language-based reports, namely, from the tertiary level of brain-mind processing.

While we wrote test items that specifically asked about "feelings" as directly as possible, we recognized that the answers people would give us would inevitably include their reflections about their feelings rather than a pure "direct brain readout" of their primary affects. We avoided writing items like "I yell at other people less than my friends do" because this required the subject to make a logical comparison that would depend on how much those in his or her circle of acquaintances resorted to yelling. Rather, we tried to write items that could access the primary affective feeling level as directly as possible from a tertiary, language/thinking-based perspective. An example would be "I almost never yell at other people." Our intention was to write items that would allow people to respond as directly as possible from the primary feelings that are embedded in their personal experiences of themselves.

Getting Started

After several iterations of writing items, testing students, and rewriting items, we finally had produced six clearly emotional personality scales (seven overall, counting Spirituality, which we discuss later). They had adequate reliabilities, which basically meant we had developed items for each scale that could be shown statistically to be consistently measuring the same underlying concept. We named the new assessment the Affective Neuroscience Personality Scales (ANPS) and started evaluating how well it worked in the real world, yielding several cycles of refinement of this new instrument as more and more data rolled in. In brief, college students were requested to complete the ANPS along with the short seventy-item test measuring the Big Five traits, as practical laboratory exercises in their ongoing psychology courses, first in Panksepp's lab, followed by Ken Davis and Larry Normansell, and now many others across the world. For readers wishing to study the ANPS as revised in 2011, it is reprinted as Appendix A.

Even though we did not consider the Big Five to adequately measure primary emotions, we still wanted to determine how these six affective ANPS traits related to the Big Five dimensions, especially because that had become the most widely accepted human personality model. In fact, we predicted from previous work that our PLAY scale would correlate with Big Five Extraversion, SEEKING would correlated with Openness, CARE would line up with Agreeableness, and RAGE/Anger, FEAR, and PANIC/Sadness would all clump together with Emotional Stability. Thus, we also hypothesized that, as indicated above, there would be significant cases where the Big Five may have blurred major distinctions between primary emotions.

ORIGINAL ANPS RESEARCH FINDINGS

The results showed that each of the six ANPS scales correlated most strongly, as predicted, with one of the Big Five dimensions, as shown in Table 2.1, which summarizes findings from our first ANPS publication (Davis et al., 2003). Among the positive affects, the PLAY scale lined up best with Extraversion, SEEKING linked clearly with Openness to Experience, and CARE correlated predominately with Agreeableness. Among the negative affects, RAGE (which we originally called ANGER), FEAR, and PANIC (which we originally called SADNESS) all correlated very highly with lower Emotional Stability. RAGE/Anger also showed a second relationship by lining up with low Agreeableness. The Big Five Conscientiousness scale correlated negatively with each of the three ANPS negative affects, although at a degree of magnitude lower than their correlations with Emotional Stability.

Thus, we obtained evidence that the foundations of human personality may be laid in the old emotional parts of mammalian brains, and hence also the human brain, suggesting that the ancient instinctual action-based emotional-affective networks, originating in deep subcortical brain regions, may be major "drivers" of human personality dimensions. Even though we had left LUST out of our scale, we decided to include a tertiary Spirituality scale because of its general importance in human affairs, especially addiction treatment programs such as Alcoholics Anonymous, where clients are encouraged to develop more spiritual ways of dealing with life.

Table 2.1. Correlation of Affective Neuroscience Personality Scales and Spirituality Scales with Big Five Personality Scales: Early Results

Affective Neuroscience Personality Scales	Big Five Personality Scales				
	Extra-version	Agreeable-ness	Conscien-tiousness	Emotional Stability	Openness to Experience
PLAY	**0.46*****	0.29***	0.00	0.12	0.13
SEEKING	0.13	−0.01	−0.01	0.01	**0.47*****
CARE	0.25**	**0.50*****	0.12	−0.07	0.06
FEAR	−0.19*	−0.17*	−0.24**	**−0.75*****	−0.05
ANGER	−0.04	**−0.48*****	−0.30***	**−0.65*****	−0.08
SADNESS	−0.21**	−0.13	−0.30***	**−0.68*****	−0.00
Spirituality	0.15	0.26***	0.14	0.09	0.17*

Student sample, $n = 171$ (50 males, 121 females). Adapted with permission from Davis et al. (2003). *$p < 0.05$; **$p < 0.01$; ***$p < 0.001$ (all two-tailed).

Simple Scale-Level Interpretation

The data supported the conclusion that each of the ANPS scales, which were based on extrapolations of the primary emotional systems of mammalian brains, were strongly related to one or another of the Big Five dimensions. RAGE/Anger was the only ANPS scale to be strongly associated with two Big Five dimensions. Parenthetically, we again note that the full capitalizations in the ANPS are official names for the primary-process emotional systems, but we will typically use the more vernacular designators, in lowercase, for discussing the fuller human-emotional complexities of personality. We do this because we have no direct neuroscientific way to monitor and probe the deep primal emotional systems of human brains, even though certain kinds of brain imaging (e.g., positron emission tomography) can visualize many of these systems (see Damasio, 1999; Damasio, Grabowski, Bechara, & Damasio, 2000). However, we assume that our language-based measures are actually making contact with the personality dynamics that are linked to (indeed, partly emerge from) such primal emotional strengths and weaknesses.

So what do these results mean in primal terms? We hypothesized that brain's PLAY system is the "root" of Big Five Extraversion. Likewise, the SEEKING system appeared to be the biological foundation of Openness to Experience. Emotional Stability seemed to be a conglomeration of all three negative primary affects: RAGE/Anger, FEAR, and PANIC/Sadness. Lastly, Agreeableness in Big Five terms seemed to be a bipolar "love-hate" dimension, with CARE on the love end and RAGE/Anger on the hate end. These data thus supported our cross-species affective neuroscience perspective that the biological sources of personality arise substantially from the primary emotion networks embedded in subcortical brain regions (often mistakenly called the subcortex).

It seemed ever more likely that these ancestral foundations of affectively motivated (perhaps even purposeful) behaviors, extensively documented in mammals and birds, were also operating in humans. Our approach further suggested that the sensitivity of these six genetically endowed unconditional emotional response systems could be adjusted and adapted to our particular environments at the secondary level by ongoing affectively guided learning (i.e., "reinforcement" may reflect how affective circuits control memory formation). Also, the diverse expressions of the six primary emotions and the secondary-level refinements could be regulated or amplified at the tertiary level by our thoughts and ruminations (more on processing levels in Chapter 5). However, at the core of each of these personality dimensions lies the ancient genetics, molded by survival needs for millions of years, creating primal affective tools for living within ancient regions of the BrainMind that continuously shaped attitudes and behaviors that helped us survive. For some reason this is a radical idea in psychology, but that may be partly due to the behaviorist tradition, which still guides much animal research, as well as the fact that most psychologists remain poorly trained in the cross-species affective neurosciences.

Conscientiousness

Conscientiousness was the only Big Five dimension that did not prominently correlate with any of the ANPS scales. This suggested to us that Conscientiousness did not represent a primary emotion. Indeed, conducting yourself in an organized, systematic manner and carefully planning your activities would seem to represent a fairly high-level cognitive trait, perhaps commonly pursued in the absence of strong primal emotional feelings. There were some lower, but still statistically significant, negative correlations of Conscientiousness with the three aversive ANPS scales—RAGE/Anger, FEAR, and PANIC/Sadness. Because higher Conscientiousness scores were associated with lower negative affect scores, this suggested the idea that Conscientiousness is reducing (perhaps regulating) the emotional expression of at least the three negative primary emotions. But, in contrast to the other results, this finding has not always been confirmed in subsequent cross-cultural research. Yet, it is possible that conscientious people have a natural faculty or have acquired the ability to limit the unpleasant effects of negative emotion systems in their lives. However, one could argue even more broadly that the Big Five Conscientious dimension is measuring the personality capacity to regulate emotionality in general, both positive and negative, depending on each individual's particular emotional sensitivities.

To Lump or Not to Lump

Why do the Big Five statistics place the three traits measured by the RAGE/Anger, FEAR, and PANIC/Sadness scales on a single trait, namely, the Emotional Stability personality dimension? Each of the ANPS scales represents a separate powerful emotion with distinct implications for pathological as well as more everyday behaviors. For example, a patient coming to a psychologist with a spider phobia would be treated differently than one complaining about depression and a litany that "life did not seem worth living." Further, a patient with temper issues would be approached very differently than a patient with anxiety problems. Why would affects as different as RAGE/Anger, FEAR, and PANIC/Sadness all be lumped together? However, because statistical results drive the Big Five more than theory, a better question might be why the statistics defining the Big Five personality model show such close associations between all three negative primary-process emotions.

Difficulty Differentiating Among Emotions at the Tertiary-processing Level

A possible explanation to the question above is that many humans have difficulty verbally differentiating among the three primary negative emotions. Hence, their rating of questions asking about different sorts of unpleasantness may not be distinctive enough to statistically drive the anger, fear, and sadness types of items into distinct factors. For example, in working with patients suffering from panic attacks, Donald Klein has reported that, after patients were given a drug that reduced their panic attacks (which may reflect sudden PANIC circuit arousals), patients reported no beneficial effect. Further analysis showed that the patients had not noticed any improvement because they still experienced strong general anxieties (FEAR) that they might have another panic attack (Klein, 1993).

Therapists often report that patients have difficulty accurately describing their feelings. Therapists have experimented with techniques, such as writing about experiences, to enrich patients' descriptions and improve progress in therapy (Paez, Velasco, & Gonzalez, 1999). Distinctions among loneliness, worry, and irritation may not seem very clear to many patients, at least linguistically, even though they may be quite distinct experientially. Maybe language gets in the way and it is sometimes difficult for people to link feelings to descriptive language. The primary emotional action systems evolved long before human spoken language.

People also seem to vary in how much they even notice their feelings (Gasper & Bramesfeld, 2006). When prodded to explain what is bothering them, people are likely to offer vague responses like "I don't know," or "It's hard to describe." Regarding work, you might hear responses like "I just don't have any energy," or "I just can't seem to get motivated." We are often no better at explaining why we like or dislike things. For whatever reason, it seems the neocortical function of human speech and the learned conceptual distinctions at the tertiary level of analysis are not always fully integrated with older subcortical mammalian brain functions. Further, a little-studied function of the neocortex is to provide inhibition to and regulation over primary-process emotional arousals. In other words, diverse neocortical inhibition may be common in enculturated human adults, even to the point where they can't easily talk about feelings. Indeed, the failure to have good language for emotions is called alexithymia.

Factor Analysis and Latent Factors

Another explanation of why the Big Five mixes all the negative affects into a single dimension may have to do with the Big Five being derived from factor analysis, a statistical method for identifying latent factors in correlational data. If, as described previously, people sometimes have difficulty describing the subtle differences of their negative emotions, why would we be surprised that factor analysis might lump them together in one statistical bucket regardless of the diversity of underlying affective processes? So, perhaps more than anything, that the Big Five does not differentiate well among the RAGE/Anger, FEAR, and PANIC/Sadness systems and lumps them into a single dimension illustrates the limitations of factor analysis. It is not that factor analysis is something personality theorists should avoid—it is a valuable tool for many psychologists. It is just that for statistical reasons it might not always produce an accurate representation of our neurobiologically dictated emotional nature.

Should Factor Analysis Limit Our Thinking About Personality?

A related question is why theorists have allowed factor-analytic statistics to limit their thinking about personality structure. Why should personality theorists accept factor analysis as the standard for parsing human personality space? A partial answer is that, prior to the widespread acceptance of factor analysis in psychology, there were many competing personality theories and competing psychological assessments, which were difficult to differentiate and integrate. Psychological personality tests produced various numbers of trait scores. For example, Eysenck (1967) claimed there were only three psychological traits, Extraversion, Neuroticism, and Psychoticism; the Myers-Briggs Type Indicator following Jung's theory claimed four, Extraversion-Introversion, Sensing-Intuiting, Thinking-Feeling, and Judging-Perceiving; Harrison Gough (Gough & Bradley, 1996) produced twenty empirically defined "folk" traits; Douglas Jackson generated twenty factor-analytically defined traits; and there are many others with intermediate numbers of personality traits.

Factor analysis came into its own with the advent of more powerful computers to carry out the heavy computational demands and promised to become a "theory-free" way to objectively decide not only how many but also what factors were needed to explain personality. While this issue is still debated, the Big Five emerged as a widely accepted model, perhaps prematurely. Our argument is that we have to understand the neurobiology of basic emotional states to have a more comprehensive and accurate assessment of human personality, and when neuroscience can demonstrate clear cross-species distinctions among various instinctive emotional systems, perhaps neuroscience should be given priority over statistics.

BIG FIVE SUMMARY

The Big Five represents the statistical analysis of how human linguistic descriptors (especially adjectives) characterize behavior, without considering whether they are comprehensive, equally balanced descriptors (i.e., how many adjectives actually relate to the various basic emotions). Human language has recorded the collective observations of behavior honed over millions of years. The wisdom and knowledge embedded in diverse language traditions are of course subject matter for the fascinating field of linguistics. The simplest descriptors of behavior are adjectives such as "outgoing," "friendly," "methodical," "anxious," and "creative." Rating behavior using such adjectives was the method used by Lewis Goldberg (1990), in many respects the "father" of the Big Five, to repeatedly demonstrate the statistical parsing of behavior ratings into five personality traits. Although factor-analyzing simple descriptive sentences such as "I prefer people who are quiet and reserved," as well as ratings of adjectives, has consistently produced support for the Big Five personality dimensions, perhaps it is time to stop relying purely on statistics to identify the "latent," underlying personality dimensions, especially because affective neuroscience has already provided extensive evidence for distinct universal emotional action systems in the mammalian brain.

In other words, the Big Five might, in part, be a statistical artifact of human language processing at the tertiary level. Certainly the Big Five model is not a direct representation of primary brain processes. Indeed, prior to a cross-species affective neuroscience (Panksepp, 1998a), there was no comprehensive brain model to link the Big Five factors to brain emotional systems. We are not suggesting that human language does not contain valuable information about human experience, only that allowing language to determine the primary dimensions of human personality may be getting the cart before the horse. It is the diverse manifestations of evolved mammalian primary-process emotions, which long preceded language, that human language is attempting to describe and that subsequently factor analysis is attempting to parse.

Prior to the advent of neuroscience, the factor analysis of language descriptor ratings may have been the most objective (and theory-free) guide for the parsing of personality, and it still remains a useful personality tool. However, given the extensive direct neuroscience evidence for primary brain emotional networks, it seems counterproductive to allow our studies of personality, and resulting conclusions, to be limited simply to statistical language analysis.

It also does not seem that sensory and homeostatic affects are typically seen as relevant for personality. Why is that? Perhaps because we typically interact with one another with a continuous background of emotional feelings rather than sensory and homeostatic ones, and personality is fundamentally about our interpersonal emotional affective strengths and weaknesses rather than the many other affective feelings (e.g., homeostatic and sensory) that are really important for governing both physical health and our immediate psychological sense of well-being. It would appear that the time is ripe for personality theory to both broaden and narrow its perspective and integrate reliable neuroscience-based emotional research into the tools used to parse the human BrainMind into meaningful and useful personality dimensions. As a step toward this integration process, we constructed the Affective Neuroscience Personality Scales.

This topic is discussed further in later chapters devoted specifically to the Big Five/Five-Factor Model, but for now, we suggest that the medieval approaches to human personality—from sanguine and melancholic to choleric and phlegmatic—were closer to what should be conceptualized as foundational issues for understanding human personality than the modern theory-free Big Five that has captivated the field of personality psychology. We now return to the main historical threads that led to the Big Five, and modern personality theory in academic psychology.

CHAPTER 3
Darwin's Comparative "Personality" Model

*My first child was born December 27th, 1839, and I at once com-
menced to make notes on the first dawn of the various expressions
which he exhibited, for I felt convinced, even at this early period, that
the most complex and fine shades of expression must all have had a
gradual and natural origin.*

—Charles Darwin, *Autobiography*

How can we gain a coherent perspective on the seemingly chaotic
multitude of existing personality models? If it's an evolutionary
grounding in personality theory you are looking for, Charles Darwin is
a pretty good place to start. Indeed, the scientific study of personality
really began with Darwin. Even though he did not focus explicitly on that
aspect of his work, he forever changed how science viewed the human
experience. Centuries earlier Copernicus and then Galileo changed how
science viewed man's place in the universe. Prior to Copernicus and
Galileo, the earth was seen as the center of the universe, with the sun,
moon, planets, and stars all orbiting around the earth. Once Copernicus
showed that the earth and the solar planets rotated around the sun and
especially after Galileo with his telescope showed that Jupiter also had
orbiting moons, our understanding of earth's relationship to the greater
universe was transformed.

It was no different when Darwin clarified our ascent from prehuman,
even premammalian, ancestors. After he published *On the Origin of Species* in 1859 and *The Descent of Man* in 1871, the relationship of *Homo
sapiens* to the rest of animal life on earth was likewise transformed.

However, Darwin did not just document the relationship of our
physical forms to the physical forms of other animals. Darwin devoted

his entire third book to emotions, namely, *The Expression of Emotions in Man and Animals* (1872) in which he evolutionarily linked human emotions to those of other mammals. In the process, of establishing the relationship of human emotions to the emotions of other mammals, he offered powerful testimony to how central emotions are to human lives.

In *Expression*, as Darwin outlined an evolutionary approach to thinking about human behavior and emotion, he did not simply invent his ideas. He based his thinking about emotions on data—carefully collected observational evidence (of the ethological as opposed to experimental variety)—just like he had done more quantitatively with the beaks of birds and other physical characteristics. For Darwin, evolutionary thinking did not involve *imagining* the challenges faced by our Stone Age human ancestors and extrapolating insights about human nature. For Darwin, evolutionary thinking consisted of examining and *comparing* the actions of many very distantly related ancestors, such as chimpanzees, monkeys, dogs, cats, and farm animals. When this comparative approached revealed a consistent pattern of behavior and emotion across multiple mammalian species, Darwin was convinced he had not deceived himself about the evolutionary importance of *homologous* (having a corresponding origin, function, and structure) inherited characteristics.

Thus, Darwin was the first to scientifically document the primary emotions shared by all mammals, including humans. Resonant with these Darwinian insights, and as we discuss in previous and following chapters, drawing a closer relationship between primal emotions and personality is one of the contributions of a cross-species affective neuroscience—a main theme of this book that allows us to begin putting human personality on a sound evolutionary foundation.

Darwin forever erased the great divide between humans and nonhumans. He used the power of his comparative observations to challenge the view of human life widely held at the time—driven by 2,500-year-old philosophical and theological assumptions—that only humans were sentient beings (indeed, at times rational), whereas the lives of other animals were governed only by mindless behavioral instincts (Beach, 1955). Darwin recognized that such emotional instincts also govern our own lives and that they are not simply unconscious behaviors, as some twentieth-century scientists continued to believe. Neuroscience has now definitively located the foundation of these instinctual emotions, and associated feelings, within diverse subcortical brain networks. The existence of positive and negative feelings is monitored by the explicit rewarding and punishing states engendered by direct brain stimulation (DBS) of various subcortical emotional circuits (Panksepp, 1982, 1998a, 2005). Research has consistently shown that organisms approach (work for) DBS that evokes SEEKING, LUST, CARE, and PLAY. They escape DBS that evokes RAGE/Anger, FEAR, and PANIC/Sadness. These measures signify the existence of emotional feelings in animal brains.

Clearly the lack of the neocortex at birth in humans does not destroy consciousness, only our capacity for language, complex perceptions, and thoughts—the complexity of our cognitions (Merker, 2007). The basic emotional life survives. And now we know, and Darwin did not, that if we massively destroy emotional circuits of the subcortical brain regions, the higher mind also collapses (Panksepp, 1998a, 2007a). The simple lesson for human personality studies is that we are not wise to neglect the brain's instinctual emotional systems as a critical aspect of the diversity of human personalities. However, some psychological groups, namely, cognitive behaviorists, do not accept that the key to unlocking human personality lies in first unlocking the affective mysteries in the old midline brain structures of our mammalian ancestors, only partly because that would also entail accepting that other mammals affectively experience their bodies and worlds much as humans do. That is not welcome news in some academic quarters.

However, clearly for Darwin, humans had evolved from earlier life forms and only differed from other animals *by degree*. He provided evidence that animals also had some capacity to "reason" and, conversely, that human behavior was subject to emotional instincts. This left open the possibility that instincts are a primal foundation for our ways of reasoning, making ethics dependent explicitly on affects, as the philosopher David Hume had already surmised, a view that has been refreshed by some modern philosophers (e.g., Greene, 2013). We must now conceive of human minds, at least their affective foundations, as residing on an evolutionary continuum with other animals. Thereby, insights into basic human mental characteristics could be gained from an understanding of other animals' instinctual behaviors and affective experiences. This remains a radical perspective for academic psychology, as well as the field of personality research.

Using comparative observation, Darwin came very close to the framework of emotional affects set out empirically by affective neuroscience over one hundred years later and, perhaps even more important, laid the foundation for later work on human emotion and personality (Davis & Panksepp, 2011), as well the better understanding and treatment of psychiatric disorders (Panksepp, 2005, 2015, 2016). Because of such achievements, a brief review of this beloved (and, in some quarters, reviled) thinker's writings on the evolution of emotions is in order. Readers who are already familiar with Darwin's writing may wish to skip the remainder of this chapter.

CHARLES DARWIN'S EMOTIONAL INSIGHTS
AND AN EMERGENT NEUROSCIENCE

Darwin provided the foundation for the scientific study of modern human behavior and personality, even though he was not explicitly a personality theorist. All of his conclusions about behavior and the origins of behavior were not precisely accurate (to this day no one's are). However, with his theory of human origins and his keen evolutionary observations, he pointed us in the right direction. In addition to describing the evolution of our physical bodies, he demonstrated the value of comparative research highlighting the similarities of behaviors and emotions across species and in so doing moved us conceptually closer to finding answers about the sources of human motivation and temperament. The neuroscience could not be done until the 1950s, when investigators first demonstrated the rewarding and punishing properties of DBS to brain systems from which emotional actions could be evoked (Delgado et al., 1954; Olds & Milner, 1954), a project that was extended by Panksepp (1974, 1982, 1998a, 2005, 2011b, 2011c, 2015) and many of his students.

The theory of evolution had implications far beyond religion and philosophy. If, as the theory of evolution contended, there was biological-evolutionary continuity in the vast family of life on earth, it meant that humans were not altogether unique. Our bodily origins could be traced to other species. Importantly, one could infer that there would be many mental similarities between humans and other vertebrate species with which humans shared a common heritage. Because of our evolutionary descent, we would expect to discover not only many bodily but also mental homologies, that is, ancestral similarities, especially between humans and other mammals. However, the similarities would not only be physiological; they would also be behavioral and motivational. In fact, at every level of analysis, scientists could expect to find observations that would generalize from one species of animal to another. Work on the neuroanatomies, neurochemistries, and neurophysiologies of the brain has amply borne that out, especially during the past century. There are abundant detailed differences, for sure, but the underlying patterns and themes speak loudly for evolutionary continuities.

For our purposes here, we note that in his most famous, second book, *The Descent of Man* (1871), subtitled *and Selection in Relation to Sex*, Darwin was quite clear on the topic of whether animals have subjective feelings: "The lower animals, like man, manifestly feel pleasure and pain, happiness and misery. Happiness is never better exhibited than by young animals, such as puppies, kittens, lambs, etc., when playing together, like our own children." He proceeded promptly to note that "the fact that the lower animals are excited by the same emotions as ourselves is so well established that it will not be necessary to weary the reader by many details" (Darwin, 1874, p. 55). He fleshed out these arguments in his remarkably prescient, third most famous, and psychologically relevant book *The Expression of Emotions in Man and Animals* (1872). Although Darwin was no expert on the brain, he realized that emotions were ancient solutions for successful animal life on earth.

He could not have known that the primary-process emotions were constructed by very ancient brain processes situated below the cortex. Indeed, only a few physiologists before the middle of the twentieth century recognized that primal emotional feelings emerged from subcortical brain regions that all mammals share, for example, most prominently Walter Cannon (1872–1945), of the famous Cannon-Bard theory, whose theory argued that emotional feelings arose from subcortical thalamic regions (Cannon, 1927, 1931), supplemented by the work of his most famous graduate student, Phillip Bard (1898–1977), whose dissertation focused more on hypothalamic contributions (Bard, 1928). These empirical breakthroughs, which challenged William James's speculations about higher brain (cortical) read-outs of bodily autonomic commotions causing emotional feelings, inspired the postulation that subcortically situated circuits formed coherent networks for emotionality, as proposed by James Papez (1937), and dramatically extended by Paul MacLean (1950, 1990) and Panksepp's *Affective Neuroscience* (1998a), which is resonant with these historical antecedents. (For a summary of William James's theory of how bodily physiological "read-outs" to upper brain regions may engender emotional feelings, see the January 2014 issue of *Emotion Review*.)

SPECIFIC EMOTIONS IN ANIMALS

In *Expression*, Darwin began with chapters on bodily emotional displays in animals. On the negative affect side, what we would recognize as the RAGE/Anger and FEAR systems are discussed for dogs cats, horses, and monkeys. The PANIC/Sadness system is discussed with reference to monkeys, which is included in paragraphs on "painful emotions."

On the positive affect side, he discussed how ticklish orangutans and chimpanzees were, along with discussions of their "laughter," which has only recently been empirically studied by others (Davila Ross, Owren, & Zimmermann, 2009), and extended to even lowly laboratory rats (Burgdorf & Panksepp, 2006; Panksepp & Burgdorf, 2003). Darwin's remarks certainly qualify as the first empirical discussion of a potential PLAY system in the brain. Obviously Darwin was well versed in LUST and CARE systems, although he, as well as practically all neuroscientists to the present day, had not conceptualized evidence indicating that the so-called brain reward system is better conceptualized as a SEEKING/

Enthusiasm system (Panksepp, 1981b, 1982, 1998a; for more recent discussions, see Panksepp & Biven, 2012; Panksepp & Wright, 2009; Wright & Panksepp, 2009).

SPECIFIC EMOTIONS IN HUMANS

Darwin became more definitive as he presented the expression of emotions from a human perspective, but he continued to integrate examples from animals in the discussion of human emotions. To avoid duplication, the summary that follows here of the various emotions presented by Darwin blends his animal and human discussions. Darwin's descriptions are not just insightful and useful; with only a few exceptions they are consistent with modern affective neuroscience. We provide enough flavor and detail from *Expression* to allow comparisons with the primary emotions in the Affective Neuroscience Personality Scales (Davis & Panksepp, 2011).

Hatred, Rage, and Anger: RAGE

In *Expression*, Darwin offered an operational definition of rage: "Unless an animal does thus act, or has the intention, or at least the desire, to attack its enemy, it cannot properly be said to be enraged" (Darwin 1872/1998, p. 78). He observed that when even moderately angry one's heart will beat more rapidly, one's face is likely to redden, and a specific facial expression is displayed, which features a strongly marked frown, that is, the drawing in of the "corrugators" or furrowing of the brow. Darwin noted that the reddening of the face can also be seen in monkeys and human infants and also pointed out that because of the strong affect of anger on the heart "not a few men with heart disease have dropped down dead under this powerful emotion" (p. 235).

He observed that angry humans often exposed their clenched teeth, which he argued revealed the evolutionary descent of this anger display, because, unlike animals, men seldom used their teeth in fighting (Darwin 1872/1998, p. 238). In a similar vein, when discussing human displays of anger and rage, Darwin also touched on the "sneer" in which canine teeth were uncovered by drawing up the outer upper lip, which we have all seen in snarling dogs. Again, Darwin thought such facial displays illuminated our animal heritage, because if a human did try to bite his or her enemy during a fight, the bite would not be made with the canine teeth the individual was displaying.

Darwin also noted in humans an "angry tone of voice" (Darwin 1872/1998, p. 242). Indeed, all over the world, angered individuals hurled verbal abuse upon their adversaries with bodies and heads leaning toward their opponents. At the level of infantile rage, he observed that enraged children screamed, kicked, and often tried to bite. In adults, the teeth and fists are often clenched. Also, the desire "to strike often becomes so intolerably strong, that inanimate objects are struck or dashed to the ground" (p. 236). Similarly, in enraged primates, emotional expressions included showing teeth, striking the ground with the hands, rolling on the ground, biting things, and sometimes "uttering terrific yells" in the case of gorillas. Highlighting another link between humans and the great apes, Darwin noted that orangutans and chimpanzees, like humans, could not move their ears, which kept them from drawing back their ears when angry as did some monkeys and all cats and dogs.

Surprise, Astonishment, Fear, Terror: FEAR

Darwin's comparative observations likewise supported a fear emotion. While affective neuroscience focuses on a more discrete primal FEAR system, Darwin believed that gradations of this emotion advanced from astonishment to fear to terror. Darwin described fear as resulting from sudden but dangerous events and used *terror* as the term for extreme fear. He stated that a frightened person "first stands like a statue motion-less and breathless" and "the skin instantly becomes pale" (Darwin 1872/1998, pp. 290–291). This description perfectly fit a bank teller the first author saw immediately after she had been robbed back in 1998 as the "base-ball-capped" bank robber walked past him on his way out of the bank. The teller was standing frozen but trying to draw attention to herself by holding her left hand in the air. Her face was totally white as she stood like a statue unable even to speak for several seconds. She was finally able to blurt out "I've been robbed" as the man was walking out the bank door.

Darwin's comprehensive description of the fear response also included the skin often breaking out in a "cold sweat" and "the hairs on the skin standing erect" (Darwin 1872/1998, p. 291). Muscles may shiver or trem-ble, and the mouth become dry. If more extreme, fear sends the subject into flight, and there may be screams of terror. Sphincter muscles may fail as well. The forehead is wrinkled, and the eyebrows are furrowed. The mouth is open, and the eyes are wide open. When experiencing ter-ror, monkeys' lips were also drawn back, teeth were exposed, and their hair became erect, all similar to fear responses in humans.

Suffering, Weeping, Grief: PANIC/Sadness

Darwin clearly reported the elements of the PANIC/Sadness system, although he treats "suffering and weeping" separately from "low spirits, anxiety, grief, dejection, despair." In his treatment of weeping he notes that human infants do not shed tears until two or three months of age, prior to which, like other animals, distress and cries are not accompanied by tears. He also observed that human tears do not only come with suffering, because tears often accompany bouts of laughter.

Darwin specifically discussed weeping in adult elephants and reported a case of a female elephant that shed tears when her baby was taken away from her. He also mentioned several species of monkeys that cry. Darwin seems to be relying on reports from other observers here, and current evidence suggests that while other mammals emit social separation cries or whines, only humans shed tears of sorrow from their tear ducts.

When discussing painful emotions in animals, Darwin focused on loss and "grief," which encompassed many features of the PANIC/Sadness system. He also claimed that dejection is plainly observable in young chimpanzees and orangutans, and he described them as listless with fallen countenances and dull eyes, not unlike humans suffering from depression.

Love, Tender Feelings: CARE

In the chapter on joy, Darwin also discussed love, which referred to the kind of love a mother has for her infant or, as he referred to it, "the tender feeling." Even though it is one of the strongest emotions, Darwin pointed out that it has no particular expression. It may be associated with "a gentle smile and some brightening of the eyes," but it does not have a facial expression that would be easily recognized out of context. Darwin observed that this tender feeling is most typically expressed by "a strong desire to touch the beloved" (Darwin 1872/1998, p. 212). As a sign of affection, he also noted that animals from dogs to chimpanzees like to rub against and touch those to whom they are attached.

Darwin's investigations also led him to conclude that human kissing was not innate, because kissing was not known among the natives of Tierra del Fuego, whom he encountered during his five-year circumnavigation of the earth on the HMS *Beagle*. Also, his observers informed him that kissing was not known among Eskimos or the natives of New Zealand, Australia, and West Africa. He concluded, however, that many different expressions of affection, such as rubbing noses, do always include "close contact with the beloved person" (Darwin 1872/1998, p. 214).

Darwin remarked about the complexity of all the feelings that can be associated with what we might call CAREing love. He reminded us of the tears of joy shown by a father and son when reunited after a long separation—which in affective neuroscience terms would be a PANIC/Sadness response. Still, he was perplexed and wondered whether those tears might be due to thoughts going through their heads of the potential grief they would probably have felt had they not been able to reunite. He likewise noted that the tears from thinking about "long-past happy days" probably have to do with the thought "that these days will never return" (Darwin 1872/1998, p. 215) and that we may be sympathizing with ourselves. Again, these tears may come more from the sense of social loss associated with the PANIC/Sadness system responses in humans. No other species weeps so clearly as human beings, and the tears of joy may arise from higher thoughtful reflections on the agony of PANIC/Sadness.

Joy, High Spirits: PLAY

For Darwin, joy was synonymous with laughter and children playing: "Laughter seems to be the expression of mere joy or happiness. We clearly see this in children at play, who are almost incessantly laughing" (Darwin 1872/1998, p. 195). Darwin also reported that the blind and deaf are also seen to laugh and clap their hands even though they could not have learned this through imitation.

Darwin saw tickling as one way to evoke this joyous state. He noted that the tickler must not be a stranger, and the tickler's touch must be light. He noted that the parts of the body that are easily tickled are among those that are not often touched, such as armpits and the soles of the feet. He reasoned that because a child cannot tickle him or herself, the "precise point to be touched must not be known [by the child]" (Darwin 1872/1998, p. 198). From this Darwin reasoned the unexpected is a strong element in general humor.

Similar to modern affective neuroscience work on the "tickling" of rats (Panksepp & Burgdorf, 2000), Darwin pointed out that young chimpanzees and orangutans have ticklish armpits, like children, and when tickled utter "chuckling or laughing" sounds with their mouths drawn backward like in a smile. Darwin described the sound that apes make when tickled as a "reiterated sound" (Darwin 1872/1998, p. 198), which corresponds to human laughter and its "short, interrupted, spasmodic contractions of the chest" (Darwin 1872/1998, p. 199)—a description that would also fit the ultrasonic "chirps" juvenile rats emit when playing with another rat pup or being "tickled" by a human hand (Panksepp, 2007c).

Darwin went on to describe the human facial expression associated with laughter and smiling. In a full smile, the orbicularis muscles surrounding the eye socket make the eye squint. Hence, with a full natural smile "crow's feet" are formed in the corners of the eye, in contrast to a partial smile, which is probably more forced and less natural.

Darwin also suggested the principle that opposite emotions would produce opposite actions. An example would be a smile with the corners of the mouth turned up and a sad expression with the corners of the mouth turned down. Darwin argued that this idea applied to the sounds made with laughter as well. Laughter sounds are "short and broken," whereas the cries of distress are "prolonged and continuous" (Darwin 1872/1998, p. 206). These observations are consistent with Panksepp's (2007c) play chirps in rats and John Paul Scott's (1974) distress vocalizations in dogs (for the first neuroscience study, see Panksepp, Herman, Conner, Bishop, & Scott, 1978). These insightful observations across mammalian species illustrate the kind of learning and generalization that can be achieved by Darwin's comparative approach to the study of emotions, which consistently supported his important principle of continuity among species.

Anticipatory Versus Consummatory Enjoyment: SEEKING

In *Expression,* Darwin does not directly discuss curious exploration or the seeking out of resources such as food. He does, however, discuss a critical element of the SEEKING system in distinguishing between the joys of anticipation and consumption. He wrote, "It is chiefly the anticipation of a pleasure, and not its actual enjoyment, which leads to purposeless and extravagant movements of the body, and to the utterance of various sounds" (Darwin 1872/1998, p. 80). His examples here were the excitement associated with anticipating an event, for example, children clapping their hands and jumping for joy or dogs barking and bounding when they see their food arriving. This reference to the anticipation of a pleasure is significant because the primary-process SEEKING/ Enthusiasm ("brain reward") emotional system of affective neuroscience features both the anticipation of and search for rewards, but not the consumption or enjoyment phase of reward (as was once thought). A very similar conclusion was later reached by Kent Berridge (2004). In addition, the SEEKING system may also energize other emotions, as in anticipating the termination of negative affects, such as SEEKING safety in a FEARful situation.

SUMMATION OF DARWIN'S CONTRIBUTIONS TO UNDERSTANDING HUMAN EMOTIONS

In affective neuroscience terms, Darwin had described elements of the RAGE/Anger (hatred and anger), FEAR (fear and terror), PANIC/Sadness (weeping and grief), CARE (love and the tender feelings), and PLAY (joy). If we include Darwin's discussion of anticipatory motivation as representing the SEEKING system, his revolutionary synthesis of human and animal emotions covered all six of the primary-process emotions prominently related to personality and measured in the ANPS.

In a sense, a reasonably definitive modern personality theory (as is modeled in the Affective Neuroscience Personality Scales discussed in this book) could be conceptualized as having started with Darwin's insights (even though, as we later describe, only William McDougall carried such an approach to personality into the twentieth century). Darwin placed humans on a continuum with other mammals and used the comparative approach to identify commonalities—homologous expressions of emotions—between humans and other mammals. Using this comparative approach he frequently illuminated profound human-animal continuities, for example, both humans and other animals baring their teeth when angry and with hairs standing erect when fearful. Because the human evolutionary "ascent" was gradual, being able to trace behavioral as well as physical and psychological elements in humans back through our evolutionary history was the rule rather than the exception. The differences between humans and their nonhuman ancestors would be of degree and not of kind, and primal emotional feelings could still lie at the root of human experience.

Darwin not only established the evolutionary link between the behavior of humans and other animals; he also asserted that we are less likely to deceive ourselves if the behaviors we study can be observed in other animals as well as in humans. While Darwin did not use the term *personality*, he did describe the personality elements of many animals—especially chimpanzees—as well as humans. While one should remain aware of the dangers of anthropomorphizing animal behavior—giving animals human characteristics—ever since Darwin it has been equally dangerous to assume that humans are so unique that our personality structures lack counterparts in the animal kingdom.

One of the themes of this book is how our evolved biological emotional systems influence our behavior and personalities. We believe, the preponderance of evidence will continue to show that Darwin got inquiries into the sources of personality off to a remarkably clear, but typically unacknowledged, start. His focus on the comparative animal study of emotion is one of the main tenets of affective neuroscience. However, there was a long period when Darwin's *Expression* was out of favor in the world of psychology, which started to be reversed a bit when Paul Ekman, who took a Darwinian approach to the study of human facial emotional expressions, published an annotated version of Darwin's *Expression* in 1998.

Regrettably, today there are still those who conclude that the subjective experience of emotions is unique to humans, or simply cannot be empirically studied in animal models. Both views are simply incorrect, and it is time to return classic emotion approaches to the study of human temperaments, a goal we strive for with this book. Therefore, we not only summarize the history of the field but also highlight how the ANPS is a bridge toward a further synthesis of human and animal data through a new comparative neuropsychology that is essential for understanding the foundations of the human mind. As we describe in the next chapter, the life work of William McDougall attempted this, even though his work currently seems to be a footnote to an intellectual passage that never happened, at least until the emergence of an empirically sound affective neuroscience.

CHAPTER 4

William McDougall's Comparative Psychology

Toward a Naturalistic Personality Approach

It is only a comparative and evolutionary psychology that can provide the needed basis [for understanding human nature]; and this could not be created before the work of Darwin had convinced men of the continuity of human with animal evolution as regards all bodily characters, and had prepared the way for the quickly following recognition of the similar continuity of man's mental evolution with that of the animal world.

—William McDougal, *Introduction to Social Psychology*

WITH CHARLES DARWIN'S evolutionary perspective, it was not long until a young British psychologist, William McDougall (1871–1938), applied Darwin's ideas to construct a more formal theory of human personality by focusing on the emerging wisdom embodied in the comparative approach. Relying on cross-species observations, McDougall arrived at a list of primary emotions that were quite similar to those of Darwin, as well as more recent psychologists like Silvan Tomkins and his students Paul Ekman and Cal Izard, as well as Jaak Panksepp's independent neuroscience work, which was purposefully constrained by a direct study of the brains of other animals. The reason Panksepp studied animal brains was straightforward: We simply do not have access to the relevant brain mechanisms in human research.

MCDOUGALL AND THE INSTINCT
THEORY OF PERSONALITY

William McDougall, a now largely forgotten psychologist, was born in England in 1871, in the same year that *The Descent of Man* was published. With his interest in the evolution of mind, McDougall became one of the earliest British psychologists in the newly emerging academic field of social psychology, and he accepted the "doctrine of the evolution of man from animal forms" (McDougall, 1908, p. 76). In 1904 he took a position at Oxford, where he wrote what turned out to be his most famous work, *Introduction to Social Psychology* (1908), which led to his being offered the William James chair of psychology at Harvard in 1920, ten years after James died. With his *Introduction to Social Psychology* (from here on referred to as ISP), McDougall had published one of the most thorough analyses of emotions ever attempted and how these important brain processes may relate to personality. However, in the United States he was greeted by a tidal wave of behaviorism and later wrote, "I found Behaviorism ascendant and rampant. I found that, though my *Social Psychology* had enjoyed before the War a much larger vogue than I had realized, it and I were now back-numbers, relics of a bygone and superseded age" (McDougall, 1930, p. 213). History can be cruel when in our estimation we are on the right track but without a receptive audience. Therefore, while at Harvard, McDougall shifted directions and spent many years attempting to demonstrate Lamarckian transmission (the inheritance of acquired traits) in rats, without success (McDougall, 1930). Of course, this was difficult without access to modern genetics.[3]

Indeed, he was quite frustrated at Harvard, because he did not get the adulation he thought he deserved. In 1927 he moved to Duke University, where he remained until his death in 1938. In his autobiography, he described himself as arrogant, and he admitted to being attracted to grand projects. At Duke he pursued "psychical research" (now known as parapsychology) with the hope of determining for the world whether "supernormal phenomena" could be experimentally verified. Parenthetically, Alfred Russel Wallace (1823–1913), a British naturalist who had shared his own prescient theory of evolution with Darwin in 1858 (which speeded Darwin's publication of *On the Origin of Species*), like McDougall also spent much of the rest of his career studying paranormal phenomena. Even though these research activities tarnished both their reputations, McDougall felt he had pursued them with the same scientific rigor that he had applied earlier to comparative psychology.

Nevertheless, it is McDougall's earlier comparative personality work, which was written just before the advent of Watsonian radical behaviorism, that was his major contribution and that we summarize in this chapter as an example of a prebehaviorism comparative approach to understanding the workings of the mammalian mind, with implications for understanding the sources of human personality differences. Remarkably, Panksepp independently took up this quest to understand basic mammalian emotions—shifting from clinical psychology to physiological psychology in his first year of graduate school as he realized there was no other way to constitutionally understand evolved emotional feelings in humans without the neuroscience essential to take understanding to the "mechanistic" level (for a neurophilosophical synopsis of the rationale, see Panksepp, 2015).

McDougall's Social Psychology: Toward Instinct Criteria for Personality Traits

McDougall's best-known work, *Introduction to Social Psychology* (1908), was based on "the sweeping assertion that the energy displayed in every human activity might in principle be traced back to some inborn disposition or instinct" (McDougall, 1930, p. 208). However, his contribution is more than just formalizing Darwin's evolutionary ideas about emotions into a personality theory. McDougall also placed each personality-related emotion and its psychopathological extreme on the same dimension, a concept that modern psychiatry is still struggling to introduce into diagnostic practice (see Panksepp, 2005, 2008). McDougall further detailed key components of primary emotions, more comprehensively than Darwin, that continue to withstand the test of time, namely, scientific scrutiny from both human psychological (Izard, 2007) and cross-species neuroscientific perspectives (Panksepp, 1998a, 2005, 2011b).

Since the publication of Darwin's theory of evolution, hundreds if not thousands of instincts had been proposed by many authors, and along with them McDougall was widely criticized for excessive use of the instinct concept. In reality, McDougall was himself critical of those that used the instinct concept loosely. Thus, McDougall placed limiting criteria on the identification of instincts and rejected proposed instincts that did not meet his standards.

The first criterion, like Darwin, was whether certain "natural" behaviors were "clearly displayed in the instinctive activities of the higher animals" (McDougall, 1908, p. 42). That is, he was only willing to consider "primary emotions" or "simple instincts" that could be observed in humans as well as other vertebrates. With this criterion he rejected many proposed instincts, including the religious instinct.

However, McDougall added a second criterion alluded to above, namely, that a primary emotion should be observable in human abnormal behavior. That is, if an emotion appeared in human beings in an

extreme and exaggerated display, which would be considered pathological, that dysfunctional reaction would also confirm its status as a primary
emotion or simple instinct. With this second principle, McDougall placed
various pathological behaviors on the same psychological dimensions
as other personality characteristics and removed any arbitrary divides
between what would be considered "normal" or "abnormal." In effect,
he presaged the intimate link between primary-process emotions and
psychological imbalances that Panksepp (1998a, 2005) advanced almost
a century later from a rigorous neuroscientific perspective and that many
have sought to include in the "bible" of psychiatric diagnostics, the
American Psychiatric Association's *Diagnostic and Statistical Manual* ,
most recently the fifth edition (*DSM-V*; see Chapter 18). The difficulties
in such tasks are enormous, because the behaviorist revolution restricted
discussion to discretely measurable units of behavior, making discussion
of psychological processes in animals especially suspect of challenged
intellectual thinking.

In any case, McDougall was on his way to developing what may be
considered the first comprehensive psychological theory of personality. Using his two criteria, he identified eleven primary instincts, only
the first seven of which he considered well defined. However, in addition to winnowing the list of primary instincts down to eleven, McDougall added four insightful principles to his theory of personality that,
while based on the comparative (cross-species) behavioral observation
method, remain largely consistent with later thinking drawn totally independently from cross-species affective neuroscience research.

The Four Principles of McDougall's
Social Psychology

First, McDougall viewed these instincts as mental processes and thus
described them in terms of what he called "the cognitive, the affective,
and the conative aspects" (p. 23) with the latter referring to a natural
impulse toward directed effort. By *cognitive*, he meant the sensory-expe-
riential component, that is, a "complex of sensations that has significance or meaning for the animal" (p. 24). The *affective* aspect referred
to the valenced feeling components, namely, various positive (good) and
negative (bad) feelings, which were uniquely associated with particular instinctive behaviors. The *conative* part was the "striving towards or
away from that object" (p. 23). This was the desire, aversion, impulse,
craving, or uneasy sense of wanting that accompanied the instinct. So,
in McDougall's hands, an instinct became the result of an evolutionarily
relevant stimulus that once perceived was accompanied by a particular
emotional-affective excitement along with particular behaviors or at least
the impulse to such behaviors.

Second, McDougall argued that the stimulus-receptive and behavioral-action parts of an instinct could be modified. On the sensory side, experience adapts instinctive actions to match new environmental demands. McDougall reasoned that we can learn to fear stimuli that were previously neutral, that is, did not previously elicit fear. He pointed out that animals learn to fear the sight of men and guns and that we learn to feel anger toward those people who have frustrated us in the past. This learning principle is comparable to Panksepp's secondary-level processing, which, following traditional behavioral learning theory, provides for the conditioning of the instinctual unconditional response systems. It has come quite clear from modern neuroscience research that the learning mechanisms in all mammals are anatomically and neurochemically very similar (see Kandel, 2007; LeDoux, 2012)—although to this day neither of these neurobehavioristic scholars puts much stock in the view that animals affectively experience their emotional arousals.

Third, McDougall offered the important everyday observation that the hidden central feeling aspects of the instincts, the affective parts, do not change qualitatively as a function of learning. For McDougall, even though the perceptions that ignite an instinct and the behavioral expressions of the instincts can change, what we feel remains qualitatively largely unmodified, although they may become stronger or weaker and longer or shorter. McDougall held that "all the principle instincts of man are liable to similar modifications of their afferent and motor parts, while their central parts [feelings] remain unchanged and determine the emotional tone of consciousness and the visceral changes characteristic of the excitement of the instinct" (p. 36). This fundamental principle remains an important element of emotion theory (Izard, 2007) and affective neuroscience (Panksepp, 1998) and is consistent with the conclusion that primal affects remain substantial key components of the unconditional arousal of emotional action systems within the brain (Panksepp & Biven, 2012). However, this is not to deny that learning and cognitions can modify and regulate the intensity and duration of primal emotional feelings, as well as engender more complex derivative feelings that are related to environmental complexities, the concurrent arousal of several emotional systems, and various types of culturally promoted or even (at least in humans) willful regulatory strategies.

Fourth, McDougall emphasized that each primary affect could not be described adequately with language. Perhaps the greatest obstacle to discussing subjective affects is our inability to describe them as precisely as we describe objects in the world. They are *qualia*, a philosophical term meaning the experiential essence of something that cannot be verbally explicitly described but that must be directly experienced. Thus, McDougall wrote, "a person who had not experienced it [the affect] could no more be made to understand its quality than a totally colour-blind person can be made to understand the experience of colour-sensation" (p. 61).

Although we cannot say exactly what FEAR feels like to a rat or even to another human being, we are sure that both experience a subjectively aversive event that can motivate learning (e.g., acquired escape and avoidance behaviors) and thereby alter exhibited action patterns, based on environmental contingencies. Indeed, an affect, *much like the effect of gravity on objects in the world*, must be inferred from behavioral changes, but the feeling component can be evaluated (inferred) in animals by whether shifts in the induced states of emotional circuits (as with direct brain stimulation) are rewarding or punishing. Of course, in humans one can ask very direct questions about the intensity and durations of shifting feelings. In short, emotional affects have one of two *valences*: They either feel good or feel bad. The ones that feel good (SEEKING/Enthusiasm, CARE/Nurturance, and PLAY/Joy) are nature's emotional rewards; the ones that feel bad (RAGE/Anger, FEAR/Anxiety, and PANIC/Grief/Sadness) are emotional punishments.

This point needs emphasis: We can infer this from any human's or animal's behavior, because the individual subsequently attempts to repeat the pleasant rewarding affects and to avoid the unpleasant punishing affects, especially when we include preference measures. For example, nonhuman animals prefer places where their positive emotional brain systems have been stimulated with small electrical currents or micro injections of an appropriate synaptic transmitter/modulator substance, such as amphetamines or opiates; they avoid places where their negative emotions have been likewise stimulated. Corresponding statements can be made about human affective experiences. Because affects evolved many millions of years before the appearance of spoken language, they are difficult to verbally describe, but they are every bit as real as our earth's gravity that causes apples to fall from trees to the ground rather than the other way around.

In short, McDougall took important conceptual steps in fleshing out an evolutionarily grounded theory of personality, although he was not able to put those ideas on a firm neuroscience foundation, which would have required cross-species brain research of the kind now common in modern animal and human affective neurosciences. He was not willing to attribute any instinctual emotion to humans that could not also be observed behaviorally in other animals. He also only considered emotions that in their extreme expression became pathological. He allowed for adaptation and the learning of new stimuli and new responses to be associated with the core affects, which did not change with experience and which needed to be directly experienced to be subjectively understood. Indeed, without the tools of modern neuroscience, he came tantalizingly close to the affective neuroscience position on emotions and personality, but the neuroscience of his day was not mature enough to take it to the next essential step—demonstration of diverse rewarding and punishing emotional brain systems in other animals, which Panksepp's (1981b, 1982, 1998a) work has solidified. Of course, there is abundant neuroempirical work left to be done, especially at the cognitive levels, because with its massive cortical expansions (relative to body size), the human brain may be the most complex object in our known universe.

A BRIEF COMPARISON OF MCDOUGALL'S AND PANKSEPP'S BASIC EMOTION APPROACHES

McDougall's terms for his list of eleven primary instincts (with alternate language in parentheses) were *flight* (FEAR), *repulsion* (disgust), *curiosity* (SEEKING), *pugnacity* (RAGE/Anger), *self-abasement* (submissiveness), *self-assertion* (dominance), the *parental instinct* (CARE), *reproduction* (LUST), the *gregarious instinct* (PANIC/Sadness), the *instinct of acquisition,* and the *instinct of construction.*

Here we briefly consider how McDougall's views on those emotions overlap with Darwin's and Panksepp's. But first, it should be noted that there are many other psychologically-oriented emotion theorists (most prominently, Ross Buck, Paul Ekman, Cal Izard, Robert Plutchick, and especially Silvan Tomkins) whose psychological and facial analyses we do not cover here, for they did not contribute to the cross-species neural understanding of primary-process emotions. There is also an enormous number of fine young investigators using modern brain imaging, especially fMRI (functional magnetic resonance imaging) of brain blood oxygen levels as a proxy for neural firing. We will not cover brain imaging in this chapter (but see Chapter 16 on brain imaging), because their work does not yet directly impact our cross-species brain network understanding of primal emotions that guided the development of our Affective Neuroscience Personality Scales (ANPS).

To facilitate this overview, Table 4.1 compares Darwin's, McDougall's, Panksepp's, and the Big Five list of primary emotions and traits. There is a solid core of similarities, with a variety of more debatable items used by McDougall, such as "disgust," which is included by most modern human emotion theorists (for recent overview, see Tracy & Randles, 2011), but Panksepp withholds judgment, seeing it as a metaphoric usage describing social disdain in terms of a sensory bodily feeling of nausea. Hence, disgust would be a secondary or tertiary emotion rather than a primary one (see Chapter 5 for a discussion of primary, secondary, and tertiary conceptual levels of emotions).

Flight and the Emotion of Fear

The instinct of flight, accompanied by the emotional feeling of fear, was McDougall's first instinct. While this instinct begins with flight or fleeing from danger, McDougall argued that flight was often followed by "concealment." He also allowed for concealment, or what we would now call freezing or hiding, to be the initial fear response and described people

Table 4.1. Emotion Systems: Three Comparative Approaches and the Big Five

Darwin: Emotions	McDougall: Primary Instincts/ Emotions	Panksepp: Primary Emotions	Big Five: Personality Traits
Surprise, Astonishment, Fear, and Terror	Flight/Fear	FEAR	Low Emotional Stability
Disdain, Contempt, Disgust, Guilt, Pride	Repulsion/Disgust	(likely a sensory affect, not an emotional system)	—
Anticipatory vs. Consummatory Enjoyment	Curiosity/Wonder	SEEKING/ Enthusiasm	Openness to Experience
Hatred, Rage, and Anger	Pugnacity/Anger	RAGE/Anger	Low Emotional Stability
—	Self-assertion/ Elation and Self-abasement/ Subjection	(Social Dominance not well defined as a distinct brain circuit)	Possible aspect of Extraversion
Love, Tender Feelings	Parental Instinct/ The Tender Emotion	CARE	High Agreeableness
—	Reproduction	LUST	—
Suffering, Weeping, Grief	The Gregarious Instinct	PANIC/Sadness	Low Emotional Stability
—	Acquisition	(such behaviors may arise largely from SEEKING)	—
—	Construction	—	—
Joy, High Spirits	Innate Play Tendency	PLAY	Extraversion

who irrationally sought cover from strange noises at night by covering their heads with their blankets.

McDougall noted that fear brought all other activities to an end. In other words, fear stopped all ongoing positive instinctual behaviors. He described the fear emotion as the "great inhibitor of action," and the "great agent of social discipline" in primitive human societies, although it is still easy today to find examples of leaders utilizing fear to control their populations. With the emotion of fear, McDougall's system fits well with Panksepp's modern affective neuroscience blue ribbon emotions, in this case the FEAR system.

Pugnacity and the Emotion of Anger

McDougall also selected pugnacity as a primary instinct and named the emotion anger. On the sensory input side, he suggested that "opposition to the free exercise of any impulse" (p. 51) elicited this instinct. The goal of this instinct was to break down the obstruction and even "destroy whatever offers opposition" (p. 51).

McDougall suggested that "irritation" described human feelings of milder pugnacity, as when one's meal is interrupted. However, he suggested that "furious" was more appropriate when one's sex life is interfered with. McDougall also suggested that one of the main functions of anger in humans is to provide an extra surge of energy when facing something blocking one's path, and in this sense anger became an enabler, in contrast to fear the inhibitor. With the pugnacity instinct and the emotion of anger, McDougall rather accurately described the RAGE/ Anger system. So, he started out two for two in a general comparison with Panksepp's blue ribbon list.

Repulsion and the Emotion of Disgust

The only other instinct McDougall offered in the negative affect mix was "repulsion" and the emotion of "disgust." He described repulsion as an "aversion" that prompts one to "remove or reject the offending object" (p. 48). He included "creepy shudder" to slimy things with the repulsion instinct, as well as spitting something "evil-tasting" out of one's mouth.

McDougall suggested that the facial expression of disgust was similar to the facial movements made when rejecting something from the mouth, and it is this widely recognized expression that convinces many that disgust is instinctive and should be included in taxonomies of emotion (e.g., Toronchuk & Ellis, 2007). However, disgust may be better thought of as a *sensory* affective reaction that happens to be associated with a facial expression, rather than a primary, whole-body emotion response.

In contrast to the other negative affects of RAGE/Anger, FEAR, and PANIC/Sadness, it is more difficult to detect disgust just by the tone of someone's speaking voice (Adolphs, 2002), although the related concept of scorn is easier to express. This and the lack of brain evidence for a well-defined emotional disgust brain system (although the nausea response depends heavily on the ancient cortical area known as the insula) led Panksepp to suggest that disgust should be considered a simpler sensory and/or possibly a homeostatic affect rather than among the blue ribbon list of primary-process integrative emotions that are more important for manifest personality differences among individuals.

Disgust, along with the sensory reaction of surprise and the feelings of tiredness, illness, hunger, and thirst, is an example of an affect that does not seem to have much influence on personality. In fact, these are not words that people tend to list as basic emotions (Russell, 1991), although they are sometimes included in lists of mood adjectives (Watson & Tellegen, 1985). So, while repulsion and disgust probably have instinctive components, they are not as clearly important for understanding the diversity of personality traits.

Curiosity and the Emotion of Wonder

Curiosity is the first positive instinct McDougall presented, and he labeled the affect *wonder*, a word he admitted might not fit perfectly but was the most appropriate he could find. (Recall his fourth principle that language could not adequately describe affects.) He contrasted the approach impulse of curiosity with the avoidance impulse of fear and discussed how the two may alternate as when curiosity compels one to start exploring a dark cave or unlit castle, which may quickly turn to fear if the strangeness or unfamiliarity of the situation becomes too great.

McDougall stated that curiosity was one of the weaker instincts. Hence, he did not see the curiosity instinct as having a general role comparable to that of Panksepp's SEEKING system for driving us enthusiastically to explore the world and heading toward goals that meet our needs. He also did not link cocaine use, which became popular in his day (indeed, Freud had written a famous paper on his experiences), to the curiosity instinct. The closest he came to offering a pathological side to curiosity was to suggest it was unlikely that any organism could exhibit too strong a curiosity instinct without meeting "an untimely end"—as the old saying goes, curiosity killed the cat.

The Parental Instinct and the Tender Emotion

McDougall found another positive affect that he called the parental instinct, engendering a tender emotion. He contrasted reproduction in the "lower animals," such as reptiles, which produce an immense number of eggs and leave their young unprotected, with that of the "higher animals" (meaning mammals), which produce far fewer eggs and display prolonged parental support and guardianship.

For McDougall, the parental instinct could be more powerful than any of the other instincts and could override any of them including fear, as he noted in those mothers "which in all other situations are very timid, any attempt to remove the young from the protective parent, or in any way to hurt them, provokes a fierce and desperate display of all their combative resource" (p. 62). While the parental instinct is usually stronger in women, he noted that "the parental instinct is by no means altogether lacking in men" (p. 59). As a student, McDougall had spent time in Indonesia on an anthropological expedition and reported watching a father in Borneo "spending a day at home tenderly nursing his infant in his arms" (p. 59).

In humans, the tender emotion is evoked by the helplessness of children, and it is the child's cry of distress that primarily provokes the tender emotion. Although the parental instinct may be aroused more intensely by one's own child, it can also be aroused by the cry of any child. McDougall noted that if those individuals with strong parental instincts cannot respond to their parental impulse, "they cannot withdraw their attention from the sound, but continue to listen in painful agitation" (p. 63).

McDougall seems to have captured the evolutionary basis of the parental instinct, as well as its possible elaboration in other aspects of life. Thus, he clearly described a system that is easily equated with the primary CARE system of modern affective neuroscience, which is a hormonally primed, female-typical variant of mammalian brain emotional circuitry.

The Gregarious Instinct

One of McDougall's minor instincts was the gregarious instinct. While he stated that this instinct is "of greatest social importance," he also wrote that its feeling component was so weak and unspecific that he did not give it a name. He may have gotten his ideas about gregariousness from the British statistician and eugenicist Sir Francis Galton (1822–1911), who was Charles Darwin's half cousin. McDougall referred to Galton's classic description of the South African ox in Damaraland. Galton had traveled to what is currently Namibia and in 1871 published his observations in *Inquiries into Human Faculty*. McDougall quoted him: "[The ox] displays no affection for his fellows, and hardly seems to notice their existence, so long as he is among them; but, if he becomes separated from the herd, he displays an extreme distress that will not let him rest until he succeeds in rejoining it" (p. 72). From this, McDougall argued that the gregarious instinct is simply "uneasiness in isolation" and "satisfaction in being one of the herd" (p. 72). However, McDougall was looking through the wrong end of the telescope and missed the significance of "separation distress." Had he never sat up all night in the kitchen trying to sooth a distressed puppy or a young child?

It seems apparent that what McDougall called the gregarious instinct was the flip side of separation distress and the PANIC/Sadness system. While he was typically an excellent observer of behavior, he never mentioned any vocalization as part of separation distress. He also made no mention of the crying exhibited by so many young animals when separated from their mates or caregivers.

So, in our view, McDougall's gregarious instinct was not about gregariousness—it was about the primary PANIC/Sadness system and the painful separation distress we feel when we lose an important social connection. If McDougall had focused on the expression of separation distress rather than its absence, he would have scored another direct hit one hundred years ago. Psychological/behavioral progress on that topic started when psychiatrist John Bowlby (1907–1990) conceptualized the emotional importance of human relationships and Harry Harlow (1905–1981) and John Paul Scott (1909–2000) concurrently started to study social attachment processes and separation distress, especially through separation-induced crying. Panksepp was the first to initiate neurobiological manipulation of this PANIC brain system.

Sympathy, Suggestibility, Imitation, and Play

McDougall added four additional innate tendencies that he stopped short of calling instincts. He argued that sympathy, suggestibility, and imitation do not have specific perceptual triggers or well-defined responses: "There is no common affective state and no common impulse seeking satisfaction in some particular change of state" (p. 88). So, he preferred to call them "pseudo-instincts." McDougall finally came to the "tendency to play," but like sympathy, suggestibility, and imitation, he stopped short of calling it an instinct and described it instead as one of "the native tendencies of the mind." However, he did acknowledge that humans and many animals start playing "spontaneously without any teaching or example" (p. 92).

McDougall reviewed and rejected several other theories of play, including G. Stanley Hall's (1904) law of recapitulation, which claimed that play represented the cultural stages humans had traversed in their evolutionary past. For example, climbing trees represented the human "monkey" period, and camping represented our "nomadic" period.

McDougall offered some interesting observations about play on his own. He noted that if play fighting was just the immature expression of the pugnacious instinct, then animals should be angry and really trying to hurt each other, but he observed that young dogs do not exhibit anger as they "roll about together" even though they show anger in other situations. He noted puppies have sharp teeth and are capable of biting hard, but when they play they do not bite each other hard enough to draw blood. McDougall also commented that "boys are no exception to the rule" of combat without anger (p. 94).

McDougall accurately described the stereotyped running and chasing play in puppies and young children. However, PLAY, as the most recently evolved mammalian emotion, seemed too complex, especially in humans. Yet, Panksepp's seminal work with the PLAY system in rats, from development of rigorous experimental paradigms to the first neuroscience inquiries (Panksepp, Siviy, & Normansell, 1984), has led to the experimental study of play becoming an increasingly important topic of rigorous inquiry (e.g., Panksepp et al., 2015; Pellis & Pellis, 2016).

CONCEPTUAL EXCESSES VERSUS EXPERIMENTAL RIGOR

A flaw that appeared in McDougall's theory was perhaps not being content with the behavioral explanations of his eleven instincts and innate tendencies. To explain more behavior, he proposed two additional constructs: sentiments and complex emotions. A sentiment was "an organised system of emotional tendencies centered about some object" (p. 105). Love and hate for another person (the object) were two such sentiments. For example, love was a sentiment rather than a primary emotion because when a person came to "love" someone, that person became likely to experience any of a collection of emotions that somehow became encapsulated in the love sentiment. That is, when a person loves another, that person will experience caring in the presence of the loved one but also fear when the loved one is in danger, anger when the loved one is threatened, sadness when separated, joy with reunion, and so forth, depending on the situation.

Complex emotions were different than sentiments in that they arose from the simultaneous arousal of two or more emotions. One of the complex emotions McDougall offered was admiration, which blended the emotions of wonder and submission. Wonder was evident in the behavioral impulse to approach, and submission in the tendency to be humbled and perhaps childlike. However, if admiration were further blended with fear, the resulting complex emotion was awe. Further examples were scorn, a combination of anger and disgust; loathing, a combination of fear and disgust; and fascination, which added an element of approach to loathing by combining loathing with wonder.

Obviously, such higher emotional constructs are next to impossible to study in animals.

McDougall went on to give examples of complex emotions that included a sentiment. Jealousy resulted when the object of our love offers affection to a third party, such that we simultaneously feel personal pain and anger toward the third party. The vengeful emotion occurred when we are angered but are not able to assert ourselves and thus regain our positive self-feeling by "getting even." Resentment resulted from the same conditions that provoke the vengefulness, but we are able to immediately avenge the situation and regain our positive self-feeling. Shame appeared after the development of the self-regarding sentiment and resulted when our own actions cause our status in the eyes of others to be lowered and thus may be negative self-feeling combined with anger directed at ourselves. McDougall included many others.

These derived or blended emotions begin to sound like cooking recipes. Mix a cup of tender emotion with a bit of negative self-feeling, place in a sentiment, wait until something separates you from someone you care about (the object of your sentiment), and you will have a dose of sorrow. Combine equal parts of the tender emotion and anger, fuse them in the crucible of parenthood, and you will soon be spewing out reproachful statements like "Why do you do the things that you do!?" The blending of emotions seems plausible and similar to the trait blends suggested by Goldberg and colleagues (Hofstee et al., 1992), but much affective neuroscience work will be required for verification, and to this day that level of analysis has not been rigorously pursued.

Supposedly, one could discern which emotions were linked with a complex emotion by observing which primary emotion motor tendencies were activated when one of these compound emotions was experienced, a claim that apparently was never empirically validated. In any event, most of these combinations are simply incapable of being studied in animals, even though progress is being made on some, such as optimism (Rygula, Pluta, & Popik, 2012) and regret (Steiner & Redish, 2014).

AN OVERALL SUMMARY OF
MCDOUGALL'S WORK

McDougall's observations led him to conclude that ancestral instincts were essential for understanding the motivations that energize our encounters with life. These "ancient instincts" provided the window into the "native tendencies of the mind." Without instincts we would be like a steam engine without a fire to maintain hydraulic pressure in the system. He wrote, "Take away these instinctive dispositions with their powerful impulses, and the organism would become incapable of activity of any kind" (p. 38). This sounds like a statement a neuroscientist might make after observing an animal subjected to a complete lesion of the lateral hypothalamus or the periaqueductal gray, both of which destroy normal behavioral and consciousness abilities. So, we would generally concur with McDougall's vision of the primary instincts, but he did not provide solid scientific entry points, neither behavioral-experimental nor neuroscientific, into clarifying concepts such as sentiments above and beyond speculative storytelling. If he had held fast to his animal comparative and clinical pathology criteria, he might have limited himself to a taxonomy of human motivation and behavior that would not be far different from the affective neuroscience conclusions one hundred years later.

McDougall was also criticized for using instincts in an explanatory way. That is, he fell victim to the nominal fallacy—confusing naming with explaining. For example, saying that mothers care for their young because they have the parental instinct made it seem like parental behavior had been explained, but in reality, little more had been accomplished than naming the behavior. At worst, such practices rapidly became circular: the parenting instinct caused mothers to care for their young, and mothers cared for their young because they had a parenting instinct. Naming the parenting instinct added no *explanation* for why the mothers cared for their offspring, except perhaps to say that there may be evolutionary or genetic factors involved, which are reflected in the ways brains operate. Indeed, Darwin's insights about emotions, important as they are historically, had the same problem, and we are confident that both Darwin and McDougall would have recognized this had they been part of the emerging experimental revolution in psychology. Still, they chose to speak up for reasonable perspectives about our nature, before we really had the robust scientific tools to illuminate such issues. So, while comparative naturalistic observations can provide relevance by identifying key behavior patterns found across a variety of species, the behavioral observations by themselves do not provide an explanation of the behaviors, and certainly not the mental experiences, except that that they were probably evolutionarily adaptive. However, with the development of the affective, behavioral, cognitive, and comparative neurosciences, we now have the capacity to break out of the circularity cycle and look for causes by studying and manipulating relevant areas of the brain and observing behavioral changes. And equally important, we can ask animals whether they like the feelings associated with those behavioral states, namely, whether artificial activations of those brain systems, or their relevant neurochemistries, are "rewarding" or "punishing," and this currently remains our best empirical gateway to understanding their feelings.

Still, these historical limitations do not detract from the conceptually insightful comparative analysis of basic emotions that McDougall provided at the beginning of the scientific era in psychology. If the worst that could be said was that McDougall did little more than name and describe personality-relevant behaviors, the same criticism might be made of many modern personality theorists, including the Big Five proponents. Indeed, Lewis Goldberg and Gerard Saucier (1995) have stated the factor-analytic Big Five tradition produces phenotypic traits that are descriptive rather that explanatory. In other words, even after having used a psychological test scale to determine that someone is an Extravert, nothing has been said about the cause and development of extraversion. The person has just been given a descriptive label that links his or her psychologically relevant behaviors to similar behaviors exhibited by other extraverted people. Affective neuroscience has aspired to take the next step: to actually begin characterizing how feelings arise from mammalian brains.

Both McDougall and Darwin demonstrated the ageless power of the comparative method. At his best, McDougall built on Darwin's previous observations and provided a short list of principles, as well as primary instincts and emotions that are not far from the model of affective neuroscience one hundred years later, which is certainly more modest (and hence incomplete) in its reach, but also more rigorous in its scientific substance. At present, the cross-species affective neuroscience approach is the best we have for decoding primal emotional feelings, but even it does not provide explicit ways to tackle the higher (tertiary-process) emotional feelings that tempted McDougall (as they do many modern psychologists). Whether animal research can aspire to understand those higher complexities such as optimism and regret (Rygula et al., 2012; Steiner & Redish, 2014) is an open issue. In Chapter 5 we review select early conceptual models of personality and present the three-level Nested BrainMind Hierarchy, a tool for facilitating such complex conversations about emotions.

CHAPTER 5

A Brief Review of Personality Since McDougall

The Need for a Bottom-Up Model of Personality

"Dynamic" has come to be used in a special sense: to designate a psychology which accepts as prevailingly fundamental the goal-directed (adaptive) character of behavior and attempts to discover and formulate the internal as well as the external factors which determine it. In so far as this psychology emphasized facts which for a long time have been and still are generally overlooked by academic investigators, it represents a protest against current scientific preoccupations. And since the occurrences which the specialized professor has omitted in his scheme of things are the very ones which the laity believe to be "most truly psychological," the dynamicist must first perform the tedious and uninviting task of reiterating common sense.

—Henry A. Murray, *Explorations*

WHILE WILLIAM McDOUGALL was one of the first to write a book about personality, many others followed that offered comprehensive models attempting to explain how humans develop their consistent patterns of behavior. In this chapter, we briefly review a representative selection of personality models after McDougall and argue that personality theorists increasingly departed from the primary instincts and emotions that Darwin wrote about and that provided McDougall with his starting point.

At the end of this chapter, we will reinforce our view that to fully understand human personality we need first to understand how feelings arise from our subcortical brains (feelings that, in general principles of operation, are shared homologously across mammalian brains) and how those primary emotional feelings are elaborated and complexified throughout our lives. Because affective feelings are survival indicators—with all positive/good feelings signaling potential thriving and all negative/bad feelings automatically projecting potential destruction—it seems likely that these brain circuits are major controllers of what we learn about the world. We will present a three-level, Nested BrainMind Hierarchy (NBH) model that may facilitate discussions about the fundamental sources of personality by clarifying the level at which the various discussions and disputes are taking place along a continuum: from the emergence and expression of primary emotions, to secondary learning and memory mechanisms that help us adapt to our specific environments, and to tertiary-level cerebral capacities that offer us abundant neurocomputational space to advance thinking, especially through the development and use of language (and ultimately mathematics). But first, we start with a short discussion about another early personality theorist who started with a fundamental base of primary emotions.

FREUD AND PSYCHOANALYTIC
THEORIES OF PERSONALITY

Sigmund Freud (1856–1939) was a contemporary of William McDougall (1871–1938). Fifteen years older than McDougall, Freud completed his first book, *The Interpretation of Dreams*, in 1900, just eight years before McDougall's *Introduction to Social Psychology* (1908). Like McDougall, Freud based his theory on biological drives or instincts. Freud's id was the reservoir of the life and death instincts. With some literary liberty, we would translate *life* as good feelings (i.e., affects that intrinsically predict survival), and *death* as bad feelings (feelings that predict potential destruction). In his early psychoanalytic writings, Freud focused on the sex instincts, or what we would call LUST. After World War I, Freud concluded that aggression—what we would include in the RAGE/Anger system—could be as potent a motive as sex.

In his early years, before the development of psychoanalysis, Freud aspired to explain clinical disorders using cerebral anatomy (see Mark Solms's forthcoming translation of Freud's early neuroscientific investigations). However, Freud soon came to accept that the available neuroscience research tools would not provide him the answers he sought. It should be noted that the International Neuropsychoanalysis Society (founded in 2000 by Mark Solms) is dedicated to linking brain neuroscience with psychoanalysis, which is something that Freud openly dreamed about.

So for the remainder of his clinical career, Freud pursued psychological-developmental theory and the treatment of psychopathology with psychoanalysis, which was his variation of a new method of therapy he had learned from a fellow Viennese physician Joseph Breuer, in which patients were cured by talking with their physician about their symptoms—their hopes and their worries. It is now generally recognized in psychiatry that frank discussions, with a receptively intelligent other, of where patients are in their affective life is solid path toward self-understanding, acceptance of life's vicissitudes, and finding paths to well-being.

We will not delve into the details of Freud's theories—we assume the typical reader is already reasonably familiar with Freud's work. However, we feel that Freud's thinking was close to affective neuroscience in spirit, especially because he based his theory on inherited instincts that were ancestral "gifts," many present at birth, which from Freud's perspective over one hundred years ago were divided into unconscious libidinal and destructive drives. He was using *unconscious* in the typical way: not on the basis of understanding qualia (namely raw experience itself, on which affective neuroscience has focused) but, rather, on whether we are aware (ideally with some understanding) of these primal sources of mind.

Retrospectively, we might suggest that the Victorian period in which he lived misled Freud to include infant nursing in what we would label the LUST system. In affective neuroscience terms, infant feeding would more likely belong in the homeostatic HUNGER system, which we would not include as a primary influence on personality. By contrast, emotional affection and bonding emerge from maternal CARE efforts and experiences. Although there is surely a substantial role for maternal nursing dynamics in infant social bonding, Harry Harlow's experiments with surrogate artificial mothers suggested that the simple act of an inanimate "mother" feeding a baby was less relevant for socially bonding than the experience of maternal warmth and physical contact. We might also argue that maternal nursing would more likely involve maternal bonding to the infant via the mother's intrinsic CARE system. Thus, out of lack of detailed knowledge of subcortical emotional systems, perhaps Freud overemphasized concepts like the "oral period" and "infant sexuality." We simply do not yet have sufficient evidence on that point. Still, Freud's thinking remained anchored in instinctual systems even as his theorizing became increasingly linked to his clinical practice and the specific life problems of clients.

Along these lines, Freud popularized the idea of the unconscious, which he felt accounted for the phenomenon of psychological repression, the symbolic content in dreams, and "slips of the tongue." He is also credited with introducing transference, a concept that is highly developed in psychoanalysis but that for personality purposes can be thought of as how earlier significant relationships influence our subsequent relationships. Thus, Freud's theorizing became increasingly conceptual and difficult to verify or even link to primary emotions. In the section that follows we continue this theme, showing how clinically based theories after Freud lost clear linkages to the primary emotional systems and came to represent ever more conceptual psychological approaches to pathology and personality.

With the psychopharmacology revolution, Freud's theories and psychoanalytic approaches lost influence in the academy. However, this is changing with the modern neuropsychoanalytic movement (see Panksepp & Solms, 2012), where interest in the neural nature of affect is intense (see Fotopoulou, 2010).

JUNG'S ANALYTICAL PSYCHOLOGY

The young Carl Jung became Freud's closest follower, to the point that Freud, two decades older, decided Jung would be his successor. However, Jung eventually seceded from Freud's inner circle, apparently because in his own psychoanalytic theory Jung came to reject Freud's strong emphasis on sex. By 1914 Jung (1875–1961) had completely struck out on his own path.

Jung's analytical psychology did not include an id, which in many ways was replaced by his "collective unconscious." For Jung the collective unconscious was the most powerful system in the psyche, and it contained the psychic traces of the human evolutionary past, including our prehuman ancestry. For Jung, the collective unconscious was a storehouse of inherited latent memories that predisposed us to react to the world in ways that were adaptive for our forefathers.

This sounds rather Darwinian, except that Jung populated the collective unconscious with "archetypes," which sounded more like higher-order cognitive concepts than subcortical emotional action systems. Jung derived his archetypes from mythology, religion, alchemy, and astrology but also found them in dreams and art. The most basic of Jung's preformed concepts was the mother. A baby's perception of its mother was guided by its mother archetype, followed by its actual experiences with its mother. However, Jung also proposed countless other supposedly innate archetypes, such as father, child, wise old man, earth mother, god, devil, hero, trickster, birth, death, separation, initiation, marriage, power, and magic. In addition, Jung argued there were archetypes that had evolved into separate systems within the personality, such as the anima, animus, persona, and shadow, plus striving for unity, which included the self-concept and was often expressed through the mandala symbol.

Jung took his novel ideas and seceded from Freud's inner circle, but he may not have escaped Freud's Olympian stature. Jung attempted to move the Freudian system away from biologically driven conflict and development toward more cognitive motives and self-fulfillment goals. However, Jung was criticized for being mystical and outside the realm of what is needed to constitute scientific proof (as some would say, although science has only evidence for or against a theory). As such, Jung's analytical psychology never had as strong an impact on the field of psychology as Freud's psychoanalytic theories. In a survey of psychology historians, Freud was rated the most important psychological theorist, and Jung was rated 30th (Coan & Zagona, 1962). In a more recent assessment, Haggbloom et al. (2002) listed Freud as having more journal citations and textbook citations than anyone else, with Jung coming in at 50th and 40th, respectively, on these two lists.

One area that keeps Jungian ideas alive is the widespread use of the Myers-Briggs Type Indicator (MBTI; Myers & McCaulley, 1985), a popular personality assessment tool based on Jung's theory of psychological types. Jung defined two major personality "attitudes," labeled *extraversion* and *introversion*, and is credited with originating these terms. Extraversion is oriented toward the external, objective world, whereas introversion is oriented internally and subjectively. Complementing the two attitudes were Jung's four psychological functions: *thinking* and *feeling*, and *sensing* and *intuiting*. The mother-daughter team of Katharine Cook Briggs and Isabel Briggs Myers turned the opposing pair of attitudes (extraversion/introversion) and the two opposing pairs of functions (thinking/feeling and sensing/intuiting) into three bipolar scales. To this they added a fourth bipolar scale, judging/perceiving, that was initially used to determine whether an individual's primary function was judging (thinking or feeling) or perceiving (sensing or intuiting).

The MBTI test battery has been extensively studied, with many questioning how effectively it actually operationalized Jung's theory but also acknowledging how difficult a task that would be. However, some data in a research paper by Robert McCrae and Paul Costa (1989) deserves attention because of its relevance to Big Five theory, covered in more detail in Chapter 12. McCrae and Costa compared the MBTI with their own personality assessment, the Neuroticism Extraversion Openness Personality Inventory (NEO-PI; Costa & McCrae, 1985), which is a widely accepted measure of the Big Five or Five-Factor-Model dimensions (namely, Extraversion, Neuroticism (the opposite of Emotional Stability), Conscientiousness, Agreeableness, and Openness to Experience). McCrae and Costa studied men and women and compared both self-reported and peer-rated NEO-PI data with MBTI self-report data. In all cases the four MBTI scales aligned the same way with the NEO-PI scales: the NEO Extraversion scale correlated significantly with MBTI Extraversion, the

NEO Openness scale correlated significantly with MBTI Intuition, the NEO Agreeableness scale correlated highly with MBTI Feeling, and the NEO Conscientiousness scale correlated highly with MBTI Judging.

Consistent with how difficult it would be to encapsulate Jungian-type concepts in a conventional psychological test, McCrae and Costa suggested that the MBTI incarnation of Jung's personality theory worked essentially like a Big Five personality assessment such as their NEO-PI, without the Neuroticism/low Emotional Stability dimension. That is, the MBTI had no scale measuring what McCrae and Costa called Neuroticism (the opposite pole of what the Big Five would call Emotional Stability). More important for our purposes, this means there is no provision in the MBTI for Panksepp's three negatively experienced emotions, namely, RAGE/Anger, FEAR/Anxiety, and PANIC/Sadness, a finding further elaborated in Chapter 12. While Jung did include a shadow archetype, the trio of powerful negative primary emotions that are such key influences on personality and mental health were not well represented in the MBTI.

ADLER, HORNEY, AND SULLIVAN

Alfred Adler (1870–1937) was another of Freud's early followers to leave his inner circle. He was an original member of the Vienna Psychoanalytic Society, which at first met in Freud's apartment, and he later served as the society president. However, like so many of the post-Freudian theorists, Adler rejected Freud's strongly instinctual orientation. He broke with Freud in 1911, like Jung over the importance of sexuality, and began developing his own ideas, focusing on man's social orientation.

Adler felt that our social nature was inborn, as was the major human motivation "striving for superiority" (what would now be called social dominance; for a discussion of the affective neuroscience of social dominance as a possible primary emotion, see van der Westhuizen and Solms, 2015). However, his social orientation toward personality led him to argue that it was not just instincts that explained human behavior but especially our goals that spurred our striving—our "attempts to express the great upward drive" (Adler, 1930, p. 398). These strivings often came from a sense of inferiority or imperfection ranging from a social disability to a child striving for a higher level of development. Thus, Adler's theorizing moved even further away from a Freudian-styled personality based on instincts toward a more social, goal-oriented human nature. His thinking followed a post-Freudian pattern of becoming more conceptual and abstract as he attempted to explain human behavior from a clinical and educational perspective.

Karen Horney (1885–1952) was trained in medicine and psychoanalysis in Germany but moved to the United States in 1932, in advance of the wave of fascism. She became dissatisfied with orthodox psychoanalysis and was a founder of the Association for the Advancement of Psychoanalysis. She especially rejected Freud's concept of penis envy and the Oedipus complex. Like Adler, she objected to the "instinctivistic" limitations of Freudian psychoanalysis. However, Horney further separated humans from other animals and wrote: "An animal's actions are largely determined by instinct . . . and beyond individual decision. In contrast, it is the prerogative as well as the burden of human beings to be able to exert choice, to have to make decisions. We may have to decide between desires that lead in opposite directions" (1945, p. 23). Yet, she did reinforce the principle that normal and pathological behavior represented the same psychological dimensions and differ only by degree, and that "the difference, then, between normal and neurotic conflicts lies fundamentally in the fact that the disparity between the conflicting issues is much less great for the normal person than for the neurotic" (p. 31).

From her clinical experience, she defined a series of ten neurotic needs (Horney, 1942), sources of inner cognitive conflicts, which she argued the neurotic personality could not resolve realistically. She later organized these needs (Horney, 1945) into three orientations: moving toward people (affiliation and love), moving away from people (self-sufficiency and perfection), and moving against people (power, prestige, and achievement). More like Adler, she did not feel that conflict and anxiety were built into human nature but arose from difficult childhood and other social experiences. As such, Horney represented another step away from biological origins toward social-developmental influences and unique personal experiences. Hers was a less tangible, more conceptual theory of personality dealing mainly with the complex workings of the human mind.

Harry Stack Sullivan (1892–1949) was another psychiatrist who became dissatisfied with Freudian psychoanalytic theory. He was a little younger than Adler and Horney and born and educated in the United States, which may have made it easier for him to deviate even more from Freud in his approach to personality. Sullivan did not accept instincts or libido as significant sources of human motivation. Although he incorporated stages of development into his theory, "by the end of the ninth month the infant is manifesting pretty unmistakable evidence of capabilities of the underlying human animal for becoming a human being" (Sullivan, 1953, p. 150). In other words, in the process of maturation, humans gradually lose their pure biological status as animals and become social human beings.

In his interpersonal theory of psychiatry, Sullivan further adopted the position that personality was a function of interpersonal events and could only be observed in interpersonal situations: "The personality that can be studied by scientific method is neither something that can be observed directly nor something . . . of which would be any concern of the psychiatrist"; namely, "psychiatry is the study of the phenomena that occur in interpersonal situations" (Sullivan 1964, pp. 32–33). While his "dynamisms" such as "malevolence," "fear," and "lust" appear similar to Panksepp's primary emotions of RAGE, FEAR, and LUST, Sullivan has carefully separated his dynamisms from any biological roots, for example, "Like any mammalian creature, man is endowed with the potentialities for undergoing fear, but in almost complete contradistinction to infrahuman creatures, man in the process of becoming a person always develops a great variety of processes directly related to the undergoing of *anxiety*" (Sullivan, 1948, p. 3). As such, Sullivan continues the pattern of generating more intangible constructs and moving further away from biological roots.

HENRY A. MURRAY

There is another personality theorist, we would like to include here, who took a rather different approach. Henry A. Murray, who wrote the epigraph for this chapter, largely ignored the dominant behaviorist zeitgeist of his time and heroically attempted to inject life and purpose into human personality by wedding McDougall's broader instinct theory with Freud's psychoanalytic linkage of unconscious motivation, early human developmental experience, and a narrower selection of primary instincts. Murray labeled his approach "personology," which combined psychological assessments and clinical practice with an emphasis on the full understanding of each individual case within an environmental context.

Murray (1893 – 1988), a native of New York City, began his academic life as an undergraduate history major, graduating from Harvard in 1915. He then completed a medical degree from Columbia and an M.A. in biology from Columbia in 1919 and 1920, respectively. Eventually his interests led him to complete a Ph.D. in biology from Cambridge in 1927. Murray experienced a major life turning point when in 1925 he spent three weeks with Carl Jung in Switzerland and became inspired to pursue a career in psychology. Having been trained in medicine and biology, but drawn to psychology, family social connections may have provided Murray the opportunity to direct the new Harvard Psychological Clinic, which gave him the chance to pursue his psychological interests and provided the research for his most famous work, *Explorations in Personality*, published in 1938.

The zeitgeist Murray found himself in can be grasped in a quote by Dan McAdams from the foreword to the 2008 edition of *Explorations*:

Psychoanalytic ideas were new and exciting and were forbidden fruit in most proper departments of psychology. Indeed, American academic psychology in the 1930s could not have been more opposed to what Murray was trying to do at the clinic. . . . Watson had already established behaviorism as the dominant psychological ethos. . . . At Harvard, . . . E. G. Boring committed Harvard psychology to the most rigorous canons of empirical science. He took a jaundiced view of Freud, Jung, and Murray. (p. xii)

However, at the Harvard Psychological Clinic, Murray saw himself bringing together the dynamic assumptions of Sigmund Freud, other early psychoanalytic theorists, and William McDougall to put the direction, motivation, and adaptive quality into human personality that was lacking in the behaviorist approach (p. 37). At the clinic, he was able to draw together resources, including a team of researchers, to intensely investigate fifty-one individuals over a period of several years and draw his tentative conclusions laid out in *Explorations*. Like his predecessor Freud, Murray felt that the "physiologists" would someday in the distant future discover the true nature of "regnant" processes occurring in the brain and accepted this limitation. While he and his team could not directly observe these brain activities, they inferred that the personality expressions they observed were accounted for by brain processes (p. 45).

Murray is perhaps best remembered for his list of twenty manifest needs. For Murray, these needs were hypothetical constructs occurring in the brain that were associated with personality traits (Murray, 1938/2008, pp. 61–62). These twenty needs are listed in Table 5.1 along with Murray's descriptions of associated desires and effects (paraphrased and extensively abridged), as well as the likely placement of six of Panksepp's seven primary emotions.

While Murray rejected behaviorist stimulus-response descriptions, despite following the lead of McDougall and Freud by providing dynamic motivations for behavior, Murray did not base his manifest needs on instincts. Although six of these needs closely reflect Panksepp's primary emotions, Murray did not consider these needs to be of an emotional nature. Indeed, Murray distinguished his manifest needs from McDougall's instincts and wrote the following: "The instinct theory of McDougall emphasizes the impulsive, emotional type of behavior . . . found . . . very commonly in animals and not infrequently as reactions to sudden stimuli in adults (emotional needs). But, according to our experience, a theory of motivation must be carried beyond the primitive, impulsive (thalamic) level of action. It must be made to include cool, carefully planned conduct" (1938/2008, pp. 94–95).

With this statement, Murray anticipates the need to specify the level of personality behavior one is describing. While Murray prefers to focus on what we would call the tertiary level of behavior/psychology, we would argue that until there is a clearer understanding of personality at the primary level, our understanding of the tertiary, derived level of human

Table 5.1. Murray's Twenty Manifest Needs Displayed in Murray's Categorical Sequence

Need	Desires and Effects[a]	Panksepp Primary Emotion
n Dominance	To control one's human environment. To influence or direct the behavior and opinions of Os.	
n Deference	To admire and support a superior O. To yield eagerly to the influence of an allied O.	
n Autonomy	To get free, shake off restraint, break out of confinement. To resist coercion and restriction. To be independent and free to act according to impulse.	
n Aggression	To overcome opposition forcefully. To fight. To oppose forcefully or punish an O.	RAGE
n Abasement	To submit passively to external force. To accept injury, criticism, punishment.	
n Achievement	To accomplish something difficult, and attain a high standard. To rival and surpass others.	
n Sex	To form and further an erotic relationship.	LUST
n Sentience	To seek and enjoy sensuous impressions.	
n Exhibition	To make an impression. To be seen and heard.	
n Play	To act for "fun," without further purpose . To laugh and make good-natured humor, even if slightly aggressive.	PLAY
n Affiliation	To enjoyably cooperate or reciprocate with an allied O. To remain loyal to a friend.	
n Rejection	To separate onesself from an inferior O. To snub or jilt an O.	
n Succorance	The tendency to cry, plead, or ask for nourishment, love, protection, or aid. To have always a supporter.	PANIC
n Nurturance	To give sympathy and gratify the needs of an infant or any O that is weak.	CARE
n Infavoidance	To avoid humiliation. To refrain from action because of the fear of failure.	

n Defendance	To defend the self against assault, criticism, and blame.	
n Counteraction	To master or make up for failure by restriving. To overcome weaknesses.	
n Harmavoidance	To avoid pain, physical injury, and death. To escape from danger or take precautions.	FEAR
n Order	To put things in order. To achieve cleanliness, neatness, and precision.	
n Understanding	The tendency to ask or answer questions, analyze events, and be interested in theory.	
Adapted from Murray (1938/2008, pp. 144–226). [a] O = Object: any external entity (thing, animal, person) other than the subject;		

personality will remain incomplete. In fact, we hold open the possibility that, despite the intense socialization characteristic of our species, human personality may routinely include more primary-level representation than many cognitively-oriented theorists would like to recognize.

Before closing this chapter with a more detailed discussion of the three-level, nested hierarchy of behavior and psychology, which reflects brain evolutionary progressions, we note that the acceptance of Murray's manifest needs is illustrated by the development of the Edwards Personal Preference Schedule measuring fifteen of Murray's needs (Edwards, 1954) and in the ongoing use of Douglas Jackson's (1929–2004) more recent Personality Research Form, which includes measures for all twenty of Murray's manifest needs (Jackson, 1974). At the Harvard Psychological Clinic, Murray and others also developed the Thematic Apperception Test, a projective assessment designed to measure a person's underlying motivation, which is still in use and being revised (Gruber & Kreuzpointner, 2013).

THREE-LEVEL NESTED
BRAINMIND HIERARCHY

Importantly, we are not arguing that any of the discussed theorist's ideas are not valuable. Many of their books, especially those of Horney and Sullivan, were published by W.W. Norton & Company and are still in print. What we are saying is that there needs to be a way to have a clear conversation about such clinically derived ideas that are often highly conceptualized and difficult to test in humans, let alone in animal models, without diminishing the importance of the primary emotions that we feel they are built upon and embedded within. This is where the three-level nested hierarchy comes into play.

The Three-level Nested BrainMind Hierarchy (NBH) illustrates how each evolved primary-process emotion sets up secondary-process learning and, furthermore, is embedded in tertiary-process cognitions (see Figure 5.1). The red squares represent the primary-process emotions; the blue ovals depict the secondary-process learning; and the purple rectangles illustrate tertiary-process thought and language (see color insert). The shapes along with upward and downward pointing arrows are intended to model that (1) lower level brain functions provide bottom-up influence on higher levels and are integrated into higher-level brain functions and that (2) higher level brain functions eventually exert top-down activation, inhibition and regulation of lower levels. Each primary-process emotion has a distinctive affective valence—that is, each has either a positive rewarding or negative punishing experience that not only guides decision making in survival situations but also promotes learning that allows for modifying these primary ancestral action systems to better meet current environmental demands. Experimental psychologists have traditionally called these evolved affective brain processes unconditioned stimuli and unconditioned responses. Indeed, FEAR and the homeostatic affect of HUNGER have been the affects that allow for diverse "reinforcements" (as discrete "objects" in the world, for example, foot shock and food) to be used by experimental psychologists to study learning. One of the functions of the primary emotions and other affects seems to be in guiding the organization of learning and memory within their respective affective spheres. As such, the primary level coordinates learning at the secondary level, which after the learning can, in turn, provide top-down adaptive modifications of the primary-level response systems (bottom arrows in Figure 5.1).

Further complexity is added as lower-level processes guide the maturation and development of tertiary-level cortical functions. We hypothesize that the functionality of the primary and secondary processes becomes represented functionally and symbolically (especially in humans) and embedded as acquired abilities in the tertiary (large cognitive/information-processing) mind. Moreover, the maturing tertiary mind, which is largely (but not exclusively) neocortical, is gradually able to add increasing sophistication and regulation to our responses to life events (top arrows in Figure 5.1). However, even as the tertiary mind gains the capacity to provide top-down cognitive regulation to our everyday psychobiological responses, our cognitive mind may still become subservient to the primary emotions when bottom-up primary affective influences suddenly appear as more challenging issues are confronted and experienced, leading at times to extreme emotional sensitivities—namely, affective states of mind that can trigger pathological displays. Thus, two-way, circular causation becomes an adaptive feature of the human mind and perhaps of mammalian minds in general, with bottom-up development and learning initially leading the way, and top-down

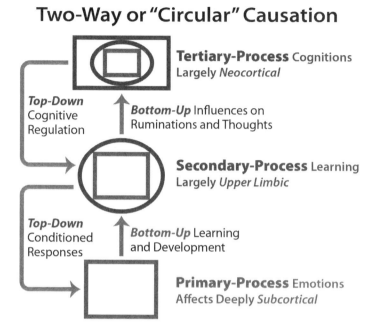

Two-Way or "Circular" Causation

Tertiary-Process Cognitions
Largely *Neocortical*

Top-Down Cognitive Regulation

Bottom-Up Influences on Ruminations and Thoughts

Secondary-Process Learning
Largely *Upper Limbic*

Top-Down Conditioned Responses

Bottom-Up Learning and Development

Primary-Process Emotions
Affects Deeply *Subcortical*

Figure 5.1. Nested BrainMind Hierarchies: Two-Way or Circular Causation. The three-level Nested BrainMind Hierarchy summarizes the hierarchical bottom-up and top-down (two-way or circular) causation proposed to operate in every primal emotional system of the brain. The diagram illustrates the hypothesis that in order for higher MindBrain functions to mature and function (via bottom-up control), they have to be integrated with the lower BrainMind functions Primary processes are depicted as red squares; secondary-process learning as blue circles; and tertiary-level processes by purple rectangles. This coding conveys the manner in which nested hierarchies integrate lower and higher brain functions to eventually exert top-down regulatory control. Adapted from Northoff et al. (2006). See insert for color.

regulations and reflections becoming part of the healthy mature (or, in extreme cases, pathological) BrainMind apparatus. The challenge of biological psychiatry and psychotherapy is to facilitate reorganization of such BrainMind dynamics.

SUMMARY

With the three-level Nested BrainMind Hierarchy (NBH), we have a coherent BrainMind conceptualization—a developmental-functional way of thinking and discussing the cognitive complexities featured by the more strictly psychological, conceptually-oriented personality theorists while still maintaining explicit links to our lower-level primary influences, which are not simply given residual status but offer a bridge to a robust animal neuroscience understanding of primal emotions that can lead to novel therapeutics (Panksepp, 2004, 2006, 2015, 2016; Panksepp et al., 2014; Panksepp & Yovell, 2014). Among Murray's list of twenty manifest needs, some, such as aggression, would seem to retain their primary-process emotions more obviously, while others seem difficult to parse in terms of primary emotions. We must also recognize the difficulties in parsing the tertiary-level mind in the same way that animal research has allowed comparative neuroscientists to probe the primary emotions through animal brain research (Panksepp, 1982, 1998a).

One question is whether the higher-level mind can create emotional feelings and novel higher-order emotions that are not based on evolved emotions in the subcortical brain. Whether the mind can create emotional subtleties beyond the raw subcortical emotions remains an open question. For instance, are there demonstrable neuroscientific differences between empathy and sympathy, or are they conceptual nuances on a theme only represented in our abstract thoughts that cannot be differentiated in the brain? The NBH way of seeing the brain and mind would suggest that some element of a primary emotion would always be present in our tertiary thoughts, although the variations possible at the secondary level might be virtually limitless.

The importance of the NBH becomes apparent as we discuss additional personality models in future chapters. For now it may be enough that the NBH can provide a richness and a level of integration to the discussions of personality theory that does not require Freud, McDougall, or Murray to be absolutely correct. Perhaps the NBH provides a way of thinking for discussions in which our evolved neurobiology, our capacity for cultural adaptation, and varying levels of individual maturation and adaptation can be reconciled.

CHAPTER 6

Bottom-Up and Top-Down
Personality Approaches

For higher MindBrain functions to mature and function (via bot-
tom-up control), they have to be integrated with the lower Brain-
Mind functions . . . in which nested hierarchies are integrating
lower brain functions into higher brain functions to eventually
exert top-down regulatory control. Affective consciousness (e.g., emo-
tional-feeling qualia) emerges from deep subcortical regions of the
brain, whereas cognitive consciousness is a higher brain function
that is permitted by the unconscious secondary-process mechanisms
of learning and memory formation. Each level of control deserves
distinct nomenclatures.

—Jaak Panksepp, "The Cross-Mammalian Neurophenomenology
of Primal Emotional Affects"

PRELUDE

It is likely that the progression of evolved primary processes (the various
"instincts" that help construct the upper mind) are critically important
in the mediation of learning and memory and thereby generating a variety of learned affective-behavioral states that enrich the mental apparatus. Indeed, the complexity of such individual and culturally facilitated
memories ultimately generates higher-order emotional feelings in *Homo
sapiens* beyond anything experienced by other species (e.g., as exemplified by our various arts and humanities). Such perspective remains
poorly developed in academic psychology, especially in personality theories. From our perspective, it is especially regrettable that psychiatric
therapies have not been more clearly based on cross-species analyses
and understandings of the evolved, fundamental (primary-process) neu-

ral nature of primal emotional feelings of our fellow species (Panksepp, 2015). This perspective is as germane for personality studies as for psychiatric practice. Our goal for this chapter is to focus on how such evolutionary perspectives may facilitate our understanding of the maturation of the neuromental infrastructure of human beings and thereby our understanding of human personality dimensions.

THEORETICAL INTRODUCTION

Why are there so many different theories of personality? Why do different researchers interpret personality so differently? One explanation is that personality theorists work a bit like the Indian parable of the blind men describing an elephant while trying to use their insights from touching only part of the beast. Their theoretical viewpoint depends greatly on where they start their analysis, the feet or body, trunk or ears. There surely must be a more systematic way to grope toward a coherent theory of personality than that, perhaps even one that can be used across multiple species, because all of us mammals, indeed all vertebrates, still share much more of the evolutionary heritage that constructed the fundamental (instinctual) neural (brain) "tools for living" than most psychologists have ever considered. If one starts from the bottom—the brain stem—there are thousands of genes that contribute to molding what different brain circuits do, even though these differences occurred many millions of years apart in ancestral times, long before humans existed. To truly understand the brain processes that all vertebrates share, one has to start at the bottom, focusing on ancient, warm-blooded, highly inquisitive, social and playful mammals such as rats, and understand how the instinctual brain systems that are concentrated below the neocortex operate. At the *bottom* of the brain, the functional circuitries and emotional similarities across species are much more dramatic than at the *top* of the brain. The human cortex is more capable of complex thoughts and cultures than that of any other species.

If one starts from the top, the neocortex, practically all the functions there have been learned rather than evolutionarily dictated—from language, to thinking, to even seeing—namely, programmed mostly by living in the world. How can we be confident of this remarkable cortical "constructivist" conclusion? Ever since neurophysiologists (Nobel Laureates of 1981, David Hubel and Torsten Wiesel) identified "feature detectors" in kitten brains they found that these cortical visual specializations *do not emerge* in cortical regions of relevant brain areas (e.g., occipital lobes) that normally receive visual input from an eye, if that eye had been prevented from seeing early in development (e.g., the eyelid sutured shut soon after birth). Supportive evidence is available from studies of human cortical plasticity observed during brain development of blind and deaf humans. If one does not use the most relevant cortical area early in perceptual development, it is hard for that tissue to catch up later in life, for sensory systems as they grow into the cortex, will tend to go to the closest cortical tissue. Thus, if very early in development one surgically redirects visual input that would normally be "destined" to become visual cortex, animals develop fine vision anyway. Indeed, as Mriganka Sur's group at MIT found (von Melchner, Pallas, & Sur, 2000), ferrets whose visual input is surgically redirected to the auditory cortex shortly after being born develop perfectly fine cortical visual abilities (i.e., the auditory cortex becomes developmentally programmed to process vision). That is, the cortex is being developmentally constructed, as opposed to being genetically dictated. Thus, we should not be looking for m(any) evolutionary specializations at the top of the brain—all those neocortical specializations seem to be *programmed by real-life experiences in the world*. In other words, the neocortex is like the massive digital storage space in a newly purchased computer—it is empty until you load programs into it via life experiences that allow you to both learn and entertain.

Perhaps the biggest news on this subject, as we were writing this book, on February 26, 2015, an article in *Science* magazine reported that a single "big brain" gene, called *ARHGAP11B*, was all that was necessary for the evolutionary expansion of our remarkably massive human neocortex (the biggest of all animals on earth relative to body size). This newly identified gene is found only in modern-day humans and in our long-lost relatives, the Neanderthals of Europe and Denisovans (the archaic human group in southern Siberia), but not in chimps (Florio et al., 2015). In mice the cortical progenitor cells divide only once and then grow into neurons, but in humans these same types of cells divide many times over and thereby, by comparison, form a huge number of neurons. Indeed, if we insert this human cortical expansion gene variant into mice, they grow much larger cortices, with sulci and gyri (grooves and mounds) that may make them smarter—an hypothesis that has not been tested, at least not at the time of this writing.

The message is humbling: The top of our brains, so essential for all of our special human cognitive qualities, from deep thoughts to profoundly mistaken ideas, was permitted by a single gene. The bottom line is humbling: Anyone who still thinks there are diverse evolutionary specializations in our "thinking caps" should be in for a rude awakening. Everything beyond the cortical functional specializations that little mice already have is probably learned. In short, we have no *evolved* "modules" for reading, writing, and arithmetic up there, no language or music instinct, nor perhaps any of our unique higher mental abilities. These higher qualities of human minds are all learned, albeit perhaps better by some brains than by others. There may be some built-in cognitive specializations that we are not yet aware of, but for present purposes it is wiser to accept that the neocortex is more like the empty random access memory (RAM) of a newly purchased digital computer than the finely engineered read-only memory (ROM) functions that allow the computer to behave so "magically." The "instinctual" emotions we are born with are more like ROM functions, albeit complexified through learning-mediated programming within more RAM-like tissues.

Clearly, our basic emotional proclivities emerge from built-in subcortical circuits that become cognitivized to fit in with the survival dictates of the world we live in, namely, developmentally refined through experience. The implications of such a nested hierarchy view of the brain and mind are germane for understanding mature human personality structures and functions. The foundational sub-neocortical tissue functions, shared more homologously by all mammals than are neocortical functions, need to be understood first to comprehend the sources and complexities of human personality. Once we have a better handle on these foundational, bottom-up processes, we will better understand the many diversifications provided by our capacity to learn. Then, how personality complexity emerges from emotional simplicity may begin to fall into place.

FROM BOTTOM-UP TO TOP-DOWN: ROUND AND ROUND WE GO

Our neuroscientific understanding of personality development needs to be first conceptualized from the bottom up, which may allow us to better understand diverse top-down processes. Most current personality theorists take a top-down approach, starting with language-based assessments of human traits. They focus on human uniqueness, emphasizing our exceptional cortical capacities, which include using our massive autobiographical memories to interpret life events. These personality theorists often rely on statistical analyses of verbal questionnaires garnering insights from our verbally expressed attitudes, opinions, preferences, and beliefs. They believe such top-down approaches are best for understanding the fundamentals of human personality. Well, it may not be the best, but it is certainly the most convenient and easily accessible. However, developmentally those fundamentals have a bottom-up trajectory.

Studies of the mind through the study of homologous behaviors and feeling patterns across species are markedly more difficult. Indeed, they are so difficult that most animal behaviorists decided a long time ago that trying to fathom animal minds simply through a study of their behaviors was foolish. Little did they realize (or at least acknowledge) that to cross that Rubicon brain research was an absolutely essential enterprise. And we think the bottom-up neuroscientific research approach to understanding basic emotions has the potential to provide a solid evolutionary foundation for personality theory.

Thus, we have chosen to take a bottom-up approach and start with the premise that the affective foundations of our personalities evolved over millions of years, indeed, long before our massive human neocortex expanded at the behest of a single gene. We further surmise that foundational elements of human personalities can be observed in other animals, especially other mammals. Accordingly, it is our position that the foundations of human personality will be better revealed through the study of the evolutionarily older subcortical *emotional* brain processes, and to a degree the other affective brain processes (e.g., the *homeostatic* and *sensory* affects), rather than by focusing on the linguistic functions of the human cortex and our most recently evolved brain expansion. Until we have a solid grasp of the fundamental emotional brain systems we are born with, we are unlikely to be able to accurately understand how those basic systems are elaborated by language and culture into complex adults with stable values, perceptions, and behavior—namely, the higher mental functions (mysteries) that get programmed into our neocortices.

Three-Level Nested BrainMind
Hierarchy Revisited

Along these lines, Jaak Panksepp has conceptualized primary, secondary, and tertiary levels of emotional processing (see Figure 5.1 in Chapter 5) and offered various *primary* subcortical brain circuits (e.g., SEEKING, PANIC/Sadness) as the starting point for the bottom-up approach to understanding animal and human minds (for a simplified rendition of cross-mammalian affects, see Panksepp, 20011b, as well as the Panksepp, 1998a, and Panksepp and Biven, 2012 monographs). In contrast, the *tertiary* process verbal level is the traditional entry point for the more cognitive and cortical top-down approaches. The *secondary* level refers to the intervening life experiences encoded by learning into memory stores, which, albeit critical for constructing all the specializations we have in the cortex, is surely important for refining our personalities but not as much for "energizing" them, a function more reserved for the primary-process emotional action systems. Initial guidance is provided by the primary emotional-temperamental differences that are genetically controlled to a substantial extent in subcortical regions and that come to influence what is learned, how fast, and for what purposes. This helps establish temperamentally unique human brain "connectomes" (Smith, 2016) that integrate the affective and cognitive sides of our personalities, for instance, the higher cognitive trait proposed by Charles Spearman in 1904 that came to be known as the "general intelligence g-factor." How this is influenced, perhaps anchored by our dispositional affective strengths and weaknesses (especially SEEKING urges), will be an exciting line of future investigation. This said, there remains the possibility that some infant nerve cells from subcortical regions may invade the neocortex during brain maturation, such as neurons releasing the corticotrophin stress hormone and oxytocin confidence-promoting neurons. Indeed, we already know that many neurochemical systems do this, such as the acetylcholine, dopamine, norepinephrine, and serotonin systems, where most neural cell bodies remain subcortically situated, even though they extend axonal branches into the cortex. We suspect such neural extensions do happen, probably to a degree under early environmental control, allowing "ancestral memories" to eventually directly guide higher brain functions.

In any event, it would avoid a great deal of confusion (especially when working with emotions, behavior, and personality), for researchers to be explicitly aware of which level of the brain-mind processing they are studying. Throughout the twentieth century, there has been a tendency to rely on our unique capacity for language to guide our thinking about personality and psychology, without recognizing that our primal affective mental foundations are dramatically shared with all the other mammals of the world, and in yet more diminutive ways with cold-blooded vertebrates, perhaps even invertebrates (Huber, Panksepp, Nathaniel, Alcaro, & Panksepp, 2011).

Difficulties Entailed in Starting
With Top-Down Approaches

Our views are unapologetically cross-species and neuroscientific, with the recognition that what came first, especially the affective subcortical survival-value networks, has led much of the cognitive parade that emerged later, not only in terms of necessary *affective* survival foundations but also all the learning and memory processes entailed in development of the upper *cognitive* mind, with its complex decision-making capacities, whereby our nuanced personality differences become seemingly infinitely complex. It is our position that a full understanding of human personality, including emotions and affective/cognitive awareness—namely, "knowing" who we are—is not possible without first understanding the emotional and other affective functions of our subcortical terrain, which emerged earlier in brain evolution. We believe that deep scientific understanding of the life-span development and workings of adult human personality structures is unlikely to succeed using mostly top-down human statistical research approaches, because such research largely ignores the intricate neuroevolutionary powers that constitute our deeply affective natures.

How we evaluate and experience our environments and our rather consistent emotional behavioral patterns remains linked to ancestral affective "memories" (intrinsic circuit functions), shared by all mammals, as they guide the maturation (and specializations) of our higher (neocortical) mental apparatus. In short, the causal, developmental infrastructure for personality development has to be bottom-up, before the top can provide regulatory guidance to the whole.

Furthermore, a top-down approach is largely correlational and cannot easily test for causal underpinnings with the kinds of neurochemical, neurophysiological, and detailed neuroanatomical research that can be conducted with animals. The top-down approach does not start with underlying evolutionary processes and mechanisms that can be evaluated neuroscientifically. At its best, it accepts top-down, statistically derived models and attempts to correlate them with possible underlying biological mechanisms (DeYoung, 2014). (For a critique of the mapping of top-down approaches onto brain structures, see Poldrack, 2010).

However, many top-down theorists seem content with correlational research when trying to reveal underlying biological mechanisms. We write *content* with tongue in cheek, of course, for we realize that the power of neuroscience is a much more recent scientific development than semantic-psychological and mathematical-statistical approaches. In fact, the kind of brain research that can be conducted on animals is simply not possible for psychologists studying humans. In any event, we are not suggesting that what has preceded us has not had value; it clearly has in laying out the broad psychological topography of personality dimensions. Our goal is to reaffirm how cross-species neuroscience and genetics have finally opened up the Pandora's box of BrainMind complexities that the great pioneers of the field simply could not consider adequately.

In sum, our perspective is that the clarification of the biological mechanisms underlying our personalities requires first achieving an evolutionary bottom-up understanding of human emotions and other affects, which requires the kind of manipulative brain research that is readily (and ethically) performed in animal models but difficult to conduct on humans. Of course, the ethics of neurobehavioral research on animals is problematic (especially for the most highly aversive negative feelings, engendered by FEAR and PAIN), but it is being done, and probably will continue to be done (hopefully, in ever better ways, as reflected in the current "gold rush" to implement optogenetic and DREADD technologies—the first being discrete stimulation of specific brain neurochemical systems with light—and the latter being designer receptors exclusively activated by designer drugs).

As our relevant knowledge base expands, many novel linkages to understanding human brains/minds will emerge. It will be on such foundations that a fuller understanding of both animal and human personalities will emerge, as well as a more satisfactory understanding of human psychopathologies and their treatment (Panksepp, 2005, 2015, 2016). Indeed, our move away from behavior-only preclinical (i.e., animal research) models of psychiatric disorders to ones that focus on the brain substrates of primary-process core affects (Panksepp, 1998a) has already yielded some promising therapeutic breakthroughs (Panksepp et al., 2014; Panksepp & Yovell, 2014), which are further discussed in Chapter 18. With these conceptual preliminaries out of the way, we now further consider how studies of human tertiary personality assessments have parsed human personality structures, without considering the relevant brain issues.

THE TOP-DOWN BIG FIVE OUTSIDE
THE LEXICAL WORLD

We conclude this chapter with a foray into the Big Five world, by way of a brief review of Colin DeYoung's ideas. DeYoung is a rising young personality psychologist at the University of Minnesota with new insights that illuminate the difficulties we have just meandered through. Colin offers a new top-down approach to personality research among a large community of researchers that still focus on traditional questionnaire measures of the five-factor model such as the revised NEO-PI (McCrae & Costa, 2010). Although not yet integrated with the kind of neuroscience approach advocated here, DeYoung offers something new within the history of personality theory. We offer the following as commentary rather than criticism.

First, what might we expect from a personality psychologist still aspiring to take a top-down approach? We would certainly expect him to take a more *cognitive* than affective approach to personality. Accordingly, DeYoung uses the Big Five as a starting point but sees behavior more in learning-theory terms and conceives of personality theory as the study of goal-directed, self-regulating systems. He has proposed the Cybernetic Big Five Theory (DeYoung, 2014), which incorporates a stimulus–response–feedback model into personality that is more consistent with a traditional cognitive-learning concept of personality than with the affective evolutionary approach espoused in this book. But this is also closer to our view, for we see affects (especially their environmentally induced shifts) as being absolutely critical ingredients in the instantiation of learning and memory.

What else might we predict? We would expect him to take a *statistical* approach to identifying personality dimensions. Correspondingly, DeYoung has theorized that the Big Five is organized on four hierarchical levels (DeYoung, Quilty, & Peterson, 2007; DeYoung, 2010). He used factor analysis to identify two metatraits that he labeled Stability and Plasticity, which together comprise the first level. This was consistent with others who had previously argued that the Big Five could be summarized with two similar higher-order factors labeled Alpha and Beta: Alpha representing the socialization processes by which "the child develops superego and learns to restrain or redirect id impulses and to discharge aggression in socially approved ways" and Beta representing "personal growth versus personal constriction" (Digman, 1997, p. 1250). Alpha "involves the common aspects of Agreeableness (vs. Hostility), Conscientiousness (vs. Heedlessness), and Emotional Stability (vs. Neuroticism)," with Beta fostered by traits such as "outgoing, adventurous, expressive, and active (Extraversion), and creative, imaginative, and open to new ideas and change (Intellect)" (pp. 1249–1250).

Going in the narrower direction, Costa & McCrae (1995) had offered six subscales, or facets, for each of their five factors. However, based on a previous twin study of five-factor facets reported by Jang et al. (2002), which found statistical evidence that two genetic factors were necessary to explain the variations in the facet scores of each of the five factors, DeYoung argued that a third layer of *aspects* needed to be inserted between the Big Five factors and their more numerous facets.

DeYoung again used factor analysis to empirically derive his third layer of ten aspects. Under Neuroticism (low Emotional Stability) he found Withdrawal and Volatility; beneath Agreeableness were Compassion and Politeness; below Conscientiousness were Industriousness and Orderliness.[4] At the next lower level for Extraversion were Enthusiasm and Assertiveness; and Openness/Intellect simply divided into the aspects of Openness and Intellect.

At the fourth level, the bottom level just below the aspects, DeYoung placed the *facets*, which were only rationally derived with no consensus regarding their number. For both the metatraits above the Big Five dimensions and the aspects inserted at a third level just below them, DeYoung relied on statistics to identify important dimensions rather than using affective neuroscience tools to grapple with what survival systems might be inherently embedded in the mammalian brain. But we think these ideas can be brought together.

Lastly, we would expect a top-down personality psychologist to overly rely on human *cortical* functions when searching for brain mechanisms underlying personality dimensions. Using neuroimaging (DeYoung et al., 2010), about 75 percent of the brain sites reported were neocortical, with fewer evolutionarily older cortical areas such as the cingulate cortex and the hippocampus, as well as two basal ganglia structures, the amygdala and the nucleus accumbens. One reason may have been that those top-brain regions are simply much larger and contain many more neurons that fire at stupendous rates (to handle the dynamic flow of real-life cognitions). Subcortical areas are tiny by comparison; their neurons fire at much lower overall rates and consequently are much harder to measure in brain imaging research.

We applaud DeYoung's focus on actual neurobiological mechanisms to help explain his identified personality aspects, but he remains in the more cognitive, top-down camp, although with the potential to integrate seamlessly with our bottom-up foundational approach. Indeed, we suspect that it is on the seamless integration of top-down and bottom-up approaches that the fecundity of future personality theories will depend.

Although DeYoung seems committed to the top-down approach to personality, we suspect he would have little problem integrating what we focus on here. Still, he has written "that personality neuroscience needs personality psychology more than the other way around. The accomplishments of the last 75 years in personality psychology should be guiding neuroscientists as they explore individual differences. We have mapped out the phenotype with remarkable success. . . . If personality neuroscience fails to avail itself of this knowledge, its results will accumulate piecemeal and will not inform us coherently about the individual as a whole" (DeYoung, 2007). So, for now, we simply note synergistic findings from our bottom-up approaches (Montag, Reuter, Jurkiewicz, Markett, & Panksepp, 2013).

Yet, having mapped out emotional phenotypes, we note that in our view two of the Big Five dimensions, Agreeableness and Emotional Stability, are compounds that comprise more than one primary emotional brain system. As reviewed in Chapter 2, we found the positive pole of Agreeableness to be associated with the subcortical CARE system, and the negative pole with the RAGE/Anger system. Similarly, the negative pole of Emotional Stability combined with all three negative primary emotions, RAGE/Anger, FEAR/Anxiety, and PANIC/Sadness. Importantly, overactivity in each of the negative primaries is associated with distinct major psychopathologies (psychopathy, anxiety disorders, depression, and panic attacks), with unique developmental trajectories and different therapeutic treatments.

What is to be gained by *not* incorporating solid affective neuroscience evidence into personality theory and giving these three brain systems, which contribute so heavily to dysfunctional lives suffering from the likes of antisocial behavior, disabling anxiety, panic attacks, and suicidal depression, the focus they deserve? Would it not be useful to consider and treat imbalances of these emotions as primary personality dimensions rather than lumping them into a single Emotional Stability/Neuroticism dimension? Similarly, why not recognize that there appears to be no higher-order Agreeableness system in the subcortical brain, and thereby increase focus on the clinical issues presented by pathologically low CARE (leading to low empathy by one path) and hypersensitive RAGE/Anger systems (leading to low empathy by another path)?

From our bottom-up perspective, the danger may be that it is the top-down research that "will accumulate piecemeal" data that may not adequately represent and prioritize our evolved human affective nature as a whole. Still, it is puzzling why so many top-down researchers do not recognize the value of our evolved, cross-species, psychobiological roots, capable of only being studied well in comparative cross-species studies, already offered by affective neuroscience. The cortex may be essential for the development of our unique human cognitive capabilities, but it is not necessary for the expression of basic mammalian affective personality characteristics. The danger of neglecting "real" affective brain-mind foundational issues for personality theory may be that, without a rich understanding of the subcortical BrainMind (which only brain research on other animals can provide), we may run the risk of failing to understand either human self-actualization or diverse pathological dysfunctions, from psychiatrically relevant personality disorders to many everyday personality problems, such as obsessive gambling and other diverse impulse control problems (e.g., addictive disorders emerging from the general-purpose SEEKING system). All of these arise from evolutionarily deeply ingrained affective systems of mammalian brains.

Humans are indeed a deeply affective species, quite similar in this respect to the other mammals. This primary level ("natural kinds") needs to be represented more explicitly in personality theorizing. Perhaps higher cortical mechanisms and cultural proclivities can elaborate our primary tools for living into other seminatural "tertiary kinds," but they should be seen as derivatives of our fundamental genetically based, psychoneurological nature. An understanding of emotional affects may be a key to bringing bottom-up cross-species affect studies and top-down human personality approaches together in a mutually beneficial synthesis.

CHAPTER 7

Our Ancestral Roots

Personality Research on Great Apes

There can be no doubt that the difference between the mind of the lowest man and that of the highest animal is immense. An anthropomorphous ape, if he could take a dispassionate view of his own case, would admit that, though he could form an artful plan to plunder a garden—though he could use stones for fighting or for breaking open nuts—yet that the thought of fashioning a stone into a tool was quite beyond his scope. Still less, as he would admit, could he follow out a train of metaphysical reasoning, or solve a mathematical problem, or reflect on God, or admire a grand natural scene. Some apes, however, would probably declare that they could and did admire the beauty of the colored skin and fur of their partners in marriage. They would admit that though they could make other apes understand by cries some of their perceptions and simpler wants, the notion of expressing definite ideas by definite sounds had never crossed their minds.

Nevertheless the difference in mind between man and the higher animals, great as it is, certainly is one of degree and not of kind.

—Charles Darwin, *The Descent of Man*

To HELP HIGHLIGHT the continuity of personality construct across species, we devote this chapter and the next two to three species: the one that is evolutionarily closest to us (chimpanzees), the one with whom we have historically had the closest relations (dogs), and one that has brought us much misery historically (plagues) yet also has served us so well in medicine and neuroscience (rats). We also briefly touch on those vertebrates that are about as distant from us as any other living vertebrate species (fish). Our hope is that this progression will help readers appreciate the gradients of personality that reach far back in evolutionary time, even as the neuropsychological (albeit not the behavioral) details get harder and harder to fathom as the evolutionary distance between ourselves and other species increases. We provide some detailed coverage for students of personality, although general readers may wish to pass over some materials.

OUR CLOSEST LIVING
EVOLUTIONARY RELATIVE

Chimpanzees are the closest living phylogenetic relatives of human beings. Humans share approximately 98.8 percent of our DNA with chimpanzees (Chimpanzee Sequencing and Analysis Consortium, 2005), and a recent analysis suggests humans and chimpanzees may share a common ancestor as recently as 4 million years ago (Hobolth, Christiensen, Mailund, & Schierup, 2007). Therefore, to the extent that personality is influenced by brain biology, one would expect chimpanzees to exhibit the most similar personalities to humans among the vast varieties of nonhumans with which we share this planet.

Indeed, many have explored how similar chimpanzees and humans actually are. Frans de Waal has written that chimpanzees form political alliances to help them maintain power and status within their social group (de Waal, 1982) and exhibit dispositions for moral behavior (de Waal, 1996). Chimpanzee cultural differences between social groups have also been described, including the use of medicinal plants (McGrew, 1992, 2004). Jane Goodall documented chimpanzees making tools and hunting small mammals (Goodall, 1986). While Goodall, in a manner of speaking, moved right into the homes of wild chimpanzees in Africa, others have adopted chimpanzees into their homes and raised them like their own children. The most famous of these human chimp parents were Allen and Beatrix Gardner (a student of Nobel Prize–winning ethologist Niko Tinbergen), who adopted Washoe into their home and taught her to communicate with them in American Sign Language. The pioneering chimpanzee researcher Robert Yerkes (1925) believed that chimps understood many of his words and had speculated that chimpanzees might learn to sign, but apparently no one ever tried to formally verify that until the Gardners. Since that pioneering work, many have now taught chimpanzees (and gorillas) to communicate using sign language or sign language equivalents.

CHIMPANZEE PERSONALITY AND
BIG FIVE CONSCIENTIOUSNESS

Up to this point in the book, we have only discussed the Big Five Conscientiousness dimension with respect to humans. In fact, in studies

using ratings of mammals using personality inventories, a Conscientiousness dimension had been lacking (Gosling & John, 1999)—until James
King and Aurelio Jose Figueredo of the University of Arizona set out
to answer the question, "How closely do chimpanzee personality factors resemble those in humans?" (King & Figueredo, 1997, p. 257), by
attempting to verify that all of the Big Five personality factors could also
be measured in chimpanzees.

Mostly drawing from Goldberg's (1990) Big Five personality taxonomy, King and Figueredo selected forty-three descriptive adjectives and
used fifty-three experienced observers to rate one hundred chimpanzees
from twelve zoological parks, obtaining an average of over four observer
ratings per chimpanzee. A factor analysis of these mean observer ratings
yielded six factors, with Dominance emerging as the first and largest
factor, which was later determined to be highly heritable in chimpanzees (Weiss, King, & Figueredo, 2000). Factors 2–6 corresponded to the
human Big Five: Surgency/Extraversion, Dependability/Conscientious-
ness, Agreeableness, Emotionality/Neuroticism, and Openness to Experience, although the Emotionality and Openness factors were small,
containing only three and two items, respectively. Confirming the validity of their findings, each of these factors except Openness was later
shown to be related to behaviors that were independently observed in
zoo settings (Pederson, King, & Landau, 2005). Indeed, for the first time
a research team had objectively documented Conscientiousness, as well
as the full Big Five personality model, in a nonhuman species, with the
wrinkle that Social Dominance was added to the mix, and they had done
so by obtaining ratings of adjective trait terms originally used to describe
human personalities.

King was also the lead author in a second factor-analytic study using
all new chimpanzee subjects, combining forty-three nonzoo chimpanzees living in a large African sanctuary in the Republic of the Congo with
seventy-four chimpanzees living in nine zoos in the United States and
Australia. In this second study, the same forty-three descriptive adjectives were used to rate the chimpanzees, although, the adjectives for the
African sanctuary chimpanzees were translated into French. Even with
this heterogeneous group, including nonzoo chimpanzees with French-
speaking raters, all six of the previously identified chimpanzee dimensions, including Conscientiousness, were obtained in this second study.
However, the small Emotionality/Neuroticism and Openness factors did
not meet statistical standards for replication, although most items loaded
the same on these two factors in both studies (King, Weiss, & Farmer,
2005). The authors concluded they needed more items on these two factors. Yet, their structure of chimpanzee personality, as revealed by factor
analysis, remained relatively constant across the two studies of different
chimpanzees regardless of the different environments, which was con-

sistent with a biological basis for personality and suggested that environmental effects on chimpanzee personalities may be relatively small.

This smooth sailing was short-lived, as a shift to orangutan subjects failed to identify a Conscientiousness factor. Although there had been an earlier failure with gorillas (Gold & Maple, 1994), with two chimpanzee successes behind them Weiss, King, and Perkins (2006) tried their hand in another large-scale study with 152 zoo-housed orangutans. The same methodology and rating instrument—expanded with five additional adjectives—replicated all of the chimpanzee dimensions except Dependability/Conscientiousness and Openness. It was largely these two dimensions that blended into the fifth factor, which Weiss and colleagues labeled Intellect based on its highest loading item, "intelligent," as well as "disciplined" from the Dependability dimension. Other adjectives identified with Dependability in the chimpanzee studies tended to load either on their Neuroticism factor, as with "impulsive," "cautious," "erratic," and "unpredictable," or on their Dominance factor, as with "persistent" and "reckless." One hypothesis for the failure to find a Dependability/Conscientiousness dimension was that the capacity for regulating the expression of aggression and irritability was not as highly developed in the orangutan, and therefore, such traits were expressed more purely as Social Dominance.

The authors also argued that the inability to replicate the Dependability factor in orangutans could suggest either that the Dependability/Conscientiousness capacity first emerged evolutionarily with chimpanzees or possibly that the conscientious regulation of especially negative primary emotions was less critical in the semisolitary orangutan. That Gosling and John (1999) were unable to identify a Conscientiousness factor in any species other than chimpanzees supported the argument that Conscientiousness first appeared in chimpanzees. However, the Darwinian principle of continuity as applied to mental functions in animals would argue for the possibility that aspects of Conscientiousness should be identifiable in orangutans and other even more distantly related species. Clearly, further work would be required to resolve such issues.

Subsequently, two additional chimpanzee studies using the original forty-three King and Figueredo (1997) items fully replicated the first four factors (Dominance, Surgency/Extraversion, Dependability/Conscientiousness, and Agreeableness) but had similar problems demonstrating statistical congruence for the last two factors (Emotionality/Neuroticism and Openness). In the first case, Weiss, King, and Hopkins (2007) added 102 new zoo animals and 175 chimpanzees housed in the Yerkes National Primate Research Center. Later, Weiss and King also teamed up with a group of five Japanese scientists (Weiss et al., 2009) to examine the personalities of 146 chimpanzees living in Japanese zoos, research institutes, and a sanctuary. Despite the same problem of not being able to statistically replicate the Emotionality/Neuroticism and Openness factors found in the original King and Figueredo (1997) report, all four studies had demonstrated a statistically replicated Conscientiousness factor. In addition, the Japanese study, in which all ratings were completed using the forty-three-adjective scales translated into Japanese, also confirmed the finding from the Republic of the Congo report that chimpanzee personality ratings were not affected by the culture of the raters, which further underscored the biological foundation of personality.

Others had pursued alternate paths to solving the chimpanzee personality puzzle. Working with Samuel Gosling, Hani Freeman wrote a dissertation that included the development and validation of a new chimpanzee personality rating scale. Her approach was to combine some adjectives from the King and Figueredo (1997) with additional trait descriptions that were unique to chimpanzees (Freeman et al., 2013). Her team tried to eliminate most redundancy and was able to reduce the list of traits to forty-one, which she used to collect ratings on ninety-nine chimpanzees at the University of Texas. In analyzing the data, several criteria finally led her to extract six factors. However, only the first five were interpretable: Reactivity/Undependability, Dominance, Extraversion, Openness, and Agreeableness. Because her Reactivity/Undependability dimension was very similar to King and Figuerado's Dependability factor, she had once again demonstrated a Conscientiousness factor in chimpanzees. The remainder of her first five factors were also similar to the King and Figueredo dimensions, except that she lacked an Emotionality/Neuroticism factor. In the Freeman et al. study, the items that would have been expected to define a Neuroticism dimension loaded on either the Reactivity/Undependability or Dominance factors. So once again, the replication of King and Figueredo's human-like Big Five plus Dominance chimpanzee personality structure remained illusive.

This story of searching for distinct personality dimensions in chimpanzees using factor analysis again demonstrates the vicissitudes of factor analysis in defining a biologically based taxonomy of personality. The first four of these chimpanzee studies suggested that results more congruent with the Big Five model would likely have been obtained if they had started with a larger, more representative pool of adjective descriptors. Even though that may be true, our position is that it is time to accept the limits of factor analysis and recognize that the next round of progress in understanding the dynamics of mammalian personality will likely emerge from an affective neuroscience analysis of how the mammalian brain responds—especially how the subcortical brain responds—to significant life events. A major theme of this book is that the remarkable homology of personality traits across mammalian species has its origin in the subcortical emotional systems of the brain, and a better understanding of these systems will be essential for discovery of the evolutionary sources of personality structures, perhaps even the sources of "human nature" from emotional pathologies to self-actualization. Indeed, this has been supported recently with Affective Neuroscience Personality Scales studies of human diverse human personality disorders (Karterud et al., 2016), discussed further in Chapter 18.

THE ANALYSIS OF ANOTHER PRIMATE

The effort to "discover" the human Big Five in the personalities of non-human primates took an interesting turn when Alexander Weiss of the University of Edinburg joined with F. Blake Morton and an international research team to study brown capuchin monkeys (*Sapajus apella*), a New World species that diverged from the human line a bit further down the evolutionary tree but one, like the Old World great apes of Africa and Asia, that has a large brain for its body size (Morton et al., 2013). Another important consideration in the project was using a revised King and Figeredo (1997) rating questionnaire called the Hominoid Personality Questionnaire, which had now been expanded from the original forty-three to fifty-four adjectives and that allowed them to better capture the Emotionality, Openness, and Conscientiousness dimensions (Weiss et al., 2009).

In this project, 127 captive brown capuchin monkeys from six sites were rated. The authors determined that their data did fit a five-factor solution, but they added further conceptual complexity to the discussion. Briefly, Morton et al. (2013) labeled their five factors Assertiveness, Openness, Neuroticism, Sociability, and Attentiveness, while acknowledging that their Assertiveness factor closely resembled King and Figueredo's (1997) original chimpanzee Dominance factor, their Openness factor was similar to King and Figueredo's Openness factor but also resembled the orangutan Extraversion factor (Weiss et al., 2006), their Neuroticism factor closely resembled the King and Figueredo's Emotionality dimension, their Sociability factor shared elements of King and Figueredo's Agreeableness and Surgency/Extraversion factors, and their Attentiveness factor most closely resembled the Conscientiousness dimension found in Japanese chimpanzees rated on the full Hominoid Personality Questionnaire by Weiss et al. (2009).

Despite these complexities, by using an expanded set of rating items, the Morton group had remarkably demonstrated Conscientiousness in capuchin monkeys, an evolutionarily older species than chimpanzees, even though earlier efforts to identify a Conscientiousness factor in gorillas and orangutans had failed to do so. This demonstration is important from a Darwinian continuity perspective and may open the way for others to look for elements of Conscientiousness even in nonprimate species. However, illustrating the difficulties of factor analysis, they failed to fully replicate the King and Figueredo (1997) Dominance factor and their Sociability factor structure blended elements of the Big Five Agreeableness and Extraversion dimensions.

BACK TO BASICS: ALTERNATIVE APPROACHES

Diane Dutton of Liverpool Hope University in the United Kingdom also developed a new personality rating scale for chimpanzees, but she started from the ground up, so to speak. That is, instead of building on an existing instrument, she used the expert knowledge of people working closely with chimpanzees and a technique developed by the American psychologist George Kelly (1955) to build a new set of rating items. In short, Dutton asked raters who had worked extensively with a group of twenty-four chimpanzees housed in the Chester Zoo to independently generate bipolar descriptors of chimpanzees, such as "aggressive-submissive," to describe differences in pairs of chimpanzee they had worked with (Dutton, Clark, & Dickins, 1997). Using such descriptors generated by expert chimpanzee observers, she intended to devise a rating scale that would be more naturalistic and perhaps more appropriate for rating chimpanzee personalities. Eventually, she produced a forty-six-item personality rating scale for chimpanzees and coordinated a study of seventy-five captive chimpanzees living in seven zoological parks in Europe, the United States, and South Africa (Dutton, 2008).

Using factor analysis, she extracted five factors that she labeled Agreeableness, Dominance, Neuroticism, Extraversion, and Intellect. Her factors included many similarities with our Affective Neuroscience Personality Scales. For example, her Agreeableness dimension included items such as "protective toward infants" and "interacts with infants and juveniles" plus "reconciles others" and "reassures others," all of which are consistent with the CARE system. Her Neuroticism dimension included "nervous," "easily frightened," "fearful for no apparent reason," and "anxious," all of which suggest the FEAR system. The Extraversion dimension included "playful" and not "withdrawn," which fit with the PLAY system. The Intellect dimension included SEEKING concepts such as "inquisitive" and "investigative." With the Dominance dimension having its highest loading on "aggressive," which is suggestive of the RAGE/Anger system, she had scales representing each of the personality-related blue ribbon emotional brain systems except PANIC/Sadness. In other words, she may have independently discovered the emotional foundations of personality in our closest evolutionary relative.

Interestingly, Dutton did not derive a Conscientiousness scale, an omission we touch on again shortly. However, in using rating items grounded in actual observations of chimpanzee natural behaviors, Dutton seems to have confirmed a theme we emphasize in this book: Relying on measures as close to the primary expression of emotional behaviors as possible is likely to keep researchers close to basic neural-system taxonomies of personality and keep them from deviating far from the foundational processes that help constitute even human personality.

"CONSCIENTIOUSNESS" CONSIDERATIONS

Conscientiousness in Big Five terms applied to humans has typically been described with such adjective pairs as "organized versus disorganized," "responsible versus irresponsible," "reliable versus undependable," and "thorough versus careless" (Goldberg, 1992) but has been difficult to identify in animal studies perhaps because of the abstract nature of these terms. By contrast, in demonstrating the first appearance of a Dependability/Conscientious factor in chimpanzees, King and Figueredo (1997) selected adjectives from Goldberg's (1990) Conscientiousness factor descriptors that seem eminently concrete and observable, such as "impulsive," "reckless," "erratic," and "disorganized"—each of which Hofstee et al. (1992) showed had its strongest loadings on Conscientiousness—plus included overtones of "defiant" and "aggressive," which might speak to the importance of regulating social dominance because it plays such a key role in chimpanzee social life. Indeed, all five chimpanzee studies reviewed above that used the forty-three King and Figueredo (1997) adjectives identified these six adjectives on their Dependability/Conscientiousness factors to some degree.

But why was Dutton not able to find a Conscientiousness factor in her chimpanzee data? Perhaps because she unfortunately included only two clear Conscientiousness items in her forty-six statements, relying on "persistent" and "unpredictable", which may not have had enough power by themselves to emerge as a sixth factor measuring Conscientiousness. King and Figueredo (1997) had included eight Big Five Conscientiousness items, four of which loaded most strongly on their Dependability factor, and six more Conscientiousness items were added to the revised fifty-four-item version of the Hominoid Personality Questionnaire that was used to identify a Conscientiousness factor in brown capuchin monkeys. Thus, it is likely that if the number of Dutton's conscientiousness-type items had been expanded, her sample would have revealed a Conscientiousness dimension as well. Such are the vagaries of the factor-analytic world.

In any case, this first clear demonstration of the Big Five human personality dimension in a nonhuman animal supported Darwin's continuity of species principle. Indeed, having demonstrated this trait in chimpanzees and then brown capuchin monkeys opens up the possibility that rudimentary forms of conscientiousness might be observable in other mammals, such as dogs and rats. Coming back to the idea that more concrete and observable descriptors were necessary to reveal conscientiousness in chimpanzees hints that even more direct interventions and measures might be necessary to identify this cognitive, regulatory dimension in other mammals, especially in even more distantly related mammals.

An intriguing neuroscience demonstration of what may be considered evidence of conscientiousness in rats was reported by J. P. C. de Bruin in 1990. He and other researchers had previously determined that lesions to the orbital prefrontal cortex increased social-agonistic interactions in rats, that is, made them more aggressive, which implied that the orbital prefrontal cortex exerted an inhibitory control over some brain region supporting the aggressive behavior. Research suggested the brain region was likely the hypothalamus. With this insight, de Bruin implanted electrodes in the hypothalamus of rats and observed whether aggression directed toward another rat was elicited by a small (40–60 microamp) current. Then, using a second prefrontal electrode, he concurrently stimulated the hypothalamus and various locations in the prefrontal cortex and determined that the greatest inhibition of hypothalamic-elicited aggression occurred when the prefrontal electrode was placed in a rat's orbital prefrontal cortex. Both the lesion data and concurrent electrical stimulation data were consistent with the conclusion that the rat orbital prefrontal cortex "exerts an inhibitory control over hypothalamic sites from which aggression can be elicited by electrical stimulation" (de Bruin, 1990, p. 492). Could this inhibition of aggressive behavior from electrodes placed in the orbital prefrontal cortex represent an induced case of conscientiousness in rats? Clearly, there is a brain mechanism in place for inhibiting rat social aggressive behavior likely stemming from the RAGE/Anger system. How this inhibitory control might be learned and expressed in rat social behavior remains to be determined. It would also be important to link orbital prefrontal activity to "conscientious" behavior in other species. In any case, this intriguing demonstration hints of a rudimentary chimpanzee-like conscientiousness inhibiting social aggression in a species much less well endowed with cortical capacity than the brown capuchin monkey.

SOCIAL DOMINANCE

The emergence of a prominent Dominance factor in chimpanzees could be explained in part by "the pervasive role of dominance and power-related activities in the social order of wild chimpanzees" and "may be further enhanced in zoo habitats where dispersal is not possible" (King & Figueredo, 1997, p. 268). However, some have emphasized dominance as a basic human personality dimension. The Hogan Personality Inventory (Hogan & Hogan, 2007) similarly expands the Big Five with a sixth scale labeled Ambition that is characterized by "status" and "competitiveness," and de Raad (1999) has also emphasized dominance as a human interpersonal personality dimension. Donne van der West-huizen, a student at the University of Cape Town in South Africa work-ing with Mark Solms, has written and published a dissertation exploring the possibility that social dominance might qualify as a primary emotion. Even though she reviewed a great deal of biological support underlying dominant and territorial behavior, her final conclusion was that there was insufficient evidence at present to classify social dominance as a primary emotion (van der Westhuizen & Solms, 2015), for dominance needs to be learned by actual social interactions. This does not mean that there are not specific brain systems that promote dominance (e.g., perhaps RAGE, LUST, and social SEEKING). In short, even though domi-nance is widespread throughout the animal world (including social rela-tions in practically all mammals), we would argue that complex social learning is essential for it to manifest in the social world, and that early social PLAY is an important factor for finding one's place in social struc-tures (Panksepp, Jalowiec, DeEskinazi, & Bishop, 1985). In any event, much work remains to be done in the area of social dominance in mam-mals, including the manner of its emergence as a key feature of primate social life.

It is also noteworthy that not being "fearful" or "dependent" both loaded on King and Figuerado's (1997) Dominance dimension rather than the Emotionality dimension, with a third adjective, "aggressive," splitting its loadings between (high) Dominance and (low) Conscien-tiousness. In affective neuroscience terms these adjectives would be associated with FEAR, PANIC/Sadness, and RAGE/Anger, respectively. By contrast, in the King and Figueredo study the Emotionality dimension was limited to the more general and less specific terms "stable," "unemo-tional," and not being "excitable," all resembling the relatively undif-ferentiated human Big Five Emotional Stability factor. Once again, one is compelled to address the limitations that factor-analytic procedures impose on parsing the workings of the mammalian BrainMind.

PRIMATE SUMMARY

Altogether, these primate studies establish that temperament in the great apes and brown capuchins can be accurately described using rating methods borrowed from human studies and resulting in the same fac-tor-analytically derived dimensions as those derived using human sub-jects. Having some difficulty replicating an Openness dimension is not surprising given the illusiveness of the smallest of the Big Five factors even in human studies (Goldberg, 1990). More generally, unresolved

issues surrounding Conscientiousness and whether it can be systematically monitored in orangutans and primates generally is bound to remain
unresolved for some time.

Yet, none of the primate studies reviewed above included a dimension for PANIC/Sadness separation distress (Panksepp, 1998a), perhaps
because relevant developmentally important social-isolation challenges
were not studied in zoo-reared primates, or because overt SADNESS-
related behaviors are rare in zoo environments, as in the death of an
infant or social companion. Yet, socially induced comforts of social contact, mediated in part by brain opioid inhibition of the PANIC/Sadness
system (Panksepp, Herman, Vilberg, Bishop, & DeEskinazi, 1980; Panksepp, 1981a), supplies the social glue that provides the cohesion observed
in the troops of intensely social animals such as chimpanzees and brown
capuchin monkeys. Without social bonding, which to a great extent is
derived from brain opioid and oxytocinergic inhibition of the PANIC/
Sadness system (Panksepp, Normansell, Herman, Bishop, & Crepeau,
1988) and the consequent alleviation of separation distress experiences,
we would not likely observe these primate species living in social troops.

Again, it is our view is that primate temperament research (indeed,
nonhuman personality research in general) could benefit from a framework for carving this psychological domain into neuroscientifically based
basic emotion dimensions. Accordingly, we suggest that a cross-species
affective neuroscience provides a new framework for understanding
some of the major sources of personality structures across all mammalian species, and thereby may provide a more scientifically meaningful
foundation for future progress than the statistical factor-analytic method
that has so far been used to classify personality traits.

SUOMI AND MACAQUES'
EARLY EXPERIENCE

Before leaving the primates, we describe how Stephen Suomi's research
on early experience in rhesus macaques illustrates complexities that
arise from variations in mothering—namely, expressions of the CARE
system—can have on primate personality. Like Scott's (1962) emphasis on critical periods of development, Suomi studied the behavior of
neonates and juveniles, believing that relatively brief early experiences
disproportionately influence behavior and temperament throughout the
life-span, and showed that early social deprivation could increase emotional reactivity and impulsiveness. Expanding on Harlow's work with
total social deprivation (Harlow, Dodsworth, & Harlow, 1965), Suomi
(2006) proceeded to explore a less severe social deprivation model in
which rhesus infants were hand-reared for one month and then housed
with same-age peers until six months of age. These laboratory hand/

peer-reared rhesus monkeys exhibited stable social-emotional deficits, such as low social dominance, little exploration, fewer play bouts, less complex play, and greater adrenocortical and noradrenergic reactions to social separation. In general, these hand/peer-reared monkeys mirrored a "high-reactive" temperament type comprising about 20 percent of rhesus monkeys reared by their mothers in naturalistic settings and also shared characteristics with an "impulsive" type accounting for 5–10 percent of mother-reared rhesus monkeys, with more aggressive social encounters, low social dominance, and low serotonergic functioning (Suomi, 1997).

Research on polymorphisms of the serotonin transporter (*5-HTT*) gene revealed that hand/peer-reared rhesus monkeys carrying a single "short" allele of the *5-HTT* gene were more emotional and distractible, with low attention and visual orientation (Champoux et al., 2002), and showed reduced serotonergic functioning and high levels of aggression (Suomi, 2006). These hand/peer-reared monkeys with a short serotonin transporter allele were also shown to become more aggressive juveniles than mother-reared monkeys with the short allele (Barr et al., 2003). Indeed, rhesus monkeys carrying either one or two short alleles that were mother-reared exhibited normal levels of aggression and serotonin metabolism, similar to rhesus monkeys carrying the long *5-HTT* allele (Higley et al.,2000). Thus, typical highly supportive maternal rearing along with normal interactions with peers was able to protect individual monkeys from the effects of the psychopathology-promoting short allele that, like in humans, has more influence on personality when expressed in the context of stressful childhood upbringing (Caspi et al., 2003).

In another example of the influence of mothering on temperament, rhesus infants bred to be either highly emotionally reactive or normally reactive were cross-fostered to well-experienced mothers selected because they were either highly nurturing or normally nurturing. The high-reactive infants reared by the highly nurturing mothers exhibited more exploration and less psychological disturbance during weaning than all other combinations. When moved into larger social groups, these high-reactive monkeys reared by the very nurturant mothers also attained top positions in the dominance hierarchy, with high-reactive monkeys fostered to normally nurturing mothers moving to the bottom of the hierarchy. Furthermore, highly reactive females reared by the highly nurturing mothers exhibited the maternal style of the foster mothers (Suomi, 1997). Such nature-nurture complexities demonstrate the dynamic character of the BrainMind that seemingly defies simple explanations. It will be interesting to learn the extent to which these maternal-gene interactions influencing temperaments of these rhesus monkeys are related to socially induced epigenetic (i.e., gene expression intensity) changes as found by Michael Meaney's (2010) work with rats—more on that subject in Chapter 15.

PRIMATE SUMMARY WITH A
HUMAN PERSPECTIVE

One of the themes running through the personality/temperament literature is the predominance of factor analysis as the tool of choice for identifying basic personality traits. Beginning with Raymond Cattell (1943)
and the eventual emergence of the Big Five human temperament factors, personality theory has become captivated by statistically derived
"latent" factors, and animal temperament research has fallen in step. Our
colleague and mentor John Paul Scott often repeated that statistics in
psychology were just tools for determining the intensities and patterns
of experimental/behavioral effects, as opposed to a way of identifying
the biological sources of those effects. Perhaps we need to think of factor analysis as just a tool that, may have been more valuable during the
"black box" era of psychology and is now superseded by the current
explosion of neuroscience approaches that allow us to peer inside the
brain and directly manipulate brain functions, such as basic emotional
networks, which we have advocated to be major contributors to human
and animal temperamental variability.

Early in the twentieth century, Walter Hess was a pioneer in providing
temperament research with improved tools to directly observe the naturally evolved "factors" within the brain (for complete summary, see Hess
1957). Notably, if one can stimulate the subcortical brain in a particular
anatomical location with a tiny and relatively crude input, and consistently observe the same coherent output, and repeat the process across
many animals, and attain the same results, one can be confident that the
input has activated an organized brain system worth investigating. By pursuing such research during the modern era, Jaak Panksepp (1971, 1998a,
2005) continued such lines of research and documented seven subcortical primary-process (innate) emotion systems in the brain: that he labeled
SEEKING, RAGE/Anger, FEAR, LUST, CARE, separation-induced PANIC/
Sadness, and PLAY, of which six (excluding LUST) are here advanced
as most relevant for personality/temperament research. Using tools that
Hess pioneered, each of these brain emotional states evoked with subcortical electrical stimulation are considered primal foundations for our core
emotional feelings—instinctual emotional-feeling systems that are critical
tools for living and perhaps the formation of personality traits.

But how can we know nonspeaking animals have any feelings at all?
This Pandora's box—the mystery of valenced experiences—was opened
up in the middle of the twentieth century by two groups of investigators
(Olds & Milner, 1954; Delgado, Roberts & Miller, 1954) using deep brain
stimulation (DBS) to simply inquire whether one can obtain rewarding or punishing effects from such brain arousals. Jim Olds found powerfully rewarding sites in many regions below the neocortex (animals

would voluntarily turn on the DBS), but not in the top of the brain that controls our sensory perceptions and thoughts. Delgado and colleagues found other sites that were punishing—animals would turn off the DBS applied to other nearby brain regions. Such effects have been found in all mammals, indeed, all vertebrates that have been studied (Wauquier & Rolls, 1976).

The working hypothesis is that such DBS studies empirically define brain systems that feel "good" and "bad" in various ways—they help define how various positively or negatively valenced states of mind arise from subcortical brain activities. Now more recent neuroscience tools are also available for further investigations, including optogenetics (light stimulation of the brain) and DREADD (designer receptors exclusively activated by designer drugs).

Thus, there is currently strong anatomical, pharmacological, and physiological evidence for these seven defined emotion systems in all mammalian brains. Several of these emotions have evolutionarily older roots (SEEKING, RAGE/Anger, and FEAR), which are evident in all vertebrates. But three (CARING, PANIC/Sadness, and PLAY) seem to be much more developed in mammalian brains. Each of these emotional systems can be aroused with DBS, and although they can operate independently, they surely interact with each ther in yet undetermined ways, as well as with a variety of higher BrainMind functions (secondary-level learning and tertiary-level thought processes) to increase the overall adaptiveness (survival ability) by interacting with diverse higher BrainMind processes (for fuller descriptions, see Panksepp, 1998a, 2005, 2010b, 2011a; Panksepp & Biven, 2012).

Much of the rest of this book is devoted to relating these ancestral emotional powers of the BrainMind to the fundamental personality infrastructures of human brains. However, we will first summarize work on the personality variability in dogs and rats—with less and less known as we progress down the phylogenetic "ladder." (*Ladder* is a misnomer—no such ladder exists, just the genetic diversification of species, because it is difficult to identify a common vertebrate ancestor that survived the last mass extinction event, namely, the last of the big die-offs of the last 500 million years—the most relevant one for mammals being the Cretaceous-Paleogene extinction event, which occurred approximately 66 million years ago.) Nevertheless, the animal and human personality complexities will undoubtedly remain poorly understood until we are able to align the major constitutional temperamental factors studied by monitoring the linguistic-questioning/answering functions of human brains with the natural (evolved) emotional/affective functions of vertebrate (especially mammalian) brains.

CHAPTER 8

The Special Case of Our Canine Companions

Besides love and sympathy, animals exhibit other qualities connected with the social instincts, which in us would be called moral; and I agree with [Louis] Agassiz . . . that dogs possess something very like a conscience.

Dogs possess some power of self-command, and this does not appear to be wholly the result of fear.

— Charles Darwin, *The Descent of Man*

THIS CHAPTER SHIFTS from our closest evolutionary relative to man's best friend, animals that have been our companions for at least 18,000 years, predating the emergence of agriculture (Thalmann et al., 2013). It is possible that our symbiotic relationship with wolves was the gateway to ultimate domestication, which led to further selection of prosocial traits (Coppinger & Coppinger, 2001; Feuerbacher & Wynne, 2012). From a Darwinian continuity perspective, a key question is how the basic temperaments of dogs may be close to traits we value in humans, while perhaps being less complex than those of chimpanzees.

Methodologies in dog personality research involve more laboratory-type measurements of dogs' responses to standard challenges, in contrast to what must necessarily be more naturalistic observational research with chimpanzees. Might using these behavioral test batteries, as opposed the observer rating approach, lead to different conclusions? The extent to which temperament findings in dogs and chimpanzees remain similar, despite shifting from more flexible observer rating studies to more laboratory-type challenges, will strengthen the evolutionary case for similar, even homologous (evolutionarily related) emotional foundations of mammalian personalities. We spend a bit more time on dogs than on monkeys and rats because dogs figure so heavily in issues of human-animal companionship. Dogs are, after all, "man's best friend," although they may not see it quite that way. Thus, we divide this chapter into two parts: first we describe Scott and Fuller's behavior genetic studies and related work that followed, and then we discuss work on quantifying socialization, including examples of puppy testing and a long-term project domesticating another canine, the fox.

With dogs, the personality discussion may move into more familiar territory for most readers, because most folks have lived with a dog or even several dogs at some point in their lives. Certainly, those who have had canine companions would agree that dogs have personalities that reflect stable behavioral and emotional characteristics that differentiate their dogs from other dogs. Of course, due to selective breeding started many centuries ago, we now have an enormous variety of dogs available for comparisons. Indeed, the American Kennel Club registers 175 different breeds, with many manifesting distinct behavioral-temperament differences. While we recognize that there are many passionate cat lovers as well, there has been much less research on cat personalities than on dogs (Gartner & Weiss, 2013). Hence, here we have selected domestic dogs, as a unique mammalian species that probably exhibits diverse genetically based personality traits both across and within subspecies, many of them arising from selective breeding for certain behavioral/psychological characteristics across the last few centuries. More important, our long historical relationship with dogs was based on the fact that we developed a symbiotic relationship long before the agricultural revolution, going back to a time when humans were still hunter-gatherers, starting perhaps some 40,000 years ago, during the peak of the last glacial period, with gradually increasing breeding of canine companions for specific utilitarian traits. As noted by Leslie Irvine (2004), "Selective cross-breeding has been done since antiquity, but it really accelerated during the 19th century." Still, it was another century before humans became interested in the scientific analysis of canine personalities, which had been pragmatically crafted to serve human needs across the past few centuries (Serpell, 1995).

ASSESSING CANINE BEHAVIOR AND PERSONALITY

Scott and Fuller: Social Behavior of the Dog

The classic work of John Paul Scott and John L. Fuller (1965), at the Jackson Memorial Laboratory in Bar Harbor, Maine, set a high quality standard for any future temperament research in dogs. J. P.Scott was recruited in 1946 to initiate a large-scale project in dog behavior genetics at the Jackson Lab. In collaboration with Fuller, Scott set out to fill a void in our understanding of the influence of heredity upon behavior, a subject that was not popular in the zeitgeist following World War II, with the residue of German genetic fantasies, such as *Übermensch,* fresh in people's minds. Overall, Scott and Fuller's work still highlights both the difficulties and promises of large-scale temperament studies in complex domestic animals, a body of work that remains to be equaled.

At least thirteen years were needed to design, set up, and carry out their extensive behavior genetic research plans. Rather than employing the selective breeding frequently used with rats, Scott's group took advantage of existing breed differences and worked on the assumption that breed differences reflected genetic differences. So, they based their work on five breeds of small dogs that spanned the temperament spectrum: Basenjis, beagles, cocker spaniels, Shetland sheepdogs, and wire-haired terriers.

Although both Scott and Fuller had backgrounds in biology, the neuroscientific and other physiological measures and manipulations that were available in the 1950s were severely limited compared to the research options that are available today. While they did collect some physiological data, they relied largely on diverse objective behavioral tests they designed to expose the dogs to environmental and behavioral challenges that might reveal individual and breed differences. These objective tests mostly allowed for timing or counting specific behavioral responses (rather than relying on subjective ratings by handlers or observers) to over twenty behavioral tests collected throughout the first year of life on large samples of all five breeds. Many of these tests were repeated throughout the dog's first year of life to quantify developmental changes; this resulted in the administration of over fifty formal tests, plus numerous incidental observations such as whether puppies could learn to hold still when being weighed during weekly health examinations. We refer to many, but not all, of these unique objective tests and behavioral observations in this brief review of their overall study (for a comprehensive summary, see Scott & Fuller, 1965). In a sense, Scott and Fuller devised the first systematic canine emotional-personality tests, which is why we cover it here in some detail.

In addition, two of these breeds, Basenjis and cocker spaniels, were selected for a more complex genetic analysis involving simple crosses of the two breeds, labeled F_1s, and crosses of those F_1 progeny called F_2s (F stands for "filial" or breeding family stock). Back-crosses from F_1s to each of these two parent breeds were also completed to check and provide initial verification of any genetic hypotheses. While Scott and Fuller showed that many breed differences could be accounted for by one and two gene models, they surprisingly found that "the vast majority of genetic effects on behavior are highly specific and restricted to one or two situations" (1965, p. 375) rather than cutting across many behavioral traits. This program of research highlighted that trans-situational temperamental variables may be rare and hence difficult to genetically analyze. It is possible that such background traits were emotional ones that are harder to select for than specific behavioral abilities, but Scott and Fuller did not neglect to focus on the emotions of their animals.

One theme running through their work was the similarity of social bonding with *conspecifics* (members of the same species) and *heterospecifics* (across other species, including humans), work that highlighted the closely related development of social emotional attachments and place attachments in young puppies. How was this determined? When old enough to maintain body temperature and move about on their own, puppies that were left alone in their home pens emitted loud "distress vocalizations" at a very high rate, signaling their aversion to social isolation. However, they send out even higher rates of distress vocalizations when isolated in a strange place, indicating that distress was amplified when puppies were no longer in a familiar place (Elliot & Scott, 1961). This heightened level of vocalization began tapering off at about eight weeks of age, at the end of what additional research later indicated was the waning of a "critical period" for social attachment (Freedman, King, & Elliot, 1961; Scott, 1958; Scott, Fredericson, & Fuller, 1951). Upon the publication of their book *Genetics and the Social Behavior of the Dog* (Scott & Fuller, 1965), Scott was invited to be the first Ohio Regent's Professor of Psychology at Bowling Green State University (BGSU), where the authors of this book worked with Scott in the early 1970s.[5]

At Scott's BGSU dog lab, Panksepp's group discovered that these distress vocalizations were specifically modulated by brain opioids (Panksepp et al., 1978) that had recently been discovered. The key finding was that tiny doses of opioids—namely "feel good" chemistries in the brains of all vertebrates that are naturally very rewarding (indeed addictive, when opioids are concentrated in various drugs)—could reduce separation distress vocalizations in young puppies. Across the late 1970s and 1980s, this led to a research program focused on the identification and description of a separation-distress brain system using direct brain stimulation procedures in guinea pigs and domestic chicks (summarized in Panksepp et al., 1988; Panksepp, 1998a). This research program highlighted a new social emotional system in vertebrates: the PANIC/Sadness system, which contributed substantially to social bonding. In other words, social bonding was partly due to addictive chemistries of the brain, helping explain why the loss of loved ones is so psychologically painful. For the first time a brain social-emotional system had been identified that no one had talked about yet. Parenthetically, at the same time Harry Harlow's group at University of Wisconsin was demonstrating how emotionally disastrous it was for young rhesus monkeys to live alone (for a poignant summary of that work, see Blum, 2002).

While Panksepp's (1982, 1998a) remaining primary-process (subcortical) brain emotional systems were worked out in rats and other species, the empirical relationships between the other brain emotion systems and dog behaviors (indirectly evident in Scott and Fuller's work) still remain to be clarified neuroscientifically. Yet this multigenerational research, spanning the careers of both Scott and Panksepp, highlights the value of how clear animal models for emotions, when combined with direct brain manipulations/understandings, have the power to impact human psychiatric practice (for summaries, see Chapter 18; see also Panksepp, 2015, 2016). The implications of such findings for the understanding of human personality remain to be fully explored, for which we developed the Affective Neuroscience Personality Scales (Davis et al., 2003; Davis & Panksepp, 2011).

Another common social behavior in dogs, enthusiastic tail wagging so common during social interactions, was measured as part of the Jackson Lab project during the research program's "handling test." These data showed that Basenjis were less attracted to human handlers and cocker spaniels and beagles were the most attracted. Correspondingly, tail wagging itself appeared two weeks later developmentally in the Basenjis than in cocker spaniels. The difference in appearance of cocker and Basenji tail wagging was highly significant and both differed from the other three breeds, which were intermediate. It was later demonstrated at the BGSU Canine Research Laboratory that tail wagging could also be manipulated in very young and juvenile puppies with opioids and the opioid blocker naloxone (Davis, 1980; Knowles, Conner, & Panksepp, 1989), which like separation distress vocalizations linked canine tail wagging to emotional social bonding/attachments and indirectly to the PANIC/Sadness system.

At Jackson Lab, Scott and Fuller (1965) had also investigated play fighting (also known as rough-and-tumble play) in their dogs. Play fighting with human handlers peaked at about fifteen weeks of age and was also associated with definite breed differences. Among the breeds studied by Scott and Fuller (1965), wirehaired terriers exhibited the most play fighting in response to standard handling tests. Basenjis, Shetland sheepdogs, and beagles played at comparable levels, while cocker spaniels exhibiting considerably less play fighting.

However, the correlation between play fighting and later real fighting between conspecifics (other dogs) was found to be low, suggesting that play fighting was not related to aggressive (RAGE/Anger) sensitivities. Indeed, these distinctions were highlighted in their findings. For example, beagles exhibited a typical high level of play fighting in the handling test (Scott & Fuller, 1965, p. 136) but exhibited the lowest level of serious fighting as observed in dominance tests (p. 155). Cockers showed low play fighting and also low levels of dominance fighting. Wirehaired terriers and Basenjis showed high levels of both play fighting and serious fighting, as manifested in "complete dominance" tests. This segregation of real fighting and play fighting likely reflected the activity of two different brain systems, one linked more to the RAGE/Anger system and the retaining of resources such as food, and the other related more to the PLAY system with its social playfulness and positive socialization, distinctions that were evident in many other species (Panksepp, 1998a). While it was not the subject of a primary research project, Scott and Fuller (1965) had already suggested that play fighting reflected a positive social experience, facilitating positive social integration. The relationship between positive affect and playfulness was later empirically confirmed in rats (as described in Chapter 9).

In the general-purpose handling test, Scott and Fuller also measured the avoidance of human handlers, which was interpreted as timidity or fear, likely reflecting the primary FEAR system. Cocker spaniels showed the lowest avoidance of human handlers. Beagles were also less avoidant in the handling test, with the other three breeds exhibiting higher avoidance levels. In addition to being among the most avoidant breeds on the handling test, Shetland sheepdogs were also the poorest performers on the motor-skill and spatial-orientation tests, both of which required climbing, which Scott and Fuller (1965) attributed to shelties being quite fearful of heights.

Another case of fear affecting test performance was on the trailing test that required dogs to track a scent down a series of branching boards leading to a fish treat. All breeds did well except the wirehaired terriers and Basenjis. However, the poor performance of Basenjis was due a "fear reaction to the apparatus" (Scott & Fuller, 1965 p. 247) and refusal to cross the board trail. Basenjis were not afraid of heights like the shelties and were skilled climbers, but their cautious reaction to the strange apparatus interfered with their scores on the motor-skills test and was another example of the highly specific nature of many instinctive fears.

The leash training test measured the tendency of juvenile puppies to adapt to being on the leash or to fight this restraint. Scott and Fuller noted that "Basenjis were outstanding in their vigorous resistance to the restraint of a collar and lead" (1965 p. 209). The heritability for fighting the restraint of the leash was estimated from 0.45 to 0.77 (with 1.0 reflecting perfect heritability). Leash fighting with juvenile puppies may be a good model reflecting the RAGE/Anger system in action, which responds to physical restraint possibly based on an evolutionary adaptation to being captured by a predator (Panksepp, 1998a). Similarly, when placed in the restrictive Pavlov stand for the reactivity test (similar to that used by Ivan Pavlov for his classic studies on canine classical conditioning of salivation), Basenjis also exhibited a strong tendency to bite. While Basenjis showed the highest and cockers the lowest percentage of biting in the Pavlov stand at all ages, the differences became greater with each successive trial. By fifty-one weeks, 83 percent of Basenjis and only 7 percent of cocker spaniels were biting the restraint. Hence, the marked personality differences between aggressiveness and fighting across species—with Basenjis and cocker spaniels being respectively at the high and low extremes—demonstrating hereditary influences from puppyhood through early adulthood, potentially in the responsivity of the RAGE/Anger system.

Scott and Fuller's (1965) overall emotional reactivity test was administered at seventeen, thirty-four, and fifty-one weeks of age, during which each dog was restrained in a Pavlov stand and subjected to ten stressful episodes with eighteen behavioral and physiological measures. Cocker spaniels showed the lowest overall reactivity scores, and Scott and Fuller interpreted the reactivity test as a measure of inhibitory training. They related the cocker's relatively calm performance during this test to the breed's historic capacity to respond to threats, especially hand motions, by ceasing all activity for a moment with no signs of emotional disturbance. This conclusion was further supported by the Jackson Lab's weekly medical checkup procedures, during which puppies, in order to be weighed, were trained to remain quiet for one minute by the handler holding his or her hands near the animal but attempting not to touch the puppy standing on the scale. By fourteen weeks of age, 80 percent of cocker spaniel puppies would remain quietly on the scale for one minute, which was more than twice the percentage for any other breed. In wirehaired terriers, also the most reactive and least inhibited breed at fifty-one weeks on the reactivity test, only 10 percent of the puppies could quietly remain on the scale for one minute. It is tempting to associate the cocker's capacity for inhibition as a cross-species form of the human Big Five Conscientiousness trait, which has been thought to represent the cortical regulation of subcortically based primary traits (Davis & Panksepp, 2011) and which in Chapter 7 was identified in chimpanzees and brown capuchin monkeys but has otherwise been difficult to identify in nonhumans.

Shetland sheepdogs showed slightly lower levels of inhibition than cocker spaniels during the reactivity test at all three ages. By contrast, wirehaired terriers, beagles, and Basenjis were consistently much more reactive and less inhibited than cockers and shelties. Like cockers, shelties were less reactive and more easily inhibited in the Pavlov stand, but in contrast to cockers, shelties exhibited high levels of fearfulness in other tests, as noted previously. In fact, among cockers, beagles, shelties, and Basenjis, all four combinations of high and low inhibition (on the reactivity test) and with high and low fear (on the human handler

Table 8.1. Segregation of Fear and Reactivity Across Four Dog Breeds		
Fear and Avoidance	**Reactivity**	
	Low	**High**
High	Shetland sheepdogs	Basenjis
Low	Cocker spaniels	Beagles
Adapted from findings reported in Scott & Fuller (1965).		

test) were exhibited, suggesting that inhibition training (low reactivity) and fearfulness (high avoidance) segregate independently genetically, as illustrated in Table 8.1.

Scott and Fuller (1965) described maternal care of puppies but only indirectly touched on the CARE system by frequently hypothesizing maternal effects, including maternal effects on aggressiveness, which have now been shown in rats (Parent & Meaney, 2008), as discussed in Chapter 9. Also, Scott and Fuller (1965) decided not to study investigative behavior, even though the investigative system was one of Scott's nine categories of behavior systems (Scott, 1958, 1972). Exploratory/investigative behavior, to monitor the status of what would relate to the primary SEEKING system, was judged to require too much space, given its relationship to hunting in the dog, and would have been too difficult to study experimentally in the field.

With a behavior genetics approach to behavior, these pioneers broadly sampled what we would view as the affective neuroscience temperament dimensions, which, for example, included demonstrations of the importance of distress vocalizations that would later be linked to Panksepp's PANIC/Sadness system. Their research also included carefully measured individual differences in the PLAYfulness, FEAR, and RAGE/Anger systems. One might also consider cocker spaniel (and to a lesser extent sheltie) inhibition as a nonhuman candidate for the Big Five dimension of Conscientiousness and the regulation of emotion. Scott and Fuller's discussion of what we would interpret as the SEEKING and CARE systems rounded out a rather complete treatment of the mammalian personality domain. In a highly objective study that predated modern neuroscience, Scott and Fuller impressively documented what Panksepp was identifying as primary mammalian emotion systems. Once again, a comprehensive analysis of mammalian behavior provided a set of traits that have been reported with remarkable consistency starting with Darwin and leading through so many other contributors to neuroscientifically documented blue ribbon emotions of affective neuroscience (Panksepp,

1981, 1982, 1998a; Panksepp & Biven, 2012). Scott and Fuller's work invites further research exploring the empirical relationships between their many observations and these brain emotion systems underlying dog behavior. In addition, their work set the stage for later dog testing, which we now selectively review.

More Canine Assessments

Scott and Fuller's work inspired subsequent behavioral dog testing. We begin with studies on dogs tested using canine behavior questionnaires and then briefly review behavioral tests for dogs in military work and one study on pets in a rescue shelter. We reserve for the second part of this chapter research on the quality of social attachments in dogs, followed by a brief review of puppy testing research on selecting guide dogs for the blind (Pfaffenberger, Scott, Fuller, Ginsburg, & Bielfelt, 1976) and police dogs, all with the goal of comparing the breadth of canine personality dimensions to Panksepp's six primary emotions related to human emotional personality issues.

Swedish Working Dog Association Studies

Svartberg and Forkman (2002) studied personalities of pet dogs using data from a dog behavior rating questionnaire developed by the Swedish Working Dog Association called the Dog Mentality Assessment (DMA). The DMA was developed mainly for dog breeders, but it became a popular general assessment with owners as well that has resulted in a massive database containing over 15,000 pet dogs from 164 breeds. The DMA evaluates dogs interacting with a familiar handler in response to ten separate subtests measuring thirty-three behavioral variables, which measure a dog's reactions to strangers, opportunities to play with a human, reactions to prey-like objects, and several potentially fearful and aggression-inducing situations. From the forty-seven most popular breeds, Svartberg and Forkman randomly selected 1,175 adult dogs that averaged about two years of age.

An exploratory factor analysis on their large dataset yielded five latent dimensions: Playfulness, Curiosity/Fearlessness, Chase Proneness (including following and grabbing behavior), Sociability, and Aggressiveness (including threat displays and attacks). The Chase Proneness factor included ratings from only a single test, and the researchers tentatively interpreted it as predatory behavior, which based on rat research (discussed in Chapter 9) would align it with Panksepp's SEEKING system. Although unpublished, some work was done in Scott's BGSU dog lab examining predatory responses of puppies to small papier-mâché animal models with rudimentary limbs and heads, which also suggested the possibility of studying canine predatory behavior as a distinct temperamental dimension.

Svartberg and Forkman were also able to document Panksepp's PLAY system with their Playfulness factor and the RAGE/Anger system with their Aggressiveness factor. They also described their Curiosity/Fearlessness factor as an "analogue to fearfulness, but inverted" (Svartberg & Forkman, 2002, p. 152) and compared it to the general fearfulness observed in other studies, which suggests their Curiosity/Fearlessness factor may be related to Panksepp's FEAR system.

Each of the behavior ratings on the Sociability factor involved initiating physical contact with a stranger along a continuum that included "intense greeting with whining and jumping" (Svartberg & Forkman, 2002, p. 137) at the high end. These social eagerness behaviors were precisely what Davis observed when opioid blockers were administered to dogs, likely activating their PANIC/Sadness systems. Morphine, an opioid, administered to dogs had the opposite effects and basically stopped dogs from initiating social contacts with a human handler or with other dogs (Davis, 1980). Thus, Svartberg and Forkman's Sociability factor seems to fit with Scott and Fuller's (1965) distress vocalization and attachment observations and later demonstrations in Scott's BGSU dog lab that the brain opioids regulate (alleviate) separation distress (Panksepp et al., 1978), which further aligns Sociability with Panksepp's PANIC/Sadness system (Panksepp, 1982, 1998a).

Altogether, Svartberg and Forkman found all of the primary personality emotions in their analysis of the DMA except for the CARE system, which like in Scott and Fuller's work was not empirically evaluated as a general temperament dimension. Using rather different methods, adult dogs from forty-seven breeds tested individually in single sessions, and relying on factor analysis, Svartberg and Forkman (2002) added further confirmation of the set of affective neuroscience dimensions that account for a substantial part of the foundation of the mammalian personality factors.

Taking a behavior genetics approach, Saetre et al. (2006), who graciously acknowledged Scott and Fuller as the pioneers of behavior genetic research on personality in dogs, used the large Swedish database of DMA behavior ratings to analyze the pedigrees of 5,964 German shepherds and 4,589 Rottweilers by integrating the DMA data with pedigrees on untested relatives back to grandparents. However, Saetre and colleagues incorporated data from an older, shorter version of the DMA and had complete data on only sixteen behavior observations that only included a single measure of Sociability, which they removed from their analysis. Using the same first-order factors previously identified by Svartberg and Forkman (excepting Sociability), the pedigree relationships and the first-order traits explained 46 percent and 39 percent of the observed genetic correlations for German shepherds and Rottweilers respectively, which supported a genetic basis for canine temperament.

C-BARQ: A Questionnaire for Dog Owners to Rate Their Pets

In dog studies, the behavioral test battery seems to have been historically more popular to identify breed as well as individual personality differences. However, trait ratings by informants—people that know the target individual well—is another method for measuring personality traits, and there is substantial evidence that in humans this approach to collecting personality data can be at least as accurate as when individuals complete the personality questionnaire themselves (Connelly & Ones, 2011).

Accordingly, Hsu and Serpell (2003) have offered a dog-rating questionnaire with sixty-eight items that dog owners can complete on their pets. The instrument was originally named the Pennsylvania Behavioral Assessment and Research Questionnaire, because the authors were at the University of Pennsylvania. However, it was later renamed the Canine Behavioral Assessment and Research Questionnaire (C-BARQ). The C-BARQ measures eleven factor-analytically derived dog temperament scales, which generally overlapped with the scales Svartberg and Forkman derived from the Swedish DMA. However, the C-BARQ scales included multiple measures of RAGE/Anger ("stranger-directed aggression" and "owner-directed aggression") and FEAR ("stranger-directed fear" and "nonsocial fear"), and a scale that combined elements of aggression and fear ("dog-directed fear or aggression"). The C-BARQ also provided three measures ("separation-directed behavior," "attachment or attention-seeking behavior," and a "trainability" scale that included items like "returns immediately when called while off leash" and "will attempt to fetch sticks, balls, and other objects"), all of which link to social contact and the primary PANIC/Sadness system that is so prominent in the study of mammalian temperaments. Further, a C-BARQ "chasing" factor was described as measuring "a tendency to engage in predatory pursuit," supporting the Svartman and Fortman chase factor and predatory behavior as a specific expression of the SEEKING dimension in canine personalities. The C-BARQ also has an "excitability" scale, which measures excited overreaction prior to events like "just before being taken for a walk," which seems like an anticipatory SEEKING response. The C-BARQ also has a scale for "pain sensitivity," which would have little to do with personality but is probably more relevant for overall veterinary care. Other than C-BARQ not having a scale for the PLAY system, the C-BARQ and Svartberg and Forkman's DMA analysis are remarkably comparable despite using very different methods.

Taking a page directly from McDougall's work, Hsu and Serpell (2003) also validated their questionnaire scales by comparing clinical diagnoses from the Veterinary Hospital of the University of Pennsylvania on two hundred dogs having clear behavior problems with the dog's C-BARQ questionnaire scores. They grouped the diagnoses into seven clusters corresponding to their first seven factor scales. Correlations between the diagnoses and questionnaire factor scores showed that particular behavior problems had the highest correlation with the corresponding questionnaire factor, strongly substantiating all three of the negative primary emotions in canine clinical work. Thus, the C-BARQ and its clinical validation confirms McDougall's principle that, in their extreme expressions, emotional personality traits can become pathological (see Chapter 4) and strongly supports the need for separate distinct scales for each of the primary negative emotions—RAGE/Anger, FEAR, and PANIC/Sadness—in mammalian personality. A future suggestion could be to add scales targeting more canine PLAYful and CAREing behaviors to broaden the C-BARQ's coverage of the primary-process positive affective temperamental domains.

Military Working Dogs

Studies of working dogs are less concerned with personality as a whole and more focused on trying to solve a very practical problem: identifying dogs that are likely to succeed in their specialty roles. That is, these behavioral tests are designed to predict narrow aptitudes for specific canine work rather than a broad set of personality dimensions. For example, Sam Gosling and colleagues (Sinn, Gosling, & Hilliard, 2010) studied military working dogs at Lackland Air Force base in San Antonio, Texas. They analyzed standardized behavioral tests collected prior to training in which observers rated a dog's reactions to exercises the military had designed to measure a dog's aptitude for patrol and detection work.

A factor analysis of twelve observer ratings yielded four factors. The authors labeled the first and largest factor "Object focus," which measured interest in chasing and playing with a rubber toy that included excited barking, pouncing, throwing, and chewing; general interest in the environment and avoiding potentially fearful distractions; and generally exhibiting no fear. This factor could be measuring predatory behavior with a playful tone in that the dog is excited and vocal rather than quiet. Lack of fear is relevant because it is very clear that fear inhibits play, an effect that has been well studied formally in juvenile rat models.

By contrast to the "vigorous vocalizations" (Sinn et al., 2010, p. 54) observed in the first factor, the second factor, Sharpness, had the highest test loadings on the dog's tendency to bite the tester's harm-protected sleeve "strongly, calmly, and quietly" (p. 55), which is strikingly similar to the quiet predatory biting elicited using electric brain stimulation in cats (Flynn, 1976; Siegel, 2004) and rats (Panksepp, 1971), a behavioral tendency that has been shown to require activation of the SEEKING system.

The third factor, Human focus, primarily measured the dog's tendency to direct aggressiveness toward the human tester with barking, snarling, tooth exposure, and piloerection, which would seem to be a direct measure of agonistic attack and Panksepp's (1998a) RAGE/Anger system. The fourth and smallest factor, Search focus, was isolated to search activity tests that may reflect Panksepp's (1998a) dopaminergic SEEKING system.

As the evolutionarily most ancient of the primary emotions, the SEEKING system has widespread influence on the widest variety of behaviors, including exploration and general activity, as well as LUST, CARE and PLAY. It is tempting to speculate that in addition to SEEKING-oriented predatory behavior, these dogs exhibited a curiosity toward the environment that military, police, and hunters take advantage of in search work. It is also relevant that these dogs seem to find the search itself rewarding, because they never get to keep the objects of their search, including the quarry they help the hunters take home. In all cases studied, the activation of the SEEKING system is a strongly positive experience and a potent reward, which relates to all primary emotions having either a subjectively experienced reward or an escape from punishing qualities.

Altogether, the Sinn et al. (2010) factor analysis included a narrower range of temperament traits focusing on what we could call the RAGE/Anger system, as well as multiple elaborations of the SEEKING system. They may also have thus distinguished playful as well the as the serious predatory behavior systems. The common link may be that the quiet predatory attack evoked by brain stimulation requires electrodes to be placed along the dopamine investigatory SEEKING circuits in the brain but with a recognition that the PLAY system (which is heavily represented in the thalamus, as opposed to just the hypothalamus; see Siviy & Panksepp, 1985) also requires substantial brain dopamine activation along the medial forebrain bundle (Panksepp, 1998a), as has been most clearly demonstrated in more recent studies with rat "laughter" (Burgdorf, Wood, Kroes, Moskal, & Panksepp, 2007; Burgdorf et al., 2008). In any case, the predatory behavior in the Sharpness scale, along with the previously described chasing factors reported in the DMA and C-BARQ studies, strongly reinforces predatory behavior as a general temperament trait in dogs.

Pet Adoption: The Need for Low RAGE/Anger

In a very practical example of a test battery, Kelly Bollen and Joseph Horowitz (2008) explored testing the suitability of shelter dogs for future adoption. They used Sue Sternberg's "Assess-a-Pet" test (Sternberg, 2002, cited in Bollen & Horowitz, 2008), which measured dogs' responses to nine common household situations, such as a human reaching into the food bowl while a dog is eating, a human taking a valued possession from a dog, and a dog meeting a human stranger. The goal was to increase the percentage of successful home placements by not placing dogs for adoption that exhibited an aggressive personality, such as lunging at the evaluator while growling and snarling, or making any attempt to bite during the tests.

Using this screening test, the shelter increased its rate of successful dog adoptions, with 3.5 percent of dogs being returned for exhibiting aggression compared to 5.1 percent the previous year, which validated Bollen and Horowitz's work. Importantly, the return rate could have been improved further by not placing "borderline" cases that during the shelter test displayed only mild aggression, such as stiffening or slight growling, because there was a significant trend for these dogs to be returned for displaying aggressive behavior in the home as well.

However, there is another basic personality question: Were there stable differences in aggressive personality tendencies in the dogs they studied? Indeed, 90 percent of the 217 dogs initially brought to the shelter because they were aggressive in their previous homes also displayed aggression during at least one of the test components evaluated in the shelter, which was almost twelve times the failure rate of dogs brought to the shelter for other reasons and highly significantly different. So, a stable aggressive personality trait was confirmed in these dogs across the two completely different settings, in the dog's previous home and at the shelter. Furthermore, the "borderline" dogs placed for adoption were more likely to be returned to the shelter than dogs exhibiting no aggression during the shelter test, demonstrating consistent aggressiveness across a third different setting. In short, Bollen and Horowitz provided evidence that a behavioral assessment could identify dogs exhibiting easily provoked RAGE/Anger that made it difficult for families to keep them as pets.

SOCIALIZATION AND DOMESTICATION

Human Social Attachment
Measures Adapted to Dogs

Social bonding has long been a subject of interest in psychology (Bowlby, 1960; Scott, 1962). In a study specifically focused on canine social attachment, Topal, Miklosi, Csanyi, and Doka (1998), working in Hungary, adapted the Ainsworth Strange Situation Test, originally used to examine attachment behavior in children (Ainsworth, 1969). The original test revealed "secure" and "insecure" social attachment styles in children by observing their reactions in a strange setting to being separated from and then reunited with their mothers, as well as interacting with a stranger. Topal and colleagues were interested in studying these attachment styles between dogs (as the child) and their human owners (as the parent). Like Mary Ainsworth, they set up a series of tests that placed each dog in a strange place with its owner, with a stranger, or alone.

In their attempt to replicate Ainsworth's attachment types in dogs, Topal et al. (1998) identified three factors: anxiety (separation distress), acceptance of stranger, and attachment to owner. They reported that some of the pet dogs clearly explored the unfamiliar room and exhibited increased play and did so significantly more with their owner present than with the stranger. This pattern was consistent with the Ainsworth (1969) secure attachment phenotype, which similarly found young children showing signs of missing the parent, but then greeting the parent upon reunion, and the child then resuming his or her activities without further interruption. Further, Topal and colleagues reported that the dogs in their study could be placed on a continuum of how securely they seemed to be attached to their owners.

However, Topal's group did not report finding dogs that matched Ainsworth's (1969) insecure attachment types, characterized by either showing extreme signs of distress when the parent left and remaining inconsolable upon the parent's return or showing little if any sign of missing the parent and avoiding and ignoring the parent when the parent reentered the test room. The Topal group did identify a cluster of five out of their fifty-one dogs exhibiting high separation anxiety, high attachment to the owner, but also with high acceptance of the stranger. That is, these dogs were eager to make contact with *any* human who was with them in the strange room. This type of social need did not appear in the Ainsworth studies, especially with the insecure children who were not consoled by strangers (Ainsworth & Bell, 1970).

In contrast to the Ainsworth findings, all of the dog's exhibiting high levels of separation anxiety when left alone in the strange room readily made contact when any human returned to the test room. Even though all of these dogs were raised in families, and Topal and colleagues argued these human-dog relationships were like the parent-child relationship, none of the dogs in the Topal study behaved like the Ainsworth insecure or insecure-avoidant types in that they all exhibited separation distress when left alone but all made contact with any human during the reunion episodes of the experiment. This pattern of data may suggest that the insecure types reflect a secondary-process personality dimension, arising from past learning-socialization experiences, rather than a primary emotional one.

Obviously, specific social attachments reflect learned secondary-process associative-learning mechanisms, with the learning of security most likely based on the primary-process PANIC/Sadness system, as well as the social reward systems of CARE and PLAY. Mammals are not born socially bonded, as was dramatically illustrated in the Scott and Fuller work in which puppies with no human contact for fourteen weeks essentially became wild animals that totally avoided humans (Freedman et al., 1961). However, in their work on the critical periods of socialization, Scott and Fuller (1965) also reported that as little as two weeks of contact with humans between four and eight weeks of age were sufficient to socialize puppies to humans. Thus, perhaps not surprisingly, Topal's group did not find pet dogs that were socially avoidant.

It is tempting to speculate that domesticated dogs have such sensitive PANIC/Sadness systems that they become socialized with even minimal contact with humans. Even though dogs and humans remain dependent on their families for many years, some human children may have sufficiently insensitive PANIC/Sadness systems that they never become securely bonded to their families, especially when surrounded by parental strife that amounts to chaos in family dynamics. As Ainsworth observed, such a child might not show separation distress when left alone and might by choice remain socially isolated when the mother returned. It is also possible that autistic children are deficient in such basic social-emotional sensitivities (Panksepp & Sahley, 1987), an understanding that may lead to novel therapeutics (Moskal, Burgdorf, Kroes, Brudzynski, & Panksepp, 2011).

Palmer & Custance (2008) added additional experimental controls and still confirmed that dog owners provided a secure base for their dogs, showing that dogs were most willing to engage in play with the owner but also more likely to play with the stranger when their owner was present than when their owner was absent. A variation on these studies by an Italian group (Mariti, Carlone, Ricci, Sighieri, & Gazzano, 2014) used Ainsworth's secure attachment paradigm to test the attachment between two dogs. They used twenty-two pairs of dogs living in the same household. One member of each dog pair was arbitrarily used as the subject and the other dog was assigned the role of the primary attachment figure, rather than using the dog's owner. A human unknown to any of the dogs was used as the stranger. Remarkably, after being left alone in the room, the dog being studied was more consoled by and made more contact with the human stranger than with the other dog that shared the same household with them, suggesting that dogs may have been genetically selected to form strong social bonds with humans (Serpell, 1995), or simply have a history of finding active comforting from humans rather than other dogs.

While more research is needed in the PANIC/Sadness-related personality differences of dogs, future attachment style research between humans and dogs might benefit from measuring specific canine appropriate social contact behaviors, such as tail wagging and face licking (e.g., Davis, 1980; Knowles et al., 1989), that could add objectivity as well as add qualitative richness to the descriptions of initial social contact the dogs made with either the owner or stranger. However, it would be especially important to include measures of separation distress vocalizations to assess the activation of the specific PANIC/Sadness system, which is characterized by a form of separation anxiety that is distinct from the anxiety generated by the FEAR system (Davis, Gurski, & Scott, 1977; Panksepp, 1998a).

An interesting new approach to detecting separation distress affect and possibly attachment style is the cognitive bias test model. This test is based on the assumption that in ambiguous situations individuals experiencing negative emotions will make more negative (pessimistic) judgments and individuals experiencing positive emotions will make more positive (optimistic) judgments, which has been confirmed in several species, including humans (Mendl, Burman, Parker, & Paul, 2009). Indeed, dogs (9 to 108 months of age) that exhibited higher levels of behaviors related to social separation distress when left alone made more pessimistic-like responses to ambiguous stimuli than dogs exhibiting less social separation distress (Mendl et al., 2010), which we would interpret as validating an animal model of the distressful PANIC/Sadness emotion biasing behavioral choices in a negative direction, and further suggest that it may be subcortical "affective bias" that is influencing these behavioral choices.

Puppy Testing Predictions

Another interesting question that arises from a discussion of early socialization is whether one can tell from examining a puppy what kind of personality it will have when it matures. This is an important question if one is deciding whether to expend the resources required to train a dog for police work or to become a guide dog for the blind. However, families also invest a great deal of money, time, and effort into raising a puppy and often would like some assurance that their new pet is going to remain a welcome addition rather than a burden to the family. This goes doubly so for selecting service companion dogs that are trained to assist medically impaired individuals, including psychiatrically challenged soldiers returning from difficult tours of duty.

While there are critics of puppy testing, especially at six to seven weeks or earlier (Riemer, Müller, Virányi, Huber, & Range, 2014; Wilsson & Sundgren, 1998), there are three validation studies with consistently positive results. These three studies all involve predicting puppies' aptitudes for later training either as guide dogs for the blind or as police dogs in the latter two studies. The guide dog study was an outgrowth of Scott's collaboration with Clarence Pfaffenberger, who was trying to reduce the number of dogs that had to be trained to produce a working Seeing Eye dog, because when the program started it could successfully train only 30 percent of its guide dog candidates. A series of thirteen behavioral tests was introduced for puppies from eight to twelve weeks of age, which included many of the kinds of tests Scott and Fuller had used in the Jackson Lab research program. A total of 239 puppies were tested and trained as guide dogs: those that were judged to have failed the tests (n = 33), those that had performed poorly (n = 18), and those that had passed (n = 188). Including puppies they thought could not be successfully trained was important to have sufficient variation in the sample to clearly show that better test results actually were related to better training results.

Four tests best predicted future success as guide dogs: the come test, the fetch test, the heel test, and the footing-crossing test. The use of these four tests improved training success rates to 60 percent, with those puppies failing the test succeeding only 20 percent of the time (Scott & Bielfelt, 1976). The first three tests could be easily conducted outdoors by a new puppy buyer. The come test involved walking a good distance away from the puppy, squatting down facing the puppy, and calling out "come puppy" while clapping or using its name (if it has one). The best result is when the puppy comes immediately. Poorer results are when the puppy has to be coaxed repeatedly or does not come at all. In the fetch test, the handler shows the puppy a small rubber ball while trying to get the puppy excited before throwing the ball several feet away and calling "puppy fetch" in a lively voice. The handler continues clapping and encouraging the puppy. The best result is when the puppy retrieves the ball to the handler immediately. For the heel test, if the puppy has never been on a leash, the puppy can be carried a short way from a familiar place, put on the leash, and encouraged to walk back on the left side of a right-handed handler. Otherwise, the puppy can be put on leash and walked away from the familiar place. The puppy can run slightly ahead of the handler, and the session is not turned into an obedience lesson. The issue (i.e., test result) is whether the puppy cooperates with the handler or fights the leash. These first three tests assess whether the puppy is motivated to interact with a human handler and, in the case of heeling on a leash, whether that extends to tolerating some physical restriction. The footing-crossing test involves a puppy being led over a patch of metal and a shallow curb. Observers rated whether the puppies were alert to these differences in their footing, which would be useful later as guide dogs.

The first of the two police dog studies was conducted in South Africa (Slabbert & Odendaal, 1999). They gave 167 young German shepherd puppies eight behavioral tests and later recorded whether the puppies passed a 103-day training course, which had to be completed by two years of age. Most of their objective tests were completed by twelve weeks of age, and three of those were most predictive of later successful training. The first was the obstacle test, a variation of the guide dog come test, in which puppies at eight weeks of age had to go through a large pipe (five feet long and two feet in diameter) and climb over stairs about eighteen inches high to reach a handler who called them. A fetch test, similar to the guide dog test, examined whether a puppy at eight weeks retrieved a small toy to its handler and was a strong predictor of later training success. At twelve weeks a startle test subjected each puppy to a stranger jumping out from behind a wall in front of the puppy. Puppies that made no effort to run away received the highest scores. A fourth test, another stranger test that the puppies received much later at six and nine months, involved a stranger provoking the puppies by striking them firmly but gently with a rag. If the dog bit the rag and held on, it received a high score; if it showed fear it received a low score. These tests were able to identify 91.7 percent of the successful dogs and 81.7 percent of the unsuccessful dogs.

The second of the police dog studies comes from the Czech Republic (Svobodová, Vápeník, Pinc, & Bartoš, 2008). In the Czech study, 206 German shepherd dogs were given ten tests and weighed at seven weeks of age. Interestingly, the strongest predictor of whether a puppy would later pass certification was its weight at seven weeks, which the authors attributed to a general preference of police to use large dogs. However, among the behavioral measures, the strongest predictors were the puppy's willingness to chase, catch, and fetch a tennis ball and whether a puppy would bite and fight a rag being drawn away from it, which the authors collectively labeled "attitude to predation." Although a weaker predictor, in three of the ten tests the puppies were exposed to loud distracting noises. Puppies that showed the most fear received the lowest scores; those that exhibited less fear and even showed exploratory interest in the noise receiver higher scores. Lastly, there was evidence that the more the puppy approached the tester in a friendly way, the more likely the puppy would later be successfully certified for police work.

All three of these studies aimed to identify dogs that could be trained to perform complex tasks. One finding all three studies have in common was a puppy fetching at an early age, which was strongly related to later training success. Scott and Bielfelt (1976) found that retrieving at later ages was not as predictive, because eventually almost all dogs in their sample could learn to fetch. However, the willingness at seven or eight weeks to fetch may indicate intense prosocial motivation that can carry into a dog's adult life and facilitate its trainability to work closely with humans. While there may be a predatory SEEKING element that energizes the chasing component of fetching, there also seems to be a strong social motivation to interact with the handler that could indicate a sensitive PANIC/Sadness or PLAY system, which makes the ensuing contact with the handler very motivating as well. Along these lines, the guide dog study and the South African study found strong evidence that a puppy's willingness and motivation to come to a human handler at eight weeks was also a strong predictor of later trainability, which could be related to the extent of human interactions in the Czech study, all of which support the idea that, in the dogs that excelled in their training, already as young puppies the PANIC/Sadness system had established a strong motivation to maintain contact with humans.

In the police studies, quiet biting (as opposed to angry noisy biting) likely reflects increased emphasis on SEEKING-based predatory behavior (with angry noisy biting more likely reflecting dispositions toward RAGE/Anger). In puppies, an aptitude for this capacity may be promoted and stimulated by taunting the puppy with a rag. This predatory (SEEKING) feature was also highlighted in the military dog training study cited above. In police or military work, biting hard and holding the bite to subdue a human target is an important tool, which the officer-handler must be able to turn on and off with commands given to the dog.

Having a less sensitive FEAR system seems to be an important affective dimension for such working dogs as well. Being able to tolerate being startled by loud noises or not being afraid of loud noises in general was a consistent predictor of future success as a police dog. Lastly, the puppy's willingness to tolerate restraint as measured by the guide dog heeling test may be a good proxy for a less sensitive RAGE/Anger system, which along with the puppy's willingness to please a human handler is an obvious requirement of all guide dog work. However, it would be surprising if this simple test were not equally effective in predicting training success in police and military working dogs.

In summary, both brain emotion network analysis and modern genetic profiling will allow investigators to have better anchored measures of emotional temperament than was available in previous eras. With ready access to modern genetic tools, such work is likely to be a major focus of future inquiries. Such analyses may already be coupled to the most remarkable canine selection study ever conducted, as described next.

The Fox Domestication Project

About fifty years ago, a selection project aimed at domesticating the Russian silver fox (*Vulpes vulpes*) was initiated to explore the domestication process in mammals. Starting with a population of silver foxes that had been farm bred for about fifty years (starting in the early twentieth century), foxes displaying the weakest fear and aggressive responses were selected to begin a line of potentially tame foxes (Trut, Oskina, & Kharlamova, 2009). Subsequent generations were subjected to attempted touching, petting, and hand feeding, and less than 10 percent of the pups exhibiting the most tameness were selected as parents for the next generation. After three generations of such selection, "aggressive and fear avoidance responses were eliminated from the experimental population" (p. 351). In the fourth generation, spontaneous tail wagging in response to humans was observed. In the sixth generation, 4 out of 213 fox pups emerged that eagerly sought human contact and wagged, whined, and licked faces like domestic dogs. The frequency of such pups increased to 17.9 percent by the 10th generation, 35 percent by the 20th generation, and 49 percent in the 30th generation. Reduced reactivity of the FEAR system seemed to have been closely involved in selection for tameness in the silver fox, because the age at which fear was first seen was shifted to about 4 months in the tame line from about 45 days in the unselected line (Trut et al., 2009). Of course, it is likely that sensitivities of PANIC/Sadness, PLAY, RAGE/Anger, SEEKING, and perhaps even CARE were also involved (as discussed further below), but without in depth neuroscience work, such issues will remain empirically unresolved.

A second line of silver foxes was selected for aggressiveness toward humans, and it was discovered that the tame and aggressive lines always exhibited different vocalizations toward humans: Tame foxes produced "cackles" and "pants," and the aggressive line "coughs" and "snorts" (Gogoleva, Volodin, Volodina, Kharlamova, & Trut, 2010). When foxes from the same lines were observed together in pairs, despite directional testing for generations, tame foxes retained their capacity for agonistic behavior and vocalizations toward other foxes and aggressive foxes retained their capacity for affiliative behavior and vocalization, suggesting the genetic independence and complexity of these emotional systems.

From video tapes of the foxes during standard tests, 311 measures of physical activities such as position in the cage, body postures, ear position, and sounds were reduced to fifty key behaviors. The first principal component (a statistical clustering) of this reduced set of behaviors provided an objective measure that accounted for 48.4 percent of the variance (a statistical measure of overall percent relatedness or how well findings are explained by the chosen measures). This first principal component distinguished the aggressive and unselected lines from the tame line, as well as the F_1 backcross to tame foxes, with the F_1 line (tame line bred with aggressive line) being intermediate (Kukekova et al., 2008), clearly demonstrating the genetic differences between the tame and aggressive lines. While no specific genetic hypotheses were offered, one must assume that many genes and brain systems must be involved considering that the proportion of foxes that could be characterized as tame almost tripled from the 10th to the 30th generation. In addition to the FEAR and RAGE/Anger systems that were selected against in the tame parent line, it is likely that the PANIC/Sadness social bonding system was selected for as well, because tail wags and face licking in response to humans—both of which are known to increase in response to opioid blockers increasing PANIC/Sadness sensitivity (Davis, 1980; Knowles et al., 1989)—amazingly emerged in the fourth and sixth generations of this remarkable selection project.

CANINE SUMMARY

In canines, many of the descriptive details of social bonding and separation-induced distress have been documented (Scott & Fuller, 1965), the C-BARQ (Hsu & Serpell, 2003) has provided a "separation-related behavior" trait scale for dogs, and Topal et al. (1998) has developed a new test of social attachment. However, fuller understanding of sensitivity to separation distress as a temperament dimension in dogs and of the range of social bonding/dependence in dogs extending to pathological separation-related behavior (Mendl et al., 2010), and their genetic and neural underpinnings, will require much additional research. Clearly, better linking the social separation experience to the mammalian brain's PANIC/Sadness system (Panksepp, 1998a) and the underlying brain and genetic mechanisms is needed to explore the canine model for separation-induced pathology in humans.

While foxes may naturally be less intensely social than dogs and wolves, the silver fox domestication project has shown that foxes possess the genetic basis for pronounced positive social motivation, including heterospecific bonding with humans. The counter suggestion that domesticated dogs have retained predatory tendencies, which are expressed toward humans, may provide insight into another pathological dimension of canine behavior in relation to humans. Although this has yet to be studied, one might start with breeds that have been found to be extra aggressive to humans historically, such as pit bulls (Sacks et al., 2000) and potentially determine whether predatory SEEKING and/or RAGE/Anger are responsible for their aggressiveness.

Another area that is once again highlighted in dog research is the confounding of fear and exploration. FEAR and SEEKING (Panksepp, 1998a) are two ancient but distinct brain emotion systems, which may often interact as animals negotiate their environments. Indeed, all the primary emotional networks tend to overlap in lower regions of the brain, such as hypothalamus and midbrain periaqueductal gray, providing many opportunities for interactions. However, a temperament profile must allow for FEAR and SEEKING to vary independently; for instance, low exploratory tendencies do not automatically imply high levels of fear. A solid understanding of temperament requires the use of models that can better distinguish the anticipatory dopaminergic SEEK-

ING system from the danger-oriented benzodiazepine-receptor-regulated FEAR system.

Overall, the key dilemma in temperament research is that there are no generally accepted experimental strategies to decode the neural nature of primary-process emotions in human subjects. A study of such brain systems in animals may eventually provide us with a causal neuroscience understanding of what it means for the mammalian/human to experience distinct affective feelings, but the primal neural mechanisms of affect simply cannot be deciphered through human research. There are at least seven emotional command networks as determined by distinct instinctual tendencies aroused by localized deep (subcortical) brain stimulation. Three of the positive affective systems, LUST, CARE, and PLAY, are all heavily dependent on the foundational influence of the general enthusiasm-promoting power of the SEEKING system, which may participate in all types of affective sentience (Panksepp, 1998a; Panksepp & Biven, 2012). However, these four as well as the three affectively negative ones (RAGE/Anger, FEAR, and PANIC/Sadness) all provide the motivation (i.e., unconditioned responses) for various kinds of learning (i.e., secondary processes) and surely higher cognitive (tertiary) processes that are very hard to systematically evaluate in animal models but that, in combination, surely guide higher cognitive-affective decision making and states of mind. Most dog owners (including Darwin) believe that their pets exhibit these higher cognitive capacities, which are so difficult to study rigorously in nonhumans.

Stated differently, a key dilemma in temperament research may be that more complete understandings at the primary-process genetic-neuroscience level are needed to provide solid foundation for all levels of personality development. Such knowledge is essential for understanding the development of higher cognitive capacities. Thus, further work on even lowly domesticated laboratory rats and mice will help provide insights and clearer empirical windows into mammalian minds, as we will discuss from genetic perspectives in the next chapter.

CHAPTER 9

Do Rats Have Personalities?

Of Course They Do!

Our children from their earliest years must take part in all the more lawful forms of play, for if they are not surrounded with such an atmosphere they can never grow up to be well conducted and virtuous citizens.

—Plato, *The Republic*

L ET US START THIS DISCUSSION of personality of our "fellow travelers" with a seemingly outrageous claim: We have learned more about the fundamental neural nature of human emotions (e.g., the subcortical neural circuits and neurochemistries) by studying the brains of laboratory rats than those of human beings. Indeed, the study of their brain emotional systems has proved to be a very effective strategy for the development of new and highly effective antidepressants, one of them from the study of the happy sounds (50 kHz chirps) they make when they play (Burgdorf, Panksepp, & Moskal, 2011; Panksepp, 2015, 2016). And when we breed males and females that show abundant "rat laughter," we have developed lines of animals that can more easily sustain positive moods and are resistant to depression. On the other hand, when we breed rats that are sourpusses (i.e., laugh very little when they are tickled), they more readily succumb to depression when stressed (Burgdorf et al., 2011; Burgdorf, Colechio, Stanton, & Panksepp, 2017; Burgdorf & Panksepp, 2006; Panksepp, Burgdorf, & Gordon, 2001).

To raise a controversial point (on which our group has more data than anyone else), we may be learning more about the subcortical fundamentals of our own laughter/joy circuits (and the neural constitution of positive affect) by studying rat brains than those of human beings—we seem to share the same fundamental subcortical circuits for such feelings (Roccaro-Waldmeyer, Babalian, Müller, & Celio, 2016). Of course, all this does not mean rats tell jokes to each other, but they surely have abundant playful fun.

Indeed, most young laboratory rats are as playful as human children, and indeed, we have learned more about the play circuitry of mammalian brains (but not their jokes) by studying rat brains than human ones. And it looks like our human laughter circuitry arises from the same ancient subcortical brain systems as rats (Burgdorf et al., 2007; Panksepp, 2000b, 2007c). Of course, for most who have not done such studies, these claims may seem outrageous.

BACKGROUND REFLECTIONS ON LABORATORY RATS (DOMESTICATED RATTUS NORVEGICUS)

Rats are mammals, but could these little beady-eyed rodents have complex interesting personalities like dogs, chimpanzees, and humans, or is that a fishy proposition (which we will touch on in the next chapter)? That surely depends, in part, on what kind of rats we are talking about. The laboratory rat, which is used extensively in medical and behavioral research, is a highly domesticated animal that has been bred for generations to accept human handling and companionship. While precise numbers are not available, the Federal Research Division of the Library of Congress found as many as 1 million rats were used for research in 2000. Data from the United Kingdom suggested that 414,335 rats were used in 2005 just in that country. These lab animals are purposely bred to be docile and in the laboratory are typically housed individually in separate cages, which has certainly altered their temperaments, perhaps making them almost immune to separation distress (for discussion, see Panksepp, 2003). The lab rat's wild relative, *Rattus norvegicus*, the common brown rat, has a major public relations problem but has so far evaded all of the human race's attempts to exterminate it. This wild relative undoubtedly has more variability in its temperament, but you may be surprised at how much personality even lowly lab rats can display when given the chance.

One of the main advantages of laboratory rats (and mice) is their combination of docility, fecundity, rapid maturation, and all the organs and all the brain systems that humans have (but in miniature, of course). Because many writers, including Darwin, have noted that being able to selectively breed for a behavior characteristic is strong evidence of its genetic basis, rodents' capacity for rapid multiplication has often made them subjects of a great diversity of selective breeding efforts. Much of what is known about rat personality comes from breeding for extreme emotional traits, and several such focused projects working with single emotions are reviewed in this chapter, in contrast to the types of projects seen with primates and dogs that attempt to assess a broad array of the animals' personalities.

The abundance of behavioral emotional research in laboratory rats (and mice) has yielded clear evidence for the heritability of more affective temperamental traits in warm-blooded mammals than have ever been demonstrated in cold-blooded vertebrates such as fish (see Chapter 10). The inheritance of the evolutionarily older RAGE/Anger and FEAR brain systems has been demonstrated multiple times in so-called gene knockout strains of mice (which have specific genes selectively inactivated) where elevations of both of these traits are evident (Crawley, 2007). Here, we focus on research using lab rats, which has confirmed the evolutionarily more ancient biologically endowed emotions of SEEKING, RAGE/Anger, and FEAR, as well as the socially oriented emotional systems of LUST, CARE/Maternal nurturing, and PLAYfulness, but perhaps less so for PANIC/Sadness (separation distress, which may have been selected against during domestication, because it was desirable for behavioral research to have animals living alone, one to a small cage; Panksepp, 2003). Most of these emotional systems are easily studied in laboratory rodents, and accordingly, we would argue they have been evolutionarily layered onto rodent personalities, which may serve as neuroscientific models for the study of the fundamentals of most primary emotional feelings. Such work may enable in-depth studies of the neural foundations of mammalian temperaments, which we believe further support a biological foundation for the primary affective traits that account for a great deal of human personality differences.

SELECTIVE BREEDING AND
THE FEAR SYSTEM

Selective breeding is nothing new in the biopsychological world. There were several early research programs of behavioral selection for temperamental fear in rodents. Calvin Hall, who spent most of his career at Western Reserve University, devised what he called a strange (i.e., novel), open-field situation, which provoked rat emotionality or excitability, or what we would label fear (Hall, 1934a). He used his new open-field test to select for and breed high and low fear strains of rats (Hall, 1941). Interestingly, Hall received his Ph.D. at the University of California, Berkeley working with Edward Tolman and Robert Tryon. At that time, Tryon was in the process of selectively breeding his maze "bright" and "dull" strains of rats to demonstrate the influence of genetics on learning processes in an era dominated by behaviorist learning theory, which emphasized that environmental rather than genetic differences controlled individual behavior differences. (Of course genetics was in its "fetal," preinfancy in those days.) Thus, it is not surprising that Hall used his open-field device so successfully to selectively breed high and low fear strains.

He placed rats in a brightly lit, eight-foot-diameter, round box that rats found stressful, because it was a strange, bright place with nowhere for a normally nocturnal prey animal to hide. He mated the male and female rats that showed the most emotional defecation and urination in the open-field test, to create a high fear line of rats, and the male and female rats showing the lowest stress-induced eliminative behaviors, yielding a low fear line (Hall, 1934b). Following this procedure for each subsequent generation, Hall found gradually increasing fear differences between the two strains during eight generations of selective breeding.

A more recent program used the elevated plus-maze to selectively breed rats for high anxiety-related behavior (HAB) and low anxiety behavior (LAB; Liebsch, Montkowski, Holsboer, & Landgraf, 1998). The elevated plus-maze was designed to elicit a rat's innate fears of open and elevated spaces. It is usually elevated about two feet from the floor and has two four-inch wide crossing arms constructed in the shape of a plus sign. One of the arms is completely open with no sides. The other arm has walls on all sides except in the center where the two arms cross, that is, a center area allowing entry into the walled or open parts of the maze. The enclosed arm is usually dark and the open arm brightly lit, which also addresses the nocturnal rat's natural preference for dark places. Typically, all rats explore the parts of the maze with walls with the more fearful animals avoiding the open arm with no walls.

In the Liebsch et al. (1998) breeding program, rats with less activity in the open arms (fewer entries and less time spent in the fear-provoking arms) were selected and bred to create the HAB line, and those with more activity in the open arms became the parents in the LAB line. Other tests showed that HAB animals spent less time in the center of an open field, thus validating that the HAB line experienced more fear than LAB animals in an open-field test. HAB animals also struggled less when first exposed to a forced swim test, which further suggested a possible depressive tendency in the HAB line (Liebsch et al., 1998).

Cross-fostering on these lines failed to reveal any maternal developmental influences (Wigger, Loerscher, Weissenbacher, Holsboer, & Landgraf, 2001), and crossbred F_1 and F_2 hybrids were intermediate to the pure HAB and LAB lines on all plus-maze fear measures, both findings consistent with genetic inheritance. We would note that human families sometimes naturally produce such crossbreeding results. That is, sometimes a person with a high fear phenotype marries a person with a low fear phenotype, and on average the couple produces children with intermediate fear sensitivities, although with the complex FEAR system, some children may track closer to the high or low fear sensitivity parent.

Interestingly, at ten days of age HAB rat pups also emitted more 40-kHz vocalizations than did LAB pups (Wigger et al., 2001). It would be relevant to determine whether these HAB rats also emitted more adult 22-kHz alarm calls, which would clearly indicate more negative affect as adults (more on rat vocalization later). Further confirming evidence included higher levels of stress indicators such as ACTH, corticosterone, and prolactin in HAB versus LAB male rats, especially when exposed to the plus-maze with no access to the enclosed arm.

Treatment for seven weeks with the SSRI antidepressant drug paroxetine (Paxil) also brought the active struggle time of the HAB rats in the forced swim test up to the level of the LAB rats (Landgraf & Wigger, 2002), which again suggested a possible depressive component in the HAB line. However, more specifically targeting fear levels, injections of the anti-anxiety drug diazepam (marketed as Valium), a highly effective antianxiety medication in the benzodiazepine group, increased the percentage of time spent in the plus-maze open arms twenty-fold in HAB rats (with a less dramatic increase of 2.5-fold in LAB animals) and increased the speed to enter the open arm sevenfold in HAB rats (only twofold in LAB line). While fear in the HAB line was dramatically relieved by diazepam, even after many generations of selection the LAB line apparently also retained the capacity to experience fear, because they also responded less fearfully after the diazepam treatment. The fact that even the LAB line continued to experience fear suggests that a potent deeply engrained FEAR system exists in the brain. Indeed, Panksepp (1971) and others have demonstrated that a powerful flight response can be evoked by stimulating specific regions in the hypothalamus, and animals given a chance will turn off the brain stimulation that activates such FEAR responses. That after the diazepam the LAB rats still experienced FEAR/Anxiety suggests that the FEAR system is likely to remain an adaptive tool for living in all mammals, regardless of their personality profiles, because it has been so essential for survival. Although highly elevated levels of fear may become maladaptive in domestic environments, presumably such systems can become overactive or sensitized not only by genetic background but also by life experiences, leading, for example, to humans developing chronic anxiety/fear disorders that may need psychiatric treatments (e.g., with benzodiazepines).

CONSPECIFIC FIGHTING AND
THE RAGE/ANGER SYSTEM

Even though rats have been domesticated for lab use for many generations, these animals retain a functional RAGE/Anger system and a corresponding capacity to become aggressive. However, in discussing anger, one must be careful to define the targeted behavior. While there are no selection studies based on fighting in highly domesticated lab rats, Panksepp (1971), using precise electrical stimulation of the brain, showed that like cats (Flynn, 1976; Hess, 1957b; Siegel, 2004) rats possess two separate brain systems capable of provoking an attack. One of these systems, for predatory attack, is characterized by a "quiet" systematic pursuit of mice, followed by a focused nape attack bite typically associated with predation, a behavioral trait rats commonly exhibit toward mice (Albert & Walsh, 1984). The other attack system is associated with defending resources and escaping physical restraint, such as might be experienced when caught by a predator. This latter type of "affective" attack behavior has been labeled the RAGE/Anger system (Panksepp, 1998a) and probably has evolutionary origins in the earliest vertebrates. In contrast, the predatory behavior is not generated by the RAGE/Anger system but is part of the general-process SEEKING system, which is essential for the search for food and all other resources needed for survival. Hence, what many think of as "bloodthirsty" hunting of prey is basically just finding a meal and has little to do with interpersonal violence.

Anger is an important temperament dimension, which has received more attention in animal temperament studies than in humans, especially because the Big Five personality model has relegated anger to either a "blend" or "facet" of Emotional Stability or the opposite of Agreeableness in a kind of "love-hate" dimension, rather than a separate primary personality dimension. This may also partly reflect the fact that most humans have been trained to regulate negative anger tendencies so that they rarely manifest as clearly as in animal models. However, just like the domesticated rats (which typically show little anger), humans certainly retain a powerful capacity for anger, which is all too frequently expressed in cases of domestic violence on the "full-blown" end of the anger dimension and with irritation and impatience on the more "toned-down" end.

One contribution of animal temperament research could be to help gain a better understanding of the basic brain processes underlying this primary-process emotional-temperament dimension as manifested in human personalities, which could also lead to enhanced recognition of the often hidden role of anger and milder forms of irritability in human conflict. The animal work can help pinpoint the underlying neurochemical factors that promote anger, which can lead to medicines to control this potentially dangerous aspect of human personalities. For example, as derived from animal work, antagonists of the brain neuropeptide synaptic transmitter (Substance P) that mediates animal RAGE may be helpful in regulating excessive anger/violence in human beings.

MATERNAL NURTURANCE
AND THE CARE SYSTEM

A very distinctive dimension of mammalian temperament is caring for young. Michael Meaney's group has studied maternal behavior in rats and found substantial individual differences in how rat mothers treated their newborns during their first week of life (Champagne, Francis, Mar, & Meaney, 2003). These maternal caregiving differences included the frequency and skill exhibited when licking, grooming, and nursing their neonatal pups. Remarkably, these researchers also found that individual differences in rat maternal care affected fear responses of their offspring as measured by open-field tests, amount eaten in a novel cage, and behavioral changes following a physical restraint tests. Specifically, offspring reared by mothers exhibiting less neonatal licking, grooming, and "arched-back nursing" (LG-ABN) showed increased hypothalamic-pituitary-adrenal responses to these stressors compared to offspring receiving more LG-ABN (Liu et al., 1997; Caldji et al., 1998). Cross-fostering experiments in which the rat pups of less attentive rat mothers were raised by more attentive rat mothers (Francis, Diorio, Liu, & Meaney, 1999) showed that high levels of LG-ABN decreased stress reactivity in the cross-fostered offspring, confirming that this stress resistance was indeed imparted by the effective mothering the rat pups had received. Furthermore, these maternal effects were passed from one generation of females to the next. That is, females born to less effective mothers but raised by more nurturant mothers became more effective mothers themselves. These researchers also showed that humans handling the pups of low LG ABN mothers—more or less simulating the increased maternal stimulation—produced females whose later maternal behavior as adults was not different from those raised by high LG-ABN mothers and who exhibited increased LG-ABN toward their own neonatal pups.

In this landmark article, Meaney's research group concluded they had demonstrated *nongenomic transmission* of significant individual differences of rat maternal behavior and stress reactivity (Francis et al., 1999). In other words, somehow this nurturing-evoked stress resistance was being passed on to the next generation. Subsequent research (Weaver et al., 2004) demonstrated that these epigenetic effects (more on this in Chapter 15) were the result of reduced DNA methylation in the offspring of high LG-ABN mothers. Reduced DNA methylation meant that the DNA itself was not changed, but its configuration was changed in a way that altered gene expression. Furthermore, cross-fostering could reverse the inherited genetic effect and produce a methylation pattern associated with the rearing mother (Weaver et al., 2004).

The Meaney group extended their groundbreaking research by further demonstrating that these maternally induced effects could also be reversed with fifty days of either postweaning social and environmental enrichment for offspring of low LG-ABN mothers or corresponding social isolation for offspring of high LG-ABN mothers (Champagne & Meaney, 2007). Meaney's group has hypothesized that these epigenetic alterations may provide a means for regulating genomic expression in response to current environmental conditions reflecting different states of environmental adversity (for further discussion, see Meaney, 2010). Thus, this research group demonstrated major differences in the maternal "personalities" of rat mothers, which had real effects on how their offspring reacted to stressors in their environments. The possible implications of what this might mean for human mothering and the corresponding impact on human personalities remain to be more fully demonstrated (more on this in Chapter 15).

SEPARATION DISTRESS ENGENDERED BY
THE PANIC/SADNESS EMOTIONAL SYSTEM

It is thought that rats vocalize in ultrasonic ranges that humans and most other mammals cannot hear in order to avoid detection by predators. Rat neonates emit a type of ultrasonic vocalization centered around 40 kHz that occurs in response to social isolation or cold stress and correspondingly elicits pup retrieval in mother rats (Panksepp & Burgdorf, 2000). There remains some ambiguity whether this call is evolutionarily related to the separation distress that has been more extensively studied in dogs, guinea pigs, and infant chickens, because it tends to disappear if testing is conducted in warm environments where fetal rat pups do not get cold (for critique, see Panksepp, 2003), a temperature effect that is also seen in young dogs before they are mature enough to thermoregulate.

Clearly investigators need to make better distinctions between the aversion of physical distress, such as getting cold, and the emotional distress from being separated from their mothers. True separation distress vocalizations have been associated in several species with the PANIC/Sadness system, which has been linked to depression in humans in part by the finding that opioids reduce both separation distress and human depression (Panksepp, 1998a, 2015, 2016). Infant rat data remain ambiguous on this issue. In any case, to demonstrate inherited influences on the distress vocalizations of very young infant rats, Susan Brunelli and colleagues at Columbia University selected lines of rats based on their high or low rates of such ultrasonic vocalizations in response to social isolation at ten days of age and selectively bred these lines for several generations (Brunelli, 2005). Of course, laboratory rats, because of traditional laboratory practices, are inadvertently bred to endure living in isolation (one rat per cage after weaning, typically done at three weeks of age, has long been standard practice). So Brunelli's group started with a highly heterogeneous strain of rats from the National Institutes of Health, hoping to maximize their chances of selecting rats experiencing high levels of separation distress. In the 20th generation, there were about four times as many isolation-induced 45-kHz vocalizations in the high-vocalization line of animals compared to a randomly selected control line, which likewise exhibited substantially more 45-kHz calls than the low vocalization line, which exhibited 45-kHz calls that averaged close to zero (Brunelli & Hofer, 2007).

In the Porsolt Swim Test, an animal model for depression, the high vocalization line showed more depression-related immobile floating than did the low vocalization line, suggesting the high vocalization line represented a depressive phenotype and heightened susceptibility to stressors. However, adult rats from the high-vocalization line were also less active in the center of an open field test, suggesting higher anxiety and increased activity of the FEAR system as well. In addition, males from the low vocalization line when paired together after social isolation exhibited fighting in 70 percent of the cases, compared to 35 percent for random line males. (The high vocalization line was not included in this study.)

Brunelli and Hofer (2007) concluded that the high-vocalization line was characterized by anxiety/depression and the low-vocalization line by aggressive/impulsive behavior. Is it possible that the RAGE, FEAR, and PANIC/Sadness systems were all inadvertently influenced by their selective breeding program? As we describe in Chapter 10 with a fish selection study for aggression (Bakker, 1994), in general it seems important for investigators to have better and more comprehensive behavioral assays for the various negative emotional systems, to determine if multiple systems were changing in response to the selection procedures. For example, lowering FEAR sensitivity in the low separation distress group may contribute to higher levels of aggressiveness (as we describe with Huntingford's fish studies in Chapter 10). Overall, it seems likely that Brunelli and her colleagues have genetically selected for high and low PANIC/Sadness sensitivity in their high and low distress vocalization lines, but it will be interesting to see in future research whether the high separation distress line would respond similarly to separation distress vocalization manipulations studied in other species, such as reduction by opioids and direct brain stimulation manipulation of key brain sites, as further evidence for the actual involvement of the PANIC/Sadness system (see Panksepp, 1998a).

Still, there are many other threads to the genetics of the personality story. Another group headed by Eva Redei at Northwestern University selectively bred two lines of rats to be either genetically susceptible or resistant to depression. Specifically, they selected sexually mature animals (seventy days old) based on their behavior in the forced swim test mentioned above. Rats that quickly gave up swimming and floated in the water were used to propagate their WMI (Wistar-Kyoto most immobile) line, with those swimming the longest selected as parents for the WLI (Wistar-Kyoto least immobile) line. By the second generation of progeny (F_2s), significant differences emerged from the different parental pools (Will, Aird, & Redei, 2003). By generation twenty-two, the two lines no longer differed in their levels of anxiety as measured, for example, by activity in the center of an open field test, behavior in an elevated plus-maze, and blood levels of corticosterone after stressful restraint, all suggesting that the "behavioral differences between the two substrains of WKYs [the Wistar-Kyoto parental rats] are not fear or anxiety driven, but rather related to depressive state" (Andrus et al., 2012, p. 52).

This group then used their two selected strains to study the inborn genetic tendencies to become depressed, in contrast to depression induced by chronic stress, which they had extensively studied in various nonselected strains (see Pajer et al., 2012). In the high endogenous depression group, they identified potential biomarker transcripts (a transcript is an RNA copy of a particular DNA segment, which is copied as the first step of gene expression) in the hippocampus or amygdala, as well as in the blood samples of the WMI and WLI strains (more on similar techniques in Chapter 18 on psychopathology). They also identified transcript differences in blood samples of humans with early-onset major depression disorder versus subjects with no disorder.

In a news-grabbing finale, the Redei group was able to extend what had begun as a search for a genetic model of depression in rats—what we might call endogenous sensitivity to depression as a likely function of the PANIC/Sadness brain emotion system—into a human blood screening test for sensitivity to adult major depression disorder and possibly even the likelihood of responding to psychotherapy (Redei et al., 2014). In short, they identified nine genetic transcripts, which can be assessed in human blood samples, that distinguished depressed from nondepressed control subjects. Three of these transcripts distinguished control subjects from those with major depression even after the depression subjects had recovered. There were even gene candidates that correlated with whether depressed patients were treated successfully with therapy. Clearly, the Redei group's research represents the value of animal research and a bottom-up approach to understanding human emotional problems. This diagnostic breakthrough is comparable to another therapeutic breakthrough that the study of animal primal emotional systems has fostered (GLYX-13), (Panksepp, 2015, 2016), which is discussed in Chapter 18.

RAT PLAY AND SEEKING SYSTEMS

If fear, anger, and social distress tendencies contribute to negativistic temperamental tendencies, the evolutionary emergence of play behavior in mammals adds a positive balance and social complexity to the domain of personality. The stable variability in playfulness among mammals suggests it is a temperamental variable, but it is a hard one to selectively breed for because it takes two animals to play, plus selection for fearfulness always reduces playfulness (Panksepp, unpublished observations). However, a new positive-affect assay for studying positive playful feelings in rats involves a human hand taking the place of a partner rat pup and simulating a "play bout" while simultaneously monitoring positive affective vocalizations that are especially common during rat pup social play (Panksepp & Burgdorf, 2000). We know these 50 kHz ultrasounds reflect positive affect because anywhere in the brain one can evoke 50 kHz ultrasonic calls with brain stimulation (mostly in subcortical sites running along the SEEKING system), animals demonstrate these states are rewarding, because they always work (self-stimulate) to obtain this positive shift in emotional state (Burgdorf et al., 2007).

Using 50-kHz ultrasonic vocalizations as an objective measure of positive social affect in these simulated play (tickling) sessions, Knutson, Burgdorf, and Panksepp (2002) selectively bred for high and low levels of this positive affective trait, yielding breeding lines that highlighted the genetic underpinning of social play (Panksepp & Burgdorf, 2003). After four generations of selective breeding, mean differences between high and low ultrasonic vocalization lines were already appearing. The high positive vocalization breeding line exhibited stronger social motivation to "play," with shorter approach latencies and less avoidance time, than either the low vocalization or the randomly bred line of rats. The high vocalization line also exhibited more play behavior with other rats, and these rats were preferred as play partners compared to low vocalization line rat pups (Panksepp et al., 2001; Panksepp & Burgdorf, 2003).

This simulated play with a human hand—sometimes referred as "tickling"—is very rewarding to rat pups and can be used to train them to approach a hand for a tickling bout. In addition, a Pavlovian conditioning procedure demonstrated the positive reinforcement value of play tickling in that a neutral signal with no initial power to elicit 50-kHz ultrasonic "chirping"—this gleeful vocalization rat pups emit when playing—elicited the chirping after being paired with hand tickling. Highlighting the appetitive nature of this positive social affect, play deprived (socially isolated) subjects exhibited stronger conditioning than did socially housed juveniles (Panksepp & Burgdorf, 2003).

This play model has also been replicated generating new lines of high and low 50-kHz vocalizing rats (Burgdorf, Panksepp, Brudzynski,

& Moskal, 2005). Again, after four generations of selection for high or low levels of the 50-kHz chirping, the high-vocalization line exhibited significantly more 50-kHz vocalizations than the other lines. In addition, research showed that negative affect 22-kHz vocalizations diverged in the opposite direction as well—happy rats complained less. Namely, they exhibited lower levels of 22-kHz distress vocalizations that have been associated with anxiety evoked by pain (Tonoue, Ashida, Makino, & Hata, 1986), addictive drug withdrawal (Mutschler & Miczec, 1998), predatory threat (Blanchard, Blanchard, Agullana, & Weiss, 1991), and social defeat (Kroes, Burgdorf, Otto, Panksepp, & Moskal, 2007). These two distinct types of ultrasonic vocalizations—50-kHz chirping versus 22-kHz distress calls—were also significantly negatively correlated in large groups of selected animals ($r = -0.59$, $p < 0.0001$; Burgdorf, Knutson, Panksepp, & Ikemoto, 2005), suggesting that the affectively positive 50-kHz vocalizations and affectively negative 22-kHz vocalizations represent polar opposite affective states in rats, confirming that these two forms of vocalizations are reciprocally related to each other (Burgdorf et al., 2001).

A variety of other emotional phenotypic differences have been evident in these replicated lines. In generation fourteen, in addition to continued playfulness and ultrasonic vocalization differences, high 50-kHz animals also exhibited diminished aggression and biting when confronted by an intruder. Also, the low 50-kHz animals behaved more like "introverts" and spent less time in contact with each other when placed in the same cage (Burgdorf et al., 2009). Perhaps the cutest finding was that young animals preferred to spend time with adults who "laughed" (chirped) a lot compared to those that laughed little (Panksepp, 2007c).

Overall, the selective breeding of highly playful rats supports the genetic basis of the PLAYful emotions within the brain. PLAY, which is the most evolutionarily recent of the six blue ribbon affective-neuroscience emotions related to personality, may also be the most complex of the six. PLAY integrates many psychological and behavioral elements providing young mammals rich social interactions and an opportunity to explore social limits in a relative safe context.

The PLAY system is indeed complex, and additional work has indicated that the 50-kHz ultrasonic vocalizations can be broken into two types. There are frequency-modulated 50-kHz calls—a kind of "trill" that covers a broader sound spectrum—that are a better measure of positive social affect than "flat" 50-kHz calls (which may be a social-sampling "hello, is anyone out there" type of call). The ability to use these frequency-modulated rat vocalizations to differentially measure positive affect has also been validated in positive anticipatory SEEKING-type situations, including food anticipation, precopulatory mating situations, and anticipation of both natural play as well as the heterospecific hand play (tickling by an experimenter). In contrast, a large variety of negative affective situations promote the 22-kHz alarm calls. Overall, this suggests these vocalizations can be used to index temperamental positive and negative affects in rats. The rewarding and punishing nature associated with these vocalizations has also been supported by operant nose poking (rat investigating activity) being increased by playback of frequency-modulated 50-kHz vocalizations and decreased by 22-kHz calls (Burgdorf et al., 2008). Again, the scientific conclusion about these calls reflecting positive affective states in animals is derived from the fact that electrical stimulation of all brain sites that generated the frequency-modulated 50-kHz trills proved to be rewarding in self-stimulation tests (Burgdorf et al., 2007). Without that kind of prediction and confirmatory data, scientists would need to keep silent about (could not draw conclusions regarding) the affective states of nonspeaking animals.

Related studies confirmed the frequency-modulated 50-kHz trills can be evoked by promoting dopamine activity, another link to the SEEKING system. Injections of amphetamine (a drug that simulates dopamine activity in the brain) into the shell of the nucleus accumbens, which is part of the mesolimbic dopamine pathway in the brain, significantly and robustly elevated the 50-kHz trills, especially in lines of rats selected for high positive affect compared to random and high negative affect lines of rats (Brudzynski et al., 2010). To further validate the neurochemical specificity of this effect and show that the increase of 50-kHz trills was mediated by dopamine, the coadministration of the dopamine antagonist raclopride attenuated the amphetamine effects, while cholinergic control drugs had no effects on these positive ultrasonic vocalizations. Indeed, because amphetamine and cocaine are addictive, it is noteworthy that the 50-kHz call can even be used as a spontaneous indicator of rats eagerly anticipating the receipt of such addictive drugs (Browning et al., 2011).

Altogether, the above findings demonstrate how easily rats can be bred to be more playful and happy, to increase play and promote high positive affect, and that dopamine has a role in enhancing this positive affect. Moreover, this work has shown that rats can indicate their affective state through emotional vocalizations provoked under standardized rat-personality testing conditions, with the 50-kHz trills reflecting a positive affective state and the 22-kHz vocalizations a negative state.

SUMMARY

In sum, yes, rats have personalities. Indeed, they exhibit complex personalities, which include expressing different levels of CAREing maternal behavior, which in turn have a direct impact on the stress tolerance of their offspring. Rats also share with cats, dogs, and other carnivorous mammals the capacity for two types of attack behavior: a predatory, quiet bite attack, which is linked to the SEEKING system, and attack behavior appropriate for defending their various resources as well as themselves, which is linked to the RAGE/Anger system.

Rats possess a complex FEAR system that psychologists have discovered is easily activated and is interwoven with all other emotional brain systems: SEEKING (curiosity), RAGE/Anger (defense), CARE (maternal nurturing), PANIC/Sadness (separation distress), and PLAY (joyful social interaction). Many times rats have been selected for high and low levels of fear expression, confirming the genetic basis of the FEAR system. Likewise, at least two labs have selected for high and low levels of PANIC/Sadness behavior, reflecting depressive tendencies. The second of these (Redei's group; see Andrus et al., 2012) recognized the importance of ensuring that elements of FEAR did not confound the behavioral differences in their high and low depression (PANIC/Sadness) lines, which allowed them to analyze gene expression in their rat subjects and ultimately generate blood screening tests for human depression. Along similar lines, Panksepp's group on three separate occasions has selected rats for high and low levels of PLAY behavior, which has resulted in the development of a drug to treat depression (Burgdorf et al., 2011; Panksepp, 2014; discussed further in Chapter 18).

CHAPTER 10
Animal Personality Summary

The distinction between emotional attitudes and habits is based on the observed fact that human beings do not always give in to their emotions, even when these have developed into an emotional attitude. . . . Animals on the other hand, do not exhibit any goal-directed actions that are not dictated by emotion or instinct.
—Magda B. Arnold, *Emotion and Personality*

In the process of natural selection, then, any device that can insert a higher proportion of certain genes into subsequent generations will come to characterize the species.
—Edward O. Wilson, *The Morality of the Gene*

INTRODUCTION

The first of William McDougall's two personality principles was to ask whether similar primary instincts and emotions could be observed in humans as well as animals. By "animals," what McDougall meant were the "higher animals," namely, mammals. However, if Darwin's continuity principle is correct, that the characteristics of humans and animals *differ by degree and not by kind*, then one should be able to trace human emotions and thereby personality characteristics back further than the evolutionary appearance of mammals. One should be able to identify relevant emotions or at least their ancestral glimmerings in our more distant evolutionary relatives as well. So, let us reflect backward in evolutionary time to put our human personalities in perspective, much like medical science, including psychiatry, studies nonhumans as a foundation for understanding human diseases.

At what point in the evolution of the animal kingdom do personality features begin to emerge? How far back in evolutionary time can we identify commonalities with human personalities? Fish are among the earliest vertebrates, meaning they have a spinal cord, along with calcified spinal vertebrae, and a central nervous system. Is it possible, for example, that even fish have personalities, that is, relatively stable personality characteristics that differentiate one fish's behavior from another's? Do even lower animals—the invertebrates—have personalities, because they presumably have some rudimentary form of consciousness (Feinberg & Mallatt, 2016)?

Indeed, there are tantalizing hints of consciousness and personality variability even among invertebrates. The nematode *Caenorhabditis elegans* is a tiny, one-millimeter-long soil-dwelling roundworm whose intimidating biological name is longer than its diminutive body. *C. elegans*, as its name is usually abbreviated, is widely studied in part because of its simple nervous system that contains only 302 neurons. In a review focused on *C. elegans*, Mario de Bono and Andres Maricq (2005) pointed out that this primitive creature, evolutionarily separated from humans for perhaps a billion years (Wang, Kumar & Hedges, 1999), contained five neurotransmitters found in vertebrates, including serotonin and dopamine, with dopamine being involved in regulating "a well-described universal foraging strategy" (de Bono & Maricq, 2005, p. 462). Could this be the early suggestion of a SEEKING system motivating this simple creature to search for a meal? Certainly dopamine figures preeminently in the diverse foraging behaviors of all mammals. Even though the discussion of such brain processes is phrased in diverse terms (Panksepp & Moskal, 2008), our preferred moniker for the primary-process manifestation of diverse forms of foraging is the SEEKING system, a universal appetitive mode aroused and directed by brain dopamine, with some of the satisfactions of this universal urge mediated by brain opioids.

Crayfish, a more sophisticated invertebrate species separated from mammals by at least 600 million years, also share neurotransmitters with mammals. Research shows that serotonin can promote aggressive tendencies in crayfish (JB Panksepp & Huber, 2002). Further, both dopamine and morphine function as powerful, possibly addictive, positive reinforcers (JB Panksepp & Huber, 2004; Nathaniel, Panksepp, & Huber, 2009). Could a crayfish's appetite for dopamine stimulants like amphetamine or cocaine be a clue that it experiences pleasant and unpleasant feelings? Does a developing fondness for morphine mean it subjectively experiences pleasures that guide preferences?

The existence of these classic brain neurotransmitters in animals genetically separated from humans for many hundreds of millions of years emphasizes the evolutionary similarities we still share with the nervous systems of these ancient creatures, suggesting deep ancestral relationships (Feinberg & Mallatt, 2016). However, the cross-species personality case becomes much more compelling when we start comparing the brains of vertebrates that have nervous systems more similar to our own. Paul MacLean, at the National Institute of Mental Health for nearly thirty years and chief of the Laboratory of Brain Evolution and Behavior, theorized the vertebrate brain had evolved in epochs, with each successive stage basically "layered" (but, of course, still massively interdigitating) with the previous one, yielding a variety of ancestral structures that still exist in the human brain. He called the oldest of these stages the "reptilian brain." Then, integrated with (but being built "on top of") the reptilian brain was the "paleomammalian brain," with features that appeared much later during mammalian evolution and associated with a new social model of living in family groups that distinguished them from reptiles. The most recent evolutionary development in the brain was the "neomammalian cortex" (or simply neocortex) that expanded mammals' capacity for much more complex learning, memory, and hence more complex decision making and better general adaptation (MacLean, 1990). The neocortex is most extensively developed in humans, although whales and dolphins also have highly developed but structurally somewhat different neocortices (i.e., their neurons are not as distinctly organized into six "layers").

MacLean argued that the brain structures primarily associated with human emotions were found in the two older, reptilian and paleomammalian brain layers. Although a simplification, if personality is linked to emotions, we can anticipate that reptiles and possibly even their vertebrate ancestors such as fish would also exhibit some recognizable personality characteristics similar to those found in mammals including humans.

So, if fish have personalities, what would we theorize their personality traits to be? Which emotions would we expect to find in these evolutionarily older vertebrates? What are the most primitive emotions, and what evidence would indicate which are the oldest emotions evolutionarily?

Actually, the brain itself can provide answers to these questions. As MacLean realized (and even Darwin recognized), the brain—unlike any other organ in the body—has evolved, with more and more modern specializations on top. Like an archeological site (note the title of the second author's previous book – *The Archaeology of Mind*), the further down one digs, the older the neuropsychological materials (i.e., brain functions) one uncovers. We must look toward the more ancient brain regions to find the evolutionarily constructed systems that are critical for the creation of emotions—it is not only reasonable to assume, but the evidence is rather overwhelming, that primal emotionality was created in very deep sub-neocortical brain regions. Indeed, those are the only brain regions where we can evoke a diversity of coherent emotional arousals simply by electrically stimulating specific brain regions (Panksepp, 1982,

1998a). Thus, we here consider the evidence-based fact that emotional arousals (and the affective foundations of personality) are mediated by the archaeologically deeper, more ancient regions of the brain. To the extent that personality is a reflection of one's emotional strengths and weaknesses, we should be very open to the idea that even fish exhibit temperamental differences in their styles of living and behaving. They too have emotional lives: such brain systems are survival systems— positive ones indicate survival and negative ones potential destruction trajectories—and fish need them as much as we do.

Based on such evolutionary reasoning, the SEEKING emotion is likely to be the oldest of the six primary emotions we focus on to understand personality variability in fish—especially psychobehavioral features such as eagerness and enthusiasm to pursue resources needed for survival, a solid foundation for the other emotions. Equally old should be the RAGE/Anger and FEAR/Anxiety systems.

Is there any credible experimental evidence that fish young exhibit any clear indices of separation-distress PANIC or PLAYfulness? Very little. These are the most recent and perhaps most complex of the basic social emotional-affective action systems. Because fish arose from very early vertebrates that predate reptiles, one might think that fish would not have evolved mammalian-type CARE, PANIC, or PLAY systems and that their temperaments would be characterized by a simpler set of personality traits featuring especially SEEKING, RAGE/Anger, and FEAR/Anxiety, but we must leave open the idea that some aspects of CARE were shuffled into their genetic "cards," with fathers often having a bigger role than mothers. After a brief review of key fish personality research, we conclude our summary of animal personality dimensions.

FISH PERSONALITY

The stage for a scientific discussion of fish temperament was set by Felicity Ann Huntingford, a psychologist at Oxford University who conducted a classic series of fish studies that tracked multiple fish behaviors across multiple settings and indeed identified three temperament dimensions (Huntingford, 1976) that we think--as already noted--can be related to the SEEKING, RAGE/Anger, and FEAR/Anxiety brain systems (Panksepp, 1998a) as brain evolution principles would have predicted.

The fish species she studied was the three-spined stickleback, *Gasterosteus aculeatus,* a commonly studied small freshwater fish that is native to some inland waters of Europe. Huntingford thought this species was a good candidate for studying temperament or personality because she had noticed that different individual sticklebacks naturally exhibited marked differences in behavior. Her strategy was to observe the fish in different experimental situations that might highlight their personality strengths and weaknesses. She basically gave each stickleback a behavioral personality test designed for fish (not unlike Scott and Fuller's approach with dogs), which required careful attention to a variety of distinct behaviors.

Huntingford first tested male sticklebacks during various stages of their nest-building and breeding cycle and found some fish consistently exhibited more aggression (defined as lunges and bites) throughout the breeding cycle. Individual patterns of lunges and bites occurred regardless of whether the intruder was a member of their own stickleback species or an unrelated species. Likewise, there were individual differences in curiosity (defined as amount of time facing an intruder). Importantly, these aggressive and curious tendencies were independent of each other; that is, fish that exhibited more aggressive behavior were not necessarily the same ones that were more curious.

To further investigate these behaviors, Huntingford also gave two additional tests to male sticklebacks in their nonbreeding phase. The first test measured their behavior in the presence of a predator fish, a young pike that had been fed to satiation just before the experiment, which had the advantage of getting the stickleback's reaction to one of its natural predators while minimizing the danger of being eaten. In this test, in addition to getting measures of apparently curious investigative behaviors, Huntingford was also able to statistically identify what she initially called "bold" behavior characterized by a lack of timidity.

The second test compared observations of sticklebacks in their home aquarium versus two different strange aquaria. One of the strange aquaria was bare of plants or other objects. Both strange aquaria were intended to function as "open field" tests, which have been used for years to measure fear in rodents. Indeed, both of the strange aquaria disturbed the fish, as indicated by less "jerky" (typical) swimming, more "still" moments (freezing), which were broken by "continuous" (faster escape) swimming, and more "spine raising" (defensive reaction).

When she statistically compared all of her tests across her subjects, she found that the fish that were least disturbed (least fearful) in the strange tanks were also the most aggressive breeding-nest defenders. Likewise, the fish that were the least timid in the predator-pike test were also the most aggressive in the reproductive tests. She concluded that the main dimension she had observed was "fearfulness," which had inhibited aggressiveness against breeding nest invaders as well as "boldness" in the pike test. In her words, "This fearfulness might be suppressing the response to a predator and to a conspecific [other three-spined stickleback intruders] to a similar extent" (Huntingford, 1976, p. 256). However, she also noted that aggression and fear had varied independently in her experiments, as did curiosity and fear. In the end, she concluded that she was observing an element of fearful inhibition in each of her experiments, which had influenced the overall behavior of her fish.

Altogether, Huntingford reported three distinct behavioral dimensions that aligned with the three evolutionarily older affective emotions: the most prominent was fear, which corresponded with the FEAR/Anxiety system of mammalian affective neuroscience; aggression, which we would hypothesize corresponded to the well-documented RAGE/Anger system in several mammalian systems (especially cats and rats); and her curiosity factor lined up with the affective neuroscience SEEKING system. Importantly, as with all dynamic creatures, she observed these emotions interacting with each other, with fear reducing the levels of aggression (RAGE/Anger) and decreasing exploratory activity (SEEKING).

Using multiple fish personality tests and measuring a variety of behaviors, Huntingford used classical psychological multitrait-multimethod technique (Campbell & Fiske 1959) to identify three personality dimensions, thus being consistent with our prediction that fish personalities, compared to mammalian personalities, would be more restricted to (but not necessarily limited to) the most evolutionarily ancient primary-process emotional action systems: SEEKING, RAGE/Anger, and FEAR/Anxiety. She also confirmed one of McDougall's observations, that fear was the great inhibitor of behavior. We await research evaluating whether the three emotional-personality dimensions of fish are controlled by some of the same neurochemistries of mammalian neural systems, including, we are willing to predict, those of primates.

REPLICATION AND TERMINOLOGY CONCERNS IN FISH PERSONALITY RESEARCH

To address testing and terminology concerns regarding fear and curiosity in fish temperament research, James Burns (2008) used guppies (*Poecilia reticulata*) and multiple measures of all tests to determine the reliability and validity of three common fish "personality" tests: an open field test (being placed in a large, unfamiliar aquarium), an emergence test (latency to leave a safe place), and a novel object test (latency to approach novel objects). Burns's (2008) data supported the use of open-field freezing as a measure of fear but cast doubt on the emergence test as a measure of fear (which may better reflect SEEKING). Still, none of the novel object measures correlated with any open field measure, which suggested that the open-field test in fish should currently be reserved as a measure of fear in fish rather than a measure of exploratory/investigatory behaviors. In any event, Burns confirmed Huntingford's findings, as well as our conclusion that the SEEKING and

FEAR systems should be carefully separated in personality research. Burns also declared that "I take shyness-boldness to be the same as fearfulness" (Burns, 2008, pp. 344–45), a conclusion also reached by other researchers (Budaev, 1997; Warren & Callaghan, 1975, 1976). We especially appreciate the willingness of Huntingford to use affective descriptors, which was not scientifically fashionable in those days.

Aggressiveness was the second of Huntingford's (1976) personality dimensions that corresponded to one of the affective neuroscience primary emotions studied in fish (but note that the necessary brain research remains to be done). However, in a real tour de force, Theo Bakker (1994) conducted a classic behavior genetic dissection of aggressiveness and the RAGE/Anger system in three-spined sticklebacks, *Gasterosteus aculeatus,* the same species studied by Huntingford. Being able to selectively breed for a trait is strong evidence for the existence of biological underpinnings. Bakker started with a natural, unselected population of freshwater sticklebacks and selectively bred multiple lines of males and females for high or low juvenile aggression, high or low territorial aggression, and high or low social dominance. His test for juvenile and territorial aggression consisted of presenting each fish with an opponent in a glass tube placed in its tank and observing acts of biting and bumping at the opponent. Juvenile aggressive tests were conducted when the fish were in their young juvenile stage of development. Territorial aggressive tests were conducted when the fish were in their mature reproductive stage. Another key feature of his triple high/low selection process was testing each generation of each line with all three aggression tests to determine how the different forms of aggression were segregating genetically.

Bakker found that selection for reduced juvenile and territorial aggression yielded significant differences from control lines of fish in both males and females after only a single generation, with larger differences observed through the third generation. However, breeding lines selected for enhanced aggression failed to produce a significant divergence from the control lines except for adult females, which yielded high and low differences in territorial fighting only after the third generation. These results suggested that there was insufficient genetic variation in Bakker's initial population to further enhance male aggressiveness, which would be consistent with the male stickleback's very aggressive reputation. Alternatively, natural selection may have already maximized juvenile and territorial aggression traits (especially in males) before the beginning of experimental selection. In any event, dominance selection was based on dominance contests between two fish in neutral tanks and produced divergence by the third generation, in which high dominance males dominated low-dominance males in 19 out of 24 contests.

Comparing correlations of the different aggression tests across selection lines revealed that selecting for juvenile aggressiveness in one line and adult female aggressiveness in a second line produced very similar juvenile and female aggressiveness in both lines, suggesting that both forms of aggression were affected by the same genes. However, correlations between juvenile and territorial aggression in male selection lines were not as strong, "suggesting that in males juvenile aggressiveness is only partly governed by the same genetic factors as territorial aggressiveness" (Bakker, 1994, p. 155). In short, selecting for reduced levels of juvenile aggressiveness did not potently influence male territorial aggression. Thus, juvenile aggressiveness may actually be an ancestral very early form of play fighting (as in many mammals) or perhaps a rather "pure" representation of the RAGE/Anger system also reflected in territorial behavior in mature males during breeding season, but including additional factors perhaps related to overall reproductive fitness.

Importantly, social dominance selection did not enhance or reduce the other forms of aggressiveness. Indeed, the degree of male red coloration accounted for most of the variation in dominance ability. This suggested that at least in the three-spined stickleback, adult intermale dominance is not closely related to either juvenile aggressiveness or adult territorial aggressiveness.

To summarize, while Bakker (1994) did not elucidate the underlying neurobiological mechanisms of aggressiveness in fish, he provided strong evidence that both juvenile aggressiveness and territorial aggressiveness were strongly influenced by genetic selection, with territorial aggressiveness perhaps being more closely linked to the RAGE/Anger system than juvenile aggression or dominance. While we are not aware of selection studies targeting fish SEEKING or FEAR systems, we would predict that such studies would confirm genetic foundations in fish for those temperament aspects of emotions as well, as has previously been well demonstrated in rodents.

ARE FISH SOCIAL ANIMALS?

Are fish personalities really just defined by SEEKING, RAGE, and FEAR sensitivities, or do fish exhibit social behavior that represents other possible personality dimensions, such as PLAY, as already noted, which may utilize many of the other emotional systems in a nonserious way? Most of the 24,000 species of teleost fish (the vast majority of bony fishes) swim together at times in groups commonly called schools, which biologists refer to as shoals, when the swimming becomes more synchronized (Faucher, Parmentier, Becco, Vandewalle, & Vandewalle, 2010). A key question is whether fish swim in groups because of the same social motivations as mammals—social bonding and separation distress associated with the PANIC/Sadness system—or for some other reason. Some biologists do refer to fish living in social groups (Colleter & Brown, 2011). However, the more common explanation is that shoaling reduces risks of predation, so perhaps reduction of FEAR is the likely emotion underlying shoaling behavior. This hypothesis seems especially reasonable, because shoaling is especially common in prey fish (Budaev, 1997; Ward, Thomas, Hart, & Krause, 2004).

A recent series of studies have argued that western mosquitofish, *Gambusia affinis*, are social, which may allow their shoaling tendencies to be used as a measure of sociability (Cote, Fogarty, & Sih, 2012). However, these authors measured sociability by placing an individual fish in the middle compartment of a tank with three compartments created by inserting two transparent glass partitions on the opposite ends of a large aquarium. One of the end compartments contained fourteen randomly selected mosquitofish. The compartment at the other end was empty. The authors defined sociability as the amount of time the individual fish spent near the compartment containing the other fish. However, in line with Burns (2008), we would argue this was more of an open field test generating FEAR rather than the separation distress of the PANIC/ Sadness emotion, but more definitive conclusions may require the use of medications that are more selective for inhibiting these two systems, namely: benzodiazepines for the FEAR system (Panksepp, 1971), and low doses of opiates for the separation-distress PANIC system (Panksepp et al., 1978).

The Cote group reported that the individual experimental fish showed signs of stress when first introduced to the novel aquarium, as indicated by constant swimming along the sides of the tank, which may be an open-field fear response corresponding to Huntingford's continuous-swimming fear measure. However, Cote et al. (2012) did not measure this behavior and also did not include any test intended to measure fear in their fish social personality test. So, their "social" fish may have spent more time near the other fish due to fear-induced shoaling, and the researchers provided no clear way of distinguishing shoaling due to social motivation from shoaling resulting from fear.

Cote et al. (2012) did report a weak positive relationship between sociability and boldness, suggesting a tendency for social fish to be less fearful, but unfortunately they used the emergence from a safe place to test for boldness, a test that has been criticized as confounded with exploratory behavior and a poor measure of fear (see Burns, 2008; Reale, Reader, Sol, McDougall, & Dingemanse, 2007).

It may be that mosquitofish exhibit a kind of group behavior that appears social, but the question for neuroevolutionary personality theory is whether this grouping behavior represents a precursor to the mammalian PANIC/Sadness system. Perhaps the most obvious argument against social bonding in fish is that they are so easy to raise in isolation. In fact, the Cote group housed their fish individually in small tanks during their experiments.

Furthermore, touching and contact comfort are key features of the mammalian PANIC/Sadness system, with physical contact providing relief from separation distress (e.g., Panksepp et al., 1980), and fish generally do not touch each other in their shoals, but they may do this indirectly by feeling water-pressure movements from adjacent fish. Fish have a "lateral line" consisting of sensory receptors from head to tail that contain hair cell bundles, which detect water movement and vibrations and enable them to maintain appropriate distances from their shoaling neighbors. Faucher et al. (2010) has shown that after inactivating the lateral line fish cannot maintain a shoal: the distance between their closest neighbor doubles, they have difficulty maintaining their orientation relative to other fish, and they frequently bump into other fish. All shoaling behaviors returned to normal as the hair cell bundles regrew. In support of their findings, Faucher et al. (2010) also cite studies showing that cohesive schooling appears only after the developmental completion of the lateral-line system. Thus, it would seem that the maturation of the fish lateral-line system, which enables fish *not* to physically touch each other (with touching apparently disrupting their "unity"), sustains highly coordinated shoaling, but no clear social motive for this has yet been identified.

Regarding a potential social emotion underlying shoaling, a computer literature search revealed no reports of social attachments in fish. There were reports of reproductive monogamy in fish, but this seemed mostly driven by dominant female fish competing for limited resources and driving away other female fish (Wong, Munday, Buston, & Jones, 2008), although other reports (Harding, Almany, Houck, & Hixon, 2003) suggest sex-specific aggression by both genders can create similar functional monogamy that has nothing to do with mate loyalty.

A related question is whether fish play; that is, do they have affective rough-and-tumble social PLAY systems in their brains? Gordon Burghardt and Vladimir Dinets of the University of Tennessee, along with James Murphy of the Smithsonian's National Zoological Park, recently published a report documenting three cichlid fish that independently acquired the behavior of repeatedly hitting a bottom-weighted thermometer sitting on the bottom of the fish's tank and letting it bounce back, which they argued qualified as object play. The fish lived separately and clearly did not learn the behavior from watching each other (Burghardt et al., 2015). These fish were clearly not playing with each other, and there has yet to be a compelling report of social play in fish. In other words, these play behaviors could be envisioned to arise as examples of object play, perhaps arising from their SEEKING systems. In short, a distinct social PLAY system in fish remains to be demonstrated, that is, affectively positive rough-and-tumble social engagements that are highest in juvenile animals and that taper off dramatically following sexual maturation (Panksepp, et al., 1984).

What about parental CARE tendencies in fish? While most fish species do not provide parental care for their young, there are cases of mouthbrooding (see Grone, Carpenter, Lee, Maruska, & Fernald, 2012 for a biological analysis). There are also cases (mostly of male fish, e.g., sticklebacks and cichlids) defending their nests and guarding their offspring against predators (see Balshine & Sloman, 2011). Although rare, there are also cases of Central American cichlids in which parental fish provide food for their young in the form of skin mucus secretions, and of African cichlids stirring up the lake floor by rapidly beating their pectoral fins to expose bottom-dwelling prey for their young (Ota & Kohda, 2015).

Despite an amazing diversity of parental care activities in fish, an evolutionary analysis of reproductive models in the very large group of ray-finned fishes (class *Actinopterygii*, a subclass of bony fishes that includes sticklebacks and cichlids) revealed no indication that female-only or biparental care was an outgrowth of a male-only care model or that biparental care has been an evolutionary stepping stone between paternal and maternal care potentially having some neuroevolutionary continuity with mammalian-style maternal parenting. However, the adaptation of females giving live birth (and thereby perhaps a more mammal-like postpartum parental reproductive pattern) has evolved independently at least eight times in ray-finned fish (Mank, Promislow, & Avise, 2005). Accordingly, such species may have antecedents of a primordial CARE system, but at present there are no researched instances of a mammalian-style CARE-type "family feeling" having emerged in fish.

Still, we suspect mammalian-type CARE in fish may have occurred, and if so, it will be most interesting to see if in those cases there are ancestral homologies in the underlying social neurochemistries that would suggest some mammalian-type continuities in fish (e.g., the ancestral variants of oxytocin, such as nine-amino-acid neuropeptides isotocin, mesotocin, and vasotocin. Indeed, it has been shown that isotocin does control paternal care in monogamous cichlid fish (O'Connell, Matthews, & Hofmann, 2012). There is a growing literature that there is some evolutionary CARE continuity from fish to mice and men—but by no means as strong as in women and mammalian mothers in general.

FISH SUMMARY

While neuroscience-type brain manipulations would be valuable in targeting specific emotions in fish, for purely observational research we would recommend more careful selection of tests to avoid the possible confusion of fearful behavior with various social, aggressive, or exploratory behaviors. Indeed, Reale et al. (2007) have recommended multiple tests of each target behavior (a la Huntingford and Burns) to clarify potential confusions.

In summary, curiosity, anger, and fear, which correspond well with the evolutionarily older SEEKING, RAGE/Anger, and FEAR brain systems, are consistently observed personality dimensions in bony fish, the most evolutionarily ancient class of vertebrates reviewed in this book. So far there is no compelling evidence for well-developed CARE, PANIC, or PLAY systems in fish that would support mammalian-like social behavior. Still, there are hints of evolutionary continuities that we suspect will get ever stronger as more neuroscience research is conducted.

HOMOLOGOUS ANIMAL AND HUMAN PERSONALITY TRAITS: A SUMMARY OVERVIEW

Here we pause to briefly summarize where we have been with this cross-species journey. Some may find it disagreeable to think that humans may share some personality traits with other animals, yet such deep homologies are no longer a surprise to psychiatrists, neuroscientists, and geneticists (e.g., Feinberg & Mallatt, 2016). That fish temperaments may be largely defined by the evolutionarily older SEEKING, RAGE/Anger, and FEAR emotion systems would also have come as no surprise to pioneers like Paul MacLean (1990), who was among the first to describe the numerous homologies across early vertebrate, mammalian, and human brains. With mammalian homologies in mind, MacLean (1990) and Panksepp (1998a) would predict that the more evolutionarily recent social emotion systems—CARE, PANIC/Sadness, and PLAY—would provide many commonalities between rats, dogs, foxes, primates, and humans with each of the six personality-focused primary-emotion BrainMind systems influencing mammalian temperaments, which is exactly what was observed. Rat, dog, and ape temperaments are incredibly complex: anticipating basic rewards, obtaining resources, and sometimes just exploring; defending those resources and life itself when necessary; avoiding danger and physical pain; caring for young and thereby unwittingly transmitting epigenetic adaptations (see Chapter 15); avoiding separation from bonded social mates and from familiar places; and learning to regulate key behaviors through socially interactive and physical play. Each of these systems was apparent in the temperament research of the three mammalian examples we summarized in the past chapters. There are echoes of certain homologies in fish, but relevant neuroscience remains scarce.

In addition, a Conscientiousness factor regulating emotional expression was identified in chimpanzees and brown capuchin monkeys (see

Chapter 7), with additional demonstrations likely forthcoming as methodological issues are refined. There was also one more unanticipated possible addition to the temperament of the domestic dog: predatory behavior expressed toward humans (see Chapter 8). This is likely part of the food foraging system and just one of the many possible species-typical predatory expressions of a basic SEEKING urge shared by all vertebrates, for instance, the "quiet biting predatory attack" that can be provoked by deep brain stimulation in both rats and cats (Siegel et al., 1999; Panksepp, 1971; Siegel, 2004). Additional basic research involving the analysis of specific brain systems will be necessary to verify homologous systems in dogs.

For humans, we thought it would be useful to have a personality test that attempts to evaluate the primary-process emotional reactivities of our own species—based upon brain emotional systems that have long been evident from cross-species affective neuroscience research (Panksepp, 1982, 1998a). As already summarized, our initial attempt to move in that direction generated a set of evolutionarily defined psychological test scales to tap into each of the primary affective brain systems except LUST (as already noted, omitted to avoid introducing unwanted "guarded" response biases) in the hope of promoting neuroscientifically anchored systematics in the field (Davis et al., 2003). Indeed, each of the six scales monitoring these basic emotional factors—from primordial SEEKING, RAGE/Anger, and FEAR to more socially sophisticated CARE, PANIC/Sadness, and PLAY—correlated highly with various Big Five dimensions except for Conscientiousness. Conscientiousness did not clearly represent any of the primary emotions, suggesting that it may be better envisioned as a cognitive rather than an affective factor, perhaps one representing higher cognitive brain functions regulating the expression of emotions, increasing behavioral sophistication, and adaptability. This idea could shed light on why Scott and Fuller (1965) found that cocker spaniels were so capable of inhibiting their emotional reactions to stressful events and suggests cockers might provide a reasonable animal model for studying an elementary form of Conscientiousness. That Conscientiousness so far has been psychometrically measured only in chimpanzees and brown capuchin monkeys suggests that Conscientiousness requires a well-developed neocortex (for an alternate view on rat prefrontal cortex, see Uylings & van Eden, 1990; for a rat model of orbital prefrontal cortex inhibition of aggressive behavior discussed in Chapter 7, see de Bruin, 1990). Even more dramatically, Frans de Waal (2009) has illuminated complex social emotions, including empathy and compassion, in our primate cousins, which may suggest other novel scales for higher anthropoid social emotions will eventually be needed.

Davis et al. (2003) showed that in humans PLAY correlated positively with Extraversion, CARE correlated positively with Agreeableness but negatively with RAGE/Anger, and SEEKING correlated positively with Openness to Experience. However, they also pointed out a basic flaw with the factor-analytically derived Big Five: RAGE/Anger, FEAR, and PANIC/Sadness all correlated negatively with Emotional Stability/low Neuroticism. Indeed, half a century ago, Walter Hess (1957b) recognized that RAGE and FEAR were two distinct primal emotions (although he did not use our primary-process terminology). MacLean (1990) also recognized that RAGE and FEAR had been major temperament dimensions for probably well over 500 million years (i.e., before the Cambrian explosion of new species), predating the evolutionary appearance of fish and agreeing with RAGE/Anger and FEAR being observable distinct personality dimensions in Huntingford's (1976) fish research. However, along with PANIC/Sadness, the Big Five lumps together all three negatively valenced emotions, which figure so prominently in psychopathology, or at best relegates them to blends or facets rather than according them the primary temperament status that is apparent in the brain of every mammal. So using the six primary emotion brain systems as a template, Davis et al. (2003; refined in Davis & Panksepp, 2011) constructed the Affective Neuroscience Personality Scales (ANPS), which was conceptualized largely as a human research tool capable of situating human subjects in primary-process affective space but that could also usefully be adapted for the study of other species. However, such a jump would be too large for many academic psychologists.

Thus, the scientific study of emotions remains a contentious topic, and the existence of emotional experiences in animals is still more controversial than it should be (for full review, see Panksepp & Biven, 2012; Panksepp, Lane, Solms, & Smith, 2017). There is also a disconnect in what scientists who work with animals claim and what intelligent nonscientists who live with animals believe. To evaluate where the latter stand on such issues, Paul Morris and colleagues from the University of Portsmouth in the United Kingdom surveyed 907 animal owners' beliefs about the existence of potential emotions in the animals they deal with on a daily basis (Morris, Doe, & Godsell, 2008). The results were striking. The vast majority of these respondents, including 337 dog owners and 272 cat owners, believed their companion animals experienced primary emotions such as anger, fear, surprise, joy/happiness, sadness, anxiety, and curiosity, and a smaller but substantial number of owners also believed the animals had what might be deemed derived emotions, such empathy, shame, pride, grief, guilt, jealousy, and embarrassment. In support of their view, consider that artificial activation of all subcortical emotional systems discussed in this book can serve as rewards and punishments in various learning tasks. Indeed, it is highly likely that the time-honored behavioristic concepts such as "reward" and "punishment" derive the capacity to mold learned behaviors because the various affec-

Two-Way or "Circular" Causation

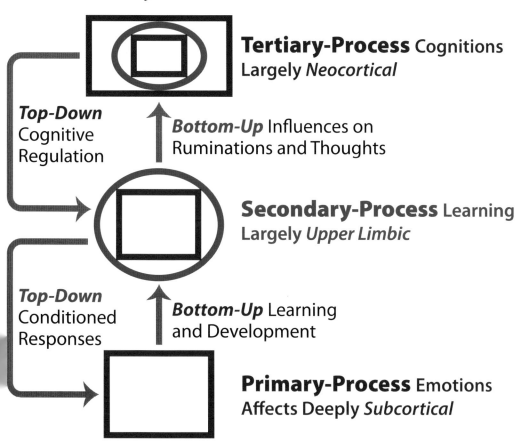

Tertiary-Process Cognitions
Largely *Neocortical*

Top-Down Cognitive Regulation

Bottom-Up Influences on Ruminations and Thoughts

Secondary-Process Learning
Largely *Upper Limbic*

Top-Down Conditioned Responses

Bottom-Up Learning and Development

Primary-Process Emotions
Affects Deeply *Subcortical*

Nested BrainMind Hierarchies

tive changes of brains were designed, in evolution, to guide learning (Panksepp, 1998a, 2005, 2010b, 2011a).

Indeed, there is overwhelming objective scientific evidence that various basic emotions are fundamental powers of the BrainMind, in both humans and other animals, and we would suggest they are of critical importance for understanding the foundations of human temperament. Cross-species affective neuroscience has the potential for scientifically mapping out the continuity of the emotional BrainMind in subcortical-limbic circuits of all vertebrate brains, as it already has for understanding various psychiatric disorders (Panksepp, 2005, 2015, 2016). We suspect that when we structure our human temperamental measures in terms of primary-process emotional issues, many of the higher aspects of personality may become easier to analyze. However, in seeking a comprehensive story, we should not forget that the higher regions of the brain are more plastic than the lower regions, and that there are environmentally relevant susceptibility factors that are not yet well understood, perhaps the most subtle of all being that the degree of environmentally induced plasticity may itself be heritable (i.e., epigenetics, discussed in Chapter 15). Clearly, such issues will never be well understood in humans unless we have corresponding animal models to study the underlying neurobiological details. We will understand our own fundamental (evolved) emotional systems and the feelings they generate largely through cross-species research, rather than just human research. This said, our neocortical expansions and capacity to speak allow us to have abundant thoughts that no other species has yet had. But little of that would exist without our grand ancestral voices and evolved primary-process affective heritage.

To summarize, working backward from this chapter through the previous three chapters, we have identified ancient neurochemistries spanning a billion years of animal evolution that humans share with the nematode *C. elegans* and have explored evidence for mammalian emotional commonalities with fish—originating perhaps 600–400 million years ago—in the SEEKING, RAGE/Anger, and FEAR emotional action systems, with glimmers of even some commonalities in our CARE system neurochemistries. Further, these ancient neural "survival systems" are still retained in the mammalian emotional affective BrainMind makeup, along with fuller elaborations of various social emotions, especially CARE, PANIC/Grief/Sadness, and PLAY. Each of these emotional affective systems is an ancestral guide for living and learning and "speak" to us in the oldest of experienced languages: They feel like something. That is, these inborn affective qualia, originating from survival systems that evolutionarily precede verbal language and are so often difficult to describe in words, each has a positive or negative valence about them that informs us about our survival paths and probabilities. Pleasant affects like the joy of CARE in nurturing infants encourage us to maintain our evolutionary-survival trajectories. Unpleasant affects like FEAR tell us we may be in danger and urge us to stop or to run—to freeze or flee—while automatically teaching us to avoid such situations in the future (via yet poorly understood "Laws of Affect" that control learning and memory formation).

These raw subjective feelings are one of life's great mysteries. No one yet knows precisely how subcortical brain networks generate such affective states of mind. We do know that they are experienced by many classes of animals, and most certainly all mammals, because they change how these animals, including humans, behave both in the moment and by altering life trajectories as they spontaneously result in learning. Animals learn to avoid the unpleasant affects and work for more of the pleasant affects. However, that these affects are experienced does not necessarily mean animals are consciously "aware" of them. They probably do not cognitively dwell on such states of mind as much as humans do, partly because of our capacity to think and speak. It is widely believed that brain cortex is required to generate conscious awareness of an affect as a kind of symbolic re-representation. Yet, as we study animals with more complex cortical development—as their cerebral cortex more closely approximates the human neocortex (especially the other anthropoid apes)—it becomes more likely that they do experience some kind of higher conscious awareness of their own affects. However, without being able to communicate with verbal language, it is difficult to know the level of any other species' actual experience, although there are tantalizing hints in animals from jackdaws to chimpanzees of some level of cognitive awareness (Bekoff, 2007; de Waal, 2009; Feinberg & Mallatt, 2016).

In any case, the increased encephalization of the brain, as perhaps best seen in chimpanzees, allows for more nuanced behavior and feelings and social learning. The expansion of the neocortex seems to allow for greater emotional regulation, as seen in the conscientiousness of chimpanzees and brown capuchin monkeys, as well as increased social sophistication, as seen in the reports of chimpanzee political alliances and examples of moral behavior. Of course, the apex of neocortical development occurs in humans. However, it is our position that even the most complex refinements and subtleties of human behavior and principles rest on the foundational values for living inherited in the form of our ancient subcortical emotional affects and their ancestral voices that speak to us in the most primal language: the spontaneous affective language of what it *feels* like to be alive—to experience life.

CHAPTER 11

Preludes to the Big Five
Personality Model

An Earlier Path To Understanding BrainMind States and Human Temperaments

Many philosophers, writers and psychologists have speculated about the basic forces or urges which impel man to respond to his environment. Some, notably McDougall, Freud, Murray, Maslow, Hull and more recently the ethologists Lorenz and Tinbergen, have argued for innate mechanisms such as drives, needs, tensions and instincts which are said to have enabled both animals and man to survive the hostilities of their surroundings. Others, like Watson and Skinner, have supposed that all patterns of motivation are acquired. . . . Whilst most of the foregoing proposals have some face validity, that is, a certain common-sense feel about them, there has been an alarming absence of appropriate experimental and analytical methods to substantiate the claims made. As they stand they scarcely belong to a mature science.

—Raymond B. Cattell and Dennis Child,
Motivation and Dynamic Structure

AT THE END OF CHAPTER 10, we summarized our position on the Big Five personality model in relation to the Affective Neuroscience Personality Scales. In this chapter, we aspire to share as readable a history as possible of the emergence of the Big Five in this important field of psychological science. Although the Big Five is claimed as the ultimate in empirical analysis of personality, as we have shown through many of the earlier chapters, the big flaw is that it is not adequately linked to the critical brain mechanisms of emotionality. The Affective Neuroscience Personality Scales is the first test that is formally grounded on the fundamental nature of our primal mammalian emotions and motivations. We return to that theme in Chapter 12, but first we will describe the remarkable history of this area of psychological research and theorizing.

Prior to the statistical approaches leading eventually to the wide acceptance of the Big Five personality model, personality theory had moved forward on the basis of the intuitions of various theoreticians, all with distinct preferences, some perhaps with extreme biases. Could statistics provide the illumination to guide personality theory out of its apparent chaos toward mathematically defined clarity? Like a voice out of the wilderness, Raymond Cattell (1905–1998) capitalized on the optimistic faith that statistics, and factor analysis in particular, could provide the objectivity needed in this chaotic field. Yet, for us the main question is whether statistics by itself could achieve a deep understanding of our emotional nature and its links to the individual styles people use to approach the world—especially the social world.

Cattell was a native of England. He received his formal education at King's College of the University of London before moving to the United States in 1937, where he rapidly moved up the ranks, from Columbia to Clark University and onward to Harvard, before being invited in 1945 to the University of Illinois at Urbana-Champaign, where he spent most of his career. At Urbana-Champaign his statistical and factor-analytic skills could be fully deployed because they had one of the first supercomputers of that era, the ILLIAC (Illinois Automatic Computer), which was needed for the large-scale factor analyses that could mathematically sift relationships among many different measures of personality.

INTRODUCTION TO RAYMOND CATTELL'S WORK

In addition to his strong statistical background, Cattell was strongly influenced by both William McDougall and Sigmund Freud, both of whom he deeply admired (Kline, 1993, p. 90). However, he also considered them "prescientific" and "speculative"—scholars whose ideas would have benefited from solid scientific approaches. It was Cattell's intention to replace earlier "observational" and "clinical" systems with "modern scientific procedures that can develop their own sets of results which can sort out of the confused mass of speculations, the dross from the gold" (Cattell & Kline, 1977, p. 7). Cattell felt that factor-analytic procedures could apply the necessary objectivity to both validate and fine-tune previous personality concepts. Later in his career he wrote that the work around dynamic (or, as he called them, *ergic*) trait structures "constitutes a quantitative development of psychoanalysis" (Cattell, 1986, p. 48).

Raymond Cattell brought an awesome intellect and energy to the task. His research and interests spanned the entire domain of psychology, from attitudes, interests, and the inheritance of personality to intelligence, which he considered part of personality. In sum, Cattell was one of the most influential psychologists of the twentieth century. An analysis of work cited in textbooks and research articles, professional achievements, and surveys of other psychologist ranked him sixteenth behind such luminaries as B. F. Skinner (no. 1), Sigmund Freud (no. 3), and William James (no. 14) (Haggbloom et al., 2002). His prolific writing yielded a lifetime bibliography that included over five hundred articles, fifty books, and thirty standardized tests. Here, we focus on key elements of his work that have contributed to present personality thinking, especially the Big Five personality model.

Factor Analysis: A Prelude to the Big Five

During his long and luminary career, Cattell pioneered the use of factor analysis as a technique to identify the basic underlying dimensions that accounted for the full spectrum of human personality. He had faith that factor analysis could objectively reveal and define all the elements of personality, including both conscious and unconscious motivations. Therefore, he felt that factor analysis had the potential to validate theoretical approaches to personality such as those proposed by Freud and the psychoanalysts.

While at the University of London, he had been a student of Charles Spearman, who was the first to develop factor analysis (Spearman, 1904). Spearman had used factor analysis—an extension of statistical correlation—to study human intelligence and had demonstrated that there was an element of "general intelligence," which he labeled "little g," in all mental ability tasks regardless of their specific content. Cattell dreamed of expanding factor analysis from the exploration of cognitive problem-solving abilities into the domain of human personality.

The Need for Computers to Make Progress on Large Data Sets

What is factor analysis? Start with a confusing array of data, stir until correlated, mix in generous portions of calculus and matrix algebra, evaluate artfully until it seems done, and ideally you will have simplified your understanding of the data by identifying a few underlying "source" factors that explain most of the variation in the mass (or "mess") of data you started with. This was Cattell's ambitious goal for exploring personality, but he faced an enormous challenge. When he started out, all mathematical calculations had to be accomplished by hand, eventually aided by electromechanical calculators, before real programmable computers like the ILLIAC emerged at the middle of the twentieth century.

Actually, Cattell probably started with a few choice "computers," in a manner of speaking, but they were the kind of computers Edwin Hubble, of expanding universe fame, had used when he worked with the first author's old astronomy professor, Clifford Crump, at the Yerkes Observatory in Geneva, Wisconsin. In 1916, Hubble and Crump both had what they called *computers*: meaning mathematically inclined human assistants who performed all of the necessary mathematical calculations (Crump, personal communication). The very first "modern" computer ever built, by Charles Babbage (1791–1871), didn't quite work because of mechanical, not conceptual, flaws in his "Analytical Engine" (see Snyder, 2011). It wasn't till the end of World War II that the first real "giant brain," named ENIAC (Electronic Numerical Integrator and Computer), was completed, half a dozen years before the first commercial computer, UNIVAC (Universal Automatic Computer) was delivered to the U.S. Census Bureau in 1951.

The chief technical limitation in those early days of factor analysis was having to do all the gruesome statistics with paper and pencil. The mathematical computations were so burdensome that many joked that any graduate student who could successfully complete the factor analysis computations in four years would automatically receive a Ph.D. In the 1930s, mechanical calculators were introduced that could multiply and divide, which lightened some of the computational load, but essentially all factor analyses were completed by hand until the development of digital computers. Supposedly, Cattell accepted his position at the University of Illinois in 1945 because the university was developing the ILLIAC, the first digital computer built and owned at any university, which would allow him to work with vastly larger data sets than could be managed by hand.

Of course, a lot of mathematical science had been accomplished before the advent of digital computers. There was Einstein's theory of relativity. Hubble had demonstrated the existence of galaxies outside of our Milky Way and had provided critical evidence for the conclusion that the universe was still expanding. Even the Manhattan Project and the development of the first atomic bomb were developed using the calculations of a small army of the original human-type computers. However, the "primitive" automated computational methods of that era meant the first factor analyses of personality measures were rather limited in scope by today's standards.

The First Glimpse of the "Big Five" in Personality Theory

Already early in his career, Cattell (1933) published an article on "temperament" traits that presaged the now widely accepted Big Five personality model. Correlating forty-six ratings on sixty-two college students, he statistically defined for the first time in a single study four factors that generally corresponded to the Big Five personality model:

> *Surgency*, or sociable-gregarious versus unsociable-shy tendencies (Big Five: Extraversion)
> *Maturity*, or a good-natured temperament versus maliciousness (Big Five: Agreeableness)
> Personal *"Will"* or *Conscientiousness* versus unreliability (Big Five: Conscientiousness)
> *Well-adjusted* versus *Maladjusted* (Big Five: Emotional Stability)

The only Big Five dimension missing was Openness to Experience. John Digman, in reviewing the history of the Big Five personality model, commented that these findings plus the Spearman "g" factor, as a measure of intellect, provided "the first glimpse of the Big Five" (1996, p. 3).

Factor-Analytic Studies Using Gordon Allport's "Dictionary Terms"

Cattell was determined to establish the broadest possible personality description covering the complete "surface" of personality. It so happened that Gordon Allport and Henry Odbert (1936), also psychologists at Harvard, had previously extracted 17,953 dictionary terms that applied to human behavior. Of these, 4,504 terms, or about 1 percent of all the words in the dictionary, were considered personality traits. Cattell, with his characteristic energy and intensity, decided to capitalize on this massive effort and to reduce these trait terms to a list that seemed practical for a manually computed factor analysis.

In 1945 and 1947, while still at Harvard and later the University of Illinois with the ILLIAC computer, Cattell used 199 subjects rated on 171 trait terms to publish papers describing twelve or thirteen personality traits extracted by factor-analytic techniques. But why didn't Cattell stop at the four or five factors he had originally found and replicate his earlier correlational study? One of the answers lies in the nature of factor analysis itself, which is somewhat of an art form in the world of statistics. Two things factor analysis does *not* do are interpret the factors it produces and, perhaps most important, determine how many total factors may be embedded in the data. These two limitations are related, because the artful statistician determines how many factors to extract, which can be influenced by whether the investigator considers them interpretable.

Another answer comes from Louis Thurstone, of the University of Chicago, the most dominant player in the factor-analytic world at that time. He advocated extracting more rather than fewer factors. Thurstone felt that extracting "too many factors can do no harm" (1947, p. 509). So, Cattell routinely extracted too many factors by today's standards and was encouraged to do so by Thurstone, the reigning factor-analytic expert of his day.

Digman, a prominent Big Five advocate, and his colleagues (Digman & Takemoto-Chock, 1981) have gone to the trouble of reanalyzing some of the data Cattell used to generate his twelve-factor solution. They concluded that Cattell would have been better advised to stop with five or six factors and that a five-factor solution would have provided a good match with current Big Five factors.

Yet, it remained difficult for psychologists to believe that only five factors were sufficient to account for the behavioral complexity observed in humans. Digman himself (1996) confessed that he assumed that more than five factors would be required to account for the childhood personalities he was studying and that both he and personality psychologist Warren Norman had fallen prey to this temptation in the 1960s. In short, how could Cattell hope to account for the seemingly countless variations of human personality with just a few factors?

In any case, Cattell, the pioneer, didn't know how many factors to expect. This was exactly the problem he was exploring as he attempted to define personality space using his factor-analytic approach. In his Sixteen Personality Factor Questionnaire (16PF), which became his most widely used and enduring standardized psychological test, he settled on sixteen scales (see Table 11.1), and he had excluded several additional possible scales to end up with his final sixteen. Further, Cattell was not alone in creating complex psychological test models. Harrison Gough later settled on twenty scales for his California Psychological Inventory, the Guilford-Zimmerman Temperament Inventory had ten scales, and Douglas Jackson's Personality Research Form had twenty scales, one for each of Henry Murray's twenty basic needs (see Chapter 5). Even the relatively revised Neuroticism Extraversion Openness Personality Inventory (NEO-PI), which is marketed as a Five-Factor Model personality instrument, has thirty scales: six separate facets for each of the five main factors.

A FOUNDATIONAL ISSUE: THE
LEXICAL HYPOTHESIS

The lexical hypothesis embraces a faith that the spoken language encompassed a profound wisdom: the ability to describe and communicate all human interpersonal behavior that had been important for survival (for a review, see Saucier & Goldberg, 1996). In reporting his derivation of sixty key variables from the 4,503 trait terms, Cattell wrote that "all aspects of human personality which are or have been of importance, interest, or utility have already become recorded in the substance of language" (1943, p. 483). He later similarly wrote that "by the pressure of urgent necessity, every aspect of one human being's behavior that is likely to affect another has come to be handled by some verbal symbol" (1957, p. 71). Furthermore, for Cattell, factor analysis was the tool to extract this "latent" understanding of the human experience that was embedded in spoken language. Parenthetically, all this may be true about tertiary-process cognitive elaborations on basic survival issues, but our view is that the primary-process emotional survival themes need to be explicitly addressed for personality scales to be optimally useful to psychiatrists and other mental health professionals.

The scientific problem that Cattell and others hoped the lexical hypothesis with factor analysis would resolve was how many distinct categories of behavior one needed to adequately describe human personality. However, Cattell also dreamed that his factor-analytically derived "source" traits would represent the fundamental "dynamic causes" of human behavior. Yet, as we have already pointed out, this marvelous statistical descriptive system has limitations when it comes to arriving at fundamental primal categories of emotional tendencies. With this statistical tool it is difficult to discern where psychologically relevant primary emotional brain systems end and higher-order tertiary personality elaborations begin. Both of these problems—identifying distinct categories of behavior and identifying the fundamental causes of personality differences— are personality issues that perhaps affective neuroscience can address more accurately than statistical factor analysis. And as soon as one identifies the foundations of personality systems useful for understanding emotional problems, often conceptualized as psychiatric disorders, one has the possibility of bridging basic brain research and clinically relevant human problems in new ways, as we describe in Chapter 18.

Cattell's Sixteen Personality Factors

Cattell ventured into the personality world armed with a rich lexical hypothesis and Thurstone's "improved" factor-analytic methods. Cattell found twelve dimensions that he could observe readily using both self-report questionnaire data (Q-data) and observer ratings (L-data). However, there were four personality dimensions he was only able to find using Q-data, which he then named Q1 through Q4. Cattell published the 16 PF, short for 16 Personality Factors, as summarized in Table 11.1—sometimes using very imaginative "cryptic" terms to describe his scales.

The Underlying Complexity of the Big Five: 16PF Source Traits

Cattell further factor analyzed his sixteen primary factors to reduce the number to eight second-order personality scales (not to be confused with our secondary-process in the Nested BrainMind Hierarchy presented in Chapter 5). Cattell later reported a second-order solution that further simplified personality profiling to five second-order factors that fit the Big Five personality model. While Cattell recognized the value of recognizing these broad themes, he consistently maintained that "greater accuracy of prediction is necessarily obtained by using primaries . . . [and] the psychologist is strongly advised to keep to the full spectrum of primaries" (Cattell, Eber, & Tatsuoka, 1970, p. 127). Again, Cattell's use of the term *primaries* referred to his basic sixteen factors and should not be confused with primary-process emotions.

Cattell's factor-analytic successors further refined his factor analyses into a clearer Big Five model, which is the subject of the next chapter. However, in closing this chapter, we take a glimpse at Cattell's factoring of more objective personality measures, which he labeled "Testing-data" or "T-data."

Instinctual Drives and Ergs

Cattell probed closer to the biological basis of personality, attempting to explore more "innate drives." The term *instinct* was very much out of favor in Cattell's time—and still remains out of favor to this day among many behavioral neuroscientists. So, for innate drives Cattell preferred to use the term *erg*, a unit of energy, a term he borrowed from physics. As explained by Cattell, an erg was "an innate psycho-physical disposition which permits its possessor to acquire reactivity (attention, recognition) to certain classes of objects more readily than others, to experience a specific emotion in regard to them, and to start on a course of action which ceases more completely at a certain specific goal activity than at any other" (1950, p. 199). This complex definition generally agrees with the affective neuroscience definition of primary emotions and aligns with the simple "APT to ACT" acronym, which summarizes four components of primary emotions: Affect, Perception, Thought, and ACtion Tendency.

Table 11.1. Brief Descriptions of Cattell's Primary Source Traits Published in the 16PF

Factor	Low Score Descriptions	High Score Descriptions
A	Sizothymia: Reserved	Affectothymia: Outgoing
B	Intelligence: Dull	Intelligence: Bright
C	Low ego strength: Easily upset	High ego strength: Emotionally stable
E	Submissiveness: Humble, easily led	Dominance: Assertive, aggressive
F	Desurgency: Sober, serious	Surgency: Enthusiastic
G	Weak superego strength: Expedient	Strong superego strength: Conscientious
H	Threctia: Shy, timid	Parmia: Socially bold
I	Harria: Tough-minded, realistic	Premsia: Tender-minded, sensitive
L	Alaxia: Trusting	Protension: Suspicious
M	Praxernia: Practical	Autia: Imaginative
N	Artlessness: Forthright, genuine	Shrewdness: Astute, polished
O	Untroubled adequacy: Self-assured	Guilt proneness: Insecure
Q^1	Conservativism: Traditional ideas	Radicalism: Liberal ideas
Q^2	Group adherence: Sound follower	Self-sufficiency: Prefers own decisions
Q^3	Low self-sentiment: Undisciplined	High self-sentiment: Controlled
Q^4	Low ergic tension: Relaxed	High ergic tension: Frustrated

Adapted from Cattell, H. B. (1989).

Cattell's "specific emotion" would generally correspond to affect; "attention, recognition" to perception and thought; and "a course of action" to action tendency. Thus, Cattell's erg components correspond closely to Panksepp's primary emotions, and for McDougall they would define emotional instincts (see Chapter 4). As is common in science, it is often hard to translate between different terminologies.

Cattell measured ergs using Testing data (T-data), which was a third kind of more direct objective data, in contrast to subjective data estimated through self-report (Q-data) or observer ratings (L-data). Examples of T-data were galvanic skin responses, word fluency tests, idea fluency tests, reaction times, and the capacity to find a particular shape embedded in a more complex drawing.

Cattell approached the identification of ergs in the same way he had come to approach other psychological questions: relying on factor analysis, although he cautioned that, "As to the actual number and naming of ergs in human beings, another decade of systematic research . . . might reasonably be expected to give us a complete picture" (Cattell & Child, 1975, p. 37). But by 1975 he concluded that adequate factor-analytic research had consistently identified ten ergs, with a few other proposed candidates. He also noted that his list was closer to McDougall's list than to those of Freud or Murray (Cattell & Child, 1975). Those ten, along with a yet-to-be-well-defined "Laughter" erg, are listed in Table 11.2 and

Table 11.2. A Comparison of Cattell's Ergs and Panksepp's Primary Emotions

Cattell's Hypothesized Ergs		
Goal Title	**Emotion**	**Panksepp's Affect or Emotion**
Food-seeking	Hunger	HUNGER (homeostatic state, not central to personality)
Mating	Sex	LUST (marginally central to personality)
Gregariousness	Loneliness	PANIC/Sadness
Parental	Pity	CARE
Exploration	Curiosity	SEEKING
Escape to security	Fear	FEAR
Self-assertion	Pride	Power/dominance (not well documented as a brain system)
Narcissistic sex	Sensuousness	? (a possible higher dimension of LUST)
Pugnacity	Anger	RAGE
Acquisitiveness	Greed	? (a possible higher dimension of SEEKING expressed in hoarding tendencies)
Laughter (proposed)	Amusement	PLAY

Adapted from Cattell and Child (1975, p. 40) and Panksepp (1998a).

compared to Panksepp's blue ribbon emotions. It should be noted that these comparisons are based on definitions, not specific data.

The agreement between the two lists is striking—yet the affective neuroscience analysis emerged from basic brain research in animals, without any linkage to or awareness of Cattell's ergs. Moreover, Cattell considered his factor-analytically derived ergs to be the main mammalian drives although his research had no connection to neurobiological brain research. They were conceived by Cattell to be in the "motivational" domain, being basic biological impulses or urges that constituted the energizing forces of personality.

In retrospect, it seems likely that Cattell's T-data were very substantially tapping into what affective neuroscience approaches would consider primary-level emotions and motivations, along with HUNGER, an affective bodily need (homeostatic feeling). Cattell's T-data seem to be accessing the primary-process and secondary-process of the Nested BrainMind Hierarchy, with the Q- and L-data likely measuring language-derived traits at the tertiary cognitively elaborated level. In other words, much personality assessment using self-report (Q-data, i.e., language) may be describing personality characteristics emerging at Panksepp's tertiary-process level, which remains difficult to link empirically to the primary-process level of affective experience. However, Cattell's ergs, estimated from objective T-data, seem to align quite readily with the primary genetically endowed emotions, which again confirms that relying on measures as close to the primary expression of emotional behaviors as possible is likely to keep researchers close to the basic foundational processes that help constitute human personality.

The similarity of Cattell's ergs with Panksepp's primary emotions continues a pattern of conceptual consistency from Darwin and McDougall to the neuroscientific work of Panksepp. Darwin and McDougall added objectivity to their selection of instinctual emotions by requiring the emotions to be observable in animals as well as humans. Panksepp used several objective criteria in making his selections: being able to neurophysiologically evoke the respective behavior patterns with electrical deep brain stimulation (DBS), specifying the anatomical brain locations associated with the various emotions, providing evidence for neurochemical systems regulating the emotions, and demonstrating that arousal of these brain systems with DBS evoked psychological feelings in animals, as evidenced by the rewarding and punishing effects (of these artificially evoked brain states (namely, animals would work for or learn to escape such DBS-induced brain states; this constituted the evidence for affects in non-speaking animals, and correspond to affective shifts seen in humans during comparable brain stimulation for more detail, see Panksepp, 1985, 1998a; Panksepp & Biven, 2012). Thus, three complementary approaches—Darwin and McDougall's comparative behavioral studies, Cattell's objective psychological analyses ot T-data, and Panksepp's neuroscientific research—have independently arrived at very similar conclusions regarding the primary affective feelings underlying human adaptive reaction tendencies that are commonly called personality traits. It is especially noteworthy that Cattell required that the drives and emotions (ergs) be interpretable from the factor analysis of T-data (directly measurable objective data). It now seems that when complex language-mediated descriptions are *not* involved in the research, a consistency emerges in the search for fundamental origins of large-scale adaptive, psychologically relevant psychobehavioral processes that are built into all mammalian brains.

Suffice it to say that wherever there is convergence on very similar organizing principles through the use of vastly different and independent scientific approaches, one has substantial assurance that nuggets of lasting knowledge are being unearthed. McDougall, a social psychologist, saw reliable patterns of animal behavior in the natural world. Cattell, a cognitively oriented psychologist, tackled the vast complexities of human personality and found similar fundamental processes especially when objective measures of human behaviors and feelings were analyzed mathematically through factor analyzes. Panksepp, a clinically-oriented neuroscientist interested in fundamental sources of human affective life so important for understanding psychiatric disorders, found evolutionarily ingrained neural systems for emotionality that exist in all mammals, and even in more distantly related creatures. And Darwin, who gave us an evolutionary view of the emergence of animal and human nature, would surely smile, for much of this was anticipated in his last two books: *The Expression of the Emotions in Man and Animals* (1872), where he said in the introduction that he had been thinking about the subject since 1838, and the second "revised and augmented" edition of *The Descent of Man, and Selection in Relation to Sex* (1874). All of this work combined tells us much about the origins of human nature, and it is remarkable that traditional psychological personality theory can be linked to the rigorous neurobiological study of primal animal emotional systems. Even though there has been much chaos and argumentation in this field, as is normal in science, when one backs away from the historical disputes, the emerging pattern is both realistic and beautiful.

CHAPTER 12

The Big Five

The Essential Core of Cattell's Factor Analysis

Psychology has not unjustly been accused through the last half century of filling libraries with theories more academic than scientific.
—Raymond B. Cattell and Dennis Child,
Motivation and Dynamic Structure

A LTHOUGH CATTELL KINDLED a factor-analytic revolution in the scientific analysis of personality, it took quite a while for it to catch on big time. One of the reasons may have been the early lack of computer power. Calculating factor analyses was an ordeal—a distinctly unpleasant task by hand, even with the time saving but irritatingly noisy mechanical calculators of the day. Even the early computers were limited in the number of variables they could analyze at one time. Then there were the massive stacks of punch cards (each about the size and texture of an airplane boarding pass), amassed in heavy boxes that contained the data, delivered by hand to the local computer operators, who fed them into the computer with IBM card readers. Users of university and business computer systems had to wait for hours, if not days, for results that arrived as massive fanfolded paper computer printouts. Those massive computers of yesteryear were way less powerful than the average laptops of today, which in seconds can produce polished graphical outputs of factor analyses from huge correlation matrixes.

However, another reason for the slow acceptance of Cattell's rigorous and sophisticated statistical breakthrough was the degree of skepticism about factor analyses and their potential for solving real problems about anything as complex and dynamic as human personality. After all, the only thing factor matrices typically provided were numerical results about people's responses to questions experimenters posed to them about their personalities. Factor analysis simply looked for mathematical grouping of types of answers to those questions. The results were statistical correlations estimating the degree of relatedness among questions, and it was still up to the scientist to make meaning out of those numerical estimates. Computers of that era did not have capacities to describe the meaning of numerical relationships—nor do the powerful machines of the current era, even IBM's computer Watson[6], which can beat humans at their own intellectual games.

Gordon Allport (1897–1967), a highly respected Harvard psychologist, was just one prominent early critic of factor analysis who skeptically wrote that "an entire population (the larger the better) is put into the grinder, and the mixing is so expert that what comes through is a link of factors in which every individual has lost his identity . . . seldom do the factors derived in this way resemble the dispositions and traits identified by clinical methods when the individual is studied intensively" (1937, p. 244). This concern reflected the fact that, at least since Sigmund Freud's revolutionary depth-psychological views about human nature, personality theory had emerged largely from clinical insight, and few believed that statistics alone could provide substantive contributions (because of the above-noted interpretive issues), let alone supersede, intense clinical analysis.

A Remarkable Replication

Putting aside the clinical versus empirical-statistical arguments for the time being, it is now recognized that the emergence of five consistent factors from diverse psychological data was a remarkable breakthrough. Why should one be able to start with an assortment of statements, which broadly sample individual personal feelings, attitudes, interests, and beliefs, reduce them to five predictable themes, and then be able to repeat the process on a second independent set of statements and individuals, with comparable results? It is because there is something there of value, especially given that the five-factor "solution" has now been replicated many times in the world of psychometrics—the science of measuring human mental traits. The responses of a few hundred people on any broad-spectrum personality test, when factor analyzed, will generally reveal five main factors resembling the Big Five personality model, regardless of how many scales the personality test reported. This phenomenon is at its most compelling with the simplified analysis of descriptive adjectives that apply to people, and with minor hiccups has been shown to work in over a dozen languages (Saucier & Goldberg,

2003, 2006). Indeed, the principle holds whether people are describing themselves or being described by people who know them well (Connelly & Ones, 2011).

Remarkably (but perhaps not surprising to William McDougall), this is a consistent pattern whether the descriptive statements are about normal everyday lives or about lives in clinical populations experiencing seriously limiting pathological feelings (Livesley, Jackson, & Schroeder, 1992). Of course, a key unresolved issue is whether this truly reflects a deep and abiding nature of human personality structures or something about the languages we have devised/invented to talk about one another. In other words, the issue is whether these five dimensions encapsulate the dynamic energizing forces that underlie our personalities or merely the conceptual, descriptive categories of our culturally generated languages, used to describe our behaviors. Of course, this is a solid scientific beginning that can have multiple implications and interpretations, all of which can be empirically linked to neurobiological processes (in research mostly yet to be done), but which do not intrinsically tell us anything about those processes.

Our position is that factor analysis by itself does not illuminate how brain systems, genetic factors, and other physiological mechanisms (hormones, etc.) might be involved with each of the statistically revealed five factors. We believe that factor analysis is a purely descriptive tool. It is easy to get caught in the classic correlation trap of assuming that finding a strong correlation means that you have found the "cause" of something. For example, the fact that liking to talk means you are extraverted is "circular," because liking to talk was part of the definition of extraversion in the first place. So the factor-analytic concept of extraversion cannot be seen as the *cause* of liking to engage in social conversion, or vice versa. We must look much further to clarify the underlying brain and psychological cause—one of our reasons for writing this book. In part, we created the Affective Neuroscience Personality Scales so we might better clarify the underlying brain processes (but more on that issue later).

The Big Five Model Is Robust

What makes the Big Five model so compelling is that it has been replicated many times across the years. The Big Five usually works regardless of the sample of individuals tested, as long as an adequate sample of personality test items (or scales) is analyzed. Start with a reasonably broad sample of personality descriptors and a population of subjects that is at least three times as large as the number of items you ask them to rate; for instance, with 70 items you would ideally have 210 subjects or more. Use a standard factor-analytic procedure to extract five factors, and the items loading on those five factors are very likely to resemble Extraversion, Emotional Stability, Conscientiousness, Agreeableness, and Openness to Experience. Given adequate samples, Extraversion, Emotional Stability, Conscientiousness, and Agreeableness are almost guaranteed. However, as many have found, identification of the most subtle of the variables, Openness to Experience, has often been more difficult, perhaps because this arises substantially from the most subtle of the emotional systems, the SEEKING system. This system, one of the oldest, in evolutionary terms (see Chapter 10), is so pervasive in everyday waking life that it tends to get molded into the opportunities that the social world provides to exercise one's natural enthusiasm to know and find more and more. In any event, when scientists find a phenomenon as robust as the Big Five, they are academically bound to agree there is *something* there. But that something has to be analyzed, neuropsychologically, neurogenetically and neurobiologically for major progress to occur. We think the Affective Neuroscience Personality Scales provides one such tool—one that bridges past affective-emotional brain research with future understanding of our underlying mental nature. But, before heading further let us flesh out the history of the field.

EMERGENCE OF THE BIG FIVE PERSONALITY MODEL

Even though Cattell, more than anyone else, promoted factor analysis as an objective personality research tool, he certainly did not originate the idea that there might be five major personality traits that could encompass most of personality. That was left to many other psychologists, and the origins of the Big Five, or the Five-Factor Model (FFM), have been well described by John Digman (1990, 1996). As noted in Chapter 11, in 1933 Cattell (1933) published a correlational analysis of forty-six bipolar items that identified four of the Big Five dimensions, including a Conscientiousness factor, which Cattell labeled "Will," and an Extraversion factor, which Cattell labeled "Surgency." In addition, Cattell identified a dimension he called "Maturity" (or the Big Five Agreeableness dimension) and a "Well-adjusted" versus Maladjusted factor, which in retrospect align with Emotional Stability. This report was an historical stepping-stone on the journey to accepting what would come to be called the Big Five personality model.

Donald Fiske: The First Validation of the Big Five

As the historical saga played out, Donald Fiske (1917–2003) of the University of Chicago came close to a full FFM solution. Using twenty-two of Cattell's rating scales, Fiske (1949) spent a year analyzing three different rating modes: self-ratings, peer ratings, and supervisor ratings. He identified five consistent dimensions in each data set. However, his five-factor solutions lacked a Conscientiousness factor. He used the labels of Social Adaptability (Extraversion), Conformity (Agreeableness), Emotional Control (Emotional Stability), and Inquiring Intellect (Openness to Experience). Unfortunately, Conscientiousness was not one of his factors, and his fifth factor was labeled Confident Self-Expression, which seemed more like an aspect of Extraversion.

Ernest Tupes: The Forgotten
Validators of the Big Five

Tupes and Christal (1961, 1992), using thirty of thirty-five Cattell scales, were the first to identify a full five-factor personality solution that is still recognized as the Big Five. Parenthetically, it is not unusual in science to forget major originators of scientific perspectives that were critical stepping-stones to the heralded achievements of others. For instance, who remembers that Oswald Avery (1877–1955) was the first scientist to identify DNA as our hereditary material (with his colleagues at Rockefeller University Hospital, published in 1944), while most other investigators in the field thought that proteins (the products of DNA and RNA) were the sources (as opposed to products) of the genes. Avery never received the Nobel Prize; Francis Crick and John Watson, who decoded the molecular structure of DNA, did in 1954 (Reichard, 2002).

In 1961 two Air Force researchers, Ernest Tupes and Raymond Christal, not only reported a stable five-factor model in their own data but also found the same five factors when they reanalyzed Cattell's and Fiske's earlier data. However, their report appeared only as an Air Force technical report, which was not widely read by personality researchers. Eventually, their paper was considered so important that it was republished in 1992 in the widely circulated *Journal of Personality*. They labeled their five broad personality factors Surgency, Agreeableness, Dependability, Emotional Stability, and Culture, which marked the beginning of the current Big Five personality model.

Tupes was working for the Air Force and trying to ensure his work would provide a sound foundation for subsequent Air Force personnel selection programs. Therefore, he used a subset of Cattell's scales that had already been used to predict high-quality performance of Air Force senior officers, as well as new second lieutenants. To ensure his studies would generalize, he sampled a broad population, including data on more than just members of the Air Force. In the initial Air Force studies, he had used Air Force officer candidates, as well as senior Air Force officers, with some airmen having only a high school education. Subsequently, he added university students and graduate students to the mix, including a reanalysis of the Cattell and Fiske data, because like Fiske he had used a subset of Cattell's scales.

His data from all eight studies were derived mostly from observer ratings rather than self-reports, and he incorporated a sampling of many different peer raters, including fellow Officer Candidate School mates, Air Force Command classmates, fellow fraternity members, female university students, clinical psychology graduate students, and "experts" such as staff clinical psychologists and psychiatrists. Clearly, his approach was a monumental effort that, in his words, sought "to isolate meaningful and relatively independent trait-rating factors which are universal enough to appear in a variety of samples, and which are not unduly sensitive to the rating conditions or situations" (Tupes & Christal, 1992, p. 227).

IBM Replication

The original Tupes and Christal (1961) study was also unique in terms of one important methodological point: after all of their analyses were completed with the electronic hand calculators available at the time, they were able to replicate one of their factor analyses on a computer. They had gained access to one of the first factor analysis software programs and an IBM 650 computer to serve up the results. Their new computer program produced results virtually identical to those they had previously generated by hand. Tupes and Christal noted that, in the future, this "will not only save many hours of labor, but will bring considerably more rigor to what has thus far been a rather loose area" (1992, p. 246). They further concluded that the consistency they found across their eight studies "has always been there, but it has been hidden by inconsistency of factorial techniques and philosophies" (p. 246).

More Factors?

Tupes and Christal (1961, 1992) found only five personality dimensions in their studies and reported that "nothing more of any consequence" (1992, p. 245) appeared in their reanalysis of Cattell's data using all thirty-five trait clusters. However, like most others that preceded them, they believed there must be more factors and almost apologized by writing that "It is unlikely that the five factors identified are the *only* fundamental personality factors. There are quite likely other fundamental concepts involved among the Allport-Odbert adjectives on which the variables used in the present study were based" (p. 247).

How prescient was their prediction! But this was not a problem to be resolved by factor analysis working with tertiary-level (language) data. The personality field had to wait for neuroscience to blossom and especially on our ever-increasing understanding of the anatomical and neurochemical nature of mammalian emotions (Panksepp, 1982, 1998a; Panksepp & Biven, 2012). As previously discussed, from an affective neuroscience perspective, the Emotional Stability dimension of the Big Five may actually be composed of three separate and distinct brain systems that generate distinct negative feelings: RAGE/Anger, FEAR, and PANIC/Sadness, and, except for Conscientiousness, the other Big Five dimensions may correspond to other distinct emotional strengths and weaknesses. In any event, just with the recognition that there are at least three primal negative emotional networks in mammalian brains, affective neuroscience could potentially add two additional emotional personality dimensions, which might yield a Big Seven list, including *Conscientiousness* (more on this later).

That said, it seems that correlational analyses of our languages have issued generalizations, such as conflating distinct negative emotions into a single category of negative emotionality. In contrast, psychiatrists and psychotherapists need a much sharper vision, including realizing that the three negative primal emotions, RAGE/Anger, FEAR, and PANIC/Sadness, have distinct brain substrates, to guide development of distinct treatments for problems in living arising from these distinct systems (Panksepp et al., 2014; Panksepp, 2015, 2016; Panksepp & Yovell, 2014).

THE WIDER ACCEPTANCE OF
THE FIVE-FACTOR MODEL

Somewhat like the young medical student and future neuroscience researcher Roger Bannister breaking the four-minute mile barrier in 1954, once broken, all great runners were up to the task. Unremarkably, everyone in human personality research now seemed able to find five major personality factors (often using slightly different semantic labels). Of course, this partly had to do with the emergence of ever more powerful computer processing, as well as more standardized factor-analytic techniques. In 1963 Warren Norman (1930–1998) of the University of Michigan, only six years out of graduate school, reported that peer ratings of twenty scales resulted in five factors, which he labeled Surgency, Agreeableness, Conscientiousness, Emotionality, and Culture (Digman, 1996). In 1964 Edgar Borgatta of the University of Washington obtained ratings of fraternity and sorority members using thirty-four scales he designed himself. Borgatta (1964) also reported five factors, which he named Assertiveness, Likeability, Responsibility, Emotionality, and Intelligence. In 1967 Gene Smith of the Harvard Medical School in Boston used forty-two bipolar scales to obtain ratings of three independent groups of first-year college students. The same five factors emerged from the factor analysis of each group, and Smith labeled the dimensions

Extraversion, Agreeableness, Emotionality, Strength of Character, and Refinement. A clear, repetitive pattern was emerging. For easier comparisons, the factor names used in these studies are listed in Table 12.1

Yet it would still be many years before the Big Five would gain wide acceptance. Alternative models were still being proposed. Eysenck (1955), Peabody (1967), and McCrae and Costa (1983) all proposed three-factor models. Block proposed a two-factor model with three subtypes (Block, 1961), and Myers and McCaulley (1985) put forth a four-factor model with sixteen types. Also, new personality instruments such as the Personality Research Form (Jackson, 1984) were published with far more than five factors.

Lewis Goldberg

In addition to reanalyzing Cattell's old data (Digman & Takemoto-Chock, 1981), John Digman and colleagues completed new studies supporting the Big Five (Digman & Inouye, 1986). Similarly, Paul Costa and Robert McCrae (1985) revised their three-factor Neuroticism Extraversion Openness Personality Inventory (NEO-PI) to incorporate five factors.

Elsewhere, Digman (1996) also describes how Lewis Goldberg, of the University of Oregon, played a central role in this Big Five renaissance. Goldberg (1990) published an influential article that was seen to definitively establish the generality of the Big Five as a robust phenomenon. He based his research on Norman's (1967) 1,431 English language adjective synonyms clustered into seventy-five scales. This was the most comprehensive set of adjectives ever used in personality research, which eliminated the argument that the five-factor solution resulted from analyzing an incomplete personality domain. In one case, students rated themselves on 1,710 trait-descriptive adjectives working in one-hour segments until they had completed this Herculean task. Of course, none of Goldberg's ambitious factor analyses would have been possible without ever more powerful modern computers.

To quash the argument that five factors would be found only with specific factor-analytic techniques, Goldberg (1990) used five mathematically different methods of extracting the factors, and also allowed the factors from each method to be either correlated with each other or completely orthogonal (a term that means the factor dimensions are mathematically "perpendicular" to each other, which basically means "independent of each other"). With each of the ten procedures (five different factoring methods, each once using correlated and once orthogonal relationships), five factors were derived with virtually identical results. Goldberg tried extracting more than five factors and found that the basic five factors remained intact. with extra factors being fragments of the basic five.

Table 12.1. Factor Names Used in Early Five Factor Model Studies					
Source	**Labels**				
Fiske, 1949	Social Adaptability	Conformity	(Missing)	Emotional Control	Inquiring Intellect
Tupes & Christal, 1961	Surgency	Agreeableness	Dependability	Emotional Stability	Culture
Norman, 1963	Surgency	Agreeableness	Conscientiousness	Emotionality	Culture
Borgatta, 1964	Assertiveness	Likeability	Responsibility	Emotionality	Intelligence
Smith, 1967	Extraversion	Agreeableness	Strength of Character	Emotionality	Refinement

One can see how several distinct negative emotions may fall under a general Emotionality factor. One function of language is to simplify complexities, to the point where psychologists often seem to believe that words are explanations for diverse preverbal psychological processes (e.g., the nominal fallacy, assuming that naming equals explaining; or the post hoc ergo propter hoc fallacy, assuming that correlation equals causation).

In any event, with his seminal paper, Goldberg demonstrated consistent replications of five factors regardless of whether people were describing themselves, rating peers they liked, or rating peers they disliked. He successfully challenged previous reservations about the generality and robustness of the Big Five personality model. Using a comprehensive collection of English language personality-descriptive adjectives, the Big Five structure had emerged regardless of samples and statistical variations. As if this weren't sufficient, Goldberg also provided one hundred Big Five "markers" to add precision to the core definitions of these five basic personality dimensions (Goldberg, 1992).

What Is the Meaning of the Big Five Personality Model?

A big question remained unanswered: What was the meaning of the Big Five personality model? Gerard Saucier and Lewis Goldberg (1996) argued that the Big Five model was phenotypic rather than genotypic. Phenotypes refer to observable characteristics (Cattell's idea of surface traits); genotypes refer to the underlying biological causes (Cattell's idea of source traits). Thus, the lexical origins of the Big Five model provided excellent descriptions but not deeper functional or psychobiological explanations. In their own words, "The lexical perspective leads to data that need explaining, not necessarily to the modes of explanation" (Saucier & Goldberg, 1996, p. 25). Saucier and Goldberg went so far as to suggest that the Big Five model should be called an "attribute" model rather than a "trait" model (p. 25). The term *trait* brought too much baggage, with assumptions about stability and genetic origin that need to be verified and not assumed. The term *attribute* was more neutral and made no assumptions about the cause or origin of the described temperamental characteristics.

Also, Goldberg (1993) stated that the Big Five were "dimensional" as opposed to "categorical" in nature. In other words, they were gradients of existence rather than distinct categories such as different kinds of fruits and vegetables. There is general agreement that levels of these five dimensions can be measured with various instruments but not on what constitutes each of these dimensions. Plus, it has not been well determined what limits there are to the categories of variables used in their measurements. For example, to what extent should evaluative terms, physical characteristics, or world views be used, and how might they alter the model that was based on descriptive adjectives? (We discuss this further in Chapter 13.)

Goldberg also preferred to use the term *Big Five* for the personality attribute model, which is derived from lexical data and remains descriptive rather than explanatory. He cited John and Robins (1993) for suggesting that the term *Five-Factor Model* (FFM) is an explanatory model that assumes the five factors correspond to specific biological origins. However, it seems unlikely that even the scientific community will be able to agree on this subtle distinction in terminology. In general, the term *Big Five* attribute model seems more neutral and open to modification than *FFM*, but we use both terms, guided by the preferences and usage of the various investigators we cite.

For Saucier and Goldberg, the Big Five are "dimensions of *perceived* personality" (1996, p. 42). It is not a theory; rather it is more a conceptual taxonomy of convenience for mapping personality variables. In any event, the dimensions constitute robust replicable findings, which can provide the basis for future research. The Big Five approaches can inform those who strive to understand personality at deeper neuropsychological levels but represent only a beginning rather than any statement about the underlying neural or psychological structures of personality based on relevant functional systems of the brain and mind.

THE CATTELL TRADITION: HOW WILL THE UNDERLYING BIOLOGY BE REVEALED?

In the tradition of Raymond Cattell's dreams, there are some like Robert McCrae and Paul Costa who see the FFM as a new empirically based personality theory that is supplanting the older more clinically based theories. They argue that the lexically derived FFM provides some support for human rationality, which stands in contrast to radical behaviorism and the psychoanalytic theories that focus on diverse unconscious processes (McCrae & Costa, 1996). Specifically, they view the factor-analytically derived FFM as having revealed the wisdom encoded in our spoken language. In other words, personality features that were important to daily social life have "trait terms" associated with them. Like Cattell, they believed that factor analysis could statistically extract the "latent" personality features embedded in language and thereby reveal the underlying biological source traits. However, this has yet to be achieved, for that requires kinds of causal/constitutive (rather than just correlational) brain research that, despite the neuroscience revolution, barely exists at the present time.

Their faith in the reality of these language indexed dimensions led McCrae and Costa (1996) to promote the FFM as an answer to the age-old problem of parsing the foundations of human personality. Thereby, they have clearly moved beyond the simply surface descriptive phase of inquiry, into the beginning of neurogenetic and neurobiological explanatory phases, without, however, having provided any roadmap or empirical clues on how such levels of explanation might be achieved. Outside of genetic heritability (Loehlin, 1992), supporting biological evidence for the FFM has come largely from modern brain neuroimaging studies, the specifics of which have sometimes been inconclusive or contradictory (as we discuss further in Chapter 16). However, brain regions frequently implicated have been cortical structures, such as the prefrontal areas, and basal ganglia structures, such as the amygdala (Canli, 2006; Mincic, 2015), which together would focus on tertiary and secondary rather than primary processes.

Researchers taking a more direct and less inferential approach are those pursuing linkages between brain, behavior, genetic, and psychological variables (Montag et al., 2013; Weaver, 2014; Weissman, Naidu, & Bjornsson, 2014). However, with the genetic-linkage analyses, which are currently proceeding ever more rapidly and efficiently (because of the vast armamentarium of modern genetic tools), the issue of how the sources of heritability will need to be linked to actual brain systems is just beginning to be addressed (e.g., Montag et al., 2013). Until the emergence of cross-species emotional neuroscience (Panksepp 1982, 1998a), the specific BrainMind emotional origins of these five factors had remained elusive.

In sum, the personality structure erected by McCrae and Costa has so far remained a surface analysis that rests largely on their trust in the factor analysis of linguistic descriptors, with the conviction that the more fundamental evidence will emerge with future research. Obviously, that will be a neuropsychologically complex story that will require a synthesis of critical lines of human and animal research. Although not yet widely recognized, animal brain research is critical for deep progress. At the very least, it will require a scientific understanding of the basic evolutionarily constructed "Darwinian" emotions that are best illuminated by cross-mammalian brain emotion studies. How those neuromental functions interact with the higher cognitive apparatus (especially language), at this point in scientific history, most critically requires deeper and deeper understanding of brain research, particularly those aspects that are shared homologously (by shared genetic factors) between humans and other animals.

Five Factors and Looking Forward to the Neurobiological Foundations of Personality

Factor analysis is a wonderful tool. However, like someone once said, if your only tool is a hammer, every problem looks like a nail. If factor analysis is the only tool for exploring personality, are we limited to explaining personality with tightly intercorrelating clusters of items that lend themselves to factor analysis? Or should factor analysis be used as the tool it really is, to simply help guide systematic research, with the caveat that there may not always be a one-to-one correspondence between statistically derived factors, based on the analysis of language, and biological systems that actually control our experiences—our diverse feelings, perceptions, and thoughts?

Like Cattell, Costa and McCrae seem to have leaped far ahead of the evidence, postulating inherited biologically based dimensions relying mainly on statistical criteria. In addition to the five factors measured by their revised NEO-PI personality assessment (Costa & McCrae, 1985), they included six narrow "facets" for each of the five higher level dimensions, reporting thirty facets altogether, and have suggested that the "psychological literature . . . provides a rich source of conceptualizations for specific facets of each of the five domains" (McCrae & Costa, 1996, p. 62). While there may easily be thirty facets operating at the tertiary level of the human personality, we believe it is unlikely that the neocortex creates new facets on its own without support from the subcortical emotional core for the "feelings" of existence that we share with the other animals.

Thus, is it really possible to "carve nature at its joints" statistically-without examining the organism itself, as is beginning to be done with cross-species affective neuroscience approaches? We propose that the foundational neuroscience of the mammalian brain is revealing the primal emotional processes that need to be understood in order to help personality theory take the next big step toward understanding the neurobiological foundations of some of the most important affective under-pinnings of human personality. We believe Goldberg was right: The Big Five is best thought of as a phenotypic, descriptive system rather than the genotypic, explanatory theory some would like it to be. We believe that affective neuroscience strategies have already provided some of the likely neurobiological foundations of personality that are currently missing from the five statistically derived personality dimensions.

It was probably inevitable that the lexical hypothesis would produce overly abstract traits. Is language itself not an abstraction? Yet, if Charles Darwin, Paul MacLean, and all the comparative affective neuroscientists that followed have taught us anything, it is that emotions appeared in the animal world long before spoken language. Why should we be surprised that our tertiary-level words, when statistically clustered, sometimes represent only metaphorical approximations of the primary-level capacities with which we confront the world and thereby experience evolved emotional qualia in various life contexts?

It may be that the Big Five attribute model does a reasonably good job with Extraversion (gregarious "hanging out," an elaboration of the PLAY/Joy emotional brain system), Agreeableness (kindness and warmth, the affects of CARE/Nurturance on the positive pole), the regulatory trait of Conscientiousness, and even Openness to Experience (curiosity and enthusiasm emerging from the SEEKING system). However, language and the Big Five seem quite inadequate when describing our capacity to experience powerful negative emotions, which are commonly transitory but which can become crystallized as affective ways of being in the world: RAGE/Anger, FEAR/Anxiety, and PANIC/Sadness. At present, the Big Five/FFM simply lumps these three affectively negative emotions together as forms of Emotional Instability. It seems unacceptable to relegate anger, fear, and separation distress as mere FFM "facets" of Neuroticism/(low) Emotional Stability, especially given the suffering (antecedent to diverse psychopathologies) created when any one of them becomes overly sensitized or imbalanced. Surely our anger and frustration, our fears and anxieties, and our social pains and distresses deserve as rich an assessment, as primal personality dimensions, as our various positive emotional systems. To emphasize their subcortical and prelanguage origins, all of these primal emotions in animal models survive removal of the upper brain (neodecortication).

The reason for the factor-analytic clustering of the negative emotions into a single factor is not clear. It could have to do with multiple negative emotions occurring simultaneously and not always coming in neat, isolated bundles. A good example comes from Don Klein's research on panic attacks (Preter & Klein, 2008). Even after medication (e.g., the tricyclic antidepressant imipramine) had stopped the occurrence of the panic attacks, his patient reported little relief (Klein, 1981). It was only

after the anticipatory "fear" of having another panic attack was eliminated that the patient felt a complete sense of relief—of having been
"cured" of those sudden lapses of a sense of social security that good
social attachments provide. A similar example came from a friend who
said that she was afraid her mother was going to die, which combined
the fear about how difficult life would be without her mother's help
with the anticipation of the separation distress she would also experience without her mother's companionship. It may be that two negative
emotions become combined in this way, with the negative emotions
augmenting each other and building an overall tertiary (upper brain),
negativistic state of mind, which can be difficult to sort out later in rational, descriptive terms. In other words, the neocortex, which cannot
generate emotional feelings by itself, may operate in a more general
dimensional (positive vs. negative) affective way, while lower BrainMind
regions have more categorical emotional systems. It may also be that
humans have various strong negative emotional experiences before we
are old enough to possess adequate language and the conscious awareness to express the distinct feelings clearly to ourselves and others.

These are among many possibilities, but regardless, we are left with
a major limitation of the lexically and hence factor-analytically derived
Big Five/FFM as an overall *theory* of personality. While it is apparent
that the unique primary emotions of RAGE/Anger, FEAR/Anxiety, and
PANIC/Sadness are supported by some overlapping systems (e.g., for
acetylcholine, norepinephrine, and serotonin neuromodulators), they
are also functionally separable brain systems (using various neuropeptides), which have differentiable effects on our behaviors and feelings
and thereby promote the solidification of different personality traits. As
we have already seen, each generates distinct psychopathological trajectories, such as explosive disorders, specific phobias, generalized anxiety,
depression, and panic attacks, the fear of which may promote chronic
anticipatory anxiety. Thus, these powerful and discrete primary negative
emotions are unsatisfactorily lumped together in the Big Five as a lack
of Emotional Stability. We now need new brain-based organizational
visions such as affective neuroscience provides, to generate diverse
objective criteria for the causal parsing of some of Cattell's source traits
and thereby bringing more neurobiological specificity and conceptual
order to the Big Five model.

We have finally reached a time when neuroscientific knowledge is
rich enough to begin taking the next major steps in understanding the
mental forces that govern personality development. Thus, it may be best
to appreciate Big Five theorizing for its highly rigorous level of *descriptive* utility than to try to make it into a major *explanatory* personality
theory in its own right. Affective neuroscience provides a clear trajectory for taking new steps in that direction and thereby expanding the

Big Five model into a more comprehensive coherent psychobiological representation of human personality, hopefully, one that can link more effectively towards understanding psychiatric disorders. In sum, providing clearer visions of our genetically derived, brain-emotional "tools for living" may allow personality theories to become ever more closely linked to variations in our genetic heritage. Furthermore, our emerging understanding of fundamental affective-emotional brain systems holds the potential of providing a new set of objective standards for *carving the foundational nature of personality at its affective joints* and thereby further illuminating what it means to be human.

CHAPTER 13

The Clarities and Confusions of the Big Five

We have met the enemy and he is us.
—Pogo (Walt Kelly, Pogo cartoonist)[7]

BIG FIVE PERSONALITY THEORY, as discussed in preceding chapters, is clearly a top-down, verbal, tertiary-level approach to understanding personality. It is openly based on the lexical hypothesis that all important human behavior has already been well described in human language, especially adjectives, and that personality can be fathomed by the clustering of these descriptors of human mental states. This chapter deals with developments in this top-down statistical approach to personality since Lewis Goldberg's research that effectively established the Big Five as the most robust human personality model (Goldberg, 1990, 1992).

Given the statistical and language basis of the top-down generated Big Five, it is perhaps not surprising that variants of the Big Five model would eventually emerge. Several of these alternates are briefly reviewed here, to show that there are chinks in what once appeared to be the solid armor of the Big Five, and that increasing numbers of top-down researchers no longer see the Big Five model as a final solution to the human "personality problem." What seemed to be a robust, almost unassailable theory of personality—the Big Five—has become more like a ball of yarn that is gradually unrolling. Challenging the Big Five's hegemony are claims for a Big Two, a Big Three, two different Big Six models, a Big Seven, and even a Big One (Saucier & Srivastava, 2015).

Even though this development may seem a bit bizarre, since the era of Raymond Cattell (see Chapter 12) and Hans Eysenck (see Chapter 14), there have been other personality models with more than or fewer than five dimensions (e.g., Douglas Jackson's Personality Research Form, and

Robert Cloninger's Tridimensional Personality Questionnaire described later in Chapter 14). What is different about the studies featured here is that, like Goldberg, these researchers also used adjectives to generate their competing personality models. However, as we describe here, these new personality models were often "discovered" by using variations in the sets of trait-descriptive terms used by Goldberg in his seminal Big Five work.

As one might imagine, given each of the various tertiary top-down approaches, small differences in language and culture can come strongly into play. Although we do not take sides on these controversies, we do note that all variants of the Big Five have led to conclusions based on statistically obtained clusters in adjectival measures of human personality. From the language analysis perspective, it is pretty obvious that trait-descriptive adjectives and nouns, including words that described highly consistent patterns, were sustained in all human languages. Thus, these approaches are by no means theory-free. They are simply capitalizing on how different human groups at different times used such descriptors. Our only aim here is to briefly review what, from our perspective, are the more significant new challenges confronting the once monolithic five-factor solution to human personality assessment.

While the Big Five descriptive personality model, first based on English language studies, had been replicated across several other languages, including Dutch, German, French, and Turkish (Saucier & Goldberg, 2006; Goldberg & Somer, 2000), other studies also began to emerge that questioned the universality of the Big Five model. Hungarian (Szirmak & De Raad, 1994) and Italian (Di Blas & Forzi, 1998) studies first pointed to a six-factor personality structure. Later, a paper by Michael Ashton et al. (2004) consolidated evidence for a six-factor model in seven different languages: In addition to the Hungarian and Italian work, Dutch, French, German, Korean, and Polish studies also found six factors.

The major difference between Ashton's six-factor model and the Big Five (summarized in Table 13.1) was the emergence of a sixth factor they labeled Honesty/Humility, which later provided the "H" in their six-factor HEXACO Personality Inventory (Lee & Ashton, 2012). The Honesty/Humility dimension was basically Conscientiousness with morality features. In fact, Ashton suggested that Morality could be an alternate name for this extra factor (Ashton et al., 2004). The new Honesty/Humility factor included adjectives such as *honest/dishonest* and *truthful/untruthful*, among others, whereas the Conscientiousness factor retained adjectives such as *orderly, careful*, and *disciplined* versus *careless* and *negligent* (Ashton et al., 2004).

Goldberg had previously included the adjectives *honest, moral*, and *truthful* in an Honesty/Morality cluster of adjectives, along with *dishonest* in a Deceit cluster, all of which were derived from Warren Norman's earlier work. Yet, these clusters did not load especially strongly in Goldberg's reported Big Five factor structure (Goldberg, 1990). Furthermore, Goldberg did not include any of these key adjectives in his lists of one hundred Big Five unipolar or fifty bipolar adjective markers (Goldberg, 1992). The adjective *moral* was included in the 540 adjectives used in the classic paper on adjectives that statistically "blended" qualities of more than one Big Five dimension, but *moral* loaded only weakly as a blend of Agreeableness and Conscientiousness (Hofstee et al., 1992). By contrast, *honest* was the most frequent high-loading Honesty/Humility adjective in the studies cited by Ashton et al. (2004), appearing in six of the seven translations, *truthful/untruthful* appeared in four of the seven translations they studied.

Overall, Goldberg included less than 40 percent of the Honesty/Humility adjectives typically appearing in the translations cited by Ashton et al. (2004). It is possible that the increased sampling from the Honesty/Humility space in these other studies was crucial for the emergence of this new factor. Indeed, this paucity of Honesty/Humility adjectives in Goldberg's Big Five work, compared to Ashton's, is reminiscent of Jack Block's (1995) critique of the Big Five, in which he noted that changing the variables in a factor analysis is likely to change the factor structure.

This discussion is not intended to be critical of Ashton et al.'s (2004) fine reanalysis and synthesis of the personality reports covering these seven languages. It seems very likely that honesty and humility are human traits that are valued in many different cultures. However, we are trying to illustrate the kinds of issues that begin appearing when starting with a tertiary top-down as opposed to a primary bottom-up approach to identifying basic personality dimensions.

OTHER "BIG" MODELS AROSE FROM THE SELECTION OF ADJECTIVES

Adding to this personality dimension conundrum, as mentioned previously, is a competing six-factor model offered by Gerard Saucier (2009) that emerged from an even different set of adjective descriptor studies (see Table 13.1). But before delving further, a short digression is needed to explain more about how different researchers have selected the adjectives for lexical personality research.

While some credit Sir Francis Galton as the first person to publish work on the lexical hypothesis (Goldberg, 1990), the systematic categorization of English-language adjectives as personality descriptors really began in earnest with Gordon Allport and Henry Odbert (1936). From the 1925 edition of *Webster's Unabridged New International Dictionary*, these investigators compiled a list of 17,953 words that were descriptive of personality or personal behavior. They placed their words

Table 13.1. Summary of Four Lexically Derived Personality Models			
Goldberg: Big Five	**Ashton: Narrow Big Six**	**Saucier: Wide Big Six**	**Tellegen & Waller, Goldberg & Somer: Big Seven**
Extraversion	Extraversion	Extraversion	Positive Emotionality
Agreeableness	Agreeableness (more anger)	Agreeableness	Agreeableness
Conscientiousness	Conscientiousness (not moral)	Conscientiousness	Dependability
Emotional Stability	Emotionality (negative)(less anger)	Resiliency versus Internalizing Negative Emotionality	Negative Emotionality
Openness to Experience	Intellect / Imagination / Unconventional	Originality / Talent / Positive Valence	Conventionality
—	Honesty / Humility	Negative Valence	Negative Valence
—	—	—	Positive Valence / Attractiveness

alphabetically in four columns, with each column corresponding to a specific category.

Column I included what they considered to be the "real traits" of personality that described stable and consistent behavior. such as *aggressive, introverted*, and *sociable*. Column II contained more "temporary states, current activities, and moods," such as *rejoicing, frantic*, and *annoyed*. Column III was reserved for evaluative words implying "social judgment," such as *worthy, coarse*, and *crude*. Column IV contained words describing "physical appearance as well as personal capacities and talents," such as *slender, pale, gifted*, and *athletic*. While Allport and Odbert clearly felt that the 4,504 adjectives in Column I were the best descriptors for stable personality characteristics, they did not consider their placements absolute and did not discourage others from exploring the other columns for additional words. And herein lies the problem with the lexical hypothesis: Different investigators have used different criteria for selecting the trait terms they choose to study as they rely on factor analysis to extract personality dimensions. In other words, experimenter choices, rather than independent criteria, are guiding ultimate research outcomes. Importantly, the Big Five typically emerges from a narrower set of mostly Column I descriptors.

In his classic 1990 paper cited by over fourteen hundred other pub-
lications, Goldberg (1990) wanted to be more inclusive than Cattell and
did include many more adjectives. Still, Goldberg had used a narrower
set of adjectives, with most of his 1,431 trait terms coming from Allport
and Odbert's neutral Column I. However, in every factor even Goldberg included exceptions, especially in the small fifth factor (Intellect/
Culture), in which seven of the twenty-eight words he used as examples were from Column III (social judgment) or Column IV (physical
appearance or capacities). The seven non-English-language studies that
Ashton et al. (2004) reanalyzed also largely followed narrower trait-term
selection criteria but sampled more broadly from the honesty-humility
domain. In other words, what you choose to include in your personality
assessment has a powerful effect on what you will find. So how does
one know what to include?

AND THE PLOT THICKENS

Gerard Saucier's (2009) alternative six-factor model was drawn from
studies in seven other languages (Chinese, English, Filipino, Greek,
Hebrew, Spanish, and Turkish) that sampled even more widely from
the domain of potential personality attributes. These studies tended to
use more trait terms from the temporary states of Column II such as
angry, and *frustrated*, and the social evaluations of Column III, such as
charming, dangerous, and *disgusting.* Saucier (2009) labeled these the
"wideband" lexical studies and referred to the group of studies used, for
example, by Ashton et al. (2004), as "narrowband" (see Table 13.1)

Saucier (2009) reexamined the eight wideband studies (two were in
English) and determined that, while six factors might be optimal for summarizing these studies, the wideband six factors did not completely replicate the narrowband six-factor model reported by Ashton et al. (2004):
The main differences were (1) a Negative Valence factor—with adjectives like *cruel, corrupt, disgusting,* and *wicked*—replaced Ashton et al.'s
Honest/Humility factor, (2) the Emotionality factor from the narrower
selection of adjectives had morphed into a Resiliency versus Internaliz-
ing Negative Emotionality factor when more evaluative trait terms like
cowardly, depressed, fearful, frustrated, gloomy, and *sad* were added,
and (3) the more traditional Intellect/Imagination factor from Ashton
et al.'s narrowband six-factor model broadened out to include more
positive-valence terms, such as *impressive, outstanding,* and *admirable,*
with fewer terms like *creative.* While there were other more minor differences between the two six-factor models, Saucier concluded that the
Big Six model would emerge differently depending on whether narrow
or wider selection criteria were used to select the trait terms, but that

in either form "the Big Six seems a more cross-culturally valid starting point than the Big Five" (2009, p. 1609).

However, Saucier also conceded that neither version of the Big Six represented a universal personality model: "The [six-factor] structure has not appeared identically in all studies in all languages. Its latent pattern can be detected across the 16 lexical studies reviewed here and by Ashton et al. (2004), but this pattern seems prone to have pieces missing in many single studies" (2009, p. 1609). In spite of Saucier's herculean effort, the language and cultural differences expressed across these lexical studies epitomize the difficulty of identifying universal personality dimensions from the top-down, tertiary, human-language starting point.

BACK TO SCIENTIFIC "BASICS": NARROWING THE FIELD ONCE MORE

The Turkish paper Saucier reexamined deserves some closer attention. Goldberg and Somer (2000) had started from scratch and broadly selected 2,200 person-descriptive adjectives from Turkish dictionaries. They narrowed their list to 1,300 adjectives by excluding many physical characteristics such as *tall* and *thin*, mere evaluations such as *good* or *bad*, and special abilities such as *good dancer*, and then further reduced the list to a manageable 498 by selecting those adjectives with the highest familiarity ratings. They concluded that seven factors best accounted for their 498-adjective data set. Each of the Big Five factors was present: Extraversion, Agreeableness, Conscientious, Emotional Stability, and Intellect (Openness to Experience). However, their set also included a Negative Valence factor and an Attractiveness factor to complete their seven factors. Notably, no Honesty/Humility factor emerged.

However, Goldberg and Somer next simulated a narrower, more restrictive item pool by eliminating terms that described physical appearance, such as *eye-catching*; one person's effect on another, such as *influential*; and words that raters rarely used to describe themselves or others, such as *idiotic*, *immoral*, *dirty*, and *uncivilized*. The factor analysis of the remaining 440 personality terms yielded a clear Big Five structure, with no additional interpretable factors.

As it turned out, they had replicated work in English that had largely identified the same seven factors from an alternate wider selection of personality descriptors (Tellegen & Waller, 1987; see below), as well as the Big Five when the adjectives were more narrowly restricted. They had also provided evidence that, even in a language as remote from English and German as Turkish, indigenous trait terms can be independently selected and a Big Five personality structure can be derived "when the item pools were restricted to terms that are less pejorative and more clearly related to personality traits" (Goldberg & Somer, 2000, p. 523). Otherwise, additional dimensions such as Negative Valence and Attractiveness are likely to emerge from the more evaluative descriptors.

ONE MORE MODEL: THE BIG SEVEN

But the question remains: Using a top-down approach, how does one know what set of adjectives to use? Tellegen and Waller (1987), opted for a purposely nonrestrictive selection of trait terms originally sourced from *The American Heritage Dictionary* and reported what they named the Big Seven personality model due to the similarity of five of their dimensions to the Big Five. However, their additional two dimensions were Negative Valence and Positive Valence, the latter replacing the Attractiveness factor found in the Turkish study (Goldberg & Somer, 2000) and in an English language study by Saucier (1997). (This also raises the issue of how to distinguish "valence" and "emotionality" in these lexical studies.)

In another study using Spanish translations of a reduced set of the ten best marker terms from each of the Big Seven factors, Benet and Waller (1995) replicated the Big Seven model in Spanish, as well as across self and peer ratings. They argued that these negative and positive valence dimensions were not statistical or response-set artifacts but were stable measures of self-image that could be observed in nonclinical as well as clinical populations. In clinical samples, borderline or narcissistic personality disorders reflected extreme forms of negative and positive self-evaluations, respectively.

However, a more ambitious attempt to replicate the Big Seven in Hebrew using a nonrestrictive set of 252 trait terms drawn from a Hebrew dictionary (Almagor, Tellegen, & Waller, 1995) was not able to replicate the seven dimensions in their original factor analysis. They were only able to identify seven factors, including Conventionality, after identifying eight Hebrew Conventionality marker terms (*erotic, sexual, unruly, liberal, individualist, permissive, naughty,* and *sensual*) and factor analyzing those with the sixty strongest markers from the other six factors, although none of their eight Conventionality markers matched the markers reported by Benet and Waller (1995).

All this may start to sound like a Tower of "Babble" for readers not initiated in academic nitpicking. In any event, Table 13.1 summarizes the four lines of research discussed above and will, hopefully, alleviate any confusion.

In discussing the results of the Greek language study, which as in the Turkish and Hebrew studies started by gleaning descriptive terms from dictionaries, Saucier, Goldberg, and colleagues suggested that "the present results are not very supportive of the cross-cultural generalizability of [personality] structures at the five- to seven-factor level" (Saucier, Georgiades, Tsaousis, & Goldberg, 2005, p. 867) and even went so far as to suggest that while all the various lexical models "are variations within some underlying scheme. It may be that factor analysis does not directly reveal this underlying scheme" (Saucier et al., 2005, p. 870).

DENOUEMENT: PULLING THE THREADS OF THIS SHAKESPEARIAN "RAVELL'D SLEEVE OF CARE"

In a sense the overall results from the many factor analyses is a nightmare. Has the mathematical method that Cattell dreamed would resolve the personality dimensions dilemma run aground on its own glacial scree? Are human languages too far removed from our primary mammalian personality sources? Is it possible that starting from the top-down using a tertiary language approach even modern computers capable of probing immense databases incorporating hundreds of people rating themselves or colleagues on hundreds of trait terms cannot parse universal features of the human BrainMind? Interestingly, after discussing the value of adjective trait terms for describing personality, Allport and Odbert (1936) offered a prescient caveat, suggesting as much:

> There is, unfortunately for scientific psychology, a second influence determining our lexicon of trait-names, namely the tendency of each epoch to characterize human qualities in the light of standards and interests peculiar to the times. Historically, the introduction of trait-names can be seen to follow this principle of cultural (not psychological) determination to a striking degree. Presumably human beings through countless ages had displayed such qualities as devotion, pity, and patience, but these terms were not established with their present meanings until the Church made of them recognized and articulated Christian virtues. (p. 2)

While they had focused exclusively on potential issues with the English lexicon, this quote strongly suggests there would be even greater problems attempting to establish lexical universals across a wide variety of cultures and languages, which is exactly what seems to be playing out.

By contrast, the bottom-up cross-species approach has provided an elegant parsing of evolutionarily adaptive emotional instincts that are common to all mammals. The BrainMind allows relatively crude subcortical prods (deep brain stimulation) to inform us what well-organized adaptive systems it contains. The bottom-up DBS approach, which comports well with the natural emotional behaviors we see in the real world, supplies us a view of the most basic affective personality spaces, which is not only a real-life starting point for all humans but also remains visible and accessible throughout the human life-span, even as language and culture shape personality into more complex tertiary spaces, heavily influenced by individual learning and culture. We must accept that such complex tertiary personality spaces come to be strongly influenced by cultural learning, which also exerts abundant top-down cortical inhibition and arousal of emotions and behavior, especially in humans. This is what developmental maturation is all about.

How you behave and respond to others has enormous influences on your success as an individual—both reproductive and cultural. However, our comprehension of that tertiary complexity is likely to be limited profoundly until we appreciate the foundational importance of primary-emotional and other affective spaces in navigating interpersonal affairs. Might it not be that the emotional affects need to be understood first to gain a lasting and coherent vision of what it means to have a distinct personality? As these affective powers, along with influences arising from our bodily homeostatic needs and sensory feelings (perhaps comparatively minor in rich life-supportive environments), guide our progress, might we see a more coherent foundation for our personality structures? The major goal of this book is to share that affirmative vision, which can easily work across species, and even inform (and be informed by) studies of our genetic nature. In so doing, we may better see the deep structure of the Big Five.

CHAPTER 14

The Earlier History of Biological Theories of Personality

Hans Eysenck, Jeffrey Gray, and Robert Cloninger

We are what we feel and perceive.
If we are angry, we are the anger.
If we are in love, we are the love.
If we look at a snowy mountain peak, we are the mountain.
While dreaming, we are the dream.
> —Thich Nhat Hanh, *Silence: The Power of Quiet in a World Full of Noise*

FEW OF THE PERSONALITY THEORIES we have reviewed so far and compared to our affective neuroscience theory of personality have delved deeply into brain sources of personality variability. Some have offered speculations, but few have attempted to integrate neuroscientific thinking into their theories. In this chapter we briefly review the work of three eminent scientists who made serious efforts to not just name and describe personality traits but to consider the possible underlying neural substrates of human personality differences. We highlight the work of Hans Eysenck, who spent most of his career as professor of psychology at the Institute of Psychiatry, King's College London, and his most eminent colleague and student, Jeffrey Gray, who added the first modern neuroscientific dimensions to emotion theorizing, and conclude with the seminal work of Robert Cloninger at Washington University in St. Louis, who focused on possible neurochemical substrates of human personality. As we share the revolutionary flavor of their work, we also contrast their seminal contributions to our affective neuroscience approach.

HANS EYSENCK

Hans Eysenck (1916–1997) was born in Germany during the First World War and emigrated to England after refusing to join the German military during the tragic events leading to the Second World War. He received his Ph.D. in psychology in 1940 from the University College London and, as fate would have it, began his career in a WWII British emergency hospital treating psychiatric casualties. He was an early advocate of diagnosing psychiatric patients using psychological dimensions rather than distinct categories based on symptom states—a battle he fought with the psychiatric powers on the European side of the Atlantic. So, it is not surprising that much of his career focused on delineating psychological characteristics, which he surmised were foundational for human personality.

His approach was similar to Raymond Cattell's (see Chapter 12) in that he utilized factor analysis, which was increasingly popular at the time. However, he deviated from Cattell by shifting his emphasis from factor-analytically identified "traits" (Cattell's source traits) to higher-order superfactors derived from the lower-order traits (Eysenck, 1990). Eysenck called these higher-order factors "types" and over his career identified three, Extraversion, Neuroticism, and Psychoticism, which had considerable impact on psychiatric theorizing.

Eysenck also differed from Cattell in his source of theoretical ideas. While Cattell used many Freudian concepts, Eysenck was influenced by Pavlov. In his 1957 book *The Dynamics of Anxiety and Hysteria*, Eysenck offered Pavlov's idea of "excitation versus inhibition" in the nervous system as the basis of Introversion versus Extraversion, with introverts being characterized by more excitatory neural processes and more sensitive to sensory overload than extraverts. As the basis of his Neuroticism, Eysenck adopted Pavlov's idea of nervous system "mobility," which was the ability of the nervous system to give one impulse priority over another. In other words, Eysenck was the first to robustly link personality theorizing to the emerging neuroscientific revolution that embraced the systematic experimental study of behavior.

In 1967 Eysenck amended his theory, adding his third personality dimension, Psychoticism-Socialization, reporting that higher levels of testosterone were associated with lower levels of socialization and higher psychoticism. He also slightly adjusted his definitions of Extraversion and Neuroticism by suggesting that the ascending reticular activation system controlled the cortical arousal characteristic of Introversion-Extroversion differences, and that the emerging limbic system concept along with the sympathetic nervous system accounted for how human personalities were influenced by an underlying Neuroticism-Stability dimension. He also reported twin studies that further convinced him that biological causes played an important part in personality.

Eysenck may be most easily summarized as an early variant of the Big Five model discussed in Chapter 12. At his higher-order level, he accepted the Big Five Extraversion and Neuroticism dimensions. However, he argued that his Psychoticism dimension was a combination of the Big Five Agreeableness and Conscientiousness factors. He did not include the fifth Big Five factor, Openness to Experience, because he regarded it as a cognitive rather than a personality dimension. He later published the Eysenck Personality Questionnaire (Eysenck & Eysenck, 1975), which focused on empirically measuring his three psychiatrically focused personality dimensions: Extraversion, Neuroticism, and Psychoticism.

Although Eysenck's reliance on factor analysis places his thinking in more of a top-down than a bottom-up category, he consistently emphasized the importance of psychological science linking his thinking to neuroscientific foundations of personality. In a paper debating how many basic human personality factors actually existed, Eysenck cited the "need for a nomological or theoretical network to accompany and be part of any model. Only thus can we avoid the problems of subjectivity and the possibilities of misinterpretations attaching to the conceptualization and naming of factors" (1992, p. 670). Further on he wrote, "We need to anchor our dimensions of personality in something more concrete than the morass of factor analysis, and biology supplies us with the necessary tools" (p. 672). Had he considered affective neuroscience perspectives and the dramatic emotional consequences of deep brain stimulation, he likely would have further modified his ideas about the biological bases of personality, a step that was taken by his most illustrious student.

JEFFREY GRAY

Jeffrey Alan Gray (1934–2004) was born in London. He did not begin his studies in psychology, receiving his first university degree in modern languages before beginning graduate studies. He was also trained in Russian during his British national military service and translated the work of Russian psychologist Boris Teplov into English for Eysenck while working as his graduate student.

In contrast to Eysenck, Gray began with a more bottom-up perspective. He completed his dissertation on emotional behavior in animals, and much of his life's research dealt with diverse physiological influences on learning behavior in rats. He believed that the "reinforce-

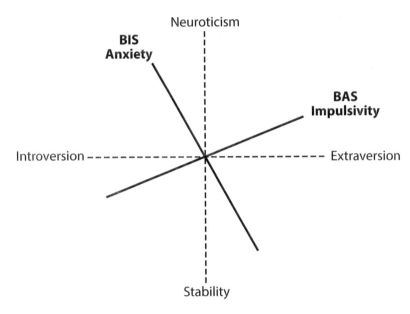

Figure 14.1. Geometrical factor alignment of Gray's behavioral activation system (BAS) and behavioral inhibition system (BIS).

ment contingencies" encountered by animals created emotions (see Gray, 1990), a view that was countered by the suggestion that shifts in emotional and other affective feelings constituted the construct of "reinforcement" (Panksepp, 1990b). From his perspective, and building upon Eysenck's seminal thoughts, he postulated that the brain has a basic Behavioral Activation System and a countervailing Behavioral Inhibition Systems.

While he built on Eysenck's factorial studies of neuroticism and extraversion, Gray argued that a geometric shift in Eysenck's model was needed to properly account for the two major personality dimensions Gray proposed: a behavioral inhibition system (BIS) that gave rise to anxiety and a behavioral approach system (BAS) that engendered impulsivity (see Figure 14.1). Gray contended the BIS and BAS constructs did not line up directly with Eysenck's extraversion and neuroticism dimensions. Gray's anxiety dimension fell between high neuroticism and low extraversion but inclined more toward neuroticism. Likewise, impulsivity aligned between high extraversion and high neuroticism, inclining more toward extraversion, as illustrated in Figure 14.1 (Gray, 1970; Corr, Pickering, & Gray, 1997). Gray argued that extraversion and neuroticism were derived from impulsivity and anxiety, which were their fundamental neurophysiological bases. In 1994, Carver and White gave a boost to research into Gray's theory by constructing personality scales to measure his hypothesized BAS and BIS systems.

In laying out his theory, Gray also deviated from classical learning theory by asserting that there was not just a single reinforcement mechanism but two: BAS reflected sensitivity to rewards, and BIS, sensitivity to punishments. However, from an affective neuroscience perspective there are many distinct reward and punishment systems: positively and negatively valenced affects manifest by the primary emotions that are closely related to personality, but there are also the homeostatic affects such as HUNGER that have been so widely utilized in rat learning research. Indeed, these powerful brain-based emotional command systems can also be thought of as evolved learning systems that facilitate ongoing adaptation to our specific environments. In other words, the shifting tides of many positive and negative affective systems constituted what behaviorists had become accustomed to calling "reinforcement" processes in the brain (Panksepp, 1990b), and to understand the affective foundations of personality one has to focus on more affective systems than just the BAS and BIS.

From Gray's learning theory perspective, the reward and punishment systems were each unidimensional. Yet, each of seven primary emotional-adaptation systems of affective neuroscience may possess different conditioning parameters in the brain, with additional, distinct *homeostatic* affects (e.g., HUNGER or THIRST, etc.) and *sensory* affects (various pains and pleasures). However, only the emotional affects are major contributors to personality development, even as they share many of the general brain chemistries for learning, such as glutamate and gamma-aminobutyric acid (GABA). For example, the SEEKING system is more of a general anticipatory reward system, whereas the CARE system may be more of a maternal-social reward system. The PLAY system may be a social emotional system that is especially robust during childhood, with some neurochemistries that are distinct from CARE and LUST. In addition, the PANIC/Sadness system may have acquired addictive-like qualities (being very strongly modulated by brain opioids), which would make its extinction patterns different from those of the FEAR system. As each of these primary emotions are thought to have evolved for distinct survival issues, serving different purposes at different times in our ancestral past, it is likely their learning parameters were evolutionarily adjusted to meet unique survival needs as well. Moreover, the development of the Affective Neuroscience Personality Scales was motivated by the need for personality psychologists to measure each of the distinct primary emotions that are most closely related to personality and psychopathology and to provide an assessment of their relative strengths and weaknesses in an individual's life. Although both Eysenck and Gray emphasized the need for personality studies to focus on brain issues, a sufficient analysis of core mammalian affects was not evident in either Eysenck's or Gray's theorizing.

In 2000, Gray and McNaughton published a revision of Gray's theory. In the revised reward sensitivity theory, the BAS remained largely unchanged. However, the BIS assumed responsibility for goal conflict resolution and became a "risk assessment" system: "the 'increased attention' output of the behavioural inhibition system" (p. 20). While the BIS once accounted for all punishment, in the revised theory it retained only its anxiety function, which was distinct from fear. Yet, BIS anxiety also included "separation anxiety" (p. 91), which was considered a childhood phenomenon and was not given any special status as in the affective neuroscience PANIC/Sadness system. Specifically, in the modified BIS, anxiety was generated by neural processing not only in the septal-hippocampal circuitry but also in the cingulate and prefrontal cortices. A proposed new brain system, the fight-flight-fear system, dealt with all defensive behavior, including fear. So, one of the more controversial positions taken by Gray and McNaughton (2000) was that fear and anxiety represented different brain systems and what we would call PANIC/Sadness was included with BIS anxiety. From our perspective, the natural emotional systems of mammalian brains were not adequately integrated into the revisions of the BAS and BIS.

Joseph LeDoux (1994) has shown that the amygdala is clearly linked to both fear and anxiety. Further, while the hippocampus provides cognitive-spatial information related to fear conditioning, it is not needed for the threat-evoked affective experiences of anxiety or fear. Others have also found that deep brain stimulation in the periaqueductal gray can generate alertness (corresponding to risk assessment and increased anxious attention), freezing, or fleeing in animal models, depending on the strength of the electrical current (Vianna, Landeira-Fernandez, & Brandão, 2001). This also applies to humans. For instance, Dean Mobbs and colleagues published a brain imaging study in humans that simulated a predator attack (Mobbs et al., 2007). They described a single "forebrain-midbrain network, which includes the vmPFC (ventromedial prefrontal cortex) at the lowest level of threat and interacts with the midbrain PAG (periaqueductal gray) as the threat level increases" (p. 1082)—meaning as predator threat is imminent, as opposed to far away, and dread increases (discussed in more detail in Chapter 16). All this is consistent with Panksepp's observations that anticipatory anxiety and raw fear are all part of the same ancient FEAR circuit. Thus, in contrast to Gray's theory, it seems likely that "anxiety" and "risk assessment" in potentially dangerous situations are tapping into the same emotional FEAR circuit that is activated when survival is imminently in jeopardy.

Perhaps when one has worked with deep brain stimulation à la Walter Hess and Jaak Panksepp, it is easier to conceptualize the foundational emotional systems embedded in the subcortical brain than when starting from a learning theory perspective. Furthermore, why not study the behavioral, biological, and psychological mechanisms of each affective brain system separately, rather than lumping all "rewards" together into a single BAS and all "punishments" together into a single BIS or FFFS? That would better allow us to consider specific and general "sensitivities" in each emotional or homeostatic affect system and further refine our definition of mammalian affective space—our genetically endowed sensitivities as well as life-span changes in sensitivities derived from addictive or traumatic experiences.

CLONINGER'S CONTRIBUTIONS: BRIDGING TO NEUROSCIENTIFIC FOUNDATIONS OF PERSONALITY

C. Robert Cloninger (born 1944) is an American psychiatrist and geneticist. He attended medical school at Washington University in St. Louis and has remained with that institution throughout his career. His personality interests and theories may fit more in the clinical tradition of personality theory. With his unified biosocial theory of personality (Cloninger, 1986), Cloninger connected clinical approaches focusing on abnormal human behaviors to the temperamental characteristics found in all humans and to emerging potential linkages to animal research. In other words, like McDougall and Eysenck before him, Cloninger advanced the view that "abnormal" disorders represented extreme cases of the same personality dimensions evident in normal people at more moderate levels (Cloninger, 1987). Thus, in line with Jeffrey Gray's work, Cloninger promoted a view that could be linked to emerging neuropsychological work in animals.

Cloninger's biosocial theory of personality hypothesized that there were three genetically inherited personality traits, which he would later call temperaments: Novelty Seeking, Harm Avoidance, and Reward Dependence, which could be measured with his Tridimensional Personality Questionnaire (TPQ; Cloninger, 1987). With the release of the TPQ, Cloninger included a discussion of how eight clinically diagnosed personality disorders from the *DSM-III* (American Psychiatric Association, 1980) could be described by his three biosocial personality scales. That is, there were eight possible combinations of high or low scores on his three TPQ scales, and he illustrated how combinations of the three biosocial personality traits potentially defined the clinical personality disorders. For example, the Antisocial personality disorder was characterized by high Novelty Seeking, low Harm Avoidance, and low Reward Dependence scores whereas the Histrionic personality disorder was described by high Novelty Seeking, low Harm Avoidance, but high Reward Dependence scores. This underscored Cloninger's belief that the underlying structure of normal personality traits was the same as that for clinically defined behavior disorders. In other words, maladaptive behavior could be placed on the same continua as behavior describing the general population.

Cloninger's Brain Systems

Around the same time, W. John Livesley (1991) was also working on a common model to bridge the divide between the clinical and normal personality worlds (for a fuller treatment, see Chapter 18), but Cloninger went further by hypothesizing that each of his three biosocial personality dimensions reflected variations in different brain systems, which were largely based on the major monoamine neural modulators (Cloninger, 1987) dopamine, serotonin, and norepinephrine (collectively called "biogenic amines") that were receiving massive neuroscience and behavioral/psychological experimental attention in the 1970s and 1980s. Figure 14.2 depicts the chemical structures of dopamine, norepinephrine, and serotonin, all of which are similar small molecules. All monoamines contain one amine group, which for dopamine and norepinephrine is connected to an aromatic benzene ring; serotonin has a more complex "indole" ring structure. We highlight his monoamine theory for historical reasons as current neuroscientific thinking has moved toward more complex/sophisticated views in the last three decades.

Cloninger argued that Novelty Seeking was primarily associated with behavior-activating dopaminergic neurons, with dopaminergic neural projections from the midbrain ventral tegmental area and substantia nigra to the forebrain. The major neural modulator in the Harm Avoidance system was postulated to be serotonin. That system had its roots in the behavior-inhibiting serotonin neurons largely located in raphe nuclei, with projections to the limbic system and the prefrontal cortex. However, Cloninger also noted that benzodiazepines, with actions similar to alcohol, block such learned behavioral inhibition via gamma aminobutyric acid GABA inhibition of serotonergic neurons. Norepinephrine was the major neuromodulator that Cloninger linked with his Reward Dependence system, with major projections from midbrain locus coeruleus to much of the brain, including the neocortex. Reward Dependence functioned as a behavioral maintenance system, with norepinephrine increasing the "signal-to-noise ratio" or salience of relevant stimuli, helping them stand out from those that are less relevant (Cloninger, 1987, pp. 576–577).

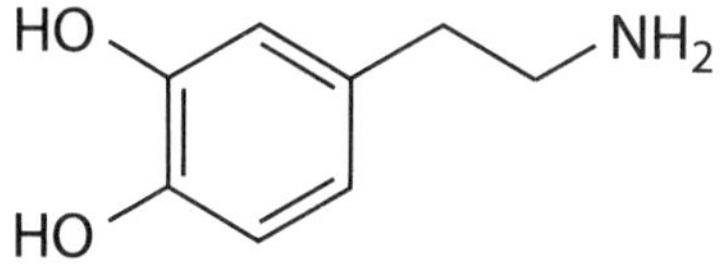

Dopamine

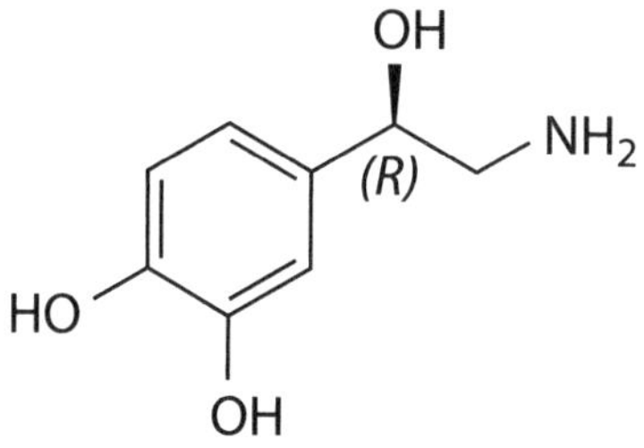

Norepinephrine

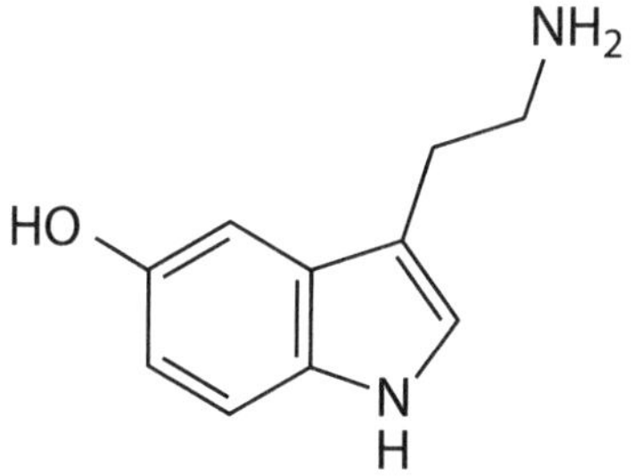

Serotonin

Figure 14.2. Molecular structures of the catecholamines, dopamine and norepinephrine, and the indoleamine, serotonin.

Novelty Seeking

Novelty Seeking represented the dopamine-promoted "heritable tendency toward intense exhilaration or excitement in response to novel stimuli or cues for potential rewards or potential relief of punishment, which leads to frequent exploratory activity in pursuit of potential rewards as well as active avoidance of monotony and potential punishment" (Cloninger, 1987, p. 574). Thus, Cloninger envisioned people characterized by high Novelty Seeking with words like impulsive, exploratory, fickle, excitable, quick-tempered, extravagant, and disorderly, versus those low in Novelty Seeking being described as reflective, rigid, loyal, stoic, slow-tempered, frugal, orderly, and persistent (p. 575). Compared to the Affective Neuroscience Personality Scales (ANPS), Novelty Seeking seems most similar to the SEEKING scale.

Harm Avoidance

Cloninger envisioned Harm Avoidance as the serotonin-promoted "heritable tendency to respond intensely to signals of aversive stimuli, thereby learning to inhibit behavior to avoid punishment, novelty, and frustrative nonreward" (Cloninger, 1987, p. 575). Those characterized by high Harm Avoidance were cautious, tense, apprehensive, fearful, inhibited, shy, easily fatigable, and apprehensive worriers, with low Harm Avoidance types being more confident, relaxed, optimistic, carefree, uninhibited, outgoing, and energetic (p. 576). The Harm Avoidance dimension has many similarities to the ANPS FEAR scale.

Reward Dependence

Cloninger's third biosocial dimension, norepinephrine-mediated Reward Dependence, was the "heritable tendency to respond intensely to signals of reward (particularly verbal signals of social approval, sentiment, and succor), and to maintain or resist extinction of behavior that has previously been associated with rewards or relief from punishment" (Cloninger, 1987, p. 575). He portrayed people who showed high Reward Dependence as "eager to help and please others, persistent, industrious, warmly sympathetic, sentimental, and sensitive to social cues and personal succor but able to delay gratification with the expectation of eventually being rewarded. In contrast, those who are lower than average in Reward Dependence are socially detached, emotionally cool, practical, tough-minded, and emotionally independent in what they choose to do" (576–577). Given a consistent association between the Big Five Extraversion and Reward Dependence (De Fruyt, Van De Wiele, & Van Heeringen, 2000; Zuckerman & Cloninger, 1996), it might be positively correlated with the ANPS PLAY scale. Overall, however, the vast diversity and complexity of brain neurochemical systems (e.g., Panksepp, 2011a) made such "aminergic" simplifications of personality open to debate even at the time they were proposed. Brain biogenic amine systems are surely critical brain arousal foundations of personality, but many other neurochemistries need to be considered in the present era, as well as various learning processes, as Cloninger well recognized.

Neuromodulator Commentary

While Cloninger argued for the dynamic interaction of the three temperaments, his attempts to link each to a major neuromodular—dopamine, serotonin, and norepinephrine—was probably painting with too broad a brush. For example, Ritalin (methylphenidate) as a dopamine stimulant should have a behavioral activation effect. However, counterintuitively, it is widely prescribed to treat hyperactive children and those diagnosed with attention-deficit hyperactive disorder making them less impulsive, with many children reporting feeling less playful and having less fun when taking Ritalin. Panksepp et al. (1984) have shown that, while moderate levels of dopamine must be present for play to occur, high levels of dopamine decrease mammalian play, illustrating the complex role dopamine can have on behavior.

Similarly, serotonin-enhancing drugs are often used as antidepressants. Many selective serotonin reuptake inhibitors (SSRIs), such as Prozac (fluoxetine), Paxil (paroxetine), and Zoloft (sertraline), are used to treat depression and act by retaining serotonin in the neuronal synapse, where it can remain active, which is consistent with Cloninger's predictions. However, the linkage of serotonin levels to Harm Avoidance has received mixed results (Paris, 2005). Further, recent reports suggest that SSRIs are only marginally effective at treating depression (Pigott, Leventhal, Alter, & Boren, 2010). In Chapter 18, we will show how opioids and other pharmaceutical treatments unrelated to the broad neuromodulator serotonin offer the promise of more effective, affectively targeted treatments for depression.

Cloninger Expands His Theory

In good novelty seeking fashion, in 1993 Cloninger, Svrakic, and Przybeck explored new personality dimensions to improve Cloninger's biosocial theory of personality and increased his eighty-item TPQ to include many more items, scales, and scale facets. Cloninger expanded his personality model beyond the biosocial neurotransmitter-based brain systems to a new psychobiological model that included a total of seven personality dimensions. With his new Temperament and Character Inventory (TCI), he also added a fourth "temperament" dimension called Persistence, although he did not provide pharmacological or other biological mechanisms for it. In addition to the temperament traits, he also introduced the concept of "character" dimensions, which he hypothesized to be (1) less genetically heritable, (2) maturing in adulthood rather than in childhood, and (3) influencing personal effectiveness through learning around self-concepts. He called his three new character dimensions Self-Directedness, Cooperativeness, and Self-Transcendence, which were thought of as being more cortical, with his original temperament dimensions being more emotional, controlled by subcortical neural systems. In other words, with the character dimensions, his personality system became considerably more cognitive.

Cloninger conceived of the three character dimensions as corresponding to one of three self-concepts, or "the extent to which a person identifies the self as (1) an autonomous individual, (2) an integral part of humanity or society, or (3) an integral part of the unity of all things" (Cloninger et al., 1993, p. 978). The Self-Directedness scale corresponded to the autonomous individual level. Cooperativeness reflected identifying with humanity. Self-transcendence was related to identifying with the universe as an interdependent whole.

Cloninger also attempted to differentiate between temperament and character dimensions based on the learning and memory systems involved. In addition to expressing inherited behavior biases, temperament personality dimensions relied on presemantic perceptual learning that basically reflected associative learning or classical and operant conditioning. This elementary level of learning required no conscious awareness and was closely related to the concepts of procedural or implicit memory (Bachevalier, 1990).

The character personality dimensions theoretically reflected conscious experiences and learning abstract concepts. The character dimensions drew on retrievable memories of facts and events. This level of learning is also referred to as declarative or explicit memory (Smith & Squire, 2005; Squire & Zola-Morgan, 1991).

In any case, the temperament scales became Cloninger's elementary components of personality. The new character dimensions added higher-level humanistic concepts to Cloninger's personality model. Beyond more concrete social bonding and nurturing that would reflect more of the primary PANIC/Sadness and CARE systems, he introduced elements to describe how we relate to our world at an abstract, conceptual level, which would seem to be positioned at a more tertiary level of BrainMind organization than the basic inherited foundations of personality. What was missing in Cloninger's early views was a clear vision of the inherited emotional proclivities in the development of personality, and the recognition that the biogenic amines modulated all of the primal emotions that the ANPS seeks to illuminate. In a sense, Cloninger's expansive additions, attempting to deal with the fuller complexities of human life (in a sense becoming a "theory of everything") diluted his initial vision of the fundamental instinctual-neural foundation of personality.

A CRITIQUE OF CLONINGER'S EXPANSIVE
THEORY OF PSYCHOLOGY

When one probes the origins of Cloninger's revised and expanded personality test, the TCI, one wonders how far Cloninger has truly extended the science of personality beyond other existing personality assessments and the factor-analytic methods he has criticized. Cloninger openly noted that the temperament scales from his original personality test, the TPQ, "were largely uncorrelated with some measures of social cooperation, such as the Agreeableness scale of the Neuroticism-Extraversion-Openness personality inventory, the Aggression scale of the Multidimensional Personality Questionnaire (MPQ), and the Hostility scale of the Profile of Mood States" (Cloninger et al., 1993, pp. 978–979). These scales were largely derived from factor-analytic analyses and must be seen as the psychometric basis for his character dimension called Cooperativeness.

He also pointed out that individual self-acceptance and self-esteem, key elements of the Self-Directedness character dimension, "were not well explained by the TPQ" (Cloninger et al., 1993, p. 979). He cited the Alienation scale of the MPQ and the Repression factor of the Minnesota Multiphasic Psychological Inventory as scales predicting positive self-regard and the acceptance of individual responsibility, including the capacity to admit to unflattering statements about oneself. These scales form the foundation of Cloninger's Self-Directedness character dimension, along with Julian Rotter's Locus of Control scale, which Cloninger cited in his discussion of Self-Directedness (Cloninger et al., 1993).

The story is the same with Auke Tellegen's MPQ Absorption scale, which Cloninger reported was not correlated with any of his four temperament traits (Cloninger et al., 1993). In a description of Self-Transcendence, Cloninger described the "absorption" that leads to "identification with things outside the individual self" (Cloninger et al., 1993, p. 982). Again, the MPQ Absorption scale may largely form the basis of Cloninger's Self-Transcendence scale.

Cloninger was able to report a factor analysis of the twenty-five facets that made up the seven scales of the TCI, in which the facet loadings were mostly consistent with how he "rationally" defined the facets (Cloninger et al., 1993, p. 986). However, this is not really surprising, because the material for the TCI character dimensions seems to have been drawn from sources that derived their scales using linear factor-analytic techniques, such as Tellegen's MPQ and Costa and McCrae's NEO.

CLONINGER ON FACTOR ANALYSIS

Cloninger has argued strongly that factor analysis is not capable of deriving adequate personality scales. He sees factor analysis as a linear statistical procedure that limits attempts to describe the human personality, which is greatly influenced by dynamic, nonlinear factors (Cloninger, 2004). Consequently, he prefers to rationally define personality scales based upon his research into the underlying causal structure of personality. He writes, "Factor analysis of individual case descriptions can only determine the minimum number of measured dimensions, and cannot decompose their underlying causal structure. Extrastatistical information is needed to specify the structure of the underlying biologic and social variability in personality traits. In other words, *descriptive data about individual behavior are not sufficient to permit any strong preference among alternative ways of summarizing personality traits*" (Cloninger et al., 1993, p. 976, italics in original).

We are in full agreement with the idea that factor analysis by itself is not adequate to specify the biological systems inherent in the BrainMind and manifested as personality. Panksepp did not derive his blue ribbon affective neuroscience emotions from a statistical analysis of descriptive data. Each of his foundational subcortical emotions reported in *Affective Neuroscience* (Panksepp, 1998a) was solidly supported with experimental brain research, such as deep brain stimulation, in which a simple electrical stimulus to a particular region of the subcortical brain produced clear, unambiguous emotional action patterns that were accompanied by diverse affective feelings, which may be foundational for the developmental complexity of the higher-order MindBrain organizations that Cloninger moved on to, without ever conceptualizing the fundamental emotional infrastructure of higher mental tendencies.

CRITIQUE BY FARMER AND GOLDBERG

Unfortunately, in the current personality research climate, psychometric criticism is likely to emerge for assessments that do not meet the requirements of the factor-analytic community. And, it is along these lines that Richard Farmer and Lewis Goldberg, two Oregon personality theorists, carefully analyzed Cloninger's TCI using their own large independent data set of TCI data (Farmer & Goldberg, 2008b). In their factor analysis of TCI facets, they were able to confirm much of the same TCI structure that Cloninger had reported earlier (Cloninger et al., 1993, p. 986), but they were able to derive only six interpretable factors. As with Cloninger's data, in their statistical analysis not all facets fell on the predicted factors. Unlike Cloninger, their Harm Avoidance and Self-Directedness facets combined to form a single factor. They were largely able to verify the Persistence, Novelty Seeking, Self-Transcendence factors and all but one of the Cooperativeness facets loaded together on the same factor. Like Cloninger, Farmer and Goldberg found the Reward Dependence facets did not load together.

When analyzing the TCI items rather than facet scores, Farmer and Goldberg were again unable to interpret seven factors or to separate Harm Avoidance and Self-Directedness into separate factors. Also, Cloninger's Novelty Seeking items split up and did not form a clear factor. However, most of the Reward Dependence items sorted onto the same factor, with similar clarity for the Cooperativeness, Persistence, and Self-Transcendence items.

Perhaps the biggest problem in the Farmer and Goldberg analyses was that Harm Avoidance and Self-Directedness loaded together on the same factor whether analyzing TCI facets or items. In other words, Farmer and

Goldberg could not distinguish between Harm Avoidance as a temperament trait and Self-Directedness as a character trait. Statistically, these two Cloninger dimensions looked like they were measuring the same thing and that Farmer and Goldberg, at best, could only account for six personality dimensions when examining Cloninger's TCI.

While a Big Five factor analysis also lumped together all three of the ANPS negative emotions, as we described in Chapter 2, Cloninger had claimed that Self-Directedness and the three character measures did not measure emotional traits and were more cortically dependent. Thus, Farmer and Goldberg's finding that Harm Avoidance and Self-Directedness formed a single factor suggested that temperament and character dimensions shared a common underlying basis. Accordingly, perhaps there weren't distinct temperament and character domains in the human personality. In our view, it is likely that both emerge from the way basic emotional strengths and weaknesses interact with developmental and life time learning experiences.

Farmer and Goldberg (2008a) further pointed out that Cloninger's claim of serotonin being specifically related to Harm Avoidance and not to character dimensions has often not been supported by outside research. Both Harm Avoidance and Self-Directedness were found to be strongly related to serotonin activity (Peirson et al., 1999), and Self-Directedness and Cooperativeness but not Harm Avoidance were strongly associated with a genetic polymorphism that modulates serotonin (Hamer, Greenberg, Sabol, & Murphy, 1999). Similarly, cognitive-behavior therapy outcomes (Dalle et al., 2007) and recovery from drug dependencies (Borman et al., 2006) have been associated with changes in both temperament and character dimensions. These findings contradicted Cloninger's prediction that pharmacological treatments would modify temperament traits with psychotherapy influencing character traits and specifically that "cognitive-behavioral therapy techniques may facilitate learning self-directed behavior" (Cloninger et al., 1993, p. 988).

Indeed, more recently Cloninger himself has softened his claim that, in contrast to the temperament dimensions, character dimensions were not genetically determined and only influenced by environment. Cloninger has conceded that data from twin studies show that "Each of the character dimensions shows moderate heritability and associations with multiple candidate genes . . . and little or no effects of environmental influences shared by siblings reared together" (2004, p. 46).[8] Cloninger later elaborated: "To my surprise, we found that the heritability of character was as great as that of temperament. This important finding suggests that the popular dichotomy in science between the neurobiological and psychosocial paradigms of human personality is not well justified" (Cloninger, 2008, p. 297). Thus, another of the three hypotheses Cloninger initially claimed distinguished his character dimensions from his temperament dimensions was not supported.

Cloninger has also backed away from his claim that character dimensions would mature in adulthood rather than childhood. He conceded that "the amounts of increase in character with age are small on average and negligible after middle age" (2004, p. 47). With that finding, all three of the pillars Cloninger hypothesized would separate character traits from temperament traits have failed to be confirmed.

CONCLUSIONS ABOUT THE CLONINGER PSYCHOBIOLOGICAL THEORY

There is substantial evidence that Cloninger's temperament and character dimensions do not represent distinct personality domains. Perhaps most telling from an affective neuroscience perspective is that both sets of dimensions exhibit significant genetic heritabilities and seem to correlate with emotions. Because we believe that there are no inherited functional "modules" in the neocortex (e.g., it is well established that even cortical vision is learned) and that all known personality dimensions have a basis in subcortical brain affective systems (or the regulation of subcortical brain emotion systems), Cloninger's lack of evidence for additional neocortical personality characteristics beyond conscientiousness strongly supports the affective neuroscience theory of personality. Although we should not exclude the possibility of the future identification of novel neocortical personality traits in addition to those regulating subcortical primary emotions, multivariate genetic analysis suggests that Cloninger's seven personality dimensions were most likely linked to the affective dynamics of the various evolved subcortical brain emotional systems (Ando et al., 2004).

With the expansion of his theory and the TCI psychological assessment in 1993, Cloninger veered significantly toward a more purely philosophical direction, advancing claims that were difficult to substantiate empirically. In his 2004 book *Feeling Good: The Science of Well-Being*, Cloninger presents ideas that end up being more humanitarian-positive psychology, with insufficient substantive brain science. His prescriptions become more sensible guides for living than evidence-based psychobiological inferences.

To his credit, Cloninger has assembled a fine personality instrument. However, while it may be one of the better instruments for diagnosing personality disorders (Farmer & Goldberg, 2008b), it is by no means the only good instrument available in this arena. One might have wished that Cloninger had attempted to refine the bottom-up neurobiological aspects of his original theory. Instead, he attempted to expand toward a more top-down approach to understanding human well-being.

Altogether, Cloninger is a creative scholar who has enlivened the field with novel perspectives, reflecting the consideration of an incredible range of information, including recent participation in a far-reaching genetic analysis of schizophrenia (Arnedo et al., 2015). However, he has yet to provide a biological theory of personality that adequately accounts for the fundamental affective infrastructure of mammalian brains.

At this point, Darwin's famous theoretical dictum about mammalian mental differences being "of degree not of kind" seems to be holding true in the world of personality theory. Along these lines, it is interesting that Cloninger has not focused on the Big Five Conscientiousness dimension as a possible cortically based character trait that may acquire the capacity to regulate subcortical primary emotions. Among the great affective neuroscience puzzles that needs more experimental attention is the developmental construction of this Conscientiousness regulatory trait, which, we assume, appeared on the neuroevolutionary scene long before the emergence of *Homo sapiens*.

The cortex, with its massive capacity to learn, provides vast diversities of mental life that are truly unique to each individual. Yet, such differences emerge from the shared emotional and other affective features of our personalities, based robustly on survival systems that evolved long before humans walked the face of the earth. That the intrinsic *genetic* and developmentally guided *epigenetic* strengths and weakness of these systems are critical for the emergence of our higher-order characterological traits seems more likely than ever, which leads us to the subject of the next chapter.

CHAPTER 15

Genetics and the Origins of Personality

Owing to the imperfection of language the offspring is termed a new animal, but it is in truth a branch or elongation of the parent; since a part of the embryon-animal is, or was, a part of the parent; and therefore in strict language it cannot be said to be entirely new at the time of its production; and therefore it may retain some of the habits of the parent-system.

—Erasmus Darwin, *Zoonomia; Or, The Laws of Organic Life*

We are survival machines—robot vehicles blindly programmed to preserve the selfish molecules known as genes. This is a truth which still fills me with astonishment.

—Richard Dawkins, *The Selfish Gene*

IN RECENT ACADEMIC HISTORY, the genetic foundations of human personality has been a contentious issue, almost as difficult for many to digest as the heritability of intelligence. To suggest that one's affective temperamental ways of being in the world could be influenced by genes was often seen as an odious way of envisioning human nature, and individuals who did so in voluble ways were commonly targets of gentle as well as strident ridicule. Of course, the classic view, from Hippocrates to Galen, was that individual differences in personality (although not called that) could be inborn, as reflected in individual temperamental variability, which was presumably controlled by basic body humors, which led people to be choleric (angry, irritable), melancholic (sad, depressive), phlegmatic (calm, unemotional, with a touch of "coldness"), or sanguine (joyful-sociable), because of their balance of distinct bodily humors. Of course, this useful scheme is now considered a historical curiosity.

Perhaps the most recent, now historically memorable example was *The Bell Curve: Intelligence and Class Structure in American Life* (1994), in which two eminent scholars, Richard Herrenstein, a professor from Harvard, and Charles Murray, asserted that "smarts" were inherited largely from smarter parents, with overtones that both social class and human diversity around the world were related to intrinsic aspects of intelligence.

Herrenstein (1930–1994), a student of B. F. Skinner, died before the commotion their book fermented fully materialized. Murray, a political libertarian and social pundit who initiated the project, has lived through the brouhaha that ensued. Reverend Jesse Jackson critiqued their effort as little more than "recapitulation of ancient garbage," while President Bill Clinton argued their thesis "goes against our entire history and our whole tradition" (Sesardic, 2005). Of course the view that "genes count," with practical consequences for all physical as well as psychological traits, has in the ensuing quarter century become accepted general knowledge, but the details have only begun to be fleshed out. And as the science of heritability has matured, new twists have been revealed (e.g., epigenetics, discussed below), making the whole topic more subtle and interesting. As we highlight here, gene expression can be dramatically molded by a host of environmental, internal chemical, and perhaps even brain emotional variables (i.e., strong, real-life experiences).

Modern genetics has revealed a Pandora's box of genetic rules, with all arguments needing to be tempered by the accruing evidence. Our goal in this chapter is to provide a snapshot of the evidence genetic analyses provide for scholarly discussion in this formerly contentious area, amplified by more recent epigenetic evidence, which has now highlighted how environmentally modulated gene expression, some of which can last a lifetime (and be passed on to offspring), adds layers of complexity to comparatively simple genetic inheritance (for a review, see, e.g., Montag et al., 2016; Montag & Panksepp, 2017; Montag & Reuter, 2014). The fact that supportive and stressful social environments can modify gene expression patterns is especially fascinating and important for the way we rear our children. But before we dip into the complex discussion of possible epigenetic controls, we focus on the classic behavioral evidence for genetic foundations of human personality.

HERITABILITY OF PERSONALITY

The traditional way to pursue this issue has been to contrast personality similarities and differences between children from the same families, with the very best data coming from the contrasting of personality traits in identical and nonidentical twins. A great deal of data exist indicating that human personality traits are highly heritable (Turkheimer, 2000), which was confirmed by extensive analyses concluding that all human traits are heritable (Montag et al., 2016; Polderman et al., 2015).

However, perhaps driven by social forces striving for gender and racial equality, as well as perpetuating a cognitive-behaviorist tradition in psychology, there remains a bias for cognitive learning theory and against genetic and epigenetic explanations, as historically characterized by a quotation from Walter Mischel: "Genes and glands are obviously important, but social learning also has a dramatic role. Imagine the enormous differences that would be found in the personalities of twins with identical genetic endowments if they were raised apart in two different families" (1981, p. 311).

Remarkably, the Minnesota Study of Twins Reared Apart took on this challenge to find out to what extent identical twins would retain their similarity if raised in different families. In 1988 the project published a study (Tellegen et al., 1988) affirming that, in contrast to the expectations of many psychologists, identical twins reared together did not have more similar personalities than identical twins separated very early in life (at a median of 2–3 months) and reared apart (with a median total separation of 33.8 years). In both cases "about 50 percent of measured personality diversity can be attributed to genetic diversity" (p. 1035). These authors further reported that the shared family environment generally played a modest role in determining personality traits, one exception being a small but significant shared environmental influence for the Social Closeness scale from the Multidimensional Personality Questionnaire (Tellegen, 1982), which measures the tendency to be warm and affectionate and to value close personal ties and turn to others for comfort and help.

These revealing studies continued beyond the realm of typical personality measures. Waller, Kojetin, Bouchard, Lykken, and Tellegen (1990) further showed that identical twins reared together or apart exhibited very similar Religiosity, a measure of religious commitment and engagement in such activities. Again, the genetic influences accounted for about 50 percent of the differences with shared environmental effects being negligible. Studying identical twins raised in different homes later showed that Religiosity was linked to Authoritarianism and Conservatism, all of which seemed to be aspects of the Traditionalism scale from the Multidimensional Personality Questionnaire, with differences accounted for by genetics consistently in the 50 percent range (Ludeke, Johnson, & Bouchard, 2013). Further pursuing the theme that all human traits are heritable, the Minnesota group (Lykken, Bouchard, McGue, & Tellegen, 1993) found again that about 50 percent of the variability of interests—including industrial arts, working with animals, buying and selling, accounting or mathematical interests, medical work, writing, and music—could be accounted for by genetics.

While these findings remain to be explained in any genetic detail, it is likely that our evolved individual variability, including personally oriented likes and dislikes coupled with our various inherited aptitudes, substantially influences how we respond to experiences in a grand endophenotype-environment interaction, which helps mediate and promote our developing temperament and interest patterns. To elaborate somewhat, this view was originally presented by Scarr and McCartney (1983) in a paper cited 1,420 times as of this writing. They proposed a behavior development theory asserting that our individual genotypes predispose us to select personally compatible environments, an "active" process that becomes increasingly prevalent as we mature and becomes more independent of our "passive" early child-rearing experiences. Specifically, they cited data that by late adolescence adopted siblings resemble each other less than previously when parental environments may have induced more similarity. Even nonidentical twin similarities begin to decline as their common early home environments give way to actively selecting experiences compatible with their individual genotypes.

Thomas Bouchard (1997) extended Scarr and McCartney's position by coming closer to defining the mechanisms driving the selection of compatible environments from the diverse available possibilities. In explicating his Experience Producing Drive theory that genes drive personality-shaping behavior, Bouchard stated, "We propose that what are inherited are specific adaptive species-typical affective motivational systems shaped by the environment of evolutionary adaptiveness" (1997, p. 62). We couldn't agree more, except to add that Bouchard's "affective motivational systems" are most likely the emotional primary rewards and punishments guiding the learning and behavioral choices of all mammals in this grand evolved endophenotype-environment interaction that allows sentient beings to adapt to their worlds. In other words, it is our emotional affects that influence our perceptions and bias our approach or avoidance of potential environmental experiences, such that one person finds backpacking in the wilderness an exciting possibility while another recoils at such a frightening venture and yet a third dismisses the idea as a childish distraction, all reflecting and amplifying our personality differences.

HERITABILITY OF THE CLASSIC BIG FIVE

For the classic Big Five personality traits (Extraversion, Agreeableness, Conscientiousness, Emotional Stability, and Openness to Experience), diverse studies during the past half century have confirmed robust genetic as well as environmental foundations for all five personality dimensions, approximating the classic 50 percent genetic influence, a finding confirmed by a meta-analysis (Vukasovic´ & Bratko, 2015). Indeed, six factors of the neuroemotionally inspired Affective Neuroscience Personality Scales (ANPS) scales could be conceptually related to the Big Five. For instance, we evaluated how emotional-personality self-reports on the ANPS related to the Big Five factors (Davis et al., 2003; Davis & Panksepp, 2011). As described in Chapter 2, each ANPS factor significantly related to one of the Big Five personality factors. Accordingly, we postulated that the core emotional systems (SEEKING/Enthusiasm, RAGE/Anger, FEAR/Anxiety, CARE/Nurturance, PANIC/Sadness, and PLAY/Joy) developmentally contribute to the emergence of the Big Five, thereby potentially providing a basic neuroemotional foundation for the psychology-only Big Five tradition.

Accordingly, with the analysis of primary emotional systems of mammalian brains, on which the ANPS was premised, one has novel ways to link the genetics of primary emotions revealed by animal research to Big Five personality dimensions derived strictly from human research. Still, there are few direct analyses of such relationships in humans. However, a collaborative study of both scales was conducted with the leadership of our German colleagues (Montag et al., 2016), who evaluated 303 identical (monozygotic) twins (77 percent female) and 172 nonidentical (dizygotic) twins (65 percent female) and found significant (moderate to strong) influences of genetics on these scales. The lowest heritability estimate was evident for the SEEKING urge (30 percent), perhaps because it influences so many basic behaviors and emotions, and highest was for PLAY (63 percent). It is worth reiterating that many personality studies during the past half century have indicated comparably robust genetic foundations for all of the Big Five traits (Johnson, Vernon, & Feiler, 2008). The Montag et al. (2016) study further highlights the usefulness of the ANPS for biologically oriented personality research such as confirming that depressed people have lower SEEKING values than nondepressed individuals as has been predicted from various animal studies (e.g., see Panksepp, 2015, 2016).

GENETIC PATHS TO PERSONALITY DEVELOPMENT?

Abundant evidence has long existed that personality has a strong genetic foundation (for a synopsis, see Montag & Panksepp, 2017). The heritability of human personality is well captured by encapsulated human wisdom in such phrases as, "She is just like her grandmother," or "He's just like his father." Animal breeders have long understood that through a knowledge of the parent's psychological temperaments, as well as their more obvious physical characteristics, they can effectively breed for many psychological as well as physical traits. These cultural truths and historical traditions in personality research are now being clarified and magnified not only by modern genetic studies of how temperamental traits can be transmitted but also by the fact that environment can have dramatic effects on how individual genes are activated or deactivated, namely, via epigenetic effects from one's social-emotional environment to environmental toxins, land infertility, or even weather fluctuations leading to famines (Skinner, 2015).

To provide an historical perspective, with the emergence of modern molecular genetics and with the definitive acceptance that DNA constitutes the molecular underpinning of inheritance, in the early 1950s Watson and Crick (1953) provided the capstone in that argument by working out the coiled structure of DNA (work that earned them the Nobel Prize in 1962). Almost until then, contrary to compelling evidence provided by Oswald Avery's group a decade earlier (Avery, MacLeod, & McCarty, 1944), most biologists believed that proteins were the proximal source of our heritability mechanisms. By the mid-1950s, after Crick and Watson beat Linus Pauling to working out the structure of DNA, everyone had accepted that the critical molecules were sequences of nucleotides in DNA (adenine, cytosine, guanine, and thymine) that could code for various messenger RNAs in various permutations (e.g., thymine being replaced with uracil), which provided the "triplet codes" for proteins that were the most manifest conveyors of inheritance. Eventually Marshall Nirenberg at the National Institutes of Health illuminated the triplet code for DNA and RNA, where three successive nucleotides coded for each of the twenty standard amino acids—he along with Gobind Khorana and Robert Holley received the Nobel Prize in 1968 for "breaking the genetic code." Only gradually did it come to be realized that Mother Nature had devised ways in which environmental events, both social and inanimate, could modulate how intensely genes were expressed, which is what epigenetics is about—that term literally means "above or beyond genetics."

This knowledge is changing the face of evolutionary psychology in ways that would amaze Charles Darwin, who first presciently plotted the paths of evolution that are now highways of solid knowledge. Clearly, this knowledge, in conjunction with modern illumination of brain circuits and neurochemistries, has enabled more lasting and ever deeper insights into the neurobiological foundations of brain systems that control animal and human nature as well as nurture, from genetics and epigenetics to social learning.

In short, this work has now affirmed the genetic foundations of our diverse personalities, both in humans and in other animals, which remain tethered to a grand ancestral heritage, but also how the foundations can be changed epigenetically through the way the genetic code can be played in different environments. Such work will eventually enrich our understanding of the basic affective foundations of human personality that lie within the deeper subcortical brain regions shared by all mammals (and many shared with all other vertebrates). Modern genetics also suggests there are genetic tethers to our cognitive abilities (for the IQ report from the Minnesota Study of Twins Reared Apart project, see Bouchard, Lykken, McGue, Segal, & Tellegen, 1990), but that is less well understood and, we assume, less important for understanding basic personality dimensions. Our focus is on inherited traits that constitute our affective strengths and weaknesses and how they are molded further by various developmental/epigenetic processes. Thus, both the qualities of nature and nurture combine in the construction of our intrinsic personality strengths and weaknesses. This is currently clearest in subcortical neural systems that are most critical for our affective lives, rather than in more purely cognitive (information-processing) qualities of our upper minds. But first, we share a few more reflections on basic genetics.

MODERN GENETICS, EPIGENETICS, AND THE HERITABILITY OF PERSONALITY TRAITS

We have already noted how investigators have been able to select for a variety of emotional-personality traits in animals (see Chapters 8–10). During the past half century, one of the most remarkable scientific achievements has been an in-depth understanding of the genetic foundations of our human nature, which is remarkably similar to that of all other mammals, with clear relationships as we go further down the evolutionary ladder or, more correctly, into the thickets of the evolutionary bush. Although it was once thought that we had at least a hundred thousand genes, with improvements in technology it fell to less than a quarter of that. Still, for most of our DNA, which contains more than 3 billion base pairs, only a small fraction are protein-coding sequences, with lots of pseudogenes (or junk DNA, as some called it) whose functions are not known, perhaps much of it being nonfunctional residues from the past, although some may facilitate protein synthesis by participating in gene regulation and expression (for a more detailed discussion, see Pennisi, 2012).

According to current estimates, there are at least twenty-two thousand human protein-coding genes, with the first draft of the human genome published on February 12, 2001 (and refined considerably since then, with the genomes of many individual humans being added to the library). This has opened up the Pandora's box of estimating the genetic contributions to many human/animal traits. Indeed, investigators are finally beginning to seek the genetic sources of various psychological traits, including the foundations of the various personality dimensions we have been discussing. We also note that the remarkable similarities in genomes across mammalian species again coaxes us to accept that we share many similarities with other mammals, including our emotional foundations, which need to be integrated into the human sciences (e.g., Panksepp et al., 2016). Indeed, genetic research on emotional traits, including personality dimensions in animals, may help clarify the foundations of our own temperamental nature. It is becoming ever clearer that certain personality traits can be inherited, and not simply from the specific genes one inherits but also by the transmission of the environmentally induced epigenetic changes in our genomes.

This story gets very complex when we consider that there are various epigenetic mechanisms that control the extent to which individual genes are expressed. During development, diverse environmental experiences, including drugs, sex, and many other life experiences, can modify the intensity of gene expressions. Remarkably, these epigenetic factors can tune our genetic orchestras to better fit the environments in which we live, and they can lead to personality changes as well as mental health issues—from increased resilience to troublesome emotional imbalances, often so extreme as to be considered psychiatric problems.

One of the great surprises of the epigenetic revolution of the past decade is the diverse ways gene regulation can be modified indirectly by environmental events (i.e., without changing the genetic code itself), and many of these effects can be passed from parents to children. In a manner of speaking, the "sins" and vicissitudes of parents can epigenetically affect their children, while positive emotional support can facilitate thriving. For instance, child abuse can leave epigenetically induced emotional scars, while well-tuned, devoted parenting can promote resilience in children. There is abundant work ranging from autism to attention-deficit hyperactive disorder (Panksepp, 2007b, 2008b) highlighting the possible long-term neurobiological consequences of rearing.

GENE REGULATION: PATHS TO BEHAVIORAL AND PERSONALITY TRAITS

The genetic and neuroscience revolutions of the past century have been the most seminal events in understanding our fundamental nature and our place in the living order. To reiterate, since 1953, the year the structure of DNA was decoded, genetic knowledge has touched all aspects of living creatures, including the sources of human and animal personalities. With the genetic revolution, we now have great assurance that the recipe for life is very similar across all mammals, indeed, all species. To a substantial degree all personality traits are heritable, with many linked to the genes we inherit and many others linked to the ability of our gene expression patterns to change dynamically, based on epigenetics.

One of the most exciting outgrowths of the modern genetic revolution is the illumination of how epigenetics (inherited and/or acquired) can impact the emotional-affective foundations of personality (for a superb review, see Weaver, 2014). The view of simple genetic determinism has been replaced with the understanding that inheritance is no longer as predetermined as it was once thought to be. Genetic science has finally revealed the joint roles of nature and nurture in guiding who we are and who we can become. And in personality theory, ruthless biological reductionism needs now to be supplemented with novel forms of environmental relativism.

In brief, the variety in the DNA sequences of our reproductive cells, called single nucleotide polymorphisms (SNPs, pronounced "snips"), provides diverse avenues for genetic changes. When rare and deleterious, they are typically called mutations, but when common (e.g., promoting trait variability), they are called SNPs. When transmitted to children, these variations can fine-tune the underlying emotional/affective tools for living that control personality styles—both strengths and weaknesses. A great number of SNPs have been discovered that contribute to behavioral and psychological effects, including various pathways to personality styles, psychobehavioral resilience, and susceptibility to mental/psychiatric disorders. There are genes that can control the intensity of people's emotional traits, such as susceptibility to anger and aggression, through well-studied mechanisms, such as the intensity of serotonin transmission in the brain (Craig & Halton, 2009), and other genes may lead to psychopathic tendencies (for an intriguing, emotional autobiography of a famous scientist who discovered that he had inherited such tendencies, see Fallon, 2013). While many genetic variants promote very specific temperamental changes, others lead to pervasive, life-damaging progressions.

THREE ROADS TO EPIGENETIC CONTROL OF PERSONALITY AND EMOTIONAL DISORDERS

Beside the sequence of nucleotides of DNA and RNA that code for amino acids in proteins, there are three major epigenetic modes of transmission. A fact that is critical for understanding such processes is that DNA is tightly packaged in a chromatin matrix within the nucleus of all cells—in a sense, DNA strands are integrated within ("wound around") a complex protein (histone and DNA) matrix that can control the extent to which DNA can be transcribed into proteins. There are three main ways that the extent of protein synthesis can be controlled: (1) the interaction of histones with DNA can be modified in various ways (e.g., histone acetylation or deacetylation), effecting rates of gene expression; (2) the chromatin matrix can be remodeled so as to modify various gene transcription factors; and (3) direct DNA methylation that can be a highly stable influence on gene expression. Each of these epigenetic regulatory processes can last a lifetime and change the intensity with which translation of DNA to RNA and ultimately protein synthesis can proceed, without any change in the DNA code itself. Thus, from a functional brain perspective, epigenetics has revealed that various factors contribute to neural development and plasticity, which ultimately can impact diverse brain processes, including the affective-emotional networks that undergird the major global personality dimensions that psychologists and neuroscientists study.

Let us consider an example: a rare childhood disorder called Rett's syndrome, characterized by Andreas Rett, a pediatrician in Vienna who first published his observations in 1966. Rett's syndrome, once thought to be an autistic spectrum disorder, typically inflicts girls, with the first symptoms, appearing at about a year of age, being loss of coherent hand movements, loss of language and social skills, and cognitive delays. Such children, doomed to a rapid regression of initial development, have severe life-long behavioral and psychological problems, including disturbing emotional symptoms, such as inconsolable crying, screaming fits, and avoidance of social contact, combined with impaired motor coordination.

This tragic disorder, with a prevalence of about 1 in 10,000 births, arises from a genetic abnormality of a specific gene, *MECP2* (methyl CpG-binding protein 2). Amir et al. (1999) discovered that most of the problems in Rett's syndrome arose from the dysfunction of this gene, whose protein product is essential for the broad regulation of the expression of various genes—this one gene plays a critical role in the epigenetic regulation of gene expressions that promote maturation. Thus, a pervasive developmental disorder emerges when this gene is dysfunctional. It is currently believed that correction of epigenetic changes in such children at an early age may prevent progression of the disorder (for a fuller description of the varieties of such developmental disorders, see Peterson and Panksepp, 2004).

A second example is the increasing evidence for epigenetic mechanisms in the development of substance abuse, for example, cocaine addiction. Coca leaves have been chewed by South American Andean natives for at least three thousand years (Biondich & Joslin, 2016), but use of whole leaves does not produce dependence, as indicated by the development of tolerance or withdrawal symptoms (Weil, 1981). However, the chemical isolation of cocaine from the leaves led to what has become a drug of abuse, with vulnerability to addiction determined roughly half by genetic and half by nongenetic factors (Nestler, 2014).

The ancestral roots of cocaine's dopaminergic reward properties have been confirmed by demonstrating cocaine-induced conditioned place preference in crayfish (Panksepp & Huber, 2004), an invertebrate species predating humans by 600 million years. It is likely that cocaine addiction, both in humans and as studied experimentally in rodents, incorporates such evolutionarily conserved brain substrates for reward, which are embedded within motivational subcortical brain systems shared homologously by all mammals. Better understanding the cross-species affective reward properties of our primary emotions is essential for understanding the motivational and behavioral changes associated with addiction, as well as exploring potential treatments for such emotional imbalances.

One of the dangers of cocaine use is the relatively rapid onset of addiction, with about 5 percent of first-time cocaine users becoming addicted by a 24-month follow-up (O'Brien & Anthony, 2005). Cocaine addiction is further characterized by drug craving and relapses—despite severe physical and social consequences—that can persist for a lifetime and outlast long periods of abstinence, suggesting the occurrence of long-lasting changes in the brain, including evidence for changes in gene expression (Robison & Nestler, 2011).

As discussed above, chromatin consists of DNA and the histone proteins that DNA is tightly coiled around. Histone acetylation allows the chromatin structure to relax and thereby facilitates gene expression. Based on the study of mouse models, it is widely thought that chromatin modification is central to the epigenetic brain changes observed in drug addiction (for a readable review, see McQuown & Wood, 2010). An acute dose of cocaine induces a process of increased histone acetylation that is balanced by corresponding deacetylation and reverts to control levels within three hours. Elevated increases in histone acetylation induced by the inhibition of histone deacetylase enzymes increase the rewarding effects of cocaine, as demonstrated by enhanced conditioned place preference even at low cocaine doses. Conversely, experimentally induced overexpression of histone deacetylase enzymes dramatically decreases cocaine's rewarding properties, as measured by conditioned place preference, providing further support that histone acetylation and deacetylation mechanisms promote the reward and behavioral changes associated with cocaine addiction (Kumar et al., 2005). Importantly, it is through chronic, not acute, cocaine exposure that a complex epigenetic process emerges, dramatically reducing histone deacetylation and providing a major mechanism for increasing the rewarding properties and associated behavior changes of cocaine addiction. Thus, the behavioral and reward changes observed in cocaine addiction may largely be the result of reducing histone deacetylation rather than directly increasing histone acetylation (Renthal et al., 2007). Eventually, such findings may lead to new treatments able to "undo" the epigenetic changes of cocaine addiction.

BEHAVIORAL, EMOTIONAL, AND
PSYCHIATRIC EPIGENETICS

Perhaps the most extensive animal research in behavioral epigenetics is the work of Michael Meaney's group at McGill University (e.g., Anacker, O'Donnell, & Meaney, 2014; Turecki & Meaney, 2016). The findings are straightforward: Rat mothers spend a lot of time licking and grooming their newborn pups during the first week of life. In general, pups that received abundant maternal touch exhibited resilience in a variety of behavioral situations, while those that did not were much more stress sensitive. Indeed, major epigenetic changes from lack of maternal care—altered expressions of a wide range of genes—were identified in neurons of the major stress axis of the brain: the hypothalamic-pituitary-adrenal system, which controls how well humans and animals can cope with a variety of environmental challenges. Such changes were clearly detrimental to young rats. Indeed, a remarkable aspect of the work lies in the demonstration that some of the adverse effects could be reversed in adulthood with pharmacological agents that could reverse early epigenetic changes (Weaver, Meaney, & Szyf, 2006).

Such work has implications for understanding comparable processes in humans and other primates as highlighted in a special issue of the journal *Hormones and Behavior* (Fleming, Lévy & Lonstein, 2016) devoted to the effect of "external regulators" such as maternal care on infant physiology, especially brain development and the resulting socioemotional developmental changes that ensue, namely, "the negative long-term consequences of the absence of needed caregiving (e.g., neglect) or the presence of harmful/aversive caregiving (e.g., physical abuse)" that "are translatable across species" (Drury, Sánchez, & Gonzalez, 2016, p. 182). Clearly, there is a possibility for cross-species translations in how negative caregiving (child maltreatment) impacts many brain and bodily processes that can have lasting negative impact on mental and physical health.

Such animal studies may have direct implications for optimal human childcare. For instance, Brody, Yu, Chen, Beach, and Miller (2016) have analyzed how negative family environments impacted diverse health issues, highlighting how parental depression when children are becoming adolescents (e.g., age eleven) can forecast accelerated epigenetic aging at age twenty, and how such deleterious effects could be ameliorated by a family-centered prevention program that sought to enhance supportive parenting and the explicit strengthening of family relationships. A total of almost four hundred families were studied, and the conclusion was that enhanced parenting guidance "can buffer the [negative] biological residue of life" (Brody et al., 2016, p. 567) in at-risk families.

Although direct translations from animal infant care often do not translate directly to humans, licking and grooming in rats may have consequences similar to attentive loving touch in humans. Indeed, Pickles, Sharp, Hellier, and Hill (2017), who had previously shown that prenatal depression and anxiety were related to diminished maternal stroking of infants, with various negative child outcomes at 29 weeks and 2.5 years (Sharp et al., 2012), evaluated whether such effects could be replicated in a much larger sample. They reported "long-term [beneficial] effects of early maternal stroking" (p. 325) on child anxiety, depressive, and aggressive symptoms. No doubt there are many psychological mirroring processes in children, and one might expect that premature infants may be especially at risk for negative epigenetic modifications. In fact, Montirosso et al., (2016) documented how preterm infants may exhibit abnormal methylation of key genes: Not only did preemies exhibit elevated negative emotionality, but Montirosso et al. also observed changes in methylation patterns of the gene *SLC6A4* that were predictive of greater negative emotionality.

Of course, there are a large number of possible mechanisms for both positive and adverse epigenetic effects (see, e.g., Gaudi, Guffanti, G., Fallon, & Macciardi, 2016). Of all the neuromodulator candidates, perhaps the most evidence has been collected for oxytocin. For instance, Haas et al., (2016) focused on the mounting evidence that oxytocin genes, which have long been associated with animal sociability, might exhibit epigenetic modifications of DNA methylation, as measured in human saliva samples. They found that people exhibiting lower oxytocin DNA methylation, which may indicate higher oxytocin expression, displayed better ability to detect facial emotional expressions, as well as more secure attachment styles. With modern brain imaging, they also found higher regional cortical arousal during emotional perspective-taking exercises in such individuals than in those whose methylation pattern indicated diminished oxytocin activity.

Modern molecular genetics will eventually impact both psychiatric diagnostics and the development of new treatments, heralding a new field of psychiatric epigenetics. Just as with animal models, there is increasing evidence that early emotional and physical traumas can promote the development of dysfunctional brain circuits, which partly reflect epigenetic changes resulting from life challenges as well as transgenerational effects, especially as arising from early life stressors (Gröger et al., 2016), which may lead to the development of various preventive measures and resilience-promoting interventions that arise directly from our understanding of epigenetics (Shrivastava & Desousa, 2016). As already noted, some of the adverse epigenetic effects can even be reversed by administration of drugs that can "erase" the adverse epigenetic markers (Weaver et al., 2006).

In sum, early life stressors, especially traumatic experiences, are major risk factors for amplifying affectively negative brain circuits, most of which currently remain to be well studied. The evidence for diverse gene × environment interactions promoting personality and other psychiatric disorders is mounting, including transgenerational epigenetic inheritance. The cycles of negative affect become ingrained as characteristic ways of being (aka shifts in personality). Conversely, early affectively positive remedial interventions can facilitate affectively positive resilience against life adversities. Indeed, the long-term consequences of poverty are among the most salient, and potentially remediable with changing social policies (Johnson, Riis, & Noble, 2016). As noted by Bruce McEwen, one of the fathers of modern neuroendocrinology and stress research, "The healthy brain has a considerable capacity for resilience, based upon its ability to respond to interventions designed to open 'windows of plasticity' and redirect its function toward better health" (2016, p. 56). Indeed, the title of one recent review proclaimed "The Miraculous Ability of the Human Genome to Adapt, and Then Adapt Again" (Gershon & High, 2015). It will be both interesting and important to see how societies respond to the growing evidence base that various social-emotional interventions can ameliorate, even prevent, psychological damage inflicted by unconscionable stress in the early life of our youngsters.

CONCLUSIONS

For centuries, animal breeders have known that they can select for practically any physical or behavioral trait by selective breeding (see Chapter 8 on fox domestication). These same lessons have been learned by generations of psychologists that have bred for specific traits (see Chapter 9 on the breeding of many specialized rat strains), but rarely have the specific genes been identified. With the clarification of the mechanisms—the molecular biology of heredity—that is now possible. In a sense Darwin's evolutionary vision has been fulfilled. But the ensuing genetic breakthroughs that are leading to powerful biomedical diagnostics and treatments are now being supplemented by the recognition that the promise of some of the other proposed paths of evolution, such as the focus on acquired traits—a view originally championed by the French biologist Jean-Baptiste Lamarck (1744–1829)—was not as far off the mark as commonly believed through most of the twentieth century.

The finding that parents can pass on characteristics to their offspring that they have acquired during their lives has now been affirmed by modern epigenetic research, including work on environmental toxins (e.g., Skinner, 2015, 2016). Indeed, it now looks like some of these characteristics can be acquired emotional personality traits. Studies of "Lamarckian inheritance" have blossomed in the twenty-first century and are amplifying our understanding of the true complexities of our human-animal nature.

The bottom line is clear for parents: As the twig is bent, so the tree will grow—now supported by the fact that children's genes are affected by more than their nucleotide sequences. Psychologically, the best inheritance parents can give their children is abundant quality emotional time each day, especially, perhaps, abundant natural social play each and every day. This may promote epigenetic pathways that diminish childhood problems like attention-deficit hyperactive disorder, reducing the need to give children medicines that are well known to be addictive (Panksepp, 2007b, 2008b). Indeed, one can envision epigenesis operating at a cultural rather than just an individual level, with social play-promoting cultural values influencing how the brains of our young people mature.

CHAPTER 16

Human Brain Imaging

The basic emotions are natural kinds that have specifiable neural substrates within the mammalian brain. If we do not come to terms with such foundation principles, we will have impoverished views of psychological and cultural complexities that ultimately arise from emotional learning.

—Jaak Panksepp, "Emotions as Natural Kinds Within the Mammalian Brain"

BRAIN IMAGING HAS BECOME a popular tool in the neurosciences. The brain imaging procedure that has become the most common and easiest to administer is functional magnetic resonance imaging (fMRI). Like computed tomography (CT), MRI is able to generate cross-sectional images of human anatomy without using X-rays. However, fMRI combines MRI technology with highly specialized statistical analyses to measure localized brain activity. Typically, fMRI uses the blood-oxygen-level dependent signal contrast to measure blood flow in a brain region. The assumption is that when brain activity increases, blood flows to that region and hence oxygen levels increase as well. While this assumption generally holds when measuring the activity of cortical regions of the brain, with their rapidly firing neurons, subcortical neurons tend to fire at much lower rates than cortical neurons creating a detection bias against finding statistically significant estimates of brain activity increases in subcortical regions. In addition, functionally relevant subcortical regions are generally smaller in size, with many nearby, overlapping functional circuits, making them even more difficult to detect.

PET ALTERNATIVE: THE DAMASIO GROUP

An alternate brain scanning procedure, positron emission tomography (PET), is more invasive but substantially more relevant for imaging emotional feelings and particularly so for the smaller, slower-firing subcortical regions of the brain. With PET, not only can general brain activity measures be monitored, typically, by measuring glucose utilization (because the main fuel for brain activity is glucose) but there is also the possibility of measuring various neurochemicals from traditional transmitters—biogenic amines such as dopamine, serotonin, and norepinephrine to more specific functional controls such as brain opioids, as long as positron emitting forms of these molecules have been synthesized.

A landmark study published in the prestigious scientific journal *Nature* by Antonio Damasio's research group, which included his wife Hanna who is a specialist in brain anatomy (Damasio et al. 2000), used PET technology to image the whole brain while their subjects actually experienced emotionally powerful states evoked by reminiscences of their own lives. In other words, their goal was to identify neuroanatomical regions whose activity correlated with the experiencing of specific personal memories of past emotional feelings. To ensure optimal results, they first screened their subjects for their ability to self-induce emotions through recalling autobiographical memories of emotionally powerful personal experiences, as well as a neutral episode recalling normal daily events.

For this project, the Damasio group investigated four target emotions: sadness, happiness, anger, and fear. Because of the emotionally taxing reenactment of these powerful experiences, for example, the death of a relative or close friend for the sadness emotion, subjects were assigned to recall only two of the four emotions, based on their prescreening demonstrations, as well as a neutral experience serving as the experimental control. Importantly, the PET brain data were collected (i.e., the radioisotope was intravenously infused) only after the subject reported actually feeling the emotion.

As might be expected, a whole-brain image analysis during the generation of different emotions would produce complex results. However, many of the remarkable correlational findings using their forty-one carefully selected human subjects were consistent with the experimental animal research using deep brain stimulation and related procedures to study primary emotions. These investigators also collected physiological measures of bodily arousals, such as skin conductance and heart rate, that had previously been used to monitor emotional states in humans.

One of the main findings from this Damasio study was the consistent activation of brainstem regions such as the periaqueductal gray (PAG) when these emotions were aroused, regions that are often cited in animal studies of primary emotions. This finding was especially interesting because up to this time "The brainstem has not been noted to be active in other human studies of emotion" (Damasio et al., 2000, p. 1052). Indeed, most previous brain imaging research studying human emotions had focused on cortical brain regions. For example, a meta-analysis (Phan, Wager, Taylor, & Liberzon, 2002) found that, of fourteen studies imaging sadness, a cortical region known as the subgenual anterior cingulate cortex (also known as Brodmann area 25, an evolutionarily older cortical midline structure located just below the anterior portion of the corpus callosum and just posterior to the prefrontal cortical region known as Brodmann area 11) was the most consistently activated brain region, which, although evolutionarily older than neocortex, was not a subcortical brain region. Thus, Damasio et al. (2000) were among the first to confirm previous primary emotion research in animals by using human subjects to illuminate the activation of subcortical brain regions during their experience of personally relevant emotional arousals, in stark contrast with the dominant picture emerging from other human brain imaging studies attempting to discern which cortical brain regions correlated with the generation of specific human emotions. For an easily interpretable picture summary of Damasio et al.'s (2000) PET imaging results, see Panksepp, 2011a, which is readily available.

Another of Damasio et al.'s (2000) findings that contrasted with the opinions of many psychologists, who believed that emotional feelings arise from neocortex, was that during the experience of strong human emotions, many neocortical brain areas were *deactivated* rather than activated. In accord with previous affective neuroscience research using animals, not only were subcortical areas consistently activated when humans experienced strong emotions but neocortical regions were, if anything, commonly deactivated, which was consistent with the animal evidence that cortical regions were not necessary for the experience of emotions. Animals as well as humans are able to express and experience a full range of primary emotions even if the neocortex had been removed at birth or, in the case of humans, when they were born without neocortex (Panksepp, Normansell, Cox, & Siviy, 1994; Merker, 2007; Solms & Panksepp, 2012).

The activation of ancient subcortical brain regions such as the PAG and the deactivation of more recently evolved neocortical brain regions, such as the dorsolateral prefrontal cortex, during the experience of primary emotions is also consistent with the idea that these physically as well as evolutionarily separate brain regions exhibit a kind of reciprocal "seesaw" interaction as the human brain contends with events that trigger or inhibit the expression of primary emotions (Liotti & Panksepp, 2004). With psychopathology, this seesaw relationship may become imbalanced as the emotional regulation processes become impaired, leading to consistent and persistent dysfunctional biases in the interpretation of socioenvironmental events, which may lead to less-regulated emotional experiences.

As the subcortical brain perceives various survival challenges and we experience intense emotional feelings, the subcortically based primal emotional systems may impose "states of mind" over many regions of the cerebral cortex, thereby altering the "color", "tone", and "interpretation" of experiences without changing the neocortical processing of specific cognitive contents (Mesulam, 2000, p. 79). While the connections from the cerebral cortex to the subcortical-limbic networks may be less extensive even in the human brain than the reciprocal subcortical to cortical connections, the recovery from emotional arousals likely involves the activation of diverse cortical-cognitive regulatory processes and thereby the reciprocal deactivation of emotional arousals as the subcortical emotional substrates are downregulated (Liotti et al., 2000). Indeed, Frank et al. (2014) have summarized the field of emotional regulation and provided consistent evidence of prefrontal cortex (PFC) regions becoming activated in service of downregulating negative emotions.

Related to the previous two findings, a third result from this Damasio study was another big surprise. One of the major areas focused on in studies of conditioned fear in animals has been the amygdala (LeDoux, 2012b). However, arousal of the amygdala in human fear experiences was not prominent in the Damasio results. Indeed, the authors noted: "There was no significant activation of the amygdala on either side [of the brain] for any of the emotion/feeling states" (Damasio et al., 2000, p. 1050). While it is clear that the amygdala plays a role in the expression and learning of fear and anger, it is also true that the amygdala is not essential for the experience and expression of fear or of anger, although its participation is more extensive for the learning of specific fear responses (Panksepp, 1998a).

Earlier animal research (preceding brain imaging technology) by A. Fernandez De Molina and Robert W. Hunsperger at the University of Zurich (building on the work of their colleague, the Nobel Laureate Walter Hess introduced in Chapter 7) strongly supports the Damasio group's third finding. These Swiss brain studies were the first to demonstrate that what we call the basic mammalian RAGE/Anger system runs from the PAG in the midbrain up to the medial hypothalamus and further up to the medial amygdala. De Molina and Hunsperger (1962) showed that the rage responses of cats can be evoked using electric brain stimulation from all three sites. However, the system is hierarchically organized, in levels of progressively increasing importance, such that aggressive responses evoked from the amygdala were abolished by lesions at the hypothalamic or PAG levels, aggressive responses elicited from the hypothalamus were dependent on the PAG but not on the amygdala, and aggression triggered from the PAG was not dependent on either of the other two "higher" brain regions. But, De Molina and Hunsperger were not satisfied by laboratory demonstrations. Cats receiving the small lesion of what they called the "hissing zone" of the PAG, "when confronted with a dog, no longer hissed or attacked" (p. 201). For a hierarchical illustration of this system, see Figure 16.1.

While the amygdala likely integrates psychological learning into the RAGE/Anger system and the hypothalamus blends in physiological influences, the PAG seems to be the primal source of RAGE/Anger responses, with damage to the PAG dramatically reducing rage evoked from the other two regions (Panksepp, 1998a). An additional corroborating demonstration in humans from the Mobbs group will be covered but first a brief summary.

In sum, the Damasio group's 2000 PET study yielded three remarkable results, which still need to be more fully integrated into psychological and psychiatric thinking about human emotions: the emphasis on *subcortical activation*, bilateral *neocortical deactivations*, and the *lack of amygdala activation* during strong emotional arousal. The Damasio et al. paper, along with the supporting animal findings, also provides compelling evidence for the affective neuroscience interpretation of where raw emotional feelings arise in the brain (Panksepp, 1998a). Indeed, the subcortical regions of the brain, which are homologously shared by all mammals (and many other vertebrates), provide more than just the evolutionary foundations of human emotional experience. In other words, their functional role in the generation of primary human emotional experiences remains as "primary" for humans as it is for other mammals.

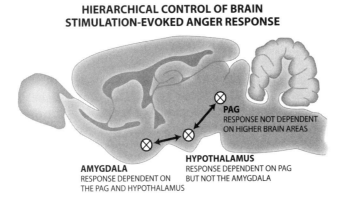

HIERARCHICAL CONTROL OF BRAIN STIMULATION-EVOKED ANGER RESPONSE

PAG
RESPONSE NOT DEPENDENT ON HIGHER BRAIN AREAS

HYPOTHALAMUS
RESPONSE DEPENDENT ON PAG BUT NOT THE AMYGDALA

AMYGDALA
RESPONSE DEPENDENT ON THE PAG AND HYPOTHALAMUS

Figure 16.1. Hierarchical control of RAGE in the brain. Lesions of higher areas do not diminish responses from lower areas, while damage of lower areas compromises the functions of higher ones.

WHEN FEAR IS NEAR: MOBBS'S
VIRTUAL PREDATOR RESEARCH

Dean Mobbs of the University College London and colleagues, took a very evolutionary approach to studying fear that largely confirmed the Damasio group's work described above, as well as De Molina and Hunsperger's work emphasizing the emotional importance of the PAG. Mobbs's group used high-resolution fMRI, rather than PET, to acquire participants' brain images during a computer-simulated survival challenge called the virtual predator and prey paradigm (Mobbs et al., 2007, p. 1080), or what they sometimes referred to as an active escape-from-pain task.

This task required volunteer subjects to escape from the virtual predator to avoid receiving a painful electric shock intended to simulate the predator's bite. It involved displaying the positions of the predator and the participant (who was the prey) on a two-dimensional maze grid that appeared on a screen, which the subject could see while in the scanner. In an initial neutral "pre-encounter" phase, the symbol depicting the inactive predator was displayed in the lower left corner of the grid or wandering about the maze but posing no immediate danger, and the symbol for the subject appeared in the upper right corner of the grid. Next, in a "postencounter" cue phase, the threat was detected: the subject saw that the "flashing" predator was active and also learned whether being captured by the predator would result in one shock (for the low level of pain) or three shocks (for the high level of pain). Then, when the predator symbol ceased flashing, the "chase" phase was on, and the participant could now attempt to move his or her symbol to escape the predator. If captured by the predator, the subject received the amount of painful shock previously indicated. Importantly, Mobbs et al.'s (2007) results showed that their subjects were motivated to escape the shocks, especially the higher level.

When the threat was first detected but not yet imminent, their analysis showed enhanced activity in frontal cortical areas such as the medial orbitofrontal cortex (mOFC; just above the eyes—orbit is another term for eye socket), the ventromedial prefrontal cortex (vmPFC) (just above the mOFC), and the anterior cingulate cortex (ACC), an adjacent older cortical area known to be involved in pain processing. During the chase phase, increased activity was observed in subcortical areas such as the PAG. As the threat became more imminent (regardless of whether subjects were caught and received the shock, or managed to escape from the virtual predator and received no shock), PAG and amygdala activity were evident, with the highest PAG activity occurring when subjects were facing the highest imminent shock level. These researchers also asked their subjects to rate the levels of "dread" of being chased and "confidence" of escaping capture that they had experienced. Increased dread and lower confidence were also associated with increased PAG activity, whereas diminished dread and higher confidence of escaping were associated with stronger prefrontal cortical activity.

To summarize, when the threat is more distant, cortical activity is more prominent, and when threat is near with increased dread and decreased confidence of escape, PAG activity is more prominent. "From an evolutionary viewpoint, higher cortical systems control behavior when the degree of threat is appraised as not-life-endangering. . . . At extreme levels of threat, the PAG may in turn inhibit more complex control processes when a fast and indeed obligatory response is required" (Mobbs et al., 2007, p. 1082). So, consistent with cross-species affective neuroscience research, and continuing the theme of this chapter, low levels of fear are accompanied by cortical arousal and corresponding cognitive threat assessment, but as the level of threat mounts, the PAG in combination with other subcortical regions inhibit cortical activity, exert increasing influence over the brain, and provides rapid reactions based on evolutionary affective memories, along with one's personal higher autobiographical history, to prepare and guide the body for survival.

Mobbs et al. (2009) repeated their simulated predator and human prey experiment and largely replicated their results. In this study, they also measured subjects' skin conductance levels (a physiological measure of anxiety) during the experiment. After subjects emerged from the scanner, researchers also asked them to rate how much anxiety they felt during the various phases of the simulation, as well as how much panic they felt during the predator encounters. These measures allowed researchers to verify that anxiety onset occurred when an encounter with the predator was signaled and that skin conductance levels, anxiety, and panic were all at their highest levels when actually being chased by the predator in the high-danger condition, when midbrain PAG activity also peaked, rather than in the low danger condition. It is relevant to note that we would prefer to reserve the term *panic* for use with the PANIC/Sadness brain system rather than an extreme expression of the FEAR system. This clearly highlights the need for a different lexicon for primary-process emotions, which we try to achieve with the convention of full-capitalization of primal emotional terms). In any case, we will continue to use Mobb's terminology.

In this replication, researchers also measured the number of button-press errors (e.g., accidentally guiding their computer icon into the wall of the maze), which likewise peaked during the high-danger chase and correlated with self-rated panic levels. Indeed, they "found that midbrain [PAG] activity increased with the amount of panic-related locomotor errors," which was consistent with "chemical stimulation of the rodent dorsolateral PAG eliciting uncoordinated panic-like behaviors" (Mobbs et al., 2009, p. 12,241). (Beside FEAR, the separation-distress PANIC response is also well represented in the PAG.) Further, the increase of "all thumbs" uncoordinated fine motor responding that Mobbs and colleagues observed is consistent with the idea that the frontal cortex motor planning functions are inhibited (or disrupted) during high levels of threat that require faster, more ancient, evolutionarily conserved escape responses, while on the other end of the affective seesaw, the prefrontal cortex can exert regulatory inhibition on subcortical regions when lower threat levels allow for more carefully planned and cognitively coordinated escape strategies.

BRIDGING THE HUMAN AND
ANIMAL PAG RESEARCH

Studies such as those by Mobbs and colleagues have encouraged other researchers to use fMRI procedures to focus more on the role of the subcortical PAG in the experience of emotions. Indeed, Buhle et al. (2013) took on the challenge of investigating whether they could replicate animal research and elicit comparable PAG activation in human subjects using negative emotional responses to pain or negative emotional responses while viewing aversive photographs (taken from the International Affective Picture System of Lang, Bradley, & Cuthbert, 2008).

All participants were subjected to high and low thermal pain as well as aversive or neutral cognitive images, and then were asked to rate how negatively they felt about the stimulus. The participants consistently reported that they experienced greater negative affect from high heat than from low heat, and from the aversive images than from the neutral images. Furthermore, the ratings for the painful heat and the aversive images did not significantly differ. Importantly, Buhle et al. noted that "Whole brain contrasts of both high vs. low pain and negative vs. neutral image viewing revealed activity in the PAG" and that "the activity did not reliably differ between the conditions [pain or aversive image]" (2013, p. 611).

As an additional check on their results, Buhle et al. (2013) identified eight independent human studies, four examining responses to high or low pain and four studying responses to negative versus neutral images. In each of the eight independent data sets, whole brain analyses identified activity in the PAG. They concluded that, combined with their own results, "these results support the hypothesis that PAG plays an important role in human negative affect, in line with previous evidence from research in animals" (p. 612). In sum, beneath our "crowning glory" of neocortex, we are like other mammals below our "thinking caps." In this context, it is important to recognize that practically all mammalian cortical functions (e.g., including vision) are probably learned (Sur & Rubinstein, 2005) rather than tightly programmed by brain evolution.

SHARPER FOCUS ON THE HUMAN PAG

Apart from examining the PAG as a whole, animal research has shown that there are distinct subregions of the PAG involving specific affective processes (Bandler & Shipley, 1994). Indeed, Sapute et al. (2013) set out to determine whether PAG subregions could be identified in humans, thus further supporting the homologies between human and animal emotions. Yet, the PAG is difficult to accurately isolate, let alone subdivide, using typical brain scanning procedures. This is in part due to the small size of the PAG—about 10 mm long (three-eighths of an inch), with a diameter of about 6 mm (less than a quarter inch) in humans. Further adding to difficulties imaging the PAG, its structure is shaped like a sleeve or hollow cylinder surrounding the cerebral aqueduct, such that the inner half of the PAG's diameter is the cerebral aqueduct, a part of the brain that, as its name implies, ensures the flow of cerebrospinal fluid, mainly downward, from the rest of the brain. During fMRI scanning, strong signals from the fluid in the cerebral aqueduct can interfere with and mask signals from the PAG. Sapute et al. (2013) addressed these problems by using an fMRI procedure incorporating an exceptionally strong 7-tesla magnet, which could provide higher scanning resolution—down to 0.75 mm—than typical fMRI equipment.

Sapute's group elicited emotions in their eleven scanning participants by showing them either neutral or highly aversive images that were related to threat, harm, and loss (again, taken from the International Affective Picture System). After having their brains scanned while viewing a set of images, participants were asked to report their emotional response to the images with five separate emotional labels: "Activated" (for arousal), "Angry," "Disgusted," "Sad," and "Scared" (for fear). The emotional labels were always presented in random order and were rated on a five-point, low-to-high scale.

An initial analysis showed that overall activity in the PAG was greater when subjects were viewing highly aversive compared to neutral images. However, an exploratory factor analysis of the high-resolution scanning results from their 7-tesla fMRI, along with subjects' self-rated emotional experiences when viewing the aversive versus neutral images, yielded three factors representing three different PAG subregions, with each of the subregions corresponding with a different emotional experience: They reported not only having "observed definitive activation in the human PAG" but also that "segmenting the PAG into both radial and longitudinal subregions illustrated that activity during negative affect was not diffuse but was concentrated along a spiral pattern from ventrolateral caudal PAG to lateral and dorsomedial rostral PAG. This [spiral-like] pattern mirrors functional and structural observations in nonhuman animals" (Sapute et al., 2013, p. 17,104). Further, spiraling around the central aqueduct from caudal to rostral (tail to head), the three PAG subregions generally corresponded to (1) disgust, arousal, and fear; (2) anger; and (3) sadness.

In short, Sapute and colleagues provided robust evidence in support of evolutionarily conserved mammalian brain homologies—from mice to men, so to speak; they had demonstrated that ultra-high-resolution fMRI procedures could be used to explore the functional architecture of the PAG, an approach that could perhaps be extended to other midbrain regions, which have so far been largely ignored in brain imaging studies of human emotion. Still, it is gratifying to see such clear functional continuities across all mammalian species that have been studied. It reinforces the conclusion that we all share a variety of evolutionarily conserved basic emotions.

REVIEWS OF NEUROTICISM AND HUMAN BRAIN IMAGING: META-ANALYSIS

Meta-analyses allow researchers to statistically combine the data from many published scientific studies and obtain a collective result that may be more valid than any of the individual studies alone. The underlying idea is that, while a single study might not report valid results because of various procedural problems or sampling errors, when the data of multiple studies are pooled something closer to a true picture is likely to emerge.

One such meta-analysis reported by Servaas et al. (2013) identified eighteen studies published from 2001 to 2011 that provided fMRI brain imaging data and self-report measures of neuroticism (also sometimes called negative emotionality or low emotional stability) using psychologically healthy subjects as participants. Their concern was that individual studies attempting to use neuroimaging to identify neurobiological correlates of neuroticism had yielded inconsistent findings. They hoped that merging these generally similar studies into a single meta-analysis would reveal more consistent data patterns and thus better validate the different roles of various brain regions than the individual studies.

Remarkably, none of the brain regions the Servaas group identified as being positively correlated with neuroticism were subcortical. Indeed, there was no mention of periaqueductal gray (PAG) activity. In search for the clearest associations with neuroticism, they identified three general brain regions that positively correlated with self-report measures of neuroticism. The first was the left parahippocampal gyrus, along with closely adjacent areas, which were primarily associated with fear-conditioning studies. The second and third areas were the left superior frontal gyrus and the dorsal and ventral regions of the right middle cingulate gyrus. These latter two areas were associated with general emotional processing, such as viewing negative emotional facial expressions, categorizing emotional words, and choice tasks resulting in the relative loss or gain of small amounts of money ($4 or less). Why the disjunction with studies monitoring immediate emotional feelings?

We would suggest that personality is ultimately an acquired result of how past primary emotional arousals have helped construct diverse brain action systems that mediate emotional activity. In the Servaas meta-analysis, each of the three general personality-relevant areas had previously been associated with cognitive emotional processing. The parahippocampal gyrus had been shown to interact with the amygdala during the encoding of negative film clips (Kilpatrick & Cahill, 2004) and in the recall of negative words (Thomaes et al., 2009). The superior frontal gyrus had been shown to be involved with maintaining human self-awareness (Goldberg, Harel, & Malach, 2006) and had been associated with general cognitive control and perhaps especially modulating the current emotional state (Frank et al., 2014). The dorsal and ventral regions of the cingulate gyrus seemed to be important in regulating the balance between external and internal attentional factors (Leech & Sharp, 2014).

Another reason that Servaas et al. (2013) did not identify any subcortical associations with neuroticism is possibly that the NEO PI-R Neuroticism scale was used to measure neuroticism in twelve of the studies they reviewed, a scale that mainly deals with a tertiary cortical cognitive appraisal of negative emotion. Items like "I have fewer fears than most people" and "Frightening thoughts sometimes come into my head" may require more cognitive reflection than a direct assessment of how the self-rater feels at the moment. Also, items like "I feel I am capable of coping with most of my problems" and "I can handle myself pretty well in a crisis" not only entail cognitive reflection but also are very general and may not tap into the patterns of specific primary emotional tendencies that have guided personality development.

A review by Montag et al. (2013) has suggested that a brain-based personality assessment such as the Affective Neuroscience Personality Scales (ANPS) might be better suited for parsing emotion-related brain regions. The ANPS was designed to address the primary-process negative emotions, namely, RAGE/Anger, FEAR, and PANIC/Sadness, and uses items that more directly tap into a self-rater's affective experience rather than relying on more general affective judgments. It is no coincidence that the ANPS negative emotionality scales target the three primary emotions Sapute et al. (2013) linked to specific regions of the periaqueductal gray using fMRI imaging: fear, anger, and sadness.

Yet another possibility is that the tasks used in the eighteen studies reviewed by Servaas et al. (2013), such as viewing negative emotional facial expressions and categorizing emotional words, are more cognitively oriented and may not strongly engage strong emotional feelings. Those tasks may be more similar to the early stage of the predator task used in the fMRI study by Mobbs et al. (2009), when there was no imminent danger and the participant had not yet encountered the predator.

In any event, the overall meta-analytic results by Servaas et al. (2013) seem more reflective of a cognitive neuroscience approach to emotions, which is inclined to look for sources of emotional brain activity in the human cortex than in subcortical regions such as the PAG originally identified in animal research, which is only recently becoming accepted as a key region for the experience of human emotion. Thus, we need to see human personality in part as an "emergent process" of how basic emotional arousals have guided the life trajectories of individual human beings. Personality may reflect how the ancient primal affective tools for living guide how one has learned to be a specific type of person in a specific environment.

EXTENDING FINDINGS WITH
MORE META-ANALYSIS

Another meta-analysis by Adina Mincic (2015) took advantage of a very active new research field, examining fifty-seven studies relating negative emotionality to brain activity and brain structure sizes, with most studies reporting cortical gray matter differences. A predominant finding was that higher negative emotionality correlated with reduced gray matter volume in the left orbitofrontal cortex (OFC)—sometimes included in the ventromedial prefrontal cortex—a region positioned just above and behind the eye sockets in humans.

Another prominent finding was greater gray matter volume in the left amygdala for participants with higher negative emotionality. Mincic (2015) also found evidence for increased volume in the hippocampus and the parahippocampal gyrus associated with higher negative emotionality scores. She only found a few studies focusing on the cingulate cortex—an evolutionarily older cortical region lying immediately above the corpus callosum—but focused on the anterior cingulate cortex ACC rather than the posterior cingulate cortex, with the reduced OFC volume extending into the rostral (very front portion) of ACC, which lies adjacent to and immediately behind the OFC. In addition, Mincic (2015) found neuroanatomical evidence for decreased volume in the left uncinate fasciculus, a Latin name for a nerve tract connecting frontal areas such as the OFC to the amygdala/hippocampal regions. All of this "supports the idea that the diminished grey matter in OFC/ACC and white matter integrity of the uncinate fasciculus may represent a structural phenotype of the NE [Negative Emotionality]-related personality traits" (p. 110). Such a conclusion highlights the top-down regulation of emotional arousal in maintaining emotional balance and well-being. However, these studies are still missing the critical midbrain emotional foundational areas, which are so apparent in the work of Damasio, Mobbs, and Sapute, as already highlighted.

Another relevant concern is the heterogeneity of results in the literature covered by these two meta-analyses. For starters, the only result the two had in common was a positive correlation in the parahippocampal region with negative emotionality. Mincic (2015) pointed out that Servaas et al. (2013) had found increased activity in the parahippocampal gyrus during negative emotional processing but, surprisingly, not in the amygdala. However, regarding Mincic's most consistent finding of reduced OFC volume associated with higher negative emotionality, she pointed out that of thirty studies investigating this particular relationship, twelve did not find this association, with two actually reporting opposite results. Similar disparities were evident for each of her conclusions.

Why is there such inconsistency in the brain imaging literature? Why did these two meta-analyses report such inconsistent results, in stark contrast to the animal studies? There are likely many reasons, including variations in the size and anatomy of human brains, the frequent use of low-resolution scanners, difficulty in the use of fMRI to identify activity in midbrain regions such as the PAG where neurons fire quite slowly relative to higher brain regions, and the fact that many studies do not even target midbrain regions. However, we may need to probe deeper into the reason for these disparities: The midbrain regions and structures like the hypothalamus have strongly inherited genetic/anatomical foundations, while the cortical regions are not as tightly genetically programmed but, rather, acquire their functions much more through individual learning and development, providing another source of cortical anatomical heterogeneity.

A theme throughout this book has been that the neocortex is not essential for the experience of emotions. The neocortex has an amazing capacity to re-represent and refine input from the more genetically defined parts of the nervous system, such as the subcortical emotional and motivational networks that guide diverse affective survival responses and to allow the rest of the brain to integrate those "survival values" with our various sensory-perceptual organs that provide information primarily about our external (rather than internal) worlds. Because cortical capacities are acquired—developmentally programmed, if you will—by our basic affective (sensory, homeostatic, and emotional) direct survival systems, there are bound to be more individual differences in cortical brain regions than the more ancient intrinsic subcortical functions. This helps explain the dramatic cortical flexibility demonstrated in Sur's animal brain research showing how temporal cortex can assume a visual function rather than its more typical auditory function (Sur & Rubenstein, 2005), as well as the dramatic cortical plasticity being demonstrated in subjects who recover from relatively minor cortical brain damage (Nudo, 2013).

Moreover, there is also convincing evidence for the recruitment of visual cortex for somatosensory processing—exercising well-developed tactile skills for reading braille or identifying objects by finger tracing—in individuals who have been blind from an early age (Cohen et al., 1997). Indeed, Sadato et al. (1998) further compared PET imaging of blind and sighted subjects and found imaging results during braille and nonbraille tasks, suggesting that tactile input usually processed in the somatosensory cortex (closer to the top of the skull) of sighted individuals was rerouted in subjects blinded early in life to occipital cortical regions that typically specialize for visual processing. Further, Weeks et al. (2000) used PET to investigate which cortical areas were activated in blind versus sighted subjects when performing auditory localization tasks. Indeed, congruent with the aforementioned work, these investigators observed auditory to visual plasticity: while sighted and blind participants both showed activated posterior parietal cortex, blind participants also showed activated right occipital cortex, a region typically identified with vision. Thus, the superior touch and hearing skills of blind individuals may be due to occipital regions (normally involved in the visual processing of sighted individuals) being "programmed" to participate in the processing of tactile and auditory information, thus providing additional cortical resources enabling expanded tactile and auditory abilities.

Perhaps one day new brain analysis tools will provide a means to show how much of the variability in cortical brain function researchers are currently observing is due to the variability in how neocortical regions are differentially "programmed" in individuals beginning life with distinct genetically promoted endophenotypes and then growing up and maturing under the influence of different environmental circumstances. One might anticipate a clearer appreciation of developmental plasticity in the cortical processing and regulation of emotions.

FIRST-ORDER EMERGENCE OF EMOTIONS: THE DAMASIO GROUP

It is fitting to close this chapter using another contribution from the Damasio group (Damasio, Damasio, & Tranel, 2013), which like the Panksepp group has challenged "the traditional view that mental states are subserved mainly or exclusively by the cerebral cortex" (p. 833). Many have proposed cortical structures as the basis for emotional experience, but A. D. "Bud" Craig (2009, 2011) has asserted that the insula, an interior region of cortex inside the cortical temporal lobe, holds the keys to the kingdom, so to speak, and is the primary neural platform for feelings of emotion.

In response to this argument, Damasio et al. (2013) reviewed subcortical evidence for the first-order emergence of emotions, but more important for this chapter, they put the insula hypothesis to the test by publishing brain images and corresponding emotional data from a person that had sustained extensive brain damage, which included bilateral insula destruction. In their 2013 paper, Damasio's group described patient B, who as a result of herpes simplex encephalitis had lost not only his insula but also his amygdala, hippocampus, and other brain cortices, including much of his orbitofrontal cortex, the temporal pole, the parahippocampal cortex, and the anterior cingulate cortex. Importantly, there was no insular cortex remaining in either hemisphere of his brain, which was clearly evident in the brain images presented by Damasio et al. (2013). They further stated that, perhaps surprising to some, "unwarned strangers interacting with him for the first time had no inkling that he had major neurological damage, the fact only becoming apparent once his dense amnesia was exposed. To put it plainly, patient-B was a whole human being suffering from a very poor episodic memory" (p. 834). Patient B's spouse completed a structured questionnaire comparing his behavior before and after his disease, with twenty-five of the questions dealing explicitly with emotions. On eighteen of the twenty-five items, his spouse rated him the same before and after he lost significant portions of his cerebral cortex. On three items she rated him up a point and on four down a point. In addition, patient B frequently and routinely expressed his pleasure or displeasure with life events, including lab procedures such as taking tape off his arm that pulled on his hairs. In short, the questionnaire data, the observations of strangers, and the observations of the research team, including psychological evaluations, all indicated patient B retained a full range of appropriate emotions after his brain disease.

The data from patient B describing his full emotional life makes it difficult to support the idea that the insula is necessary for subjective affective experiences. Indeed, this case provides compelling evidence that structures such as the amygdala, the hippocampus, the parahippocampal gyrus, the temporal pole, the orbitofrontal cortex, and the anterior cingulate cortex are not essential for the expression and experience of emotion. Thus, we agree with Damasio's group and argue that the structures essential for the generation of emotions are largely subcortical brain regions, especially the PAG and hypothalamus. Clearly, cortical regions play a big role in the full sophistication of human emotional life, but that role is largely a secondary-level one that is acquired—"programmed"—through learning resulting from life experiences, with perhaps early life experiences being especially influential. It isn't that cortical areas do not play an important emotional role—especially with humans. Many regions of cortex elaborate emotional learning. However, that function is similar to the one provided for all our sensory and motor modalities: Learning provides nuanced refinements that not only enrich and complexify our affective experiences but also offer the potential for diverse learned regulations and elaborations of our emotions—both augmenting and inhibiting (Frank et al., 2014). Without our subcortical affective systems we lose cognitive consciousness. Without our neocortices, at least if lost near birth, affective consciousness survives, without the developmentally added cognitive complexities such as the capacity for spoken language that patient B was fortunately spared.

As neuroscientists become more sophisticated in the use of brain imaging and as new techniques emerge, such as diffusion tensor imaging, which has enabled Coenen et al. (2012) to better understand subcortical deep brain stimulation options for the treatment of psychiatric disorders (Coenen et al., 2012; Panksepp et al., 2014; Panksepp, 2016), we will better understand the origins of subcortical affective imbalances and the role cortical regions contribute to both affective equilibrium and disequilibrium (Panksepp, 2015, 2016).

An important theme running throughout this book is the necessity of first understanding our subcortical primary-process emotional action-affect systems before we can hope to illuminate the subtleties of the human mind and the heights and depths it can traverse through learning and culture. At the core of our mental lives there are profound positive and negative affects, which find their origins in ancient regions of our brain that we share homologously with all the other mammals. The massive "mushrooming" of our neocortex expands our subcortical capacities and allows us complex thoughts and unique creative endeavors of our own making. With the addition of abundant neocortex instantiated and energized by our lower mind, our upper mind can reach creatively, indeed uniquely, into the depths of each human life, as it attempts to optimize its present moment as well as imagined mindscape trajectories into the future.

CHAPTER 17
Personality and the Self

A tolerance for multiple alternative representations may provide the critical ingredient that sets the special flavour of human consciousness. It is reasonable to assume that animals have a relatively simple sort of consciousness, the content of which is closely determined by the here-and-now of immediate needs and sensations. A more complex form of consciousness would be expected to emerge if some critical mass of neurons, freed from the household chores of sensation and action, could afford to form alternative and annotated representations of ambient events. One consequence of this process could be the emergence of an observing self who becomes differentiated from the sensory flux and who can therefore intentionally comment (introspect) on experience.

—M. Marsel Mesulam, "From Sensation to Cognition"

WHAT WOULD PERSONALITY be without a sense of self? The "miracle" of the mind is that humans experience themselves, and this is essential to a sense of self. The "self" is a fundamental sense of who and what we are as distinct from all other beings and all other things. This suggests that a sense of self would include our sense of our own personality, but it surely is a broader concept than personality, accounting for a wider array of behaviors and experiences than personality. Beyond personality, the experience of our own personal affects, and the basic mechanisms of learning and memory, the human self would include

  intelligence
  cognitive, physical, and social skills and abilities
  an awareness of our own and others' personal characteristics, such
      as attractiveness, size, and strength

a life story line of autobiographical memories that constitute our
   unique personal history
our relationships to other beings and to unfolding life events in
   general
a continuous experience of our mental and bodily states
an explicit sense of owning our body
a feeling of agency, meaning a sense that when our body moves,
   we are making it move
a moment-by-moment assessment of the position of our body and
   body parts in time and space
being able to distinguish our body from the external world

There are probably more, depending on how we want to slice that ineffable feeling of being a mind that exists in a world that exists, and now,
after modern science, the existential perspective of being an ineffable
"dot" in a cosmic universe that may be one among many.

This long list, which moves from more elaborate to more basic abilities (to an existential entity in the cosmos), suggests that the self is a
very complex psychological construct with a long evolutionary and cultural history. However, it is difficult to imagine a meaningful human life
without even the most elementary of these existential-mental capacities,
which is perhaps why Alzheimer's disease, with the expectation of losing various cognitive mental faculties, is such a feared diagnosis.

This chapter reviews various ideas about the self-concept from a general neuroscience research orientation, much of which focuses on the
cortex, which is easier to study in humans because of our neocortical
capacity for language. Indeed, as we described in Chapter 16, with current neuroimaging techniques cortical changes are much easier to study
than the prelinguistic subcortical functions of the brain, partly because
neuronal firing rates are much higher in cortical brain regions than in
subcortical areas where our basic emotional circuits are concentrated.
With damage to any single major region of our neocortex, we remain
sentient beings. In contrast, following relatively small damage to subcortical brain regions, the mental "light" of consciousness disappears, especially when damage is concentrated in the most ancient mid-brainstem
region of the periaqueductal gray (PAG) and very closely associated
brainstem regions that as a group have been called the reticular activating system.

In any case, a great deal of work remains to be done relating the self
to the ancient subcortical brain regions and circuits that are essential
for constituting the core of our primary emotion networks. While an
autobiographical sense of self may reach its fullest elaboration in the
recently evolved human neocortex, here we try to illuminate the SELF (a
Simple Ego-type Life Form) from a brain evolutionary perspective (see

Panksepp, 1998a; Panksepp & Biven, 2012). In this chapter we try to demonstrate the limitations of a purely neocortically based self-concept and conclude with a cross-species affective neuroscience interpretation of the core self, shared across mammals, at the very least.

Focusing first on our most basic SELF and self-related capacities, imagine yourself in a physical fight against a human attacker. What psychological self constructs would be critical for survival? First of all, you would need to experience an emotion (with all its physiological, motivational, and motor action tendencies) in response to the attack. Second, you would need to automatically distinguish your body from your attacker's body. Third, during the fight, it would be adaptive to have an automatic moment-to-moment sense of where your body and its various parts are located. Fourth, with a bit more mind power, it would also help to have a sense of agency—that you could make your body do things to achieve goals, such as using your fist to hit the attacker hard enough to undo their attack, to functionally drive him or her away.

While these four capacities seem rather elementary, they constitute quite a remarkable evolutionary accomplishment. A self that was characterized by only the four basic abilities required by our fighter would be a very elementary SELF, but these minimal features of raw existence represent real evolved solutions to problems faced by all animals with nervous systems capable of adapting to and surviving basic life challenges. Of primary importance in this chapter is that very basic cross-species mental powers remain essential for humans to maintain a coherent sense of self. We have already used several different conceptions of the self, and now we will try to flesh out the several levels of BrainMind organization that need to be considered to understand this multidimensional BrainMind process.

THE PROTO-SELF AND CORE SELF

For creatures with a brain, even a primitive or proto-self (see Damasio, 1999; Panksepp, 1998b, 2005) probably includes the capacity to respond to bodily metabolic needs in addition to the ability to spontaneously generate body movements, and the ability to implicitly distinguish self from nonself. Further on, evolution may have integrated primary sensory, homeostatic, and emotional affects and primitive coherent-instinctual, sensory-motor processes with a proto-self to create what the second author of this book has called the core SELF (Panksepp, 1998a). However, even then we are still just talking about a type of pure affective experience without the capacity to reflect on that experience with awareness, namely, as a third-party observer of sorts that neocortical self-reflective experiences allow—an explicit characteristic perhaps unique to humans, or perhaps shared implicitly with as yet undetermined numbers of other species, although without language and hence probably in a more limited capacity.

Simple amphibian vertebrates, such as the much-studied northern leopard frog, *Rana pipiens,* would be a good example of a species with a core SELF. Because frogs possess limited cortex, they would largely have subcortical body maps. Affects and sensory inputs would be processed in areas homologous to the mammalian subcortical brain, such as the PAG and the superior and inferior colliculi. Yet, even though a frog's visual acuity, for example, would not be considered 20–20 from a human viewpoint, and frogs can be easily visually fooled (Lettvin, Maturana, McCulloch, & Pitts, 1968), they still manage to fill their tummies with flies, which is no small achievement. But, their limited self-representational brain capacity relative to humans likely leaves them with a rather minimal self (for an evolutionary synthesis, see Feinberg & Mallatt, 2016).

It is generally thought that the core SELF is generated as the Brain-Mind represents somatic and visceral states in neural maps, which are able to integrate inputs from various sources to generate a sense of bodily coherence. Such neuropsychic map-like representations probably occur at many levels throughout the brain. In the lower midbrain, they are found in the PAG as well as inferior and superior colliculi; they are also found in the upper midbrain and diencephalon (that is, in the hypothalamus and midline thalamic regions), before they are re-represented with additional cognitive complexities in the forebrain. In mammals, the cerebral cortex acquires (probably through developmental learning mechanisms that are still poorly mapped) well-developed body sensory maps, motor maps, and extensive higher-order visual and auditory processing areas, which we increasingly come to rely on as we mature, and which at least in humans permit thoughts about our place in the world.

THE EMERGENCE OF SELF-AWARENESS

Humans have a subcortical brain anatomy homologous to the frog's but with many additions, including more sophisticated "switch-boards" and cortical regions for processing sensory inputs that we grow ever more dependent on from infancy to adulthood. With our ample neocortex, humans have inherited spectacular representational and re-representational upgrades, which not only provide us with self-awareness but also allows us to observe ourselves and even see ourselves from the viewpoint of others. We are able to know that mom told us not to eat any of the freshly baked cookies we love until after dinner but at the same time to be aware that mom is out on the front porch talking to the neighbor and that we have an opportunity to easily sneak one of those sugary gems up to our room and enjoy it without her ever knowing.

It is not clear how many other species are capable of this level of awareness. However, Nicola Clayton's group at Cambridge University has reported that if one scrub jay (*Aphelocoma californica*), a rather intelligent bird, notices another scrub jay watching it hide food, the first scrub jay will retrieve the food later and hide it in a new place after the onlooker has left (Dally, Emery, & Clayton, 2006), seeming to demonstrate the ability to appreciate the contents of other minds, which some earlier investigators prematurely granted only to humans. This group of researchers has also demonstrated that this is learned behavior, because some hand-reared birds do not exhibit this recaching behavior, and only birds mature enough to display Piagetian "object permanence" are able to learn the behavior.

It appears that as the self-representational capacities of mammalian brains became more elaborate, the ability to integrate varied sources of information and the complexity of the self increase correspondingly. Especially with primates, this means becoming ever more reliant on the cerebral mantle (neocortex) for more refined analyses of sensory data as the cortex learns to provide ever more sophisticated interpretations in the service of more sophisticated behavioral strategies. This mantle allows us to have more sophisticated strategies to find, construct, and hold resources, just like an overcoat allows us to survive in cold weather. However, this does not mean that a more cerebrally complex self can be sustained on its own without the continuous support of primary (evolutionarily more ancient) affective BrainMind functions. And, with the increased reliance on refined cortical abilities and interpretations, some new mental "problems" can emerge as well.

We now summarize a series of fascinating ways human self-referential bodily feelings can be projected into the inanimate world. We do this to help highlight that our sense of personal ownership of our personalities may be less stable than we commonly believe. Although how these issues relate to understanding human personality remains ambiguous, the following fascinating laboratory demonstrations show that our neocortex and the higher sense of ourselves can fool us about the sources of experience.

ANOSOGNOSIA

One interesting body ownership phenomenon is called anosognosia (a literal Greek translation is "without disease knowledge"), a deficit of self-awareness that can occur after a stroke. For example, a person whose left arm is paralyzed as a result of a stroke may deny that the paralyzed limb is part of the body. This sounds bizarre. Although the condition occurs in about 10 percent of acute stroke patients, it usually does not persist for long (Starkstein, Jorge, & Robinson, 2010).

There are also a related series of fascinating demonstrations that we can project our feelings into inanimate objects as if they were part of our body. For instance, a faulty body ownership phenomenon that can be easily induced in a laboratory is called the rubber hand illusion, in which subjects begin experiencing that an artificial hand belongs to their own body (Botvinick & Cohen, 1998). These researchers created the illusion by placing the subject's left arm on a table but hiding it from the subject's view with a small standing screen. Then a full-sized rubber model of a left arm and hand was placed on the table in front of the subject. While the subject viewed the rubber hand, two small paintbrushes were used to simultaneously stroke the rubber hand and the subject's own hidden hand. After ten minutes of "synchronous" stroking, the subject was asked to complete a questionnaire, which showed . subjects strongly agreed that "I felt as if the rubber hand were my hand" and that "It seemed as though the touch I felt was caused by the paintbrush touching the rubber hand." The researchers also asked subjects to close their eyes and slide their right index finger under the table until it aligned with the index finger of their left hand. Experimental subjects shifted their alignment an average of 2.3 centimeters toward the rubber hand, while control subjects who received "asynchronous" brushing shifted alignment away from the rubber hand.

Armel and Ramachandran (2003) took this illusion several steps further by demonstrating that, in addition to brushing, sensory tapping could also generate the illusion. They also provided what they called an absurd situation in which they successfully substituted the tabletop for the rubber hand. These researchers further showed that strong skin conductance responses, a physiological measure of autonomic arousal, were elicited if either the adopted rubber hand or adopted tabletop was "injured" despite the fact that all surprise was ruled out by showing the participants in advance the painful procedures, such as extreme finger bending or ripping off a bandage, and assuring them these would not be performed on their real hand.

Henrik Ehrsson's group at the Brain, Body and Self Laboratory at the Karolinska Institutet in Stockholm provided fMRI data to test the feeling of ownership and the extent to which the rubber hand was incorporated into the body. They were able to show that threatening the adopted rubber hand by making stabbing movements toward that hand with a needle (without actually touching the rubber hand) could induce activity in the anterior cingulate cortex (ACC) and insula—areas of the brain associated with the anticipation of pain—similar to when the subject's real hand was threatened, and the effect was stronger than the effect of just seeing the needle (Ehrsson, Wiech, Weiskopf, Dolan, & Passingham, 2007). Moreover, "the more strongly the participants felt the rubber hand to be their own hand, the greater the activity in the ACC and left insular cortex when the hand was under threat" (p. 9,831). These researchers were also able to show a positive correlation between anxiety ratings collected after the threat procedures and ACC and insular cortex brain activation during the synchronous stroking condition, with no corresponding effects during the asynchronous control condition.

Petkova and Ehrsson (2008) were able to extend this distortion of body ownership to complete "body swapping"—the feeling that another person's body is your own. Using a mannequin with cameras mounted on its head that projected its image to a head-mounted visual display worn by the subject, when the subject looked down, he or she saw the abdomen of the mannequin. In addition to this visual stimulation, the subject and mannequin both received simultaneous tactile strokes on the abdomen with a short rod. Via the headset, the subject could only view the strokes to the abdomen of the mannequin. After synchronous visual and tactile stimulation, the subject showed a significantly greater skin conductance response when the abdomen of the mannequin was threatened with a knife than when threatened by a spoon or when threatened with a knife after having received only asynchronous stimulation. While humans normally experience a spatial unity between their self and their body, a lab in Switzerland further tested the extent of these body illusions by showing how we can experimentally induce "out-of-body" experiences in which a person's sense of bodily location was shifted toward a virtual body in front of the person (Lenggenhager, Tadi, Metzinger, & Blanke, 2007).

Others had previously reported that operating a robot would lead to feeling embodied within the arms and body of the robot (Cole, Sacks, & Waterman, 2000). The robot had human-like arms and fingers, which were directly activated, after a short delay, by sensors placed on the operator's arms and hands. Cameras placed on the robot projected images of the robot's arms to a headset worn by the operator, which provided a viewpoint similar to the view of the operator's own arms and which eliminated any direct vision of the operator's own body. After a few minutes of operating the robot and experiencing the proprioceptive feedback from their unseen arms, coupled with seeing the nearly simultaneous movements of the robot's arms, participants "became at ease with the feeling of being 'in' the robot" (p. 167). The sense of embodiment was sufficiently strong that one operator had the sensation that "he had better be careful for if he dropped a wrench it would land on his leg" (p. 167), even though the robot holding the wrench was on the other side of the room. Clearly, our neocortex can easily construct delusional perspectives. But as a side note, these shifts in perspective might also relate to the human capacity for empathy, the affective foundations of which are shared with other mammals (J.B Panksepp & Panksepp, 2017).

H. Henrik Ehrsson's group (Ehrsson, Spence, & Passingham, 2004) has also conducted human experiments in which they acquired fMRI brain images during the induction of the rubber hand illusion and found that activity in the premotor cortex, an area just in front of the primary and supplementary motor cortex, is associated with the feeling of ownership of the seen rubber limb. Further, the level of brain activity in the premotor cortex was directly proportional to the degree of subjective ownership reported by the participant. These authors argued that self-attribution of body parts depended on multisensory integration occurring in the ventral premotor cortex, which is connected to visual and somatosensory (tactile) areas of the cortex. However, it should be noted that their fMRI procedures did not adequately explore subcortical regions of the brain.

This Swedish research group was also able to reverse the illusion: rather than inducing participants to adopt a rubber hand, they induced them to "disown" their own hand. This was accomplished by using a video recording of the participant's hand being stroked (made previously with the participant's eyes closed). In the experiment, participants were able to see only the video recording while their own hand was being stroked either synchronously or asynchonously with the viewed video image. On a postscan questionnaire, participants receiving stroking that was asynchronous with their viewed image strongly reported that "it felt as if I was looking at somebody else's hand." Under the asynchronous stroking condition, subjects also exhibited significantly smaller skin conductance responses when the viewed hand was threatened with a kitchen knife and did not exhibit the expected fMRI responses compared to when the tactile stroking was synchronous with their viewed image (Gentile, Guterstam, Brozzoli, & Ehrsson, 2013). This loss of self-ownership of the participant's own hand was consistent with their premise that "maintenance of updated representation of the body is an essential prerequisite for goal-directed or defensive interactions with the external world and the sense of a bodily self" (p. 13,350).

COULD THE HUMAN SELF BE
PRIMARILY CORTICAL?

While body ownership illusions and the associated brain data are impressive, these novel self-attribution adaptations are also as easily reversed as they were generated. Do they mean that in humans the core self has become a cortically induced phenomenon? Does this all mean that, like with the senses, the neocortex has also become the dominant provider of the sense of our experienced core self and hence that a complex human cognitive sense of self—what has been called the idiographic self (Panksepp & Biven, 2012)—relies on and cannot survive without these cortical representations?

Brain damage studies and other brain research suggest otherwise for at least core self processes. Indeed, even in neurologically intact humans, the core self remains deeply rooted in the subcortical emotional foundations of the brain with links to other brain structures evolutionarily older than the neocortex. The evidence does not support the idea that the cortex, especially the neocortex, is essential to maintaining a stable sense of an affective core self.

It is well documented that brain damage in humans to the frontal motor regions of the neocortex (where plans and intentions are generated) results in greater personality changes than damage to posterior sensory regions of the neocortex (Eslinger et al., 1992; Passingham, 1993). Neocortical sensory losses may include numbness or the loss of vision or hearing. Neocortical damage often influences the ability to use language. Neocortical motor losses may also include reduced muscular control, paralysis, or personality-altering reduced impulse control. Yet, these patients still have an affective sense of self and feel they are still very much the same person they always were despite their life-changing cognitive or physical limitations. Their fundamental sense of self and affective experience have not been eliminated, and as with anosognosia, any self-disturbance resulting from damage to these more lateral (more recently evolved) brain regions typically does not persist.

Nobel Prize winner Roger Sperry's famous split-brain studies (for an historical overview, see Gazzaniga, 2015) likewise do not support the idea that the cortex is essential for a coherent sense of self. At that time, almost half a century ago, the split-brain procedure had become a successful treatment for patients with severe epileptic seizures. In these patients, surgeons completely cut through the corpus callosum, the brain structure connecting the left and right cerebral hemispheres, thus separating the two cerebral hemispheres and greatly reducing the intensity of life-threatening seizures by preventing their spread from one hemisphere to the other. One might assume that this procedure would greatly disrupt the self, possibly creating two selves, if the basis that the self lies primarily in the cortex. However, no such dramatic shift occurred. Indeed, after the patients recovered from surgery there were no signs of changes to their outward behavior or functioning. Special experiments on these subjects were required to demonstrate any differences, and these differences had little to do with the self.

These patients did not exhibit split personalities and displayed fluid, whole-body intentional behavior. As Michael Gazzaniga, one of Sperry's students, pointed out in his book *The Mind's Past*, "Split-brain effects have to be exposed in a laboratory, where special techniques separately test each half-brain" (1998, p. 132). He does goes on to say that split-brain patients seem to have two minds with different skills and abilities—we might say learned cortical representations. But, also that during laboratory tests, in which the nonspeaking right hemisphere was given a command, while the speaking left brain couldn't say what command had been given to the right hemisphere, "it [the left hemisphere] didn't seem perturbed about the right brain carrying out whatever the command might be. There was never a complaint about this odd state of affairs" (p. 132).

The ease with which split-brain patients conducted their lives may relate to the fact that their entire brains had not been split; only their evolutionarily newer cortical hemispheres had been separated. The surgeon's scalpel had not entered their evolutionarily older subcortical brain regions such as the thalamus, hypothalamus, and midbrain. Because these subjects had no difficulty leading normal coherent lives, this would argue that the basis of the core self, where our action-oriented raw emotions are processed, is likely rooted in subcortical areas of the brain that had not been cut.

THE ROLE OF CORTICAL MIDLINE STRUCTURE

However, there are also evolutionarily older, more medial (closer to the middle) cortical areas, with a simpler anatomical infrastructure, that seem to be more closely linked with more primal self-related processes. These areas, often called cortical midline structures, have been examined in neuroimaging studies focusing on self-related activities. Representative studies have observed subjects performing (1) verbal tasks, such as judging whether a trait like "trustworthy" applied to oneself or to another person, (2) memory tasks, such as determining whether self-related trait adjectives would be remembered better than trait adjectives judged not to be self-related, (3) emotional processing, such as rating the self-relatedness of emotional pictures, and (4) ownership of actions, such as being aware that the circle on a computer screen was drawn by yourself or by someone else (Northoff et al., 2006).

In such studies, the brain regions most predominately activated were not in the neocortex but, rather, in the evolutionarily older cortical midline structures, especially in frontal midline regions, such as the dorsomedial prefrontal cortex, ventromedial prefrontal cortex, and pre/subgenual anterior cingulate cortex. However, it should again be noted that these fMRI studies did not typically examine subcortical regions, which are commonly difficult to monitor using fMRI procedures. Each of these evolutionarily older cortical midline structures is widely connected to other cortical and, importantly, to subcortical regions of the brain, especially subcortical regions such as the hypothalamus and PAG that are closely related with the brain's primal emotion networks. The Northoff et al. (2006) meta-analysis of brain imaging studies related to the self found that the cortical midline structures were intimately associated with the processes generating the sense that information is self-relevant. It follows that patients with brain damage to these evolutionarily older midline cortical areas would exhibit an impaired capacity for developing a coherent sense of self, as well as disturbances in their social interactions (Damasio, 1999).

SUBCORTICAL MIDLINE SYSTEM

If brain damage extends into subcortical midline systems, and into the PAG lying at the heart of subcortical affective systems, even conscious awareness can be dramatically compromised. Complete destruction of the PAG impairs all self-related processing of environmental events (Panksepp & Biven, 2012, p. 409), indeed, consciousness itself. Animals with complete PAG lesions no longer exhibit spontaneous self-care activities and no longer respond to environmental events in anticipatory ways. For instance, they no longer show anticipatory interest in food, although they will chew and swallow food placed in their mouths (Bailey & Davis, 1942, 1943). For unknown reasons, without special care, such animals spontaneously die within a few months of surgery—no physiological cause of death could be identified.

SUMMARY

As we traverse progressively more ancient medial regions of the brain related to survival, we find neural systems that are essential for generating and maintaining organismic coherence—much more than the neocortex. It is there, in those ancient brain regions, that we find the highest concentrations of all the basic emotional systems that provide an essential affective foundation for the development of personality. It would appear that a core sense of self and even consciousness itself are not possible without the support of the diverse primary emotional networks that help developmentally constitute our higher personality structures. This said, abundant higher cerebral programming is required to bring out the full richness of personality development. In the final accounting, the emotional foundations alone are essential, but not sufficient, for the full flowering of human and animal personalities.

CHAPTER 18

Affective Neuro-Personality and Psychopathology

Once these affects are re-represented in higher MindBrain regions, they tend to remain idiographically self-centered, and much of emotional education as well as psychotherapy may need to proceed by "deconditioning" and "recontextualization" of emotional self-centeredness. That allows one to accept one's negative feelings as one's own, and not of others' making.

— Jaak Panksepp, "The Primary Process Affects in Human Development, Happiness, and Thriving"

In 2013, the U.S. Department of Health and Human Services reported that 43.8 million adults in the United States eighteen or more years of age (18.5 percent of the population) had some form of mental illness in 2013, and a total of 15.7 million of these adults (6.7 percent of the population) had had at least one major depression episode (NSDUH: Mental Health Findings, 2013). Depression, of all the major psychiatric disorders, is associated with the highest risk of suicide, highlighting how the psychological pain of mental illness can erode the will to live and lead some people to take their own lives. Mortality data from the Centers for Disease Control and Prevention (2014) show that suicide is the tenth leading cause of death in the United States, with over forty thousand deaths by suicide in 2012, or 1.6 percent of all deaths in the United States. The details are frightening: (1) Suicide is the seventh leading cause of death for males and the fourteenth leading cause for females. (2) Although "females are more likely than males to have suicidal thoughts," (3) "males take their own lives at nearly four times the rate of females and represent 77.9% of all suicides" (Centers for Disease Control and Prevention, 2015).

These figures dramatize the impact of mental disorders in the general population. But what actually is mental illness? What causes these bouts of human suffering? Why do afflicted individuals have such difficulty escaping from their periods of maladaptive behavior and thought? How can we develop more effective treatments for these psychological problems? Unfortunately, the neural nature of psychological pain remains largely a mystery, at least compared to physical pain (Panksepp & Biven, 2012). However, there is a growing database highlighting how feelings of loneliness (i.e., separation distress, arising from the PANIC/Sadness system) may be foundational for the intrapsychic pain that leads to so much human suffering (Panksepp, 2016), which could be treated more easily with ultralow doses of safe opioids, such a buprenorphine and perhaps tramadol, than the medical system is willing to admit (Yovell et al., 2016).

As discussed in Chapter 4, over one hundred years ago William McDougall tried to answer the question of what mental illness is by putting forward the thesis that abnormal behavior simply represented extreme, exaggerated arousals of our normal primary instincts. In other words, psychopathology could be placed on the same personality dimensions as more moderate expressions of personality, but with imbalanced affective instinctive reactions so pronounced they became a liability to survival rather than an asset. This would be analogous to losing the ability to regulate one's normal body temperature and experiencing life-threatening fever or hypothermia. McDougall's insight suggested that many mental illnesses could best be understood as special cases of imbalanced activities of our usually adaptive primary emotional urges. In short, to understand many mental illnesses, we may not require unique categories specific to mental illness. Instead, they could fruitfully be thought of as cases in which the regulation of normal emotional behaviors and feelings were excessive or inadequate or had broken down in ways that could be demonstrated neuroscientifically (for such views, see Panksepp, 2004, 2006).

We concur with McDougall's basic point. But until recently, neuroscience has had difficulty conceptualizing how to study the neural nature of emotional feelings in humans. Many still resist the evidence-based idea that basic emotional systems are shared homologously across all other mammals, including those like laboratory rats, in which the detailed neuroscientific work can be conducted. However, this idea has become more substantive as the neuroscience revolution has revealed more and more about how our emotional feelings arise from subcortical brain activities (Panksepp, 1998a, 2004, 2006, 2016). As we have discussed throughout this book, the mammalian subcortical primary emotional systems are foundation pillars for our personalities, and many psychopathologies arise from imbalances of such primary brain emotional systems. Both personality disorders and other psychopathologies arise when these fundamental BrainMind systems become imbalanced. In such affectively disordered states, our emotional systems can create distressing feelings (as well as excessive joy, as in mania), often accompanied with distorted and extreme thoughts and behaviors. For instance, the psychological pain that leads people to commit suicide can arise from sustained overactivity of the PANIC/Sadness system, which can lead to depression (e.g., Panksepp & Yovell, 2014; Panksepp, 2015, 2016) and can be treated by medicines that reduce the painful feelings of separation distress (Yovell et al., 2016).

Yet, it is important to consider how the older subcortical areas of our brains seem able to overwhelm the more recently evolved cerebral cortex and its remarkable capacity for spoken language and reflective thinking. The reason seems straightforward: A basic tenet of affective neuroscience is that the subcortical emotion systems prevail in early development and remain foundational not only for our normal, everyday emotional feelings and personality traits but also our imbalanced adult emotional feelings.

For a complementary perspective, the eminent neurologist Marsel Mesulam of Northwestern University's School of Medicine explained it as follows: These subcortical systems can "rapidly shift information processing states throughout the cerebral cortex . . . [and] alter the tone, coloring, and interpretation of experience rather than its content" (2000, pp. 78–79). The mechanism mediating these old brain influences may lie in the distinction between cortical "channel" and subcortical affective "state" brain-mind functions (Mesulam, 2000). For state modulation, each cortical area receives inputs arising from subcortical brain regions, such as the vast biogenic amine systems, involving norepinephrine, serotonin, and dopamine, ascending from ancient brain stem regions along with various more specific neuropeptide systems (reviewed in Panksepp, 1993). These regions regulate not only many subcortical emotional circuits but also the entire cerebral cortex, thereby concurrently regulating both specific cognitive and more ancient affective messages. These connections determine the state of information processing rather than the content being transmitted along the point-to-point cortical channels that instantiate thoughts, through the "fine weave" of more rapidly acting local excitatory glutamate and inhibitory GABA systems of neocortex. These affect modulating "corticopetal" (Latin for cortex-seeking) biogenic amine projections to upper brain regions are not balanced by thoughtful "corticofugal" (Latin for cortex-fleeing) connections from the cerebral cortex to older regions of the brain. But without the cortex, the brain cannot "put the brakes on" extreme emotional feelings that arise from below.

Our affective states of mind strongly influence not only what our senses and thoughts perceive but also our interpretations of the emotional importance of incoming messages. Thereby the affective tone of our thoughts can be shifted positively or negatively, giving personal meaning to our diverse cognitive experiences. To the extent that individuals are chronically biased toward experiencing excessively negative emotional states (and perceive, think, and act correspondingly), their pessimistic thoughts and behaviors become progressively problematic, leading to increasing life difficulties. The underlying brain changes that promote such problems in living (e.g., depression and anxiety) have been the focus of abundant brain and genetic research in the past half century. Such modern findings affirm William McDougall's hypothesis that "morbidly exaggerated" emotions may instigate psychiatric as well as personality disorders. We will only touch upon a few high points, but first we focus on the close relationship of psychopathology and personality dimensions.

THE COMMON DIMENSIONS OF
NORMAL AND DISORDERED LIVES

Many studies have shown how normal brain affective mechanisms, taken to extremes, can promote various difficulties in living. Accordingly, many psychologists and psychiatrists have explored the relationship between personality and psychopathology. Specifically, there have been efforts to link diagnoses of mental illness to the Big Five/Five-Factor Model personality dimensions (Livesley, Schroeder, Jackson, & Jang, 1994; Krueger & Markon, 2014; Widiger, Costa, & McCrae, 2013). In one of the earlier more prominent efforts, John Livesley (Livesley et al., 1992) and Lee Anna Clark (1993) independently generated assessment tools that specify psychopathologies in terms of the dimensions of the Big Five/Five-Factor Model.

More recently there have been attempts to incorporate psychometric measures of maladaptive personality elements into the *DSM-V* psychiatric diagnostic process. While most such efforts have failed, one partial success was the inclusion of Section III in the *DSM-V*, which addresses "personality disorders" in terms of the Big Five/Five-Factor Model, thereby providing specific experimental assessments to describe and classify patients. In doing this, the *DSM-V* retained the traditional medical model that seeks to more explicitly demarcate normality from abnormality. Accordingly, the *DSM-V* retained Section II of the previous version, which delineates the old diagnostic categories of personality disorders. Thus, the categorical versus factorial debate continues, with the dominant categorical diagnostic model still based on clinical authority and collective wisdom rather than emerging research evidence, which ideally, in the future, would be based on primary-process emotional inquiries.

Table 18.1. Personality Inventory for DSM-5 personality disorder facets

Facet	Brief Definitions
Emotional lability	Exhibiting unstable emotions that are inconsistent to the event experienced.
Anxiousness	Feelings of tenseness including apprehensiveness in uncertain situations.
Separation insecurity	Dread of being socially rejected by or separated from one's social contacts.
Submissiveness	Adapting to the interests or desires of others even when contrary to one's own interests or desires.
Hostility	Frequent feelings of anger or irritation even in response to minor conflicts.
Perseveration	Persistence of a behavior despite that behavior not being effective.
Withdrawal	Avoiding social contacts and preferring to be alone.
Intimacy avoidance	Avoiding close or sexual relationships.
Anhedonia	Lacking the capacity to enjoy life events or take an interest in doing things.
Depressivity	Feeling hopeless and pessimistic including possible thoughts of suicide.
Restricted affectivity	Blunted reactions to normally emotionally arousing situations and remaining indifferent in such circumstances.
Suspiciousness	Expectations of being mistreated by others and questioning their loyalty or intent.
Manipulativeness	Attempting to influence or control others to achieve one's own ends.
Deceitfulness	Dishonesty including misrepresentation and fabrication in communications to others.
Grandiosity	Feeling superior to others and entitled to special treatment.
Attention seeking	Exhibiting behavior intended to make one's self the focus of attention.
Callousness	Lacking concern for others and lacking remorse after harming others in some way.

Irresponsibility	Disregarding commitments and obligations including carelessness with others' property.
Impulsivity	Frequently acting spontaneously without a plan or assessing possible outcomes.
Distractibility	Having one's attention easily distracted from a task and difficulty staying focused on a goal.
Risk taking	Engaging in risky activities regardless of the level of potential danger involved.
Rigid perfectionism	Insisting on flawless performance by self and others including the belief that there is only one correct way.
Unusual beliefs and experiences	Believing one possesses supernatural abilities and has unusual experiences that seem to include delusional elements.
Eccentricity	Exhibiting odd behavior, appearance, and speech including having strange thoughts.
Cognitive and perceptual dysregulation	Having unusual thought experiences including being detached from one's self and the external world seeming unreal.
Adapted from Krueger and Markon (2014).	

For those with such interests, Section III of the *DSM-V* does provide experimental assessments, the main one being an extensive 220-item questionnaire (Krueger, Derringer, Markon, Watson, & Skodol, 2012) that measures twenty-five statistically derived scales or facets that essentially represent the maladaptive extremes of the five-factor personality model (see Table 18.1 for the full list of facets). These facets were factor analytically summarized into five factors that very closely resemble the Big Five/Five-Factor Model. This new assessment is called the Personality Inventory for *DSM-V* (PID-5) and is owned and provided by the American Psychiatric Association (for a lucid discussion of this transition process and the ten-year-long political process that resulted in the American Psychiatric Association board *not* endorsing the personality disorder dimensional model, see Krueger and Markon 2014).

In contrast, the Affective Neuroscience Personality Scales (ANPS) is a categorical assessment. It provides measures of six primary emotions, which can be useful for placing disordered lives as well as more normal personalities in affective space (which can also be conceptualized dimensionally). The PID-5 has three facets that more or less correspond to primary emotions: The ANPS RAGE/Anger, FEAR, and PANIC/Sadness scales would likely line up closely with the PID-5 Hostility, Anxiousness, and Separation Insecurity scales. However, many of the corresponding PID-5 items have a more tertiary than primary flavor. For example, one of the PID-5 Hostility items reads, "I always make sure I get back at people who wrong me." One of the PID-5 Anxiousness items reads, "I always expect the worst to happen," and a Separation Insecurity item reads, "I'd rather be in a bad relationship than be alone." Most troubling from an affective neuroscience perspective is the absence of scales that closely correspond to the SEEKING, CARE, or PLAY emotional systems. For example, does a low level on the PID-5 Withdrawal scale equate to a high level of PLAY? As we discuss later in this chapter, the absence of positive emotions may be as critical to maintaining mental health as regulating the negative emotions. In sum, much work is needed to relate the primary mammalian brain emotions credibly to psychiatric symptoms, many of which undoubtedly are mixtures of primary emotions, with many others representing more tertiary expressions. The ANPS provides an explicit neuroscience-based anchoring tool that may better help us proceed systematically from primary-process affective issues to tertiary-process levels of cognitive complexity.

ANPS DIMENSIONS OF AFFECTIVE IMBALANCE; OR, ONE WAY TO AVOID DIAGNOSTIC CONFUSION

Here we show that the ANPS may be usefully deployed to describe and discriminate between psychiatric diagnostic categories such as type I bipolar disorder (BPD-I), type II bipolar disorder (BPD-II), and major depressive disorders. BPD-I and BPD-II are similar, but BPD-I is symptomatically more severe and perhaps more indicative of the classic manic-depression diagnosis. In BPD-II, the manic phase is less debilitating and is often seen as actually increasing personal effectiveness due to increased energy and goal-directed activity. In BPD-II, the high energy phase is thus called hypomania, which may also be characterized by increased irritability (e.g., possibly a combination of high SEEKING and RAGE/Anger).

According to the quantitative genetic model of bipolar spectrum illness (Evans et al., 2005), the same genetic variants contribute to the development of affective temperaments such as depression, as well as psychiatric problems such as BPD, in which periods of mania and depression may occur successively. In a study of the distribution of affective personality traits in families with members having a BPD diagnosis, Savitz, Merwe, and Ramesar (2008a) found that the ANPS PANIC/Sadness scale was significantly higher in BPD-I–diagnosed family members than in two control groups made up of unaffected family members or family members with a *DSM-IV* diagnosis other than depression, such as alco-

holism or generalized anxiety disorder. Consistent with the model, both
the ANPS PANIC/Sadness and FEAR scores were highest for individuals
diagnosed with BPD-I or BPD-II but generally lower for individuals with
recurrent major depression or that had only had a single depressive episode and lowest for the two control groups. However, after controlling
for self-rated depression using the Beck Depression Inventory (Beck &
Steer, 1993) or mania using the Altman Self-Rating Mania Scale (Altman,
Hedecker, Peterson, & Davis, 1997), only the PANIC/Sadness scale continued to differentiate significantly between groups, perhaps suggesting
the relative importance of this primary emotion in these disorders.

In a related paper, Savitz, Merwe, and Ramesar (2008b) also reported
that the ANPS RAGE/Anger scale differentiated BPD-II subjects better
than BPD-I subjects compared to unaffected family members. BPD-II
patients, who are often characterized by an irritable mood, also had
significantly higher RAGE/Anger scores than individuals with previous
depressive episodes or unaffected relatives. Savitz et al. (2008b) reported
in this study that Beck Depression Inventory scores were significantly
correlated with higher RAGE/Anger scores and lower SEEKING and
PLAY scores, a finding that supports research on the importance of promoting positive emotions (e.g., SEEKING and PLAY) in the treatment of
depression (Panksepp et al., 2014; Panksepp & Yovell, 2014) (also discussed later in this chapter). Another research team (Sawaya et al., 2015)
similarly reported that, compared to a control group, a group of patients
who had experienced a major depressive episode showed significantly
lower ANPS SEEKING and PLAY scores, as well as significantly higher
RAGE/Anger, FEAR, and PANIC/Sadness scores. Thus, we continue to
see that lower positive affects in addition to elevated negative affect systems are important considerations for disordered personalities.

In a Norwegian study, Sigmund Karterud's group (Karterud et al.,
2016) reported ANPS data on over five hundred patients with specific
personality disorder diagnoses, focusing on the two largest diagnostic
categories, which together accounted for over 70 percent of the patients:
borderline and avoidant personality disorders. Regression analyses on
these two largest groups showed that the borderline group had high
SEEKING scores, while the avoidant group had low SEEKING scores
as well as low PLAY scores. Again, the positive emotions played an
important role in distinguishing between the two groups. The regression analysis also showed that high FEAR was also a key factor in the
avoidant group. Otherwise, the avoidant group showed lower RAGE/
Anger, with the borderline group showing higher RAGE/Anger as well
as higher PANIC/Sadness. Karterud's work has reinforced the ideas not
only that positive primary emotions also play a prominent role in personality disorders but also that personality disorders can be defined on
the same continua as the ANPS-monitored primary emotional founda-

tions of personality in general and that psychiatrically significant personality disorder diagnoses may not require special categories unique to "mental illness."

While there has not yet been any ANPS research on the serotonin transporter gene (5-HTT) discussed in Chapter 7, a research group at the University of Bonn has investigated the relationship of ANPS scales and other genes. For example, Reuter, Weber, Fiebach, Elger, and Montag (2009) investigated links between ANPS RAGE/Anger scores and the DARPP-32 (dopamine- and cAMP-regulated phosphoprotein 32 kDa) gene (a C→T single nucleotide polymorphism) based on previous demonstrations that RAGE/Anger was influenced by the dopamine system. DARPP-32 is a key regulatory molecule in the dopaminergic signaling pathway. The C-allele is more common in sub-Saharan Africa but rather infrequent in European populations. The genetic analysis of German subjects without psychopathology showed that carriers of the T-allele (either TT or TC) had significantly higher ANPS RAGE/Anger scores, and subjects with the CC genotype had significantly lower RAGE/Anger scores. MRI data on a subsample of subjects also revealed that higher RAGE/Anger scores were associated with lower gray matter volume in the left amygdala, a subcortical brain structure whose corticomedial regions are associated with RAGE/Anger circuitry (Panksepp, 1998a).

Reuter, Panksepp, Schnabel, Kellerhoff, Kempel, & Hennig (2005) also demonstrated a link between the ANPS SEEKING scale and creativity. Using figural, verbal, and numeric creativity tests, subjects with higher SEEKING scores had higher numeric creativity scores and were significantly superior on figural and verbal creativity. SEEKING scores also explained more than 15 percent of the variance of total creativity. Using intelligence tests as a covariate indicated that the relationship of SEEKING to creativity was not related to measures of intelligence. Because of an interest in hormonal influences on creativity, subject's testosterone was also measured. While testosterone did not predict creativity levels, subjects with higher testosterone had higher SEEKING scores, which may help explain the past finding of positive relations between testosterone levels and monotony avoidance (Mattsson, Schalling, Olweus, Löw, & Svensson, 1980). A path analysis using LISREL 8.51 software showed that 39 percent of the variance in SEEKING scores could be predicted by testosterone and creativity levels, with testosterone and creativity being nearly equal but uncorrelated predictors.

Ideally, the ANPS will continue to be a useful tool for providing explicit assessment of primary brain emotion systems strengths and weaknesses for psychological and genetic research, as well as providing a useful tool for clinicians evaluating where their clients are situated temperamentally in emotional-affective space. Because these basic brain emotion systems influence the affective quality of mental life, clinicians can use the ANPS to evaluate individual profiles of key emotional dimensions for clues about emotional forces that may have become imbalanced (for a clinical case study that relied upon such ANPS results, see Turnbull, Evans, & Owen, 2005).

OPIOID TREATMENT OF DEPRESSION

A 1978 research report in the journal *Biological Psychology* (Panksepp et al., 1978) showed that very low doses of opioids such as morphine could easily quell plaintive separation distress cries in an animal model. The original demonstration was with young puppies in John Paul Scott's canine research lab (see Chapter 8). This was soon followed by more extensive analyses with guinea pigs and chicks (for reviews, see Panksepp et al., 1980; Panksepp, 1998a). Of course, separation distress cries are well known to anyone who has been around human children and young mammals in general. These feelings of social pain and distress continue throughout life in the aftermath of a broken relationship or the death of a loved one. Humans have even developed a special evolved means for expressing the psychic pain of separation, namely, tears, as well as an odd affinity for songs and stories dealing with "broken hearts."

John Bowlby's classic volumes on attachment and loss (Bowlby, 1960, 1980) had made the links between excessive early social separation, problematical parental bonding, and depression occurring later in life. So, it would seem a short step to treating an overactive PANIC/Sadness system cascading into depression with opioid drugs. It turns out that opiates were actually used to treat depression until the mid-1950s (Bodkin, Zornberg, Lukas, & Cole, 1995; Tenore, 2008). It was around then that new antidepressant drugs, knows as monoamine oxidase inhibitors and tricyclic antidepressants, emerged, which gave psychiatrists an alternative to the addiction problems with opiates. The tricyclic drug Tofranil (imipramine) was first tried as a treatment for psychotic disorders, where it failed, but was later tried more successfully with depressed patients. Imipramine, like most tricyclics, increases the availability of the neuromodulators norepinephrine and serotonin. Soon, Eli Lilly introduced Prozac (fluoxetine), which was a more selective serotonin reuptake inhibitor (SSRI) with fewer side effects, and the SSRIs became the new drug of choice for depression. However, even the SSRIs have never had a sterling track record for treating depression (as highlighted by the STAR-D report: Sinyor, Schaffer, & Levitt, 2010), with some SSRIs even thought to increase the probability of suicide. Prozac was first reported to lead to suicide in 1990 (Healy & Aldred, 2005).

But what about those individuals where loss of love, and resulting "broken hearts," promotes suicide? What if there were an opioid that could help with depression-related suicide but that was less addictive, or perhaps not addictive at all (Panksepp & Yovell, 2014)? A study out of Harvard (Bodkin et al., 1995) reported that buprenorphine, a "safer" opioid with much reduced dependence and abuse liabilities, produced significant improvements in patients with major depression that had never previously responded to conventional antidepressant treatments. The term "conventional" should be emphasized here since buprenorphine has never been approved by the FDA for treating depression.

Although it has been demonized as a gateway drug to opiate addiction, buprenorphine is in fact one of the safest opioids: it produces much less respiratory depression, which can be lethal, while retaining opioid analgesic qualities that could directly reduce psychological pain at very low doses (Dahan et al., 2006). Hypothesizing that it is the "psychological pain" that leads to increased suicidal thoughts, Jaak Panksepp and Yoram Yovell (2014) designed a double-blind pilot study to see if very low doses of buprenorphine could help depressed patients who were already receiving treatment but still had frequent thoughts of committing suicide. The project was finally completed in Israel because it could not be approved in the United States.[9] After two weeks, results showed that those patients receiving the buprenorphine reported fewer depressive symptoms and fewer suicidal thoughts. Based on the encouraging pilot results, a much larger and equally successful phase 3 clinical trial was completed (Yovell et al., 2016). Thus, focusing on primary emotional affects can make a substantial difference in treatment of psychiatric disorders characterized by psychological pain. Buprenorphine specifically targets the opioid receptors that can reduce the psychological pain of the PANIC/Sadness system, in contrast to the more broadly acting SSRI drugs, which increase serotonin levels but are not particularly effective in reducing depression (remember the STAR-D report by Sinyor et al., 2010), and which mildly subdue many other primary affects, both positive and negative.

TREATING DEPRESSION WITH DEEP BRAIN STIMULATION

Major depression is not just extremely psychologically debilitating; it is commonly very difficult to treat. Various treatments for depression have shown some early promise that subsequently proved overly optimistic (Sinyor et al., 2010). Cognitive therapy (CT) is the most popular form of psychotherapy for depressed patients and theoretically works by teaching patients new sets of cognitive skills, which they can use to control their depression. However, success with CT has been difficult to demonstrate versus control groups, including those on antidepressant medications. In a critical review of research into evidence-based explanations for psychotherapeutic interventions, Yale University's Alan Kazdin concluded, "whatever may be the basis of changes with CT [cognitive therapy], it does not seem to be the cognitions as originally proposed" (2007, p. 8), implying that effective therapeutic interventions may typically impact affective dimensions of the BrainMind more than just the cognitive, information-processing ones (a theme we revisit in Chapter 19). As a last line of intervention for patients with major depressive disorders, electroconvulsive therapy, often referred to as shock treatment, is still effectively used in cases of treatment-resistant depression, although about half the responders relapse within a year (Jelovac, Kolshus, & McLoughlin, 2013).

Because as many as 33 percent of patients with major depression do not respond to depression treatments (Rush et al., 2006), treatment-resistant depression remains a major psychiatric challenge. Affective neuroscience research suggests that more effective treatments are likely to emerge by addressing primary-process emotional affects. Specifically, an affective neuroscience approach to depression, has proposed "that sustained over activity of the PANIC and under activity of the SEEKING and PLAY networks substantially contribute to depression" (Panksepp et al., 2014, p. 477; see also Panksepp & Yovell, 2014). When these emotional systems are out of balance, depression is likely to occur.

One hypothesis is that increasing activity of the SEEKING brain system could be a viable treatment option for treatment-resistant patients. This is exactly what a German research group has done, by using tiny electrical currents to the brain to increase activity of the SEEKING system. In an initial study with three treatment-resistant patients, they first selected the nucleus accumbens as a therapeutic target for deep brain stimulation (DBS) of treatment-resistant patients (Schlaepfer et al., 2008), thus arousing a subcortical way station that is heavily controlled by the mesolimbic dopaminergic pathway, a key node of the brain SEEKING network. Their results were remarkable in that two patients after only sixty seconds of stimulation spontaneously mentioned plans to engage in interesting activities (one wished to take up bowling again). In a follow-up study involving ten treatment resistant patients, 50 percent of the patients exhibited sustained antidepressant effects after twelve months of DBS, including elevated enthusiasm and positive active planning for the future (Bewernick et al., 2010). However, a further study achieved even greater results by shifting the placement of the electrodes slightly to the "heart" of the medial forebrain bundle, a central part of the mesolimbic pathway and the most rewarding DBS site in the SEEKING system (for the human anatomy of this system, see Coenen et al., 2012) This adjustment led to the highest recovery rate in treatment-resistant depression ever reported. Six of the seven patients in the study improved over 50 percent on a standard measure of depression within three weeks and were still above that mark at the end of the thirty-three-week study (Schlaepfer, Bewernick, Kayser, Madler, & Coenen, 2013). A single patient may not have responded because of surgical problems (minor vascular damage at one of the DBS sites).

It is important to note that after DBS of their SEEKING systems, which probably included activation of dopamine systems, these patients did not act like cocaine or amphetamine users. They were not wildly euphoric, and they did not report any explicit "rewarding" or "pleasurable" feelings during their brain stimulation. Their experiences were not of consummatory pleasures, as one might experience eating exquisite Belgian chocolate, for example; theirs was an anticipatory enthusiasm, as when a chocolate lover approaches the Belgian chocolate shop and looks in its appetizing, well-stocked window. Their SEEKING system affect was one of energetically looking forward to life's rewards, which may have also explicitly counterbalanced the psychological pain engendered by overactive PANIC/Sadness separation distress networks. The mesolimbic pathway also projects to the frontal cortical areas (see Coenen et al., 2012), where DBS may have positively colored their perceptions and thoughts, with life beginning to look more inviting again. It is also notable that no negative psychological side effects were observed in any of the patients that have received this treatment so far.

TREATING DEPRESSION
WITH PLAYFUL JOY

Most of you probably cannot image playing with a rat. Most people do not like rats. People have even been diagnosed with "musophobia," or the fear of mice and rats, and even elephants have a reputation for being afraid of mice.

So, who wants to play with a rat? Actually, the second author has acquired a reputation for playing with rats, so much so he has been nicknamed the "rat tickler." Rats, like all mammals, love (and perhaps even need) to play. However, play is the domain of the young, and rats, along with humans, decline in their tendency to play and respond to tickling as they age. But while they are young, little play-prone rats love to be tickled by a human hand and, like human children, are always ready for more.

Is it possible that Ponce de Leon was looking in the wrong place as he searched for the fountain of youth? Is it possible that the fountain of youth is not a geographical place but might actually be found in the BrainMinds of playful little rat pups and happy human beings? That was one of novel therapeutic ideas developed by the extended affective neuroscience group at the Falk Center for Molecular Therapeutics at Northwestern University. They were building on research from Bowling Green State University where extensive research on "rough-and-tumble" play in rat pups began in the late 1970s (Panksepp, 1981c; Beatty & Costello, 1982; Panksepp et al., 1984) but especially on later work discovering that rats frequently emitted 50-kHz ultrasonic vocalizations during rat play sessions that could be used as a psychological assay for positive affect in rats (see Chapter 9). It turns out these 50-kHz vocalizations are also promoted by many positive events, such as the anticipation of sexual activity, daily feeding, being tickled, rewarding brain stimulation, and addictive psychostimulants. Notably, rats will work to receive DBS at all brain sites that evoke 50-kHz calls (Burgdorf et al., 2007). Also, rats will approach places where they have emitted these 50-kHz "chirps" as if anticipating finding some positive event (Wohr & Schwarting, 2007).

During social play, juvenile rat pups abundantly emit these ultrasonic 50-kHz rat chirps that are akin to the laughter of joyful children playing. While rat pups, like dog puppies, normally give each other little nips during their play bouts, if one rat pup bites too hard, the play and the joyous chirping (rat laughter?) are at least temporarily interrupted. Indeed, these enthusiastic ultrasonic chirps also halt at the hint of cat smell (as well as to practically all aversive experiences), during which animals often begin to emit 22-kHz "complaints," which can be used as a validated psychological-affective assay for unpleasant feelings in rats, as indicated by the fact that, if given the chance, rats readily avoid or turn off playback of such sounds.

Overall, the study of rat play and laughter led to a profound proposition: that we could neuroscientifically begin to understand the feelings of social joy in an animal model, and that such a state of mind in rats is dramatically diminished in clinical depression. Further, these assays of playful social joy in rats could lead to the study of the gene expression patterns of the brain that might reveal new pathways for antidepressant development (for overviews, see Panksepp, 2015, 2016). In short, the Falk affective neuroscience group wondered whether play could increase the production of brain chemicals that would give clues to the development of new antidepressants. The key question was what genes were being overexpressed in the brains of rats that had just played for half an hour, and whether some of the identified neurochemistries could be targets for novel antidepressants (Burgdorf et al., 2011).

This search led to a variety of possible novel medications, some of which did not have the safety profiles needed to go into human testing. However, one of the most intensely expressed genes was selected as a very safe pathway, and potential medicinal agents were constructed (Burgdorf et al., 2011). The key molecule, a neuropeptide named GLYX-13, was "a partial agonist for glycine sites on N-methyl-D-aspartate receptors, promoting glutamate transmission in low doses and blocking it in high doses" (Moskal et al., 2011). As hypothesized, GLYX-13 promoted the positive-affective 50-kHz ultrasonic vocalizations in rats during social play (Burgdorf et al., 2011). More importantly, GLYX-13 passed all toxicology trials, and in human phase 2b clinical trials has so far demonstrated robust and sustained antidepressant effects, with a rapid onset of antidepressant activity in as little as two hours (Preskorn et al., 2015)—this may be the *first novel psychiatric medicine* that has come from human knowledge of animal emotional processes. Many more are bound to emerge as more investigators understand the power of "affective modeling" of psychiatric disorders rather than the traditional "never-mind" behavior-only modeling that remains so abundant in the field.

SUMMARY

We believe all three of these new antidepressant treatments, which were all developed from focusing on the affective nature of the mammalian BrainMind, highlight the value of an affective neuroscience approach to psychopathology (Panksepp, 2015, 2016). Affective imbalances can best be approached from an understanding of the homologous mammalian subcortical anatomies that control primal animal emotionality and thereby our own deeply affective nature. As we gain a fuller understanding of the affective brain systems that we have inherited as ancestral birthrights, hopefully additional evidence-based treatments, based on taking the affective processes of other animals as models for our own, will be discovered. But at this point, affective neuroscience orientations to research in this field are still disproportionately small, because of a century of belief that the feelings of other animals could not be empirical penetrated.

With respect to personality, the ANPS is the first human psychological inventory that has arisen directly from our understanding of primal emotional processes in animal brains. We suspect that some future version of the *DSM* will focus on such brain systems as the very foundation of understanding the diverse psychiatrically significant affective traits that need to be carefully monitored (and modeled) to have better understandings (and treatments) of human affective disorders. Also, new psychological measurement tools that respect these foundations of normal and psychologically disordered human personality development need to be constructed. (For further discussion of these topics, see the next chapter).

CHAPTER 19

Fleshing Out the Complexities

Feeling, in the broad sense of whatever is felt in any way, . . . is the mark of mentality. In its most primitive forms it is the forerunner of the phenomena that constitute the subject matter of psychology. Organic activity is not psychological unless it terminates, however remotely or indirectly, in something felt. . . .

The thesis I hope to substantiate here is that the entire psychological field—including conception, responsible action, rationality, knowledge—is a vast and branching development of feeling.

—Susanne K. Langer, *Mind: An Essay on Human Feeling*

HUMANS ARE A PROFOUNDLY affective species. Our affects constitute a language of their own, not a verbal, orally spoken language but a nonverbal, felt language. It is perhaps the oldest language of consciousness, the original source of vital information that we experience as a part of living. Raw affective experiences are "the ancestral voices of the genes," to use Ross Buck's felicitous phrase, that speak to us directly as we experience life with its various levels of survival encounters and positive and negative life choices. Some of our emotional affects alert us to the possible loss of resources (RAGE/Anger), the loss of our social connections (PANIC/Sadness), and various dangers to life and limb (FEAR), thus teaching us what sorts of things to avoid, because they feel "bad," or aversive. On the positive feel "good" side, our emotional affects also make us aware of opportunities to harvest and hunt for resources and to pursue safety and other life-sustaining outcomes (SEEKING), namely, energized psychobehavioral activities devoted to opportunities to get all resources needed for survival. Our positive emotional affects also move us to tenderly help significant others, especially babies (CARE), and affectively excite us to physically interact and engage socially with others just for the fun of it (PLAY), thus teaching us how to live best with others. Included in the overall mix of basic emotions after puberty, although perhaps less closely related to personality, maturing animals and humans experience positive exciting arousals associated with identifying and becoming more intimate with potential mating partners (LUST). Many of these emotions relate directly to the nature of social bonding, which is essential for the formation of families and mutually supportive working communities.

In short, our primal emotions along with their powerful affects continuously guide our perceptions, thoughts, and actions. In addition to the emotional affects, there are also various sensory affects, for example, tastes and touches, but also feelings of disgust that compel us to spit out nasty things and possibly smack slimy, creepy things off our skin. Plus, there are homeostatic affects that inform us about our internal bodily states—survival needs such as food (HUNGER), water (THIRST), warmth (or cool shade), rest (tiredness), and sleep (sleepiness). However, it is the emotional affects that are largely responsible for guiding our moment-by-moment choices as we maneuver through the dynamic complexities of our worlds.

The primary-process manifestations of such affective states are instinctual—inherited tools for living that often remain inadequately addressed by those who study animal brains and behaviors to understand our intrinsic survival-value systems. For such research, affects cannot be seen directly but have to be inferred from behaviors. Of course with humans we can make judgments based on what subjects say and do.

In either case, it is a marvel to observe the coordinated interactions of new mammalian infants and parents as they learn to coordinate and navigate in their new social world. These interactions are very different in ungulates, such as sheep and horses, which are born ready to run and bond with their mother, compared with other mammals, such as dogs and humans, who are born very immature and require longer periods of maternal care. Ungulate infants and mothers bond rapidly, as indicated by prompt distress calls if they become separated, while other mammals take much longer to show such responses. But in both precocious (born quite mature) and altricial (born very immature) species, these separation distress calls help inform parents that their infants are distressed and activate parent-infant reunion behaviors and emotions.

Importantly, all primary-process emotions are also learning systems, such that each time an emotion's powerful rewarding or punishing affects are aroused, the associated behaviors are rewarded or punished according to the valence of the emotional affects experienced, a process that can take place without conscious awareness—namely, valenced experiential states without cognitive correlates. Also remember that in classical learning theory, the termination of a punishment, such as a foot shock, can serve as a reward—ambiguously called "negative reinforcement," which does not mean something positive happened, simply a response that avoids negative outcomes. But clearly a sophisticated psychology requires more realistic affective concepts than that. Let us consider real-life situations more common than the termination of electric shock.

For instance, it seems likely that, after an infant's perceived separation, reunion with the parent, accompanied by renewed physical contact, creates a two-edged learning event: learning to avoid painful social separation and learning the soothing contact comfort of physical reunion. Much has been written about parent-infant bonding, and many researchers believe that when an infant learns that he or she can rely on the parent returning, a secure social bond is created, with the infant gradually learning to tolerate longer periods of separation and independent activity (Ainsworth, 1969; Ainsworth & Bell, 1970). However, the potent positive affect of social reunion should not be called "negative reinforcement" unless one refuses to conclude, as many behaviorists did, that their shocked animals actually experience something like relief when shock is terminated.

An instinctive emotional foundation does not make humans and other mammals mechanical robots, but treats them as active agents engaging and adapting to their worlds. Importantly, all primary-process emotional action systems are also learning systems allows creatures—human and nonhuman alike—to extend their genetically endowed instinctive responses and adapt to novel environments that their inborn, evolved capacities did not specifically anticipate. This phenomenon of emotional action systems, promoting and "encapsulating" learning in memories, extends beyond mammals, even to invertebrates such as crayfish that form place attachments to locations where they have received opioids (Huber et al., 2011) and perhaps even to fruit flies (Gibson et al., 2015).

THE THREE-LEVEL NESTED
BRAINMIND HIERARCHY REVISITED

The complexity that emerges from our primary-process emotional action systems, with their powerful affects, has been conceptualized in what we call the three-level Nested BrainMind Hierarchy (NBH; see Chapter 5), starting with the expression of primary emotions, which leads to secondary learning as we interact with life events and experience the primary emotions with their rewarding or punishing valenced affects, which in turn (especially in humans) results in tertiary cognitive processes of reflecting and ruminating (thinking) about past outcomes and future possibilities.

A single primary-process emotional affect in its pure form—that is, by itself and not experienced in combination with another primary affect, a condition that may not often exist in nature—can be thought of as a kind of affective least common denominator. Each primary emotional affect can be experienced at various levels of intensity. Each is a reward or punishment with its own distinct, initially intrinsic nature, or qualia, which cannot be adequately described in language or understood by anyone who has not experienced it—such as McDougall's example of trying to explain to a person who has been blind since birth what the color red looks like. In addition, each emotional affect creates its effect on learning without requiring anything else in addition to itself. Each emotional affect, as part of an emotion, is also accompanied by altered thoughts and perceptions, as well as an activity or an urge to act that is consistent with its primary emotion. In short, each emotional affect is a unique qualia that requires nothing else in order to actuate its motivational effect as well as the experience of the affect itself.

These emotional primes provide a good basic tool kit with which to start life but would yield a rather simple creature if it were not for the "Law of Affect," (Panksepp & Biven, 2012, p. 58), that is, their effects on learning and memory formation, and consequent adaptability and survivability. While evolution endows its creatures with a set of crucial survival skills, it is the rewarding or punishing impact of the affects (some of them packaged as the primary emotions where raw affect and instinctual behaviors go together in the brain) that allows each sentient being the capacity to adopt novel responses to life challenges and to adapt to environments and cultures that Mother Nature did not foresee.

Affective learning proceeds automatically, and this secondary-process learning can proceed unconsciously and does not require awareness (which requires higher conscious reflections). While this secondary conditioning allows us, for example, to acquire many new fears, the element in the affective equation that theoretically does not change qualitatively is the feeling of FEAR itself. Still, successful learning (e.g., "negative reinforcement," in behaviorist parlance) can help attenuate and regulate such aversive states of mind. As illustrated in the three-level NBH (see Figure 5.1), at its core each newly acquired fear remains rooted in the primary emotion from which it was derived (e.g., in the present example FEAR). While the intensity and duration of the aroused affect may vary as a function of learning, the foundational affect itself does not qualitatively change, but the psychological end result in the present case is "relief," not the artificial terminology of "negative reinforcement" created by behaviorists, seemingly throwing away the mind in the behaviorist bathwater.

It remains a mystery when self-awareness first appeared in evolutionary history: perhaps only in the highest "branches" of the evolutionary bush, such as higher primates, with animals sufficiently endowed with the tertiary-level cognitive processes subsumed by the highest level of the NBH. At such tertiary levels of processing, cognitive awareness allows for thinking about and reflecting on one's emotional experiences as a kind of third-party observer. At least in humans, our highly developed cerebral cortex, as well as spoken language, adds further complexity to our emotional experiences, with the emergence of cognitively derived or promoted emotional affects, such as jealousy, guilt, and shame, along with additional verbal labels perhaps describing shades of emotional affects, all of which lead us into the largely unchartered waters of a tertiary-level neuroscience, that modern human brain imaging is attempting to explore (Takahashi et al., 2004; Michl et al., 2014).

At the tertiary level, while primary-process emotions continue to provide the foundation for emotional experience, one can no longer say that emotions and affects at cortical levels remain *primary* in the strictest sense: They are occurring only in the present moment and sufficient by themselves, because they likely also depend on "re-represented" thoughts and perceptions that can be kindled and rekindled over time with, for example, RAGE/Anger potentially emerging as an ongoing cold "hate" and SEEKING appearing as a perpetually harbored "wonderful" or "inappropriate" desire. At this tertiary, cognitive, and (for humans) verbal level there is the possibility for exceeding complexity, as well as many opportunities for personal confusions (plus misunderstandings across individuals as well as cultures). For example, it can be challenging to know when one is truly in love or how best to respond when such social bonds are threatened or broken. This is where the arts and humanities may be more successful than the sciences.

It is our position that emotional events at the more abstract, tertiary level remain firmly grounded in the basic mammalian emotional action systems. We believe that all personal values are rooted in experiences with the positive or negative affects, which include, at the very least, sensory, homeostatic, and emotional affects. Further, it is likely that all thoughts include affective elements. Humans are profoundly affective creatures, with affective features likely integrated with all aspects of our lives and our most moving arts.

So, on the face of it, what starts as an instinctive repertoire of ancestral survival skills at the primary-process level, through learning becomes expanded into a system of adapted behavior limited only by the capacities of the individual, all culminating in affective-cognitive subtleties elaborated uniquely, to some extent, in human minds.

The Emotional PLAY System
Conceptualized Within the NBH

The emotional PLAY system is one of the brain's blue ribbon primary emotional action systems. It is has been observed in practically all mammals studied, with few exceptions (e.g., it may have been bred out of some strains of laboratory mice), yet it has been difficult to document in nonmammalian species. The PLAY system is most frequently studied at the primary-process level and is typically expressed in young mammals as chasing and wrestling accompanied by distinctive vocalizations. In human children these vocalizations can take the form of ear-piercing shrieks of delight. In rodents, play vocalizations are necessarily ultrasonic (not audible to humans) to avoid detection by predators. In addition to the back-and-forth chasing seen, for example, in human children and juvenile dogs, play in young mammals also frequently takes the form of a kind of rough-and-tumble wrestling, which can appear like fighting to human observers but which is a positively energized experience for the young participants. One characteristic of these play tussles is that if one participant begins to win more than 70 percent of the time, the losing partner will diminish playing with that partner, suggesting that both participants need to experience the positive affect of "ending up on top" around half the time in order to sustain play motivation. Stuart Brown has provided a dramatic example of this PLAY system principle of a wild polar bear playing with a chained sled dog: with the polar bear lying on its back, allowing the sled dog to chew on its neck as if it were winning the play bout (Brown & Vaughan, 2009). His TED talk, including pictures, can be found at "https://www.ted.com/talks/stuart_brown_says_play_is_more_than_fun_it_s_vital".

However, human children, especially boys when given the opportunity, will begin to spontaneously organize pickup team games as a form of play that entails an order of magnitude greater complexity than the more elementary rough-and-tumble play. Team sports have not been observed in other species and require a level of cognitive abstraction in the form of rules of play that need to be accepted and followed by all players. As such, we can conceptualize playing baseball as an example of a tertiary-level PLAY activity. Yet, it is likely no coincidence that three primary PLAY system components, (1) running, (2) occasional physical contact, and (3) near to a 50 percent chance of winning, are "nested" even in such involved games with the explicit rules that humans are more expert at than any other species. Thus, even at this tertiary play level, in these afterschool games, usually of children's own devising, it remains important to develop methods to divide the players as equally as possible, often according to skill level, in order to maintain the plausibility that either team could win.

Without such a feeling of quid pro quo, play has difficulty getting energized, which reflects the anticipatory enthusiasm of the SEEKING system. In our personal experiences, that usually meant the two best players became informal captains of opposing teams who then alternated selection of team members to assure that a clique of more skilled players did not always play on the same team and dominate the play activities, for example, in baseball by making fewer outs, enabling them to stay up at bat for extended periods. Thus, both teams retain the potential of winning, which nests this primary PLAY-SEEKING principle into the tertiary PLAY experience. Variations of such honest means of dividing players into well-matched teams seem to work equally well for afterschool basketball or football games in the United States. Of course when it comes to formal team sports in high school and college, those courtesies are dispensed with, and it becomes much more of a cultural power game. Such social reflections of "my team" often lead to outright aggression among groups.

A tertiary quality to these pickup baseball games of middle youth is their being governed by rules, which the children often devise themselves to accommodate special local circumstances. For example, children might need to define boundaries often on marginal play sites that are not set up to define foul ball areas. As another example, when smaller children are included, they might be given easier pitches to give them better chances of hitting the ball and keeping them motivated to play. Such participant-defined and participant-enforced rules seem to go beyond anything observed in nonhuman play and adapt the rules of what is already a comparatively complex sport to specific circumstances. Handball or "stick ball" played in the streets and alleys of many megacities (e.g., NYC) provide similar tertiary adaptations for "make-shift" available circumstances.

Another primary process characteristic of PLAY is that children and other young mammals actually *need* to play. Research has shown that animals deprived of play opportunities are more motivated to play and play more than nondeprived control subjects when finally given the opportunity (Panksepp, 1981c; Siviy & Panksepp, 1987), which would be no surprise to any teacher of young school children. As another feature of what is perhaps the most complex mammalian primary emotion, it is likely that social play actually contributes to the developmental maturation of frontal cortex brain regions (Siviy & Panksepp, 2011), areas frequently involved in planning and emotional regulation that may develop more slowly than other brain regions. Thus, the primary-process mammalian need to play may foster the maturation of cortical regions that typically contribute to the development of social skills and the maintenance of social cohesion, which may in turn enhance tertiary-level social play and strategizing as well.

That children need to play has not been lost on Mike Lanza, a Menlo Park, California, parent of three boys who sensed that his children were not having the same spontaneous, unsupervised play experiences he benefitted from growing up in Pittsburgh. Mike and his wife turned their front and backyards into a childhood fantasy playground that inspired their entire "playborhood" (Thernstrom, 2016). Mike's only rule was that if parents brought their kids over to play, the parents had to leave and participate in the kind of "benign neglect" that allowed children to play and work out their problems on their own. Needless to say, the Lanza yard, although controversial with some parents, became very popular with kids, who were allowed to play there whether the Lanzas were home or not.

A related indication of the growing public awareness of the importance of play in children's lives takes us to Finland. A Hechinger Report (Doyle, 2016) tells how students with ample opportunities to play consistently perform strongly on academic achievement tests. Among other well-rounded, designed school experiences, preschool teachers are required not only to give children as many as four outdoor free-play breaks each day but also to design play-based classroom learning experiences such as selling ice cream to fellow students. In an era in which even American kindergarteners are having instruction time replace play time, a Finnish preschool teacher is quoted in an article amusingly titled "The Joyful, Illiterate Kindergartners of Finland": Children "learn so well through play. They don't even realize that they are learning because they're so interested" (Walker, 2015).

While little academic research has been focused on access to free-play activities in schools, emerging research is providing evidence that elementary school teachers do rate children's in-school performance higher if the children are allowed to participate in a preschool play sanctuary before each school day (Scott & Panksepp, 2003). There is also evidence that there may be a cultural price for limiting children's play: the development of attention-deficit hyperactive disorder and consequent drug sensitivities created by overprescribing medications for the condition (Andersen, Arvanitogiannis, Pliakas, LeBlanc, & Carlezon, 2002). Further, we may be "improving children's sustained attention at the expense of other vital cognitive functions," such as important plasticity in the prefrontal cortex (Urban & Gao, 2013, p. 7). It may be that we ignore the mammalian need for childhood PLAY system activities at our own peril.

Psychopathology

William McDougall concluded that an important criterion for identifying a primary instinct would be whether in its extreme expression the behavior became pathological. Indeed, many psychopathologies are closely related to primary-process emotional action-affect systems. As we described in Chapter 18, depression and suicidal ideation were linked to the PANIC/Sadness system, with strong evidence that safe opioid medications such as buprenorphine could be an effective treatment. In addition to an overly sensitized PANIC/Sadness system contributing to major depression, we also described that depression might be the result of a functionally diminished (one might say sluggish) SEEKING system that no longer supported normal living, which could be successfully treated by deep brain stimulation to the medial forebrain bundle, reactivating mesolimbic dopamine circuits.

Our view is that psychopathology is largely the result of emotions becoming imbalanced. As such, a main goal of therapy is to identify and label emotions that are imbalanced and explore them from a bottom-up perspective within a "therapeutic alliance," that is, a caring, empathetic, and supportive relationship with a therapist (Shedler, 2010). However, one of the currently most popular psychotherapy modalities is cognitive therapy (CT), which uses a top-down approach aiming to help patients uncover and change distorted thoughts and perceptions that are theoretically causing psychological distress. A central tenet of CT is that life events generate thoughts that in turn give rise to emotions, and that creating more realistic cognitive beliefs will result in healthier, less distressing feelings. Of course, this approach is bound to produce benefits, especially if clients feel CAREed for by therapists whom they trust, again suggesting that a supportive affective alliance is essential in the best psychotherapeutic approaches.

As mentioned in Chapter 18, a detailed analysis of actual CT therapist practices and patient outcomes has shown "that improvements can readily occur without changes in cognitions . . . [and] whatever may be the basis of changes with [cognitive therapy], it does not seem to be the cognitions as originally proposed" (Kazdin, 2007, p. 8). We concur and note that our primary-process emotional energies evolutionarily preceded human language and thought by well over 100 million years, perhaps much longer (Feinberg & Mallatt, 2016). When these ancestral mental energies become disrupted, patients would likely benefit most from having them addressed more directly, with affective cushioning, rather than indirectly through cognitive maneuvers (for a fuller discussion, see Smith, 2017). We argue that therapists who are able to recognize the distinct affective dynamics of basic emotions are likely to be more helpful than therapists less skilled at working at the primary-process emotional level or those who intentionally and exclusively focus on the cognitive, tertiary level. Indeed, the bottom-up affective voices featured in this book, arising from ancient subcortical brain circuits, powerfully influence the whole cognitive domain, and therapists who remain alert to opportunities to recruit the often latent positive affective resources in their patients are likely to facilitate beneficial shifts in patient thinking as well.

It is likely that primary affects are also important elements in the therapeutic use of memory reconsolidation. Every time a previously consolidated memory is retrieved, it enters a labile phase after which new elements concurrently being experienced can be incorporated into the original memory during an active process required to make the new memory stable again, namely, reconsolidation. One idea is that, in the context of a CAREing, empathetic, emotionally warm/supportive therapy session, especially after sharing a painful memory, the patient's old original memory may incorporate elements from the accepting, supportive therapeutic experience during the reconsolidation of the old memory, thus softening the memory and making the reconsolidated memory less emotionally intrusive and hence more bearable. It isn't that the old memory disappears, but in the context of a supportive therapeutic alliance in which the therapist resonates with the client's psychological pain, the healing that takes place may involve tempering the original traumatic experience with "a warm therapeutic experience" through the process of memory reconsolidation. Any of the positive primary emotions, CARE, SEEKING, PLAY, and perhaps in special circumstances, even LUST, could be used to therapeutically reconsolidate painful memories.

A therapeutic technique known as eye movement desensitization and reprocessing (EMDR; Shapiro, 1989) provides another possible reconsolidation example. During an EMDR procedure, the patient recalls distressing images while receiving sensory input such as side-to-side eye movements. EMDR may work by activating a visually induced positive SEEKING exploratory urge that facilitates reconsolidation, that is, restructures the traumatic memory into a less debilitating and more manageable psychic structure (Bisson et al., 2007).

Thus, it seems that targeting primary affects in supportive therapies facilitate healing. For example, simply imagining the motor imagery of PLAYful laughter can be sufficient to significantly increase happy mood ratings (Panksepp & Gordon, 2003). However, dealing with affects more directly, perhaps merely capturing a mutually shared PLAYful, humorous experience during a therapy session, might be a surer step toward restructuring a difficult aversive memory.

Any reader involved in a romantic relationship can try the following personal experiment. While having a spat with your romantic partner, try to look for an opportunity during which the two of you might touch each other and tenderly draw physically together. In this moment, notice how your thoughts change. You might find yourself reconsidering some of the things you said while you were arguing, which could lead to a gentler resolution of the quarrel. Likely, your partner will be having a similar experience. We would see this as an example of a bottom-up process in which a primary emotion and its distinctive affect—in this case perhaps even supportive romantic LUST—naturally guides positive thoughts and perceptions much better than trying to resolve the quarrel by focusing on a purely cognitive top-down process of adjusting distorted thoughts and perceptions. Good luck trying to convince your partner that his or her thoughts and ideas are the ones that are distorted, which is likely a recipe for more disasters.

This little experiment could provide an example of how individuals themselves can learn to tap into their own psychic energies to help reframe personal thoughts and perceptions into new psychic structures that might be more adaptive. Indeed, we believe that everyone could benefit from becoming better educated about the emotional primes and how to recognize and deal with them, perhaps with the guidance of a supportive, affectively oriented therapist. One way to situate anyone in affective space is by using the Affective Neuroscience Personality Scales, which addresses each of the primary emotions except LUST.

SUMMARY

It feels like *something* to be alive, to be awake and sentient. These feelings are raw affective states that are experienced subjectively as either desirable or undesirable, pleasant or unpleasant. They are age-old evolutionary survival tools, with the unpleasant affects informing us what to avoid and the pleasant ones what to approach. While there are sensory affects like disgust and homeostatic affects like hunger and thirst, it is the emotional affects that generally guide our major life choices. For humans and perhaps our more cerebrally gifted animal relatives, shifts in these emotional affective states change the color and tone of our cognitive experiences; they alter our perceptions, thoughts, and memories, in ways that have adaptively guided our actions for millennia.

We are never far from these primary-level emotions, and as illustrated in the three-level Nested BrainMind Hierarchy (NBH) presented in Chapter 5 and discussed again in this chapter, our primary emotions are embedded in everything we do. They are also learning systems, which organize all of our positive and negative memories in a state-dependent manner that allows them to be accessible in similar situations in the future. We define this as the secondary-level process, which allows us to incorporate new experiences and refinements into our emotional action systems repertoire.

However, humans are also highly cognitive creatures, and tertiary processing is more prevalent in our species than in any other. This is also the level of spoken language. However, as the NBH illustrates, the primary emotions are embedded at this level as well. Although humans attempt to describe their emotional experiences verbally, their feelings are qualia, which evolutionarily preceded spoken language by many millions, perhaps hundreds of millions, of years. Thus, as psychoanalysts discovered early in the twentieth century, humans often have difficulty accurately expressing their emotional experiences in words.

Even though we are highly cognitive creatures, is it possible that all our motivations are linked to ancestral affects? While there is no absolute answer yet, the SEEKING system clearly seems to be the most pervasive BrainMind motivator, and it is currently barely recognized in the psychological sciences. It is likely linked to all anticipatory goal seeking, with evidence that consumer-purchasing decisions can be reliably predicted by the activation of one of the major upper nodes of this system: the nucleus accumbens, an area incredibly rich in dopamine receptors (Knutson et al., 2007). It was the dopaminergic SEEKING system that Olds and Milner (1954) found, without fully realizing what they had discovered, which they later dubbed "the brain reward system," although we now know there are several distinct reward systems in the mammalian brain. It is also no coincidence that cocaine, amphetamine and other dopaminergic drugs are highly addictive, because the SEEKING system is so closely linked to brain dopamine, and people love the feeling of heightened enthusiasm. From primary-level to tertiary-level processing, the SEEKING system probably provides a foundation for practically all of our drives and positive (and many negative) motivations.

However, the PANIC/Sadness system also looms large in human social motivations and affective affairs. At the primary process level, opiates such as heroin, morphine, and oxycodone are also highly addictive. On the more strictly psychiatric end of the spectrum, it seems many children diagnosed with autism may be experiencing excessive surges of their internal (endogenous) opioids, which can markedly diminish their social motivation and concern for the perspectives of others. Also, a history of insecure social bonding is common in suicidal patients, a condition that, we have found, is effectively treatable with low-dose opioid drugs (Yovell et al., 2016). Indeed, at the tertiary-process level, broken relationships are a very prevalent theme in movies and songs.

In addition, the FEAR system is involved in many psychiatric diagnoses, such as anxiety disorders and phobias. Benzodiazepines (e.g., Librium and Valium) are often used to treat anxiety disorders, which reflect, in part, overarousal of the FEAR System. Yet, because alcohol acts within the brain almost like a benzodiazepine, much social drinking may be a form of self-medication to reduce FEAR-induced psychological tension (i.e., anxiety) and thereby to promote relaxation and a feeling of well-being, which in too many cases can cascade into a prevalent form of alcoholism-like addiction.

Although we humans are highly cognitive creatures, it is clear that we are not liberated from ancient emotional arousals. Indeed, many of our memories have emotional components, and many of our thoughts are emotionally tinged and triggered—to what extent remains a fascinating question yet to be answered. Ideally, more and more psychologically-oriented investigators of mind will pursue the many research challenges that are emerging from such understanding of the ancestral emotional forces that guide and govern human minds.

In any event, it is becoming clear that our primary-process emotions provide solid foundations for the emergence and manifestations of our personalities. At their more extreme, imbalanced emotional processes account for many psychopathologies that afflict our species. The study of these shared emotional processes in animal models is providing a new and solid foundation for psychiatric/psychoanalytic thinking. From mania to depression, from phobias and fears to angry antisocial behaviors and related emotional imbalances, extreme, out-of-control emotions can gallop rough-shod over our cognitions, thereby disrupting not only our own lives but also those who are close to us. We designed the Affective Neuroscience Personality Scales to assess the relative strengths and weaknesses of these emotional action systems and how their pervasive affects guide our lives. It is the first personality test based on a cross-species understanding of our affective heritage.

On more individual levels, we may all benefit from becoming more aware of our individual emotional tendencies and their influences on our cognitive apparatus. In short, we all need better emotional education and may profit from becoming more aware of how our perceptions and thoughts are influenced in real time by our affective states. Learning to regulate and manage these emotional evolutionary foundations of personality can be a lifelong task leading to what Aristotle called *phronesis*—learning how to behave with emotional wisdom, and thereby better knowing who we are and what we want to become.

Appendix: Scoring the ANPS 2.4

The ANPS 2.4 was published in 2011 (Davis & Panksepp, 2011) and was a revision of the original ANPS published in 2003 (Davis, Panksepp & Normansell, 2003). The ANPS 2.4 revision aimed to increase some of the scale reliabilities. Future revisions can be expected as well.

The ANPS 2.4 items are arranged in fourteen blocks using the following item sequence: SEEKING, FEAR, CARE, ANGER, PLAY, SADNESS, Spirituality (with only twelve items), followed by a filler research question. The items in the even blocks are reverse-scored. All items use a four-point response scale running from "Strongly Disagree" to "Disagree" to "Agree" to "Strongly Agree." However, an easy way to hand score the ANPS 2.4 and compare scores to the norms published in the 2003 paper is to use a 3 for the highest responses ("Strongly Agree" except for reversed-scored items) and a 0 for the lowest responses. This procedure allows for the possibility of a low score of zero on each scale with scores on the six primary-process scales featured in this book ranging from 0 to 42. If you use 4 for the highest responses and 1 for the lowest responses, scores on the six primary scales will range from 14 to 56.

For example, each of the positively worded SEEKING scale items (numbers 1, 17, 33, 49, 65, 81, and 97) would be scored as follows: Strongly Agree=3, Agree=2, Disagree=1, and Strongly Disagree=0. Correspondingly, each of the negatively worded SEEKING scale items in the even blocks (numbers 9, 25, 41, 57, 73, 89, and 105) would be reverse scored as follows: Strongly Agree=0, Agree=1, Disagree=2, and Strongly Disagree=3. Again, the order of the six primary-process ANPS 2.4 items always follows the following order: SEEKING, FEAR, CARE, ANGER, PLAY, and SADNESS with filler items separating the blocks.

The following are simple hand scoring formulas for the six primary-process ANPS 2.4 scales, which use a 3 for the highest response and a 0 for the lowest response for each item.

SEEKING score = +(anps1) +(anps17) +(anps33) +(anps49) +(anps65) +(anps81) +(anps97)
+(3 -anps9) +(3 -anps25) +(3 -anps41) +(3 -anps57) +(3 -anps73) +(3 -anps89) +(3 -anps105).

FEAR score = +(anps2) +(anps18) +(anps34) +(anps50) +(anps66) +(anps82) +(anps98)
+(3 -anps10) +(3 -anps26) +(3 -anps42) +(3 -anps58) +(3 -anps74) +(3 -anps90) +(3 -anps106).

CARE score = +(anps3) +(anps19) +(anps35) +(anps51) +(anps67) +(anps83) +(anps99)
+(3 -anps11) +(3 -anps27) +(3 -anps43) +(3 -anps59) +(3 -anps75) +(3 -anps91) +(3 -anps107).

ANGER score = +(anps4) +(anps20) +(anps36) +(anps52) +(anps68) +(anps84) +(anps100)
+(3 -anps12) +(3 -anps28) +(3 -anps44) +(3 -anps60) +(3 -anps76) +(3 -anps92) +(3 -anps108).

PLAY score = +(anps5) +(anps21) +(anps37) +(anps53) +(anps69) +(anps85) +(anps101)
+(3 -anps13) +(3 -anps29) +(3 -anps45) +(3 -anps61) +(3 -anps77) +(3 -anps93) +(3 -anps109).

SADNESS score = +(anps6) +(anps22) +(anps38) +(anps54) +(anps70) +(anps86) +(anps102)
+(3 -anps14) +(3 -anps30) +(3 -anps46) +(3 -anps62) +(3 -anps78) +(3 -anps94) +(3 -anps110).

Please note that women tend to obtain higher CARE scores than men. Also, individual scores tend to reflect a degree of "social desirability" such that scores for the FEAR, ANGER, and SADNESS scales tend to be lower than the scores for the SEEKING, CARE, and PLAY scales depending on how concerned the individual is about the ANPS results making a good impression.

Affective Neuroscience Personality Scale 2.4   Name: _____

Age: [ ] Sex: (M) (F)   Please mark bubbles like this ●

	Str Disagree	Disagree	Agree	Str Agree
1. Almost any little problem or puzzle stimulates my interest.	①	②	③	④
2. People who know me well would say I am an anxious person.	①	②	③	④
3. I often feel a strong need to take care of others.	①	②	③	④
4. When I am frustrated, I usually get angry.	①	②	③	④
5. I am a person who is easily amused and laughs a lot.	①	②	③	④
6. I often feel sad.	①	②	③	④
7. Feeling a oneness with all of creation helps give more meaning to my life.	①	②	③	④
8. I like to be the one in a group making the decisions.	①	②	③	④
9. I do not get much pleasure out of looking forward to special events.	①	②	③	④
10. I am not frequently jittery and nervous.	①	②	③	④
11. I think it is ridiculous the way some people carry on around baby animals.	①	②	③	④
12. I never stay irritated at anyone for very long.	①	②	③	④
13. My friends would probably describe me as being too serious.	①	②	③	④
14. I seem to be affected very little by personal rejection.	①	②	③	④
15. Feeling like a part of creation is not an important source of meaning for my life.	①	②	③	④
16. I will gossip a little at times.	①	②	③	④
17. I really enjoy looking forward to new experiences.	①	②	③	④
18. I often think of what I should have done after the opportunity has passed.	①	②	③	④
19. I like taking care of children.	①	②	③	④
20. My friends would probably describe me as hotheaded.	①	②	③	④
21. I am known as one who keeps work fun.	①	②	③	④
22. I often have the feeling that I am going to cry.	①	②	③	④
23. I am often spiritually touched by the beauty of creation.	①	②	③	④
24. I usually avoid activities in which I would be the center of attention.	①	②	③	④
25. I am usually not highly curious.	①	②	③	④
26. I would not describe myself as a worrier.	①	②	③	④
27. Caring for a sick person would be a burden for me.	①	②	③	④
28. I cannot remember a time when I became so angry that I wanted to break something.	①	②	③	④
29. I generally do not like vigorous games which require physical contact.	①	②	③	④
30. I rarely become sad.	①	②	③	④
31. I rarely rely on spiritual inspiration to help me meet important challenges.	①	②	③	④
32. I always tell the truth.	①	②	③	④
33. Seeking an answer is as enjoyable as finding the solution.	①	②	③	④
34. I often cannot fall right to sleep because something is troubling me.	①	②	③	④
35. I love being around baby animals.	①	②	③	④
36. When I get angry, I often feel like swearing.	①	②	③	④
37. I like to joke around with other people.	①	②	③	④
38. I often feel lonely.	①	②	③	④
39. For me, experiencing a connection to all of life is an important source of inspiration.	①	②	③	④
40. When I play games, it is important for me to win.	①	②	③	④
41. I usually feel little eagerness or anticipation.	①	②	③	④
42. I have very few fears in my life.	①	②	③	④
43. I do not especially like being around children.	①	②	③	④
44. When I am frustrated, I rarely become angry.	①	②	③	④
45. I dislike humor that gets really silly.	①	②	③	④
46. I never become homesick.	①	②	③	④
47. For me, spirituality is not a primary source of inner peace and harmony.	①	②	③	④
48. Sometimes I feel like swearing.	①	②	③	④
49. I enjoy anticipating and working towards a goal almost as much as achieving it.	①	②	③	④
50. I sometimes cannot stop worrying about my problems.	①	②	③	④
51. I feel softhearted towards stray animals.	①	②	③	④
52. When someone makes me angry, I tend to remain fired up for a long time.	①	②	③	④
53. People who know me would say I am a very fun-loving person.	①	②	③	④
54. I often think about people I have loved who are no longer with me.	①	②	③	④
55. Contemplating spiritual issues often fills me with a sense of intense awe and possibility.	①	②	③	④
56. If my peers have outperformed me, I would still be happy, if I have nearly met my goals.	①	②	③	④

47321

mdanps24

Please mark bubbles like this ● and not like this ⊗ or ⊙

	Str Disagree	Disagree	Agree	Str Agree
57. I am usually not interested in solving problems and puzzles just for the sake of solving them.	①	②	③	④
58. My friends would say that it takes a lot to frighten me.	①	②	③	④
59. I would generally consider pets in my home to be more trouble than they are worth.	①	②	③	④
60. People who know me well would say I almost never become angry.	①	②	③	④
61. I do not particularly enjoy kidding around and exchanging "wisecracks."	①	②	③	④
62. It does not particularly sadden me when friends or family members are disapproving of me.	①	②	③	④
63. My sense of significance and purpose in life does not come from my spiritual beliefs.	①	②	③	④
64. I have never "played sick" to get out of something.	①	②	③	④
65. My curiosity often drives me to do things.	①	②	③	④
66. I often worry about the future.	①	②	③	④
67. I feel sorry for the homeless.	①	②	③	④
68. I tend to get irritated if someone tries to stop me from doing what I want to do.	①	②	③	④
69. I am very playful.	①	②	③	④
70. I tend to think about losing loved ones often.	①	②	③	④
71. Feeling a connection with the rest of humanity motivates me to make more ethical choices.	①	②	③	④
72. When I play games, I do not mind losing.	①	②	③	④
73. I rarely feel the need just to get out and explore things.	①	②	③	④
74. There are very few things that make me anxious.	①	②	③	④
75. I do not like to feel "needed" by other people.	①	②	③	④
76. I rarely get angry enough to want to hit someone.	①	②	③	④
77. I do not tend to see the humor in things many people consider funny.	①	②	③	④
78. I rarely have the feeling that I am close to tears.	①	②	③	④
79. The goals I set for myself are not influenced by my spirituality.	①	②	③	④
80. There have been times in my life when I was afraid of the dark.	①	②	③	④
81. Whenever I am in a new place, I like to explore the area and get a better feel for my surroundings.	①	②	③	④
82. I often worry about whether I am making the correct decision.	①	②	③	④
83. I am the kind of person that likes to touch and hug people.	①	②	③	④
84. When things do not work out the way I want, I sometimes feel like kicking or hitting something.	①	②	③	④
85. I like all kinds of games including those with physical contact.	①	②	③	④
86. I frequently feel downhearted when I cannot be with my friends or loved ones.	①	②	③	④
87. Spiritual inspiration helps me transcend my limitations.	①	②	③	④
88. I am not satisfied unless I can stay ahead of my peers.	①	②	③	④
89. I am not the kind of person that likes probing and investigating problems.	①	②	③	④
90. I rarely worry about my future.	①	②	③	④
91. I do not especially want people to be emotionally close to me.	①	②	③	④
92. I hardly ever become so angry at someone that I feel like yelling at them.	①	②	③	④
93. I do not frequently ask other people to join me for fun activities.	①	②	③	④
94. I rarely think about people or relationships I have lost.	①	②	③	④
95. My choices are not guided by a sense of connectedness with all of life.	①	②	③	④
96. I have never intentionally told a lie.	①	②	③	④
97. I often feel like I could accomplish almost anything.	①	②	③	④
98. I often feel nervous and have difficulty relaxing.	①	②	③	④
99. I am a person who strongly feels the pain of other people.	①	②	③	④
100. Sometimes little quirky things people do really annoy me.	①	②	③	④
101. I see life as being full of opportunities to have fun.	①	②	③	④
102. I am a person who strongly feels the pain from my personal losses.	①	②	③	④
103. When working on a project, I like having authority over others.	①	②	③	④
104. Being embarrassed or looking stupid are among my worst fears.	①	②	③	④
105. I am not an extremely inquisitive person.	①	②	③	④
106. I almost never lose sleep worrying about things.	①	②	③	④
107. I am not particularly affectionate.	①	②	③	④
108. When people irritate me, I rarely feel the urge to say nasty things to them.	①	②	③	④
109. Playing games with other people is not especially enjoyable for me.	①	②	③	④
110. It would not bother me to spend the holidays away from family and friends.	①	②	③	④
111. Striving to be better than my peers is not important for me.	①	②	③	④
112. Fear of embarrassment often causes me to avoid doing things or speaking to others.	①	②	③	④

47321

mdanps24

References

Adler, A. (1930). Individual psychology. In C. Murchisan (Ed.), *Psychologies of 1930* (pp. 395–405). Worcester, MA: Clark University Press.

Adolphs, R. (2002). Neural systems for recognizing emotions. *Current Opinions in Neurobiology, 12,* 169–177.

Ainsworth, M. D. S. (1969). Object relations, dependency and attachment: A theoretical review of the infant-mother relationship. *Child Development, 40,* 969–1025.

Ainsworth, M. D. S., & Bell, S. M. (1970). Attachment, exploration, and separation: Illustrated by the behavior of one-year-olds in a strange situation. *Child Development, 41,* 49–67.

Albert, D. J., & Walsh, M. L. (1984). The inhibitory modulation of agonistic behavior in the rat brain: A review. *Neuroscience and Biobehavioral Reviews, 6,* 125–143.

Allport, G. (1937). *Personality: A psychological interpretation.* New York, NY: Holt.

Allport, G. W., & Odbert, H. S. (1936). Trait names: A psycho-lexical study [Special issue]. *Psychological Monographs, 47*(1).

Almagor, M., Tellegen, A., & Waller, N. (1995). The Big Seven model: A cross-cultural replication and further exploration of the basic dimensions of natural language of trait descriptions. *Journal of Personality and Social Psychology, 69,* 300–307.

Altman, E., Hedeker, D., Peterson, J. L., & Davis, J. M. (1997). The Altman Self-Rating Mania Scale. *Biological Psychiatry, 42,* 948–955.

American Psychiatric Association. (1980). *Diagnostic and Statistical Manual of Mental Disorders* (3rd ed.). Washington, DC: Author.

American Psychiatric Association. (2013). *Diagnostic and statistical manual of mental disorders* (5th ed.). Washington, DC: Author.

Amir, R., Van den Veyver, I., Wan, M., Tran, C., Francke, U., & Zoghbi, H. (1999). Rett syndrome is caused by mutations in X-linked MECP2, encoding methyl-CpG-binding protein 2. *Nature Genetics, 23,* 185–188.

Anacker, C., O'Donnell, K., & Meaney, M. (2014). Early life adversity and the epigenetic programming of hypothalamic-pituitary-adrenal function. *Dialogues in Clinical Neuroscience, 16,* 321–333.

Andersen, S., Arvanitogiannis, A., Pliakas, A., LeBlanc, C., & Carlezon, W., Jr. (2002). Altered responsiveness to cocaine in rats exposed to methylphenidate during development. *Nature Neuroscience, 5,* 13–14.

Ando, J., Suzuki, A., Yamagata, S., Kijima, N., Maekawa, H., Ono, Y., & Jang, K. (2004). Genetic and environmental structure of Cloninger's temperament and character dimensions. *Journal of Personality Disorders, 18,* 379–393.

Andrus, B. M., Blizinsky, K., Vedell, P. T., Dennis, K., Shukla, P. K., Schaffer, D. J., . . . Redei, E. E. (2012). Gene expression patterns in the hippocampus and amygdala of endogenous depression and chronic stress models. *Molecular Psychiatry, 17,* 49–61.

Armel, K. C., & Ramachandran, V. S. (2003). Projecting sensations to external objects: Evidence from skin conductance response. *Proceedings of the Royal Society B: Biological Sciences, 270,* 1499–1506.

Arnedo, J., Svrakic, D. M., Del Val, C., Romero-Zaliz, R., Hernández-Cuervo, H., Molecular Genetics of Schizophrenia Consortium, . . . Zwir, I. (2015). Uncovering the hidden risk architecture of the schizophrenias: confirmation in three independent genome-wide association studies. *American Journal of Psychiatry, 172,* 139–153.

Ashton, M. C., Lee, K., Perugini, M., Szarota, P., De Vries, R. E., Di Blas, L., . . . De Raad, B. (2004). A six-factor structure of personality-descriptive adjectives: Solutions from psycholexical studies in seven languages. *Journal of Personality and Social Psychology, 86,* 356–366.

Avery, O. T., MacLeod, C. M., & McCarty, M. (1944). Studies on the chemical nature of the substance inducing transformations of pneumococcal types: Induction of transformation by a desoxyribonucleic acid fraction isolated from pneumococcus type III. *Journal of Experimental Medicine, 79,* 137–158.

Bachevalier, J. (1990). Ontogenetic development of habit and memory formation in primates. *Annals of the New York Academy of Sciences, 608,* 457–477.

Bailey, P., & Davis, E. W. (1942). Effects of lesions of the periaqueductal gray matter in the cat. *Proceedings of the Society for Experimental Biology and Medicine, 51,* 305–306.

Bailey, P., & Davis, E. W. (1943). Effects of lesions of the periaqueductal gray matter on the *Macaca mulatta. Journal of Neuropathology and Experimental Neurology, 3,* 69–72.

Bakker, T. C. M. (1994). Genetic correlations and the control of behavior, exemplified by aggressiveness in sticklebacks. *Advances in the Study of Behavior, 23,* 135–171.

Balshine, S., & Sloman, K. A. (2011). Parental care in fishes. In A. P. Farrell (Ed.), *Encyclopedia of fish physiology: From genome to environment* (Vol. 1, pp. 670–677). San Diego: Academic.

Bandler, R., & Shipley, M. T. (1994). Columnar organization in the midbrain periaqueductal gray: Modules for emotional expression? *Trends in Neurosciences, 17,* 379–389.

Bard, P. (1928). A diencephalic mechanism for the expression of rage with special reference to the sympathetic nervous system. *American Journal of Physiology, 84,* 490–516.

Barr, C. S., Newman, T. K., Becker, M. L., Parker, C. C., Champoux, M., Lesch, K. P., . . . Higley, J. D. (2003). The utility of the non-human primate model for studying gene by environment interactions in behavioral research. *Genes, Brain and Behavior, 2,* 336–340.

Beach, F. A. (1955). The descent of instinct. *Psychological Review, 62,* 401–410.

Beatty, W. W., & Costello, K. B. (1982). Naloxone and play fighting in juvenile rats. *Pharmacology, Biochemistry and Behavior, 17,* 905–907.

Beatty, W. W., Dodge, A. M., Dodge, L. J., Whike, K., & Panksepp, J. (1982). Psychomotor stimulants, social deprivation and play in juvenile rats. *Pharmacology Biochemistry and Behavior, 16,* 417–422.

Beck, A. T., & Steer, R. A. (1993). *Manual for the Beck Depression Inventory.* San Antonio, TX: Psychological Corporation.

Bekoff, M. (2007). *The emotional lives of animals.* Novato, CA: New World Library.

Benet, V., & Waller, N. G. (1995). The Big Seven factor model of personality description: Evidence for its cross-cultural generality in a Spanish sample. *Journal of Personality and Social Psychology, 69,* 701–718.

Berridge, K. C. (2004). Pleasures, unfelt affect, and irrational desire. In A. S. R. Manstead, N. Frijda, & A. Fischer (Eds.), *Feelings and emotions: The Amsterdam Symposium* (pp. 243–262). Cambridge, UK: Cambridge University Press.

Bewernick, B. H., Hurlemann, R., Matusch, A., Kayser, S., Grubert, C., Hadrysiewicz, B., . . . Schlaepfer, T. E. (2010). Nucleus accumbens deep brain stimulation decreases ratings of depression and anxiety in treatment-resistant depression. *Biological Psychiatry, 67,* 110–116.

Biondich, A., & Joslin, J. (2016). Coca: The history and medical significance of an ancient Andean tradition. *Emergency Medicine International, 2016,* 1–5.

Bisson, J., Ehler, A., Matthew, R., Pilling, S., Richards, D., & Turner, S. (2007). Psychological treatments for chronic post-traumatic stress disorder: Systematic review and meta-analysis. *British Journal of Psychiatry, 190,* 97–104.

Blanchard, R. J., Blanchard, D. C., Agullana, R., & Weiss, S. M. (1991). Twenty-two kHz alarm cries to presentation of a predator, by laboratory rats living in visible burrow systems. *Physiology and Behavior, 50,* 967–972.

Block, J. (1961). *The Q-sort methodology in personality assessment.* Springfield, IL: Thomas.

Block, J. (1995). A contrarian view of the five-factor approach to personality description. *Psychological Bulletin, 117,* 187–215.

Blum, D. (2002). *Love at Goon Park: Harry Harlow and the science of affection.* New York, NY: Perseus.

Bodkin, J. A., Zornberg, G. L., Lukas, S. E., & Cole, J. O. (1995). Buprenorphine treatment of refractory depression. *Journal of Clinical Psychopharmacology, 15,* 49–57.

Bollen, K. S., & Horowitz, J. (2008). Behavioral evaluation and demographic information in the assessment of aggressiveness in shelter dogs. *Applied Animal Behaviour Science, 112,* 120–135.

Borgatta, E. (1964). A very short test of personality: The Behavioral Self-Rating (BSR) form. *Psychological Reports, 14,* 275–284.

Borman, P. D., Zilberman, M. L., Tavares, H., Surís, A. M., el-Guebaly, N., & Foster, B. (2006). Personality changes in women recovering from substance-related dependence. *Journal of Addictive Diseases, 25,* 59–68.

Botvinick, M., & Cohen, J. (1998). Rubber hands "feel" touch that eyes see. *Nature, 391,* 756.

Bouchard, T. (1994). Genes, environment, and personality. *Science, 264,* 1700–1701.

Bouchard, T. (1997). Experience producing drive theory: How genes drive experience and shape personality. *Acta Paediatrica 422*(suppl.), 60–64.

Bouchard, T., Lykken, D., McGue, M., Segal, N., & Tellegen, A. (1990). Sources of human psychological differences: The Minnesota Study of Twins Reared Apart. *Science, 250,* 223–228.

Bowlby, J. (1960). Separation anxiety. *International Journal of Psychoanalysis, 41,* 89–113.

Bowlby, J. (1980). *Attachment and loss: Vol. 3. Loss: Sadness and depression.* New York, NY: Basic Books.

Brody, G. H., Yu, T., Chen, E., Beach, S. R., & Miller, G. E. (2016). Family-centered prevention ameliorates the longitudinal association between risky family processes and epigenetic aging. *Journal of Child Psychology and Psychiatry, 57,* 566–574.

Brown, S. (accessed September 14, 2017). *Play is more than just fun.* https://www.ted.com/talks/stuart_brown_says_play_is_more_than_fun_it_s_vital

Brown, S., & Vaughan, C. (2009). *Play: How it shapes the brain, opens the imagination, and invigorates the soul.* New York, NY: Avery.

Browning, J. R., Browning, D. A., Maxwell, A. O., Dong, Y., Jansen, H. T., Panksepp, J., & Sorg, B. A. (2011). Positive affective vocalizations during cocaine and sucrose self-administration: A model for spontaneous drug desire in rats. *Neuropharmacology.* 61, 268–275.

Brudzynski, S. M., Silkstone, M., Komadoski, M., Scullion, K., Duffus, S., Burgdorf, J., . . . Panksepp, J. (2010). Effects of intraaccumbens amphetamine on production of 50 kHz vocalizations in three lines of selectively bred Long-Evans rats. *Behavioural Brain Research, 217,* 32–40.

Brunelli, S. A. (2005). Selective breeding for an infant phenotype: Rat pup ultrasonic vocalization (USV). *Behavior Genetics, 35,* 53–65.

Brunelli, S. A., & Hofer, M. A. (2007). Selective breeding for infant rat separation-induced ultrasonic vocalizations: Developmental precursors of passive and active coping styles. *Behavioural Brain Research, 182,* 193–207.

Budaev, S. V. (1997). "Personality" in the guppy (*Poecilia reticulata*): A correlational study of exploratory behavior and social tendency. *Journal of Comparative Psychology, 111,* 399–411.

Buhle, J., Kober, H., Ochsner, K., Mende-Siedlecki, P., Weber, J., Hughes, B., . . . Wager, T. (2013). Common representation of pain and negative emotion in the midbrain periaqueductal gray. *Social and Cognitive Affective Neuroscience, 8,* 609–616.

Burgdorf, J., Colechio, E. M., Stanton, P., & Panksepp, J. (2017). Positive emotional learning induces resilience to depression: A role for NMDA receptor-mediated synaptic plasticity. *Current Neuropharmacology, 15,* 3–10.

Burgdorf, J., Knutson, B., Panksepp, J., & Ikemoto, S. (2001). Nucleus accumbens amphetamine microinjections unconditionally elicit 50 kHz ultrasonic vocalizations in rats. *Behavioral Neuroscience, 115,* 940–944.

Burgdorf, J., Kroes, R. A., Moskal, J. R., Pfaus, J., Brudzynski, S. M., & Panksepp, J. (2008). Ultrasonic vocalizations of rats (*Rattus norvegicus*) during mating, play, and aggression: Behavioral concomitants, relationship to reward, and self-administration of playback. *Journal of Comparative Psychology, 122,* 357–367.

Burgdorf, J., & Panksepp, J. (2006). The neurobiology of positive emotions. *Neuroscience and Biobehavioral Reviews, 30,* 173–187.

Burgdorf, J., Panksepp, J., Brudzynski, S. M., Beinfeld, M. C., Cromwell, H. C., Kroes, R. A., & Moskal, J. R. (2009). The effects of selective breeding for differential rates of 50-kHz ultrasonic vocalizations on emotional behavior in rats. *Developmental Psychobiology, 51,* 34–46.

Burgdorf, J., Panksepp, J., Brudzynski, S. M., & Moskal, J. R. (2005). Breeding for 50-kHz positive affective vocalizations in rats. *Behavior Genetics, 35,* 67–72.

Burgdorf, J., Panksepp, J., & Moskal, J. R. (2011). Frequency-modulated 50 kHz ultrasonic vocalizations: A tool for uncovering the molecular substrates of positive affect. *Neuroscience and Biobehavioral Reviews, 35,* 1831–1836.

Burgdorf, J., Wood, P. L., Kroes, R. A., Moskal, J. R., & Panksepp, J. (2007). Neurobiology of 50-kHz ultrasonic vocalizations in rats: Electrode mapping, lesion, and pharmacology studies. *Behavioral Brain Research, 182,* 274–283.

Burghardt, G. M., Dinets, V., & Murphy, J. B. (2015). Highly repetitive object play in a cichlid fish (*Tropheus duboisi*). *Ethology, 121,* 38–44.

Burns, J. G. (2008). The validity of three tests of temperament in guppies (*Poecilia reticulata*). *Journal of Comparative Psychology, 122,* 344–356.

Caldji, C., Tannenbaum, B., Sharma, S., Francis, D., Plotsky, P. M., & Meaney, M. J. (1998). Maternal care during infancy regulates the development of neural systems mediating the expression of fearfulness in the rat. *Proceedings of the National Academy of Sciences of the USA, 95,* 5335–5340.

Campbell, D. T., & Fiske, D. W. (1959). Convergent and discriminant validation by the multitrait-multimethod matrix. *Psychological Bulletin, 56,* 81–105.

Canli, Turhan. (2006). Genomic imaging of extraversion. In T. Canli (Ed.), *Biology and personality and individual differences* (pp. 93–115). New York, NY: Guilford.

Cannon, W. B. (1927). The James-Lange theory of emotions: A critical examination and an alternative theory. *American Journal of Psychology, 39,* 10–124.

Cannon, W. B. (1931). Again the James-Lange and the thalamic theories of emotion. *Psychological Review, 38,* 282–295.

Carver, C. S., & White, T. L. (1994). Behavioral inhibition, behavioral activation, and affective responses to impending reward and punishment: The BIS/BAS Scales. *Journal of Personality and Social Psychology, 67,* 319–333.

Caspi, A., Sugden, K., Moffitt, T. E., Taylor, A., Craig, I. W., Harrington, H., . . . Poulton, R. (2003). Influence of life stress on depression: Moderation by a polymorphism in the 5-HTT gene. *Science, 301,* 386–389.

Cattell, H. B. (1989). *The 16PF: Personality in Depth.* Champaign: Illinois. Institute for Personality and Ability Testing, Inc.

Cattell, R. B. (1933). Temperament tests. II. Tests. *British Journal of Psychology, 24,* 20–49.

Cattell, R. B. (1943). The description of personality: Basic traits resolved into clusters. *Journal of Abnormal and Social Psychology, 38,* 476–506.

Cattell, R. B. (1950). *Personality: A systematical theoretical and factual study.* New York, NY: McGraw-Hill.

Cattell, R. B. (1957). *Personality and motivation structure and measurement.* New York, NY: World Book.

Cattell, R. B. (1986). The actual trait, state, and situation structures important in functional testing. In R. B. Cattell & R. Johnson (Eds.), *Functional psychological testing: Principles and instruments* (pp. 33–53). New York, NY: Brunner/Mazel.

Cattell, R. B., & Child, D. (1975). *Motivation and dynamic structure.* New York, NY: Wiley.

Cattell, R. B., Eber, H., & Tatsuoka, M. (1970). *Handbook for the Sixteen Personality Factor Questionnaire (16PF).* Champaign, IL: Institute for Personality and Ability Testing.

Cattell, R. B., & Kline, P. (1977). *The scientific analysis of personality and motivation.* New York, NY: Academic.

Centers for Disease Control and Prevention. (2014, November 26). *LCWK9: Deaths, percent of total deaths, and death rates for the 15 leading causes of death: United States and each State, 2012.* Retrieved from http://www.cdc.gov/nchs/data/dvs/LCWK9_2012.pdf

Centers for Disease Control and Prevention. (2015). *Suicide: Facts at a glance,*

2015. National Center for Injury Prevention and Control, Division of Violence Prevention. Retrieved from http://www.cdc.gov/violenceprevention/pdf/suicide-datasheet-a.pdf

Champagne, F., Francis, D. D., Mar, A., & Meaney, M. J. (2003). Variations in maternal care in the rat as a mediating influence for the effects of environment on development. *Physiology and Behavior, 79,* 359–371.

Champagne, F. A., & Meaney, M. J. (2007). Transgenerational effects of social environment on variations in maternal care and behavioral response to novelty. *Behavioral Neuroscience, 121,* 1353–1363.

Champoux, M., Bennett, A., Shannon, C., Higley, J. D., Lesch, K. P., & Suomi, S. J. (2002). Serotonin transporter gene polymorphism, differential early rearing, and behavior in rhesus monkey neonates. *Molecular Psychiatry, 7,* 1058–1063.

Chimpanzee Sequencing and Analysis Consortium. (2005). Initial sequence of the chimpanzee genome and comparison with the human genome. *Nature, 437,* 69–87.

Clark, L. A. (1993). *Manual for the Schedule for Nonadaptive and Adaptive Personality (SNAP).* Minneapolis, MN: University of Minnesota Press.

Clark, W. E. L. (1938). *The hypothalamus.* London: Oliver and Boyd.

Cloninger, C. R. (1986). A unified biosocial theory of personality and its role in the development of anxiety states, *Psychiatric Developments, 3,* 167–226.

Cloninger, C. R. (1987). A systematic method of clinical description of classification of personality variants. *Archives of General Psychiatry, 44,* 573–588.

Cloninger, C. R. (2004). *Feeling good: The science of well-being.* New York, NY: Oxford University Press.

Cloninger, C. R. (2008). The psychobiological theory of temperament and character: Comment on Farmer and Goldberg (2008). *Psychological Assessment, 20,* 292–299.

Cloninger, C. R., Svrakic, D. M., & Przybeck, T. R. (1993). A psychobiological model of temperament and character. *Archives of General Psychiatry, 50,* 975–990.

Coan, R. W., & Zagona, S. V. (1962). Contemporary ratings of psychological theorists. *Psychological Record, 12,* 315–322.

Coenen, V. A., Panksepp, J., Hurwitz, T. A., Urbach, H., & Mädler, B. (2012). Human medial forebrain bundle (MFB) and anterior thalamic radiation (ATR): Diffusion tensor imaging of two major subcortical pathways that may promote a dynamic balance of opposite affects relevant for understanding depression. *Journal of Neuropsychiatry and Clinical Neurosciences, 24,* 223–236.

Cohen, L., Celnik, P., Pascual-Leone, A., Corwell, B., Faiz, L., Dambrosia, J., . . . Hallett, M. (1997). Functional relevance of cross-modal plasticity in blind humans. *Nature, 389,* 180–183.

Cole, J., Sacks, O., & Waterman, I. (2000). On the immunity principle: A view from a robot. *Trends in Cognitive Sciences, 4,* 167.

Colleter, M., & Brown, C. (2011). Personality traits predict hierarchy rank in male rainbowfish social groups. *Animal Behaviour, 81,* 1231–1237.

Comings, D. E., Gade-Andavolu, R., Gonzalez, N., Wu, S., Muhleman, D., Blake, H., . . . MacMurray, J. P. (2000). A multivariate analysis of 59 candidate genes in personality traits: The temperament and character inventory. *Clinical Genetics, 58,* 375–385.

Connelly, B., & Ones, D. (2010). An other perspective on personality: Meta-analytic integration of observers' accuracy and predictive validity. *Psychological Bulletin, 136,* 1092–1122.

Coppinger, R., & Coppinger, L. (2001). *Dogs: A startling new understanding of canine origin, behavior and evolution.* New York, NY: Scribner.

Corr, P. J., Pickering, A. D., & Gray, J. A. (1997). Personality, punishment, and procedural learning: A test of J. A. Gray's anxiety theory. *Journal of Personality and Social Psychology, 73,* 337–344.

Costa, P., & McCrae, R. (1985). *The NEO Personality Inventory manual.* Odessa, FL: Psychological Assessment Resources.

Costa, P. T., Jr., & McCrae, R. R. (1995). Domains and facets: Hierarchical personality assessment using the revised NEO Personality Inventory. *Journal of Personality Assessment, 64,* 21–50.

Cote, J., Fogarty, S., & Sih, A. (2012). Individual sociability and choosiness between shoal types. *Animal Behaviour, 83,* 1469–1476.

Craig, A. D. (2009). How do you feel—now? The anterior insula and human awareness. *Nature Reviews Neuroscience, 10,* 59–70.

Craig, A. D. (2011). Significance of the insula for the evolution of human awareness of feelings from the body. *Annals of the New York Academy of Sciences, 1225,* 72–82.

Craig, I. W., & Halton, K. E. (2009). Genetics of human aggression. *Human Genetics, 126,* 101–113.

Crawley, J. N. (2007). *What's wrong with my mouse? Behavioral phenotyping of transgenic and knockout mice* (2nd ed.). New York, NY: Wiley.

Crews, D., Gillette, R., Miller-Crews, I., Gore, A. C., & Skinner, M. K. (2014). Nature, nurture and epigenetics. *Molecular and Cellular Endocrinology, 398,* 42–52.

Dahan, A., Yassen, A., Romberg, R., Sarton, E., Teppema, L., Olofsen, E., & Danhof, M. (2006). Buprenorphine induces ceiling in respiratory depression but not in analgesia. *British Journal of Anesthesiology, 96,* 627–632.

Dalle, G. R., Calugi, S., Brambilla, F., Abbate-Daga, G., Fassino, S., & Marchesini, G. (2007). The effect of inpatient cognitive-behavioral therapy for eating disorders on temperament and character. *Behaviour Research and Therapy, 45,* 1335–1344.

Dally, J. M., Emery, N. J., & Clayton, N. S. (2006). Food-caching western scrub-jays keep track of who was watching when. *Science, 312,* 1662–1665.

Damasio, A. (1999). *The feeling of what happens: Body and emotion in the making of consciousness.* New York, NY: Harcourt Brace.

Damasio, A., Damasio, H., & Tranel, D. (2013). Persistence of feelings and sentience after bilateral damage of the insula. *Cerebral Cortex, 23,* 833–846.

Damasio, A., Grabowski, T., Bechara, A., Damasio, H., Ponto, L., Parvizi, J., Hichwa, R. (2000). Subcortical and cortical brain activity during the feeling of self-generated emotions. *Nature, 3,* 1049-1056.

Darwin, C. (1859). *On the origin of species by means of natural selection, or, the preservation of favoured races in the struggle for life.* London: J. Murray.

Darwin, C. (1874). *The descent of man, and selection in relation to sex.* London: John Murray.

Darwin, C. (1958). *The autobiography of Charles Darwin 1809–1882.* Nora Barlow (Ed.). London: Collins.

Darwin, C. (1998). *The expression of emotions in man and animals: Definitive edition.* Introduction, afterword, and commentaries by Paul Ekman. New York, NY: Oxford University Press. (Original work published 1872)

Darwin, C. (2004). *Descent of man and selection in relation to sex.* New York, NY: Barnes and Noble. (Original work published 1871)

Davila Ross, M., Owren, M. J., & Zimmermann, E. (2009). Reconstructing the evolution of laughter in great apes and humans. *Current Biology, 19,* 1106–1111.

Davis, K. L. (1980). *Opioid control of canine social behavior* (PhD thesis). Bowling Green, OH: Bowling Green State University.

Davis, K. L., Gurski, J., & Scott, J. P. (1977). Interaction of separation distress with fear in infant dogs. *Developmental Psychobiology, 10,* 203–212.

Davis, K., & Panksepp, J. (2011). The brain's emotional foundations of human personality and the Affective Neuroscience Personality Scales. *Neuroscience and Biobehavioral Reviews, 35,* 1946–1958.

Davis, K. L., Panksepp, J., & Normansell, L. (2003). The affective neuroscience personality scales: Normative data and implications. *Neuropsychoanalysis, 5,* 21–29.

de Bono, M., & Maricq, A. V. (2005). Neuronal substrates of complex behaviors in *C. elegans. Annual Review of Neuroscience, 28,* 451–501.

de Bruin, J. P. C. (1990). Social behaviour and the prefrontal cortex. *Progress in Brain Research, 85,* 485–496.

De Fruyt, F., Van De Wiele, L., & Van Heeringen, C. (2000). Cloninger's psychobiological model of temperament and character and the five-factor model of personality. *Personality and Individual Differences, 29,* 441–452.

Delgado, J., Roberts, W., & Miller, N. (1954). Learning motivated by electrical stimulation of the brain. *American Journal of Physiology, 179,* 587–593.

De Molina, A.F. & Hunsperger, R.W., (1962). Organization of the Subcortical System Governing Defence and Flight Reactions In the Cat. *J. Physiology.* 160, 200-213.

Depaulis, A., & Bandler, R. (Eds.). (1991). *The midbrain periaqueductal gray matter: Functional, anatomical, and neurochemical organization.* New York, NY: Plenum.

Depue, R. A. (1995). Neurobiological factors in personality and depression. *European Journal of Psychology, 9,* 413–439.

de Raad, B. (1999). Interpersonal lexicon: Structural evidence from two independently constructed verb-based taxonomies. *European Journal of Psychological Assessment, 15,* 181–195.

de Waal, F. B. M. (1982). *Chimpanzee politics: Power and sex among apes.* New York, NY: Harper and Row.

de Waal, F. B. M. (1996). *Good natured: The origins of right and wrong in humans and other animals.* Cambridge, MA: Harvard University Press.

de Waal, F. (2009). *The age of empathy: Nature's lessons for a kinder society.* New York, NY: Harmony Books.

DeYoung, C. G. (2007). Remembering Memphis—J. S. Tanaka Dissertation Award winner talk: Colin DeYoung. *Online Newsletter for Personality Science,* no. 1. Retrieved from http://www.personality-arp.org/html/newsletter01/page5c.html.

DeYoung, C. G. (2010). Personality neuroscience and the biology of traits. *Social and Personality Psychology Compass, 4,* 1165–1180.

DeYoung, C. G. (2014). Cybernetic Big Five theory. *Journal of Research in Personality, 56,* 33–58.

DeYoung, C. G., Hirsh, J., Shane, M., Papademetris, X., Rajeevan, N., & Gray, J. (2010). Testing predictions from personality neuroscience: Brain structure and the Big Five. *Psychological Science, 21,* 820–828.

DeYoung, C. G., Quilty, L., & Peterson, J. (2007). Between facets and domains: Ten aspects of the Big Five. *Journal of Personality and Social Psychology, 93,* 880–896.

Di Blas, L., & Forzi, M. (1998). An alternative taxonomic study of personality descriptors in the Italian language. *European Journal of Personality, 12,* 75–101.

Digman, J. M. (1990). Personality structure: Emergence of the five-factor model. *Annual Review of Psychology* 41, 417–440.

Digman, J. M. (1996). The curious history of the five-factor model. In J. S. Wiggins (Ed.), *The five-factor model of personality* (1–20). New York, NY: Guilford.

Digman, J. (1997). Higher-order factors of the Big Five. *Journal of Personality and Social Psychology, 73,* 1246–1256.

Digman, J. M., & Inouye, J. (1986). Further specification of the five robust factors of personality. *Journal of Personality and Social Psychology, 50,* 116–123.

Digman, J. M., & Takemoto-Chock, N. K. (1981). Factors in the natural language of personality: Re-analysis, comparison, and interpretation of six major studies. *Multivariate Behavioral Research, 16,* 149–170.

Doyle, W. (2016). OPINION: How Finland broke every rule — and created a top school system. *Hechinger Report,* February 18, 2016.

Drury, S. S., Sánchez, M. M., & Gonzalez, A. (2016). When mothering goes awry: Challenges and opportunities for utilizing evidence across rodent, nonhuman primate and human studies to better define the biological consequences of negative early care giving. *Hormones and Behavior, 77,* 182–192.

Dutton, D. M. (2008). Subjective assessment of chimpanzee (*Pan troglodytes*) personality: Reliability and stability of trait ratings. *Primates, 49,* 253–259.

Dutton, D. M., Clark, R. A., & Dickins, D. W. (1997). Personality in captive chimpanzees: Use of a novel rating procedure. *International Journal of Primatology, 18,* 539–552.

Economist. (2013, April 6). Personality testing at work: Emotional breakdown.

Edwards, A. L. (1954). *Edwards Personal Preference Survey.* Seattle, WA: University of Washington.

Ehrsson, H. H., Spence, C., & Passingham, R. E. (2004). That's my hand! Activity in premotor cortex reflects feeling of ownership of a limb. *Science, 305,* 875–877.

Ehrsson, H. H., Wiech, K., Weiskopf, N., Dolan, R. J., & Passingham, R. E. (2007). Threatening a rubber hand that you feel is yours elicits a cortical anxiety response. *Proceedings of the National Academy of Sciences of the USA, 104,* 9828–9833.

Elliot, O., & Scott, J. P. (1961). The development of emotional distress reactions to separation, in puppies. *Journal of Genetic Psychology: Research and Theory on Human Development, 99,* 3–22.

Eslinger, P. J., Grattan, L. M., Damasio, H., & Damasio, A. R. (1992). Developmental consequences of childhood frontal lobe damage. *Archives of Neurology, 49,* 764–769.

Evans, L., Akiskal, H. S., Keck, P. E., Jr., McElroy, S. L., Sadovnick, A. D., Remick, R. A., & Kelsoe, J. R. (2005). Familiality of temperament in bipolar disorder: Support for a genetic spectrum. *Journal of Affective Disorders, 85,* 153–168.

Eysenck, H. J. (1955). Psychiatric diagnosis as a psychological and statistical problem. *Psychological Reports, 1,* 3–17.

Eysenck, H. J. (1957). *The dynamics of anxiety and hysteria.* New York, NY: Praeger.

Eysenck, H. J. (1967). *The biological basis of personality.* Springfield, IL: Charles C. Thomas.

Eysenck, H. J. (1990). Biological dimensions of personality. In L. A. Pervin (Ed.), *Handbook of personality: Theory and research* (pp. 244–276). New York, NY: Guilford.

Eysenck, H. J. (1992). Four ways five factors are not basic. *Personality and Individual Differences, 13,* 667–673.

Eysenck, H. J., & Eysenck, S. B. G. (1975). *Manual of the Eysenck Personality Questionnaire.* San Diego, CA: EdITS.

Fallon, J. (2013). *The psychopath inside: A neuroscientist's personal journey into the dark side of the brain.* New York, NY: Penguin.

Farmer, R. F., & Goldberg, L. R. (2008a). Brain modules, personality layers, planes of being, spiral structures, and the equally implausible distinction between TCI-R "temperament" and "character" scales: Reply to Cloninger (2008). *Psychological Assessment, 20,* 300–304.

Farmer, R. F., & Goldberg, L. R. (2008b). A psychometric evaluation of the revised Temperament and Character Inventory (TCI-R) and the TCI-140. *Psychological Assessment, 20,* 281–291.

Faucher, K., Parmentier, E., Becco, C., Vandewalle, N., & Vandewalle, P. (2010). Fish lateral system is required for accurate control of shoaling behaviour. *Animal Behaviour, 79,* 679–687.

Feinberg, T. E., & Mallatt, J. M. (2016). *The ancient origins of consciousness: How the brain created experience.* Boston, MA: MIT Press.

Feuerbacher, E. N., & Wynne, C. D. (2012). Relative efficacy of human social interaction and food as reinforcers for domestic dogs and hand-reared wolves. *Journal of the Experimental Analysis of Behavior, 98,* 105–129.

Fiske, D. (1949). Consistency of the factorial structure of personality ratings from different sources. *Journal of Abnormal and Social Psychology, 44,* 329–344.

Fleming, A., Lévy, F. & Lonstein, J. (Eds.). (2016) Parental Care. *Hormones & Behavior,*77, 1-284.

Florio, M., Albert, M., Taverna, E., Namba, T., Brandl, H., Lewitus, E., . . . Huttner, W. (2015). Human-specific gene *ARHGAP11B* promotes basal progenitor amplification and neocortex expansion. *Science, 347,* 1465–1470.

Flynn, J. P. (1976). Neural basis of threat and attack. In R. G. Grenell & S. G. Abau (Eds.), *Biological foundations of psychiatry* (pp. 275–295). New York, NY: Raven.

Fotopoulou, A. (2010). The affective neuropsychology of confabulation and delusion. *Cognitive Neuropsychiatry, 15,* 38–63.

Fraga, M., Ballestar, E., Paz, M., Ropero, S., Setien, F., Ballestar, M., . . . Esteller, M. (2005). Epigenetic differences arise during the lifetime of monozygotic twins. *Proceedings of the National Academy of Sciences of the USA, 102,* 10604–10609.

Francis, D., Diorio, J., Liu, D., & Meaney, M. J. (1999). Nongenomic transmission across generations of maternal behavior and stress responses in the rat. *Science, 286,* 1155–1158.

Frank, D., Dewitt, M., Hudgens-Haney, M., Schaeffer, D., Ball, B., Schwarz, N., . . . Sabatinelli, D. (2014). Emotion regulation: Quantitative meta-analysis of functional activation and deactivation. *Neuroscience and Biobehavioral Reviews, 45,* 202–211.

Freedman, D. G., King, J. A., & Elliot, O. (1961). Critical period in the social development of dogs. *Science, 133,* 1016–1017.

Freeman, H. D., Brosnan, S. F., Hopper, L. M., Lambeth, S. P., Schapiro, S. J., & Gosling, S. D. (2013). Developing a comprehensive and comparative questionnaire for measuring personality in chimpanzees using a simultaneous top-down/bottom-up design. *American Journal of Primatology, 75,* 1042–1053.

Gartner, M. C., & Weiss, A. (2013). Personality in felids: A review. *Applied Animal Behaviour Science, 144,* 1–13.

Gasper, K., & Bramesfeld, K. (2006). Should I follow my feelings? How individual differences in following feelings influence affective well-being, experience, and responsiveness. *Journal of Research in Personality, 40,* 986–1014.

Gaudi, S., Guffanti, G., Fallon, J., & Macciardi, F. (2016). Epigenetic mechanisms and associated brain circuits in the regulation of positive emotions: A role for transposable elements. *Journal of Comparative Neurology, 524,* 2944–2954.

Gazzaniga, M. (1998). *The mind's past.* Berkeley, CA: University of California Press.

Gazzaniga, M. (2015). *Tales from both sides of the brain: A life in neuroscience.* New York, NY: HarperCollins.

Gentile, G., Guterstam, A., Brozzoli, C., & Ehrsson, H. (2013). Disintegration of multisensory signals from the real hand reduces default limb self-attribution: An fMRI study. *Journal of Neuroscience, 33,* 1350–1366.

Gershon, N. B., & High, P. C. (2015). Epigenetics and child abuse: Modern-day Darwinism—The miraculous ability of the human genome to adapt, and then adapt again. *American Journal of Medical Genetics Part C: Seminars in Medical Genetics, 169,* 353–360.

Gibson, W., Gonzalez, C., Fernandez, C., Ramasamy, L., Tabachnik, T., Du, R. R., . . . Anderson, D. A. (2015). Behavioral responses to a repetitive visual threat stimulus express a persistent state of defensive arousal in *Drosophila. Current Biology, 25,* 1401–1415.

Gillespie, N. A., Cloninger, C. R., Heath, A. C., & Martin, N. G. (2003). The genetic and environmental relationship between Cloninger's dimensions of temperament and character. *Personality and Individual Differences, 35,* 1931–1946.

Gogoleva, S. S., Volodin, I. A., Volodina, E. V., Kharlamova, A. V., & Trut, L. N. (2010). Vocalization toward conspecifics in silver foxes (*Vulpes vulpes*) selected for tame or aggressive behavior toward humans. *Behavioural Processes, 84,* 547–554.

Gold, K. C., & Maple, T. L. (1994). Personality assessment in the gorilla and its utility as a management tool. *Zoo Biology, 13,* 509–522.

Goldberg, I., Harel, M., & Malach, R. (2006). When the brain loses its self: Prefrontal inactivation during sensorimotor processing. *Neuron, 50,* 329–339.

Goldberg, L. R. (1990). An alternative "description of personality": The Big-Five factor structure. *Journal of Personality and Social Psychology, 59,* 1216–1229.

Goldberg, L. R. (1992). The development of markers for the Big-Five factor structure. *Psychological Assessment, 4,* 26–42.

Goldberg, L. R. (1993). The structure of phenotypic personality traits. *American Psychologist, 48,* 26–34.

Goldberg, L. R., & Saucier, G. (1995). So what do you propose we use instead—A reply to Block. *Psychological Bulletin, 177,* 221–225.

Goldberg, L. R., & Somer, O. (2000). The hierarchical structure of common Turkish person-descriptive adjectives. *European Journal of Personality, 14,* 497–531.

Goodall, J. (1986). *The chimpanzees of Gombe: Patterns of behavior.* Cambridge, MA: Harvard University Press.

Gosling, S. D., & John, O. P. (1999). Personality dimensions in nonhuman animals: A cross-species review. *Current Directions in Psychological Science, 8,* 69–75.

Gough, H. G., & Bradley, P. (1996). *CPI manual* (3rd ed.). Palo Alto, CA: Consulting Psychologists.

Gray, J. A. (1970). The psychophysiological basis of introversion-extraversion. *Behaviour Research and Therapy, 8,* 249–266.

Gray, J. A. (1982). *The neuropsychology of anxiety: An enquiry into the function of the septohippocampal system.* New York, NY: Oxford University Press.

Gray, J. A. (1990). Brain systems that mediate both emotion and cognition. *Cognition and Emotion, 4,* 269–288.

Gray, J. A., & McNaughton, N. (2000). *The neuropsychology of anxiety: An enquiry into the functions of the septo-hippocampal system.* Oxford, UK: Oxford University Press.

Greene, J. (2013). *Moral tribes: Emotion, reason, and the gap between us and them.* New York, NY: Penguin.

Gröger, N., Matas, E., Gos, T., Lesse, A., Poeggel, G., Braun, K., & Bock, J. (2016). The transgenerational transmission of childhood adversity: Behavioral, cellular, and epigenetic correlates. *Journal of Neural Transmission (Vienna), 123,* 1037–1052.

Grone, B., Carpenter, R., Lee, M., Maruska, K., & Fernald, R. (2012). Food deprivation explains effects of mouthbrooding on ovaries and steroid hormones, but not brain neuropeptide and receptor mRNAs, in an African cichlid fish. *Hormones and Behavior, 62,* 18–26.

Gruber, N., & Kreuzpointner, L. (2013). Measuring the reliability of picture story exercises like the TAT. *PLoS One, 8,* e79450. http://dx.doi.org/10.1371/journal.pone.0079450

Haas, B. W., Filkowski, M. M., Cochran, R. N., Denison, L., Ishak, A., Nishitani, S., & Smith, A. K. (2016). Epigenetic modification of OXT and human sociability. *Proceedings of the National Academy of Sciences of the USA, 113,* E3816–E3823.

Haggbloom, S. J., Warnick, R., Warnick, J. E., Jones, V. K., Yarbrough, G. L., Russell, T. M., . . . Monte, E. (2002). The 100 most eminent psychologists of the twentieth century. *Review of General Psychology, 6,* 139–152.

Hall, C. S. (1934a). Drive and emotionality: Factors associated with adjustment in the rat. *Journal of Comparative Psychology, 17,* 89–108.

Hall, C. S. (1934b). Emotional behavior in the rat I: Defecation and urination as measures of individual differences in emotionality. *Journal of Comparative Psychology, 18,* 385–403.

Hall, C. S. (1941). Temperament: A survey of animal studies. *Psychological Bulletin, 38,* 909–943.

Hall, G. S. (1904). *Adolescence: Its psychology and its relations to physiology, anthropology, sociology, sex, crime, religion, and education* (2 vols.). New York, NY: Appleton.

Hamer, D. H., Greenberg, B. D., Sabol, S. Z., & Murphy, D. L. (1999). Role of the serotonin transporter gene in temperament and character. *Journal of Personality Disorders, 13,* 312–328.

Harding, J. A., Almany, G. R., Houck, L. D., & Hixon, M. A. (2003). Experimental analysis monogamy in the Caribbean cleaner goby, *Gobiosoma evelynae. Animal Behaviour, 65,* 865–874.

Harlow H. F., Dodsworth, R. O., & Harlow, M. K. (1965). Total social isolation in monkeys. *Proceedings of the National Academy of Sciences of the USA, 54,* 90–97.

Healy, D., & Aldred, G. (2005). Antidepressant drug use and the risk of suicide. *International Review of Psychiatry, 17,* 163–172.

Herrenstein, R., & Murray, C. (1994). *The bell curve: Intelligence and class structure in American life.* New York, NY: Free Press.

Hess, W. (1957a). *Diencephalon: Autonomic and extrapyramidal functions.* New York, NY: Grune and Stratton.

Hess, W. R. (1957b). *The functional organization of the diencephalon.* New York, NY: Grune and Statton.

Higley, J. D., Bennett, A., Heils, A., Long J., Lorenz, J., Champoux, M., . . . Lesch, K. P. (2000). Early rearing and genotypic influences on CNS serotonin and behavior in nonhuman primates. *Biological Psychiatry, 47,* S10–S11.

Hobolth, A., Christiensen, O. F., Mailund, T., & Schierup, M. H. (2007). Genomic relationships and speciation times of human, chimpanzee, and gorilla inferred from a coalescent hidden Markov model. *PLoS Genetics, 3,* 294–304.

Hofstee, W. K., de Raad, B., & Goldberg, L. R. (1992). Integration of the Big Five and circumplex approaches to trait structure. *Journal of Personality and Social Psychology, 63,* 146–163.

Hogan, R., & Hogan, J. (2007). *Hogan Personality Inventory manual.* Tulsa, OK: Hogan Assessment Systems.

Horney, K. (1942). *Self-analysis.* New York, NY: Norton.

Horney, K. (1945). *Our inner conflicts.* New York, NY: Norton.

Hsu, Y., & Serpell, J. A. (2003). Development and validation of a questionnaire for measuring behavior and temperament traits in pet dogs. *American Veterinary Medical Association Journal, 223,* 1293–1300.

Huber, R., Panksepp, J. B., Nathaniel, T., Alcaro, A., & Panksepp, J. (2011). Drug-sensitive reward in crayfish: An invertebrate model system for the study of SEEKING, reward, addiction, and withdrawal. *Neuroscience and Biobehavioral Reviews, 35,* 1847–1853.

Huntingford, F. A. (1976). The relationship between anti-predator behaviour and aggression among conspecifics in the three-spined stickleback, *Gasterosteus aculeatus. Animal Behaviour, 24,* 245–260.

Irvine, L. (2004). *If you tame me: Understanding our connection with animals.* Philadelphia, PA: Temple University Press.

Izard, C. E. (2007). Basic emotions, natural kinds, emotion schemas, and a new paradigm. *Perspectives on Psychological Science, 2,* 260–280.

Jackson, D. N. (1974). *Personality Research Form manual.* Goshen, NY: Research Psychologists.

Jackson, D. N. (1984). *Personality Research Form manual.* Port Huron, MI: Research Psychologists.

James, W. (2014, January). *Emotion Review.*

Jang, K. L., Hu, S., Livesley, W. J., Angleitner, A., Riemann, R., & Vernon, P. A. (2002). Genetic and environmental influences on the covariance of facets defining the domains of the five-factor model of personality. *Personality and Individual Differences, 33,* 83–101.

Jelovac, A., Kolshus, E., & McLoughlin, D. M. (2013). Relapse following successful electroconvulsive therapy for major depression: A meta-analysis. *Neuropsychopharmacology, 38,* 2467–2474.

John, O. P., & Robins, R. W. (1993). Gordon Allport: Father and critic of the five-factor model. In K. H. Craik, R. Hogan, & R. N. Wolfe (Eds.), *Fifty years of personality psychology* (pp. 215–236). New York, NY: Plenum.

Johnson, A. M., Vernon, P. A., & Feiler, A. R. (2008). Behavioral genetic studies of personality: An introduction and review of the results of 50+ years of research. In G. J. Boyle, G. Matthews, & D. H. Saklofske (Eds.), *The Sage handbook of personality theory and assessment: Vol. 1. Personality theories and models* (pp. 145–173). London: Sage.

Johnson, S. B., Riis, J. L., & Noble, K. G. (2016). State of the art review: Poverty and the developing brain. *Pediatrics, 137,* e20153075. http://dx.doi.org/10.1542/peds.2015-3075

Kandel, E. (2007). *In search of memory: The emergence of a new science of mind.* New York, NY: Norton.

Karterud, S., Pedersen, G., Johansen, M., Wilberg, T., Davis, K., & Panksepp, J. (2016). Primary emotional traits in patients with personality disorders. *Personality and Mental Health, 10,* 261–273.

Kazdin, A. E. (2007). Mediators and mechanisms of change in psychotherapy research. *Annual Review of Clinical Psychology, 3,* 1–27.

Kelly, G. A. (1955). *The psychology of personal constructs.* New York, NY: Norton.

Kilpatrick, L., & Cahill, L. (2004). Amygdala modulation of parahippocampal and frontal regions during emotionally influenced memory storage. *Neuroimage, 20,* 2091–2099.

King, J. E., & Figueredo, A. J. (1997). The five-factor model plus dominance in chimpanzee personality. *Journal of Research in Personality, 31,* 257–271.

King, J. E., Weiss, A., & Farmer, K. H. (2005). A chimpanzee (*Pan troglodytes*) analogue of cross-national generalization of personality structure: Zoological parks and an African sanctuary. *Journal of Personality, 73,* 389–410.

Kinley, N., & Beh-Hur, S. (2013). *Talent intelligence: What you need to know to identify and measure talent.* San Francisco, CA: Jossey-Bass.

Klein, D. F. (1981). Anxiety reconceptualized. In D. F. Klein & J. Rabkin (Eds.), *Anxiety: New research and changing concepts* (pp. 235–264). New York, NY: Raven.

Klein, D. F. (1993). False suffocation alarms, spontaneous panics, and related conditions. *Archives of General Psychiatry, 50,* 306–317.

Kline, P. (1993). *Personality: The psychometric view.* New York, NY: Routledge.

Knowles, P. A., Conner, R. L., & Panksepp, J. (1989). Opiate effects on social behavior of juvenile dogs as a function of social deprivation. *Pharmacology Biochemistry and Behavior, 33,* 539–543.

Knutson, B., Burgdorf, J., & Panksepp, J. (2002). Ultrasonic vocalizations as indices of affective states in rat. *Psychological Bulletin, 128,* 961–977.

Knutson, B., Rick, S., Wimmer, G.E., Prelec, D., & Loewenstein, G. (2007). Neural predictors of purchases. *Neuron, 53,* 147–156.

Kroes, R. A., Burgdorf, J., Otto, N. J., Panksepp, J., & Moskal, J. R. (2007). Social defeat, a paradigm of depression in rats that elicits 22-kHz vocalizations, preferentially activates the cholinergic signaling pathway in the periaqueductal gray. *Behavioral Brain Research, 182,* 290–300.

Krueger, R. F., Derringer, J., Markon, K. E., Watson, D., & Skodol, A. E. (2012). Initial construction of a maladaptive personality trait model and inventory for *DSM-V. Psychological Medicine, 42,* 1879–1890.

Krueger, R. F., & Markon, K. E. (2014). The role of the *DSM-V* personality trait model in moving toward a quantitative and empirically based approach to classifying personality and psychopathology. *Annual Review Clinical Psychology, 10,* 477–501.

Kruk, M. R., Halász, J., Meelis, W., & Haller, J. (2004). Fast positive feedback between the adrenocortical stress response and a brain mechanism involved in aggressive behavior. *Behavioral Neuroscience, 118,* 1062–1070.

Kukekova, A. V., Trut, L. N., Chase, K., Shepeleva, D. V., Vladimirova, A. V., Kharlamova, A. V., . . . Acland, G. M. (2008). Measurement of segregating behaviors in experimental silverfox pedigrees. *Behavior Genetics, 38,* 185–194.

Kumar, A., Choi, K. Renthal, W., Tsankova, N., Theobald, D., Truong, H., . . . Nestler, E. (2005). Chromatin remodeling is a key mechanism underlying cocaine-induced plasticity in striatum. *Neuron, 48,* 303–314.

Landgraf, R., & Wigger, A. (2002). High vs low anxiety-related behavior rats: An animal model of extremes in trait anxiety. *Behavior Genetics, 32,* 301–314.

Lang, P. J., Bradley, M. M., & Cuthbert, B. N. (2008). *International Affective Picture System (IAPS): Affective ratings of pictures and instruction manual.* Gainesville, FL: University of Florida.

Langer, S. (1988). *Mind: An essay on human feeling.* G. Van Den Heuvel (Ed.). Baltimore, MD: Johns Hopkins University Press. (Original work published 1967)

LeDoux, J. (1994). Emotion, memory and the brain. *Scientific American, 270,* 50–59.

LeDoux, J. (2012a). A neuroscientist's perspective on debates about the nature of emotion. *Emotion Review, 4,* 375–379.

LeDoux, J. (2012b). Rethinking the emotional brain. *Neuron, 73,* 653–676. http:// dx.doi.org/10.1016/j.neuron.2012.02.004

Lee, K., & Ashton, M. (2012). *The H factor of personality: Why some people are manipulative, self-entitled, materialistic, and exploitive—and why it matters.* Waterloo, ON: Wilfrid Laurier University Press.

Leech, R., & Sharp, D. (2014). The role of the posterior cingulate cortex in cognition and disease. *Brain, 137,* 12–32.

Lenggenhager, B., Tadi, T., Metzinger, T., & Blanke, O. (2007). Video ergo sum: Manipulating bodily self-consciousness. *Science, 317,* 1096–1099.

Lettvin, J. Y., Maturana, H. R., McCulloch, W. S., & Pitts, W. H. (1968). What the frog's eye tells the frog's brain. In W. C. Corning & M. Balaban (Eds.), *The mind: Biological approaches to its functions* (pp. 233–258). New York, NY: Interscience.

Liebsch, G., Montkowski, A., Holsboer, F., & Landgraf, R. (1998). Behavioural profiles of two Wistar rat lines selectively bred for high or low anxiety-related behaviour. *Behavioral Brain Research, 94,* 301–310.

Liotti, M., Mayberg, H., Jones, V., Agan, L., Cook, C., Woldorff, M., . . . Fox, P. (2000). Interactive effects in the anterior cingulate of sadness and selective attention: A PET study [abstract]. *Biological Psychiatry, 47,* S125–S126.

Liotti, M., & Panksepp, J. (2004). Imaging human emotions and affective feelings: Implications for biological psychiatry. In J. Panksepp (Ed.), *Textbook of biological psychiatry* (pp. 33–74). Hoboken, NJ: Wiley.

Liu, D., Diorio, J., Tannenbaum, B., Caldji, C., Francis, D., Freedman, A., . . . Meaney, M. J. (1997). Maternal care, hippocampal glucocorticoid receptors, and hypothalamic-pituitary-adrenal responses to stress. *Science, 277,* 1659–1662.

Livesley, W. J. (1991). Classifying personality disorders: Ideal types, prototypes, or dimensions? *Journal of Personality Disorders, 5,* 52–59.

Livesley, W. J., Jackson, D. N., & Schroeder, M. L. (1992). Factorial structure of traits delineating personality disorders in clinical and general population samples. *Journal of Abnormal Psychology, 101,* 432–440.

Livesley, W. J., Schroeder, M. L., Jackson, D. N., & Jang, K. L. (1994). Categorical distinctions in the study of personality disorder: Implications for classification. *Journal of Abnormal Psychology, 103,* 6–17.

Loehlin, J. C. (1992). *Genes and environment in personality development.* Newbury Park, CA: Sage.

Ludeke, S., Johnson, W., & Bouchard, T. (2013). "Obedience to traditional authority": A heritable factor underlying authoritarianism, conservatism and religiousness. *Personality and Individual Differences, 55,* 375–380.

Lykken, D., Bouchard, T., McGue, M., & Tellegen, A. (1993). Heritability of interests: A twin study. *Journal of Applied Psychology, 78,* 649–661.

MacLean, P. (1950). Psychosomatic disease and the "visceral brain": Recent developments bearing on the Papez theory of emotion. *Psychosomatic Medicine, 11,* 338–353.

MacLean, P. (1990). *The triune brain in evolution: Role in paleocerebral functions.* New York, NY: Plenum.

Mank, J. E., Promislow, D. E. L., & Avise, J. C. (2005). Phylogenetic perspective in the evolution of parental care in ray-finned fishes. *Evolution, 59,* 1570–1578.

Mariti, C., Carlone, B., Ricci, E., Sighieri, C., &Gazzano, A. (*2014*). Intraspecific attachment in adult domestic dogs (*Canis familiaris*): Preliminary results. *Applied Animal Behaviour Science, 152,* 64–72.

Mattsson, A., Schalling, D., Olweus, D., Löw, H., Svensson, J. (1980). Plasma testosterone, aggressive behavior, and personality dimensions in young male delinquents. *Journal of the American Academy of Child Psychiatry, 19,* 476–490.

McCrae, R. & Costa, P. (1983). Joint factors in self-reports and ratings: Neuroticism, extraversion and openness to experience. *Personality and Individual Differences, 4,* 245–255.

McCrae, R., & Costa, P. (1989). Reinterpreting the Myers-Briggs Type Indicator from the perspective of the five-factor model of personality. *Journal of Personality, 57,* 17–40.

McCrae, R., & Costa, P. (1996). Toward a new generation of personality theories: Theoretical contexts for the five-factor model. In J. S. Wiggins (Ed.), *The five-factor model of personality* (pp. 51–87). New York, NY: Guilford.

McCrae, R. R., & Costa, P. T., Jr. (2010). *NEO Inventories: Professional manual.* Lutz, FL: Psychological Assessment Resources.

McDougall, W. (1908). *Introduction to social psychology.* London: Methuen.

McDougall, W. (1930). William McDougall. In C. Murchison (Ed.), *A history of psychology in autobiography* (Vol. 1, pp. 191–223). New York, NY: Russell and Russell.

McEwen, B. S. (2016). In pursuit of resilience: Stress, epigenetics, and brain plasticity. *Annals of the New York Academy of Sciences, 1373,* 56–64.

McGrew, W. C. (1992). *Chimpanzee material culture: Implications for human evolution.* Cambridge, UK: Cambridge University Press.

McGrew, W. C. (2004). *The cultured chimpanzee: Reflections on cultural primatology.* Cambridge, UK: Cambridge University Press.

McQuown, S., & Wood, M. (2010). Epigenetic regulation in substance use disorders. *Current Psychiatry Reports, 12,* 145–153.

Meaney, M. J. (2010). Epigenetics and the biological definition of gene × environment interactions. *Child Development, 81,* 41–79.

Mendl, M., Brooks, J., Basse, C., Burman, O., Paul, E., Blackwell, E., & Casey, R. (2010). Dogs showing separation-related behaviour exhibit a "pessimistic" cognitive bias. *Current Biology, 20,* R839–R840.

Mendl, M., Burman, O. H. P., Parker, R. M. A., & Paul, E. S. (2009). Cognitive bias as an indicator of animal emotion and welfare: Emerging evidence and underlying mechanisms. *Applied Animal Behaviour Science, 118,* 161–181.

Merker, B. (2007). Consciousness without a cerebral cortex: A challenge for neuroscience and medicine. *Behavioral and Brain Sciences, 30,* 63–134.

Mesulam, M. M. (2000). *Principles of behavioral and cognitive neurology* (2nd ed.). New York, NY: Oxford University Press.

Michl, P., Meindl, T., Meister, F., Born, C., Engel, R., Reiser, M., & Hennig-Fast,

K. (2014). Neurobiological underpinnings of shame and guilt: A pilot fMRI study. *Social Cognitive and Affective Neuroscience, 9,* 150–157.

Mincic, A. M. (2015). Neuroanatomical correlates of negative emotionality-related traits: A systematic review and meta-analysis. *Neuropsychologia, 77,* 97–118.

Mischel, W. (1981). *Introduction to personality* (3rd ed.). New York, NY: Holt, Rinehart, and Winston.

Mobbs, D., Marchant, J., Hassabis, D., Seymour, B., Tan, G., Gray, M., . . . Frith, C. (2009). From threat to fear: The neural organization of defensive fear systems in humans. *Journal of Neuroscience, 29,* 12236–12243.

Mobbs, D., Petrovic, P., Marchant, J., Hassabis, D., Weiskopf, N., Seymour, B., . . . Frith, C. (2007). When fear is near: Threat imminence elicits prefrontal-periaqueductal gray shifts in humans. *Science, 317,* 1079–1083.

Montag, C., Hahn, E., Reuter, M., Spinath, F. M., Davis, K., & Panksepp, J. (2016). The role of nature and nurture for individual differences in primary emotional systems: Evidence from a twin study. *PLoS One, 11,* e0151405. http://dx.doi.org/10.1371/journal.pone.0151405

Montag, C., & Panksepp, J. (2017). Primary emotions and personality. *Frontiers in Psychology, 8,* 1–15.

Montag, C., & Reuter, M. (2014). Disentangling the molecular genetic basis of personality: From monoamines to neuropeptides. *Neuroscience and Biobehavioral Reviews, 43,* 228–239.

Montag, C., Reuter, M., Jurkiewicz, M., Markett, S., & Panksepp, J. (2013). Imaging the structure of the human anxious brain: A review of findings from neuroscientific personality psychology. *Reviews in the Neurosciences, 24,* 167–190.

Montirosso, R., Provenzi, L., Giorda, R., Fumagalli, M., Morandi, F., Sirgiovanni, I., . . . Borgatti, R. (2016). SLC6A4 promoter region methylation and socio-emotional stress response in very preterm and full-term infants. *Epigenomics, 8,* 895–907. http://dx.doi.org/10.2217/epi-2016-0010

Morris, P. H., Doe, C., & Godsell, E. (2008). Secondary emotions in non-primate species? Behavioural reports and subjective claims by animal owners. *Cognition and Emotion, 22,* 3–20.

Morton, F. B., Lee, P. C., Buchanan-Smith, H. M., Brosnan, S. F., Thierry, B., Paukner, A., . . . Weiss, A. (2013). Personality structure in brown capuchin monkeys (*Sapajus apella*): Comparisons with chimpanzees (*Pan troglodytes*), orangutans (*Pongo* spp.), and rhesus macaques (*Macaca mulatta*). *Journal of Comparative Psychology, 127,* 282–298.

Moskal, J. R., Burgdorf, J., Kroes, R. A., Brudzynski, S. M., & Panksepp, J. (2011). A novel NMDA receptor glycine-site partial agonist, GLYX-13, has therapeutic potential for the treatment of autism. *Neuroscience and Biobehavioral Reviews, 35,* 1982–1988.

Murray, H. A. (2008). *Explorations in personality.* With foreword by Dan P. McAdams. New York, NY: Oxford University Press. (Original work published 1938)

Mutschler, N. H., & Miczec, K. A. (1998). Withdrawal from a self-administered or non-contingent cocaine binge: Differences in ultrasonic distress vocalizations in rats. *Psychopharmacology, 136,* 402–408.

Myers, I. B., & McCaulley, M. H. (1985). *Manual: A guide to the development and use of the Myers-Briggs Type Indicator.* Mountain View, CA: Consulting Psychologists.

Nathaniel, T. I., Panksepp, J., & Huber, R. (2009). Drug-seeking behavior in an invertebrate system: Evidence of morphine-induced reward, extinction and reinstatement in crayfish. *Behavioural Brain Research, 197,* 331–338.

Nestler, E. (2014). Epigenetic mechanisms of drug addiction. *Neuropharmacology, 76,* 1–16.

Norman, W. T. (1963). Toward an Adequate Taxonomy of Personality Attributes: Replicated factor structure in peer nomination personality ratings. *Journal of Abnormal & Social Psychology,* 66, 574-583.

Norman, W. T. (1967). *2800 personality trait descriptors: Normative operating characteristics for a university population.* Ann Arbor, MI: University of Michigan, Department of Psychology.

Northoff, G., Heinzel, A., de Greck, M., Bermpohl, F., Dobrowolny, F., & Panksepp, J. (2006). Self-referential processing in our brain—A meta-analysis of imaging studies on the self. *NeuroImage, 31,* 440–457.

Nudo, R. J. (2013). Recovery after brain injury: Mechanisms and principles. *Frontiers in Human Neuroscience, 7,* 1–14.

O'Brien, M., & Anthony, J. (2005). Risk of becoming cocaine dependent: Epidemiological estimates for the United States, 2000–2001. *Neuropsychopharmacology, 30,* 1006–1018.

O'Connell, L. A., Matthews, B. J., & Hofmann, H. A. (2012). Isotocin regulates paternal care in a monogamous cichlid fish. *Hormones and Behavior, 61,* 725–733.

Olds, J., & Milner, P. (1954). Positive reinforcement produced by electrical stimulation of the septal area and other regions of rat brain. *Journal of Comparative and Physiological Psychology, 47,* 419–427.

Ota, K., & Kohda, M. (2014). Maternal food provisioning in a substrate-brooding African cichlid. *PLoS One, 9,* 1–4.

Paez, D., Velasco, C., & Gonzalez, J. L. (1999). Expressive writing and the role of alexythimia as a dispositional deficit in self-disclosure and psychological health. *Journal of Personality and Social Psychology, 77,* 630–641.

Pajer, K., Andrus, B. M., Gardner, W., Lourie, A., Strange, B., Campo, J., . . . Redei, E. E. (2012). Discovery of blood transcriptomic markers for depression in animal models and pilot validation in subjects with early-onset major depression. *Translational Psychiatry, 2,* 1–10.

Palmer, R., & Custance, D. (2008). A counterbalanced version of Ainsworth's strange situation procedure reveals secure-base effects in dog-human relationships. *Applied Animal Behaviour Science, 109,* 306–319.

Panksepp, J. (1971). Aggression elicited by electrical stimulation of the hypothalamus in albino rats. *Physiology and Behavior, 6,* 311–316.

Panksepp, J. (1974). Hypothalamic regulation of energy balance and feeding behavior. *Federation Proceedings, 33,* 1150–1165.

Panksepp, J. (1981a). Brain opioids: A neurochemical substrate for narcotic and social dependence. In S. Cooper (Ed.), *Progress in theory in psychopharmacology* (pp. 149–175). London: Academic.

Panksepp, J. (1981b). Hypothalamic integration of behavior: Rewards, punishments, and related psychobiological process. In P. Morgane & J. Panksepp (Eds.), *Handbook of the hypothalamus* (pp. 289–487). New York, NY: Marcel Dekker.

Panksepp, J. (1981c). The ontogeny of play in rats. *Developmental Psychobiology, 72,* 261–264.

Panksepp, J. (1982). Toward a general psychobiological theory of emotions. *Behavioral and Brain Sciences, 5,* 407–467.

Panksepp, J. (1985). Mood changes. In P. Vinken, G. Bruyn, & H. Klawans (Eds.), *Handbook of clinical neurology: Vol. 45. Clinical neuropsychology* (pp. 271–285). Amsterdam: Elsevier Science.

Panksepp, J. (1990a). Can "mind" and behavior be understood without under-standing the brain? A response to Bunge. *New Ideas in Psychology, 8,* 139–149.

Panksepp, J. (1990b). Gray zones at the emotion/cognition interface: A commentary. *Cognition and Emotion, 4,* 289–302.

Panksepp, J. (1993). Neurochemical control of moods and emotions: Amino acids to neuropeptides. In M. Lewis & J. Haviland (Eds.), *Handbook of emotions* (pp. 87–107). New York, NY: Guilford.

Panksepp, J. (1998a). *Affective neuroscience.* New York, NY: Oxford University Press.

Panksepp, J. (1998b). The periconscious substrates of consciousness, affective states and the evolutionary origins of the SELF. *Journal of Consciousness Studies, 5,* 566–582.

Panksepp, J. (2000a). Emotions as natural kinds within the mammalian brain. In M. Lewis & J. M. Haviland-Jones (Eds.), *Handbook of emotions* (2nd ed., pp. 137–156). New York, NY: Guilford.

Panksepp, J. (2000b). The riddle of laughter: Neural and psychoevolutionary underpinnings of joy. *Current Directions in Psychological Sciences, 9,* 183–186.

Panksepp, J. (2003). Can anthropomorphic analyses of "separation cries" in other animals inform us about the emotional nature of social loss in humans? *Psychological Reviews, 110,* 376–388.

Panksepp, J. (Ed.). (2004). *Textbook of biological psychiatry.* Hoboken, NJ: Wiley.

Panksepp, J. (2005). Affective consciousness: Core emotional feelings in animals and humans. *Consciousness and Cognition, 14,* 19–69.

Panksepp, J. (2006). Emotional endophenotypes in evolutionary psychiatry. *Progress in Neuro-psychopharmacology and Biological Psychiatry, 30,* 774–784.

Panksepp, J. (2007a). Affective consciousness. In M. Velmans and S. Schneider (Eds.), *The Blackwell companion to consciousness* (pp. 114–129). Malden, MA: Blackwell.

Panksepp, J. (2007b). Can PLAY diminish ADHD and facilitate the construction of the social brain? *Journal of the Canadian Academy of Child and Adolescent Psychiatry, 10,* 57–66.

Panksepp, J. (2007c). Neuroevolutionary sources of laughter and social joy: Modeling primal human laughter in laboratory rats. *Behavioral Brain Research, 182,* 231–244.

Panksepp, J. (2008a). Cognitive conceptualism—Where have all the affects gone? Additional corrections for Barrett et al. (2007). *Perspectives on Psychological Science, 3,* 305–308. http://dx.doi.org/10.1111/j.1745-6924.2008.00081.x

Panksepp, J. (2008b). PLAY, ADHD and the construction of the social brain: Should the first class each day be recess? *American Journal of Play, 1,* 55–79.

Panksepp, J. (2009). Core consciousness. In T. Bayne, A. Cleeremans, & P. Wilken (Eds.), *The Oxford companion to consciousness* (pp. 198–200). Oxford, UK: Oxford University Press.

Panksepp, J. (2010a). The basic affective circuits of mammalian brains: Implications for healthy human development and the cultural landscapes of ADHD. In C. M. Worthman, P. M. Plotsky, D. S. Schechter, & C. A. Cummings (Eds.), *Formative experiences: The interaction of caregiving, culture, and developmental psychobiology* (pp. 470–502). New York, NY: Cambridge University Press.

Panksepp, J. (2010b). Evolutionary substrates of addiction: The neurochemistries of pleasure seeking and social bonding in the mammalian brain. In J. D. Kassel (Ed.), *Substance abuse and emotion* (pp. 137–168). Washington, DC: American Psychological Association.

Panksepp, J. (2011a). The basic emotional circuits of mammalian brains: Do animals have affective lives? *Neuroscience and Biobehavioral Reviews, 35,* 1791–1804.

Panksepp, J. (2011b). Cross-species affective neuroscience decoding of the primal affective experiences of humans and related animals. *PLoS One, 6,* 1–15.

Panksepp, J. (2011c). Empathy and the laws of affect. *Science, 334,* 1358–1359. http://dx.doi.org/10.1126/science.1216480

Panksepp, J. (2011d). The primary process affects in human development, happiness, and thriving. In K. Sheldon, T. Kashdan, & M. Steger (Eds.), *Designing positive psychology: Taking stock and moving forward* (pp. 51–88). New York, NY: Oxford.

Panksepp J. (2014). Crossing the brain-mind Rubicon: How might we scientifically understand basic human emotions and core affective feelings of other animals? *Neuropsychoanalysis, 16,* 39–44.

Panksepp, J. (2015). Affective preclinical modeling of psychiatric disorders: Taking imbalanced primal emotional feelings of animals seriously in our search for novel antidepressants. *Dialogues in Clinical Neuroscience, 17,* 363–379.

Panksepp, J. (2016). The cross-mammalian neurophenomenology of primal emotional affects: From animal feelings to human therapeutics. *Journal of Comparative Neurology, 524,* 1624–1635. http://dx.doi.org/10.1002/cne.23969

Panksepp, J., & Biven, L. (2012). *Archaeology of mind: The neuroevolutionary origins of human emotions.* New York, NY: Norton.

Panksepp, J., & Burgdorf, J. (2000). 50k-Hz chirping (laughter?) in response to conditioned and unconditioned tickle-induced reward in rats: Effects of social housing and genetic variables. *Behavioral Brain Research, 115,* 25–38.

Panksepp, J., & Burgdorf, J. (2003). "Laughing" rats and the evolutionary antecedents of human joy? *Physiology and Behavior, 79,* 533–547.

Panksepp, J., Burgdorf, J., & Gordon, N. (2001). Toward a genetics of joy: Breeding rats for "laughter." In A. Kazniak (Ed.), *Emotion, qualia, and consciousness* (pp. 124–136). Singapore: World Scientific.

Panksepp, J., & Gordon, N. (2003). The instinctual basis of human affect: Affective imaging of laughter and crying. *Consciousness and Emotion, 4,* 197–206.

Panksepp, J., Herman, B., Conner, R., Bishop, P., & Scott, J. P. (1978). The biology of social attachments: Opiates alleviate separation distress. *Biological Psychiatry, 13,* 607–618.

Panksepp, J., Herman, B. H., Vilberg, T., Bishop, P., & DeEskinazi, F. G. (1980). Endogenous opioids and social behavior. *Neuroscience and Biobehavioral Reviews, 4,* 473–487.

Panksepp, J., Jalowiec, J., DeEskinazi, F. G., & Bishop, P. (1985). Opiates and play dominance in juvenile rats. *Behavioral Neuroscience, 99,* 441–453.

Panksepp, J., Lane, R. D., Solms, M., & Smith, R. (2017). Reconciling cognitive and affective neuroscience perspectives on the brain basis of emotional experience. *Neuroscience and Biobehavioral Reviews, 76,* "Part B, 16" 187–215. http://dx.doi.org/10.1016/j.neubiorev

Panksepp, J., & Moskal, J. (2008). Dopamine and SEEKING: Subcortical "reward" systems and appetitive urges. In A. Elliot (Ed.), *Handbook of approach and avoidance motivation* (pp. 67–87). New York, NY: Psychology Press.

Panksepp, J., Normansell, L., Cox, J., & Siviy, S. (1994). Effects of neonatal decortication on the social play of juvenile rats. *Physiology and Behavior, 56,* 429–443. http://dx.doi.org/10.1016/0031-9384(94)90285-2

Panksepp, J., Normansell, L. A., Herman, B., Bishop, P., & Crepeau, L. (1988).

Neural and neurochemical control of the separation distress call. In J. D. Newman (Ed.), *The physiological control of mammalian vocalizations* (pp. 263–300). New York, NY: Plenum.

Panksepp, J., & Panksepp, J. B. (2013). Toward a cross-species understanding of empathy. *Trends in Neurosciences, 36,* 489–496.

Panksepp, J., & Sahley, T. (1987). Possible brain opioid involvement in disrupted social intent and language development of autism. In E. Schopler & G. Mesibov (Eds.), *Neurobiological issues in autism* (pp. 357–382). New York, NY: Plenum.

Panksepp, J., Siviy, S., & Normansell, L. A. (1984). The psychobiology of play: Theoretical and methodological perspectives. *Neuroscience and Biobehavioral Reviews, 8,* 465–492.

Panksepp, J., & Solms, M. (2012). What is neuropsychoanalysis? *Trends in Cognitive Sciences, 16,* 6–8.

Panksepp, J., & Wright, J. S. (2009). On SEEKING: A foundational source of affective, behavioral and cognitive enthusiasm, volition, and will-power. *Neuropsychoanalysis, 14,* 59–75.

Panksepp, J., Wright, J. S., Döbrössy, M. D., Schlaepfer, T. E., & Coenen, V. A. (2014). Affective neuroscience strategies for understanding and treating depressions: From preclinical models to novel therapeutics. *Clinical Psychological Science, 2,* 472–494.

Panksepp, J., & Yovell, Y. (2014). Preclinical modeling of primal emotional affects (Seeking, Panic and Play): Gateways to the development of new treatments for depression. *Psychopathology, 47,* 383–393. http://dx.doi.org/10.1159/000366208

Panksepp, J. B., & Huber, R. (2002). Chronic alterations in serotonin function: Dynamic neurochemical properties in agonistic behavior of the crayfish, *Orconectes rusticus. Journal of Neurobiology, 50,* 276–290.

Panksepp, J. B., & Huber, R. (2004). Ethological analyses of crayfish behavior: A new invertebrate system for measuring the rewarding properties of psychostimulants. *Behavioural Brain Research, 153,* 171–180.

Papez, J. (1937). A proposed mechanism of emotion. *Archives of Neurological Psychiatry, 38,* 725–743.

Parent, C. I., & Meaney, M. J. (2008). The influence of natural variations in maternal care on play fighting in the rat. *Developmental Psychobiology, 50,* 767–776.

Paris, J. (2005). Neurobiological dimensional models of personality: A review of the models of Cloninger, Depue, and Siever. *Journal of Personality Disorders, 19,* 156–170.

Passingham, R. E. (1993). *The frontal lobes and voluntary action.* New York, NY: Oxford University Press.

Patrick, C., Curtin, J., & Tellegen, A. (2002). Development and validation of a brief form of the Multidimensional Personality Questionnaire. *Psychological Assessment, 14,* 150–163.

Peabody, D. (1967). Trait inferences: Evaluative and descriptive aspects. *Journal of Personality and Social Psychology, 46,* 639–646.

Pederson, A. K., King, J. E., & Landau, V. I. (2005). Chimpanzee (*Pan troglodytes*) personality predicts behavior. *Journal of Research in Personality, 39,* 534–549.

Peirson, A. R., Heuchert, J. W., Thomala, L., Berk, M., Plein, H., & Cloninger, C. R. (1999). Relationship between serotonin and the Temperament and Character Inventory. *Psychiatry Research, 89,* 29–37.

Pellis, S. M., & Pellis, V. C. (2016). Play fighting in Visayan warty pigs (*Sus cebifrons*): Insights on restraint and reciprocity in the maintenance of play. *Behaviour, 153,* 727–747.

Pennisi, E. (2012). ENCODE project writes eulogy for junk DNA. *Science, 337,* 1159–1161.

Peterson, B., & Panksepp, J. (2004). The biological psychiatry of childhood disorders. In J. Panksepp (Ed.), *Textbook of biological psychiatry* (pp. 393–436). New York, NY: Wiley.

Petkova, V. I., & Ehrsson, H. H. (2008). If I were you: Perceptual illusion of body swapping. *PLoS One, 3,* 1–9.

Phan, K., Wager, T., Taylor, S., & Liberzon, I. (2002). Functional neuroanatomy of emotion: A meta-analysis of emotion activation studies in PET and fMRI. *Neuroimage, 16,* 331–348.

Pickles, A., Sharp, H., Hellier, J., & Hill, J. (2017). Prenatal anxiety, maternal stroking in infancy, and symptoms of emotional and behavioral disorders at 3.5 years. *European Child and Adolescent Psychiatry, 26,* 325–334.

Pigott, H. E., Leventhal, A. M., Alter, G. S., & Boren, J. J. (2010). Efficacy and effectiveness of antidepressants: Current status of research. *Psychotherapy and Psychosomatics, 79,* 267–279.

Plutchik, R., & Conte, H. (1997). *Circumplex models of personality and emotions.* Washington, DC: American Psychological Association.

Plutchik, R., & Kellerman, H. (1980). *Emotion: Theory, research, and experience: Vol. 1. Theories of emotion.* New York, NY: Academic.

Polderman, T. J. C., Benyamin, B., De Leeuw, C. A., Sullivan, P. F., van Bochoven, A., Visscher, P. M., & Posthuma, D. (2015). Meta-analysis of the heritability of human traits based on fifty years of twin studies. *Nature Genetics, 47,* 702–709. http://dx.doi.org/10.1038/ng.3285

Poldrack, R. (2010). Mapping mental function to brain structure: How can cognitive neuroimaging succeed? *Perspectives on Psychological Science, 5,* 753–761.

Preskorn, S., Macaluso, M., Mehra, V., Zammit, G., Moskal, J. R., & Burch, R. M. (2015). Randomized proof of concept trial of GLYX-13, an N-methyl-D-aspartate receptor glycine site partial agonist, in major depressive disorder nonresponsive to a previous antidepressant agent. *Journal of Psychiatric Practice, 21,* 140–149.

Preter, M., & Klein, D. F. (2008). Panic, suffocation false alarms, separation anxiety and endogenous opioids. *Progress in Neuro-psychopharmacology and Biological Psychiatry, 32,* 603–612.

Ravven, H. M. (2013). *The self beyond itself: An alternative history of ethics, the new brain sciences, and the myth of free will.* New York, NY: New Press.

Reale, D., Reader, S. M., Sol, D., McDougall, P. T., & Dingemanse, N. J. (2007). Integrating animal temperament within ecology and evolution. *Biological Review, 82,* 291–318.

Redei, E. E., Andrus, B. M., Kwasny, M. J., Seok, J., Cai, X., Ho, J., & Mohr, D. C. (2014). Blood transcriptomic biomarkers in adult primary care patients with major depressive disorder undergoing cognitive behavioral therapy. *Translational Psychiatry, 4,* 1–7.

Reichard, P. (2002). Osvald T. Avery and the Nobel Prize in Medicine. *Journal of Biological Chemistry, 277,* 13355–13362. http://dx.doi.org/10.1074/jbc.R200002200

Renthal, W., Maze, I., Krishnan, V., Covington, H., Xiao, G., Kumar, A., . . . Nestler, E. (2007). Histone deacetylase 5 epigenetically controls behavioral adaptations to chronic emotional stimuli. *Neuron, 56,* 5517–5529.

Reuter, M., Panksepp, J., Schnabel, N., Kellerhoff, N., Kempel, P., & Hennig, J. (2005). Personality and biological markers of creativity. *European Journal of Personality, 19,* 83–95.

Reuter, M., Weber, B., Fiebach, C. J., Elger, C., & Montag, C. (2009). The biological basis of anger: Associations with the gene coding for DARPP-32 (PPP1R1B) and with amygdala volume. *Behavioural Brain Research, 202,* 179–183.

Riemer, S., Müller, C., Virányi, Z., Huber, L., & Range, F. (2014). The predictive value of early behavioural assessments in pet dogs—A longitudinal study from neonates to adults. *PLoS One, 9,* 1–13.

Robison, A., & Nestler, E. (2011). Transcriptional and epigenetic mechanisms of addiction. *Nature Reviews Neuroscience, 12,* 623–637.

Roccaro-Waldmeyer, D. M., Babalian, A., Müller, A., & Celio, M. R. (2016). Reduction in 50-kHz call-numbers and suppression of tickling-associated positive affective behaviour after lesioning of the lateral hypothalamic parvafox nucleus in rats. *Behavioural Brain Research, 298,* 167–180.

Rush, A. J., Trivedi, M. H., Wisniewski, S. R., Nierenberg, A. A., Stewart, J. W., Warden, D., . . . Fava, M. (2006). Acute and longer-term outcomes in depressed outpatients requiring one or several treatment steps: A STAR*D report. *American Journal of Psychiatry, 163,* 1905–1917.

Russell, J. A. (1991). Culture and the categorization of emotions. *Psychological Bulletin, 110,* 426–450.

Rygula, R., Pluta, H., & Popik, P. (2012). Laughing rats are optimistic. *PLoS One, 7,* e51959.

Sacks, J. J., Sinclair, L., & Gilchrist, J. (2000). Breeds of dogs involved in fatal human attacks in the United States between 1979 and 1998. *Journal of the American Veterinary Medical Association, 217,* 836–840.

Sadato, N., Pascual-Leone, A., Grafman, J., Deiber, M. P., Ibanez, V., & Hallett, M. (1998). Neural networks for braille reading by the blind. *Brain, 121,* 1213–1229.

Saetre, P., Strandberg, E., Sundgren, P., Pettersson, U., Jazin, E., & Bergström, T. F. (2006). The genetic contribution to canine personality. *Genes, Brain and Behavior, 5,* 240–248.

Sapute, A., Wager, T., Cohen-Adad, J., Bianciardi, M., Choi, J., Buhle, J., . . . Barrett, L. (2013). Identification of discrete functional subregions of the human periaqueductal gray. *Proceedings of the National Academy of Sciences of the USA, 110,* 17101–17106.

Saucier, G. (1997). Effects of variable selection on the factor structure of person descriptors. *Journal of Personality and Social Psychology, 73,* 1296–1312.

Saucier, G. (2009). Recurrent personality dimensions in inclusive lexical studies: Indications for a big six structure. *Journal of Personality, 77,* 1577–1614.

Saucier, G., Georgiades, S., Tsaousis, I., & Goldberg, L. R. (2005). The factor structure of Greek personality adjectives. *Journal of Personality and Social Psychology, 88,* 856–875.

Saucier, G., & Goldberg, L. R. (1996). The language of personality: Lexical perspectives on the five-factor model. In J. S. Wiggins (Ed.), *The five-factor model of personality: Theoretical perspectives* (pp. 21–50). New York, NY: Guilford.

Saucier, G., & Goldberg, L. (2003). The structure of personality attributes. In M. R. Barrick & A. M. Ryan (Eds.), *Personality and work: Reconsidering the role of personality in organizations* (pp. 1–29). San Francisco, CA: Jossey-Bass.

Saucier, G., & Goldberg, L. R. (2006). Personnalité, caractère et tempérament: La structure translinguistique des traits (Personality, character and temperament: The cross-language structure of traits). *Psychologie Française, 51,* 265–284.

Saucier, G., & Srivastava, S. (2015). What makes a good structural model of personality? Evaluating the Big Five and alternatives. In M. Mikulincer, P. Shaver, M. L. Cooper, & R. Larsen (Eds.), *APA handbook of personality and social psychology: Vol. 4. Personality processes and individual differences* (pp. 283–305). Washington, DC: American Psychological Association

Savitz, J., van der Merwe, L., & Ramesar, R. (2008a). Dysthymic and anxiety-related personality traits in bipolar spectrum illness. *Journal of Affective Disorders, 109,* 305–311.

Savitz, J., van der Merwe, L., & Ramesar, R. (2008b). Hypomanic, cyclothymic and hostile personality traits in bipolar spectrum illness: A family-based study. *Journal of Psychiatric Research, 42,* 920–929.

Sawaya, H., Johnson, K., Schmidt, M., Arana, A., Chahine, G., Atoui, M., . . . Nahas, Z. (2015). Resting-state functional connectivity of antero-medial prefrontal cortex sub-regions in major depression and relationship to emotional intelligence. *International Journal of Neuropsychopharmacology, 18,* 1–9.

Scarr, S., & McCartney, K. (1983). How people make their own environments: A theory of genotype-environment effects. *Child Development, 54,* 424–435.

Schlaepfer, T. E., Bewernick, B. H., Kayser, S., Madler, B., & Coenen, V. A. (2013). Rapid effects of deep brain stimulation for treatment-resistant major depression. *Biological Psychiatry, 73,* 1204–1212.

Schlaepfer, T. E., Cohen, M. X., Frick, C., Kosel, M., Brodesser, D., Axmacher, N., . . . Sturm, V. (2008). Deep brain stimulation to reward circuitry alleviates anhedonia in refractory major depression. *Neuropsychopharmacology, 33,* 368–377.

Scott, E., & Panksepp, J. (2003). Rough-and-tumble play in human children. *Aggressive Behaviour, 29,* 539–551.

Scott, J. P. (1958). *Aggression.* Chicago, IL: University of Chicago Press.

Scott, J. P. (1962). Critical periods in behavioral development. *Science, 138,* 949–958.

Scott, J. P. (1972). *Animal behavior* (2nd ed., rev.). Chicago: University of Chicago Press.

Scott, J. P. (1974). Effects of psychotropic drugs on separation distress in dogs. *Excerpta Medica International Congress Series, 359,* 735–745.

Scott, J. P., & Bielfelt, S. W. (1976). Analysis of the puppy testing program. In C. J. Pfaffenberger, J. P. Scott, J. L. Fuller, B. E. Ginsburg, & S. W. Bielfelt (Eds.), *Guide dogs for the blind: Their selection, development and training* (pp. 39–76). New York, NY: Elsevier.

Scott, J. P., Fredericson, E., & Fuller, J. L. (1951). Experimental exploration of the critical period hypothesis. *Personality, 1,* 162–183.

Scott, J. P., & Fuller, J. L. (1965). *Genetics and the social behavior of the dog.* Chicago, IL: University of Chicago Press.

Serpell, J. (1995). *The domestic dog: Its evolution, behaviour, and interactions with people.* Cambridge, UK: Cambridge University Press.

Servaas, M., van der Velde, J., Costafreda, S., Horton, P., Ormel, J., Riese, H., & Aleman, A. (2013). Neuroticism and the brain: A quantitative meta-analysis of the neuroimaging studies investigating emotion processing. *Neuroscience and Biobehavioral Reviews, 37,* 1518–1529.

Sesardic, N. (2005). *Making sense of heritability.* New York, NY: Cambridge University Press.

Shapiro, F. J. (1989). Efficacy of the eye movement desensitization procedure in the treatment of traumatic memories. *Journal of Traumatic Stress, 2,* 199–223.

Sharp, H., Pickles, A., Meaney, M., Marshall, K., Tibu, F., Hill, J. (2012). Frequency of infant stroking reported by mothers moderates the effect of prenatal depression on infant behavioural and physiological outcomes. *PLoS ONE* 7, 1-10.

Shedler, J. (2010). The efficacy of psychodynamic psychotherapy. *American Psychologist, 65,* 98–109.

Shrivastava, A., & Desousa, A. (2016). Resilience: A psychobiological construct for psychiatric disorders. *Indian Journal of Psychiatry, 58,* 38–43. http://dx.doi.org/10.4103/0019-5545.174365

Siegel, A. (2004). *Neurobiology of aggression and rage.* Boca Raton, FL: CRC.

Siegel, A., Roeling, T., Gregg, T., & Kruk, M. (1999). Neuropharmacology of brain-stimulation-evoked aggression. *Neuroscience & Biobehavioral Reviews,* 23, 359-389.

Sinn, D. L., Gosling, S. D., & Hilliard, S. (2010). Personality and performance in military working dogs: Reliability and predictive validity of behavioral tests. *Applied Animal Behaviour Science, 127,* 51–65.

Sinyor, M., Schaffer, A., & Levitt, A. (2010). The Sequenced Treatment Alternatives to Relieve Depression (STAR*D) trial: A review. *Canadian Journal of Psychiatry / Revue canadienne de psychiatrie, 55,* 126–135.

Siviy, S., & Panksepp, J. (1985). Dorsomedial diencephalic involvement in the juvenile play of rats. *Behavioral Neuroscience, 99,* 1103–1113.

Siviy, S., & Panksepp, J. (1987). Sensory modulation of juvenile play. *Developmental Psychobiology, 20,* 39–55.

Siviy, S., & Panksepp, J. (2011). In search of the neurobiological substrates for social playfulness in mammalian brains. *Neuroscience and Biobehavioral Reviews, 35,* 1821–1830.

Skinner, M. K. (2015). Environmental epigenetics and a unified theory of the molecular aspects of evolution: A neo-Lamarckian concept that facilitates neo-Darwinian evolution. *Genome Biology and Evolution, 7,* 1296–1302. http://dx.doi.org/10.1093/gbe/evv073

Skinner, M. K. (2016). Epigenetic transgenerational inheritance. *Nature Reviews Endocrinology, 12,* 68–70. http://dx.doi.org/10.1038/nrendo.2015.206

Slabbert, J. M., & Odendaal, J. S. J. (1999). Early prediction of adult police dog efficiency—A longitudinal study. *Applied Animal Behaviour Science, 64,* 269–288.

Smith, C., & Squire, L. R. (2005). Declarative memory, awareness, and transitive inference. *Journal of Neuroscience, 25,* 10138–10146.

Smith, G. M. (1967). Usefulness of peer ratings of personality in educational research. *Educational and Psychological Measurement, 27,* 967–984.

Smith, J. (2017). *Psychotherapy: A practical guide.* Cham, Switzerland: Springer.

Smith, S. (2016). Linking cognition to brain connectivity. *Nature Neuroscience, 19,* 7–9. http://dx.doi.org/10.1038/nn.4206

Snyder, L. (2011). *The philosophical breakfast club: Four remarkable friends who transformed science and changed the world.* New York, NY: Random House.

Solms, M. (Forthcoming). *The complete neuroscientific works of Sigmund Freud* (4 vols.). London: Karnac and Institute of Psychoanalysis.

Solms, M., & Panksepp, J. (2012). The "id" knows more than the "ego" admits: Neuropsychoanalytic and primal consciousness perspectives on the interface between affective and cognitive neuroscience. *Brain Science, 2,* 147–175.

Spearman, C. (1904). "General intelligence" objectively determined and measured. *American Journal of Psychology, 15,* 201–293.

Spielberger, C. D. (1975). The measurement of state and trait anxiety: Conceptual and methodological issues. In L. Levi (Ed.), *Emotions: Their parameters and measurement* (pp. 713–725). New York, NY: Raven.

Spielberger, C. D. (1983). *Manual for the State-Trait Anxiety Inventory* (Form Y). Palo Alto, CA: Consulting Psychologists.

Squire, L. R., & Zola-Morgan, S. (1991). The medial temporal lobe memory system. *Science, 253,* 1380–1386.

Starkstein, S. E., Jorge, R. E., & Robinson, R. G. (2010). The frequency, clinical correlates, and mechanism of anosognosia after stroke. *Canadian Journal of Psychiatry / Revue canadienne de psychiatrie, 55,* 355–361.

Steiner, A. P., & Redish, A. D. (2014). Behavioral and neurophysiological correlates of regret in rat decision-making on a neuroeconomic task. *Nature Neuroscience, 17,* 995–1002.

Sullivan, H. S. (1948). The problem of anxiety in psychiatry and in life. *Psychiatry: Journal for the Study of Interpersonal Processes, 11,* 1–13.

Sullivan, H. S. (1953). *The interpersonal theory of psychiatry.* New York, NY: Norton.

Sullivan, H. S. (1964). *The fusion of psychiatry and social science.* New York, NY: Norton.

Suomi, S. J. (1997). Early determinants of behaviour: Evidence from primate studies. *British Medical Bulletin, 53,* 170–184.

Suomi, S. J. (2006). Risk, resilience, and gene × environment interactions in rhesus monkeys. *Annals of the New York Academy of Sciences, 1094,* 52–62.

Sur, M., & Rubenstein, J. (2005). Patterning and plasticity of the cerebral cortex. *Science, 310,* 805–810. http://dx.doi.org/10.1126/science.1112070

Svartberg, K., & Forkman, B. (2002). Personality traits in the domestic dog (*Canis familiaris*). *Applied Animal Behaviour Science, 79,* 133–155.

Svobodová, I., Vápeník, P., Pinc, L., & Bartoš, L. (2008). Testing German shepherd puppies to assess their chances of certification. *Applied Animal Behaviour Science, 113,* 139–149.

Szirmak, Z., & De Raad, B. (1994). Taxonomy and structure of Hungarian personality traits. *European Journal of Personality, 8,* 95–118.

Takahashi, H., Yahata, N., Koeda, M., Matsuda, T., Asai, K., & Okubo, Y. (2004). Brain activation associated with evaluative processes of guilt and embarrassment: An fMRI study. *NeuroImage, 23,* 967–974.

Teitelbaum, P., & Epstein, A. (1962). The lateral hypothalamic syndrome: Recovery of feeding and drinking after lateral hypothalamic lesions. *Psychological Review, 69,* 74–90.

Tellegen, A. (1982). *Brief manual for the Differential Personality Questionnaire.* Unpublished manuscript, University of Minnesota, Minneapolis, MN.

Tellegen, A., Lykken, D. T., Bouchard, T. J., Jr., Wilcox, K. J., Segal, N. L., & Rich, S. (1988). Personality similarity in twins reared apart and together. *Journal of Personality and Social Psychology, 54,* 1031–1039.

Tellegen, A., & Waller, N. G. (1987). Re-examining basic dimensions of natural language trait descriptors. Paper presented at the 95th annual convention of the American Psychological Association.

Tenore, P. L. (2008). Psychotherapeutic benefits of opioid agonist therapy. *Journal of Addictive Diseases, 27,* 49–65.

Thalmann, O., Shapiro, B., Cui, P., Schuenemann, J., Sawyer, S. K., Greenfield, D. L., . . . Wayne, R. K. (2013). Complete mitochondrial genomes of ancient canids suggest a European origin of domestic dogs. *Science, 342,* 871–874.

Thernstrom, M. (2016, October 19). The anti-helicopter parent's plea: Let kids play! *New York Times Magazine.* Retrieved August 14, 2017, from https://www.nytimes.com/2016/10/23/magazine/the-anti-helicopter-parents-plea-let-kids-play.html

Thomaes, K., Dorrepaal, E., Draijer, N. P. J., de Ruiter, M. B., Elzinga, B. M., van Balkom, A. . . . Veltman, D. J. (2009). Increased activation of the left hippocampus region in complex PTSD during encoding and recognition of emotional words: A pilot study. *Psychiatry Research: Neuroimaging, 171,* 44–53.

Thurstone, L. L. (1947). *Multiple-factor analysis: A development and expansion of the vectors of mind.* Chicago, IL: University of Chicago Press.

Tonoue, T., Ashida, Y., Makino, H., & Hata, H. (1986). Inhibition of shock-elicited ultrasonic vocalization by opioid peptides in the rat: A psychotropic effect. *Psychoneuroendocrinology, 11,* 177–184.

Topal, J., Miklosi, A., Csanyi, V., & Doka, A. (1998). Attachment behavior in dogs (*Canis familiaris*): A new application of Ainsworth's (1969) Strange Situation Test. *Journal of Comparative Psychology, 112,* 219–229.

Toronchuk, J. A., & Ellis, G. F. R. (2007). Disgust: Sensory affect or primary emotional system? *Cognition and Emotion, 21,* 1799–1818.

Tracy, J. L., & Randles, D. (2011). Four models of basic emotions: A review of Ekman and Cordaro, Izard, Levenson, and Panksepp and Watt. *Emotion Review, 3,* 397–405.

Trut, L., Oskina, I., & Kharlamova, A. (2009). Animal evolution during domestication: The domesticated fox as a model. *BioEssays, 31,* 349–360.

Tupes, E., & Christal, R. (1961). An air force technical report.

Tupes, E., & Christal, R. (1992). Recurrent personality factors based on trait ratings. *Journal of Personality, 60,* 225–251.

Turecki, G., & Meaney, M. (2016). Effects of the social environment and stress on glucocorticoid receptor gene methylation: A systematic review. *Biological Psychiatry, 79,* 87–96.

Turkheimer, E. (2000). Three laws of behavior genetics and what they mean. *Current Directions of Psychological Science, 9,* 160–164.

Turnbull, O. H., Evans, C. E., & Owen, V. (2005). Negative emotions and anosognosia. *Cortex, 41,* 67–75.

Urban, K., & Gao, W.-J. (2013). Methylphenidate and the juvenile brain: Enhancement of attention at the expense of cortical plasticity? *Medical Hypotheses, 81,* 1–15.

U.S. Department of Health and Human Services. (2014, November). *Results from the 2013 National Survey on Drug Use and Health: Mental health findings.* Substance Abuse and Mental Health Services Administration, Center for Behavioral Health Statistics and Quality. Retrieved August 14, 2017, from https://www.samhsa.gov/data/sites/default/files/NSDUHmhfr2013/NSDUHmhfr2013.pdf

Uylings, H. B., & van Eden, C. G. (1990). Qualitative and quantitative comparison of the prefrontal cortex in rat and in primates, including humans. *Progress in Brain Research, 85,* 31–62.

van der Westhuizen, D., & Solms, M. (2015). Basic emotional foundations of social dominance in relation to Panksepp's affective taxonomy. *Neuropsychoanalysis, 17,* 19–37.

Vianna, D. M., Landeira-Fernandez, J., & Brandão, M. L. (2001). Dorsolateral and ventral regions of the periaqueductal gray matter are involved in distinct types of fear. *Neuroscience and Biobehavioral Reviews, 25,* 711–719.

von Melchner, L., Pallas, S. L., & Sur, M. (2000). Visual behaviour mediated by retinal projections directed to the auditory pathway. *Nature, 404,* 871–876.

Vukasović, T., & Bratko, D. (2015). Heritability of personality: A meta-analysis of behavior genetic studies. *Psychological Bulletin, 141,* 769–785.

Walker, T. D. (2015, October 1). The Joyful, Illiterate Kindergartners of Finland.

Atlantic Monthly. Retrieved August 14, 2017, from https://www.theatlantic
.com/education/archive/2015/10/the-joyful-illiterate-kindergartners-of-finland
/408325/.

Waller, N., Kojetin, B., Bouchard, T., Lykken, D., & Tellegen, A. (1990). Genetic
and environmental influences on religious interests, attitudes and values: A
study of twins reared apart and together. *Psychological Science, 1,* 138–142.

Wang, D. Y., Kumar S., & Hedges, S. B. (1999). Divergence time estimates for
the early history of animal phyla and the origin of plants animals and fungi.
Proceedings of Biological Science, 266, 163–171.

Ward, A. J. W., Thomas, P., Hart, P. J. B., & Krause, J. (2004). Correlates of boldness in three-spined sticklebacks (*Gasterosteus aculeatus*). *Behavioral Ecology and Sociobiology, 155,* 561–568.

Warren, E. W., & Callaghan, S. (1975). Individual differences in response to an
open field test by the guppy—*Poecilla reticulata* (Peters). *Journal of Fish
Biology, 7,* 105–113.

Warren, E. W., & Callaghan, S. (1976). The response of male guppies (*Poecilla
reticulata,* Peters) to repeated exposure to an open field. *Behavioral Biology,
18,* 499–513.

Watson, D., & Tellegen, A. (1985). Toward a consensual structure of mood. *Psychological Bulletin, 98,* 219–235.

Watson, J. D., & Crick, F. C. (1953). Molecular structure of nucleic acids: A structure for deoxyribose nucleic acids. *Nature, 171,* 737–738.

Wauquier, A., & Rolls, E. R. (Eds.). (1976). *Brain-stimulation reward.* Amsterdam: North-Holland.

Weaver, I. C. G. (2014). Integrating early life experience, gene expression, brain
development, and emergent phenotypes: Unraveling the thread of nature via
nurture. *Advances in Genetics, 86,* 277–307.

Weaver, I. C. G., Cervoni, N., Champagne, F. A., D'Alessio, A. C., Sharma, S.,
Seckl, J. R., . . . Meaney, M. J. (2004). Epigenetic programming by maternal
behavior. *Nature Neuroscience, 7,* 847–854.

Weaver, I. C., Hellstrom, I. C., Brown, S., Andrews, S., Dymov, S., Diorio, J., . . .
Meaney, M. (2014). The methylated-DNA binding protein MBD2 enhances
NGFI-A (egr-1)-mediated transcriptional activation of the glucocorticoid
receptor. *Philosophical Transactions of the Royal Society of London, Series B,
Biological Sciences, 369,* 1–11.

Weaver, I. C. G., Meaney, M. J., & Szyf, M. (2006). Maternal care effects on the
hippocampal transcriptome and anxiety-mediated behaviors in the offspring
that are reversible in adulthood. *Proceedings of the National Academy of Sciences of the USA, 103,* 3480–3485.

Weeks, R., Horwitz, B., Aziz-Sultan, A., Tian, B., Wessinger, C. M., Cohen, L.
G., . . . Rauschecker, J. P. (2000). A positron emission tomographic study of
auditory localization in the congenitally blind. *Journal of Neuroscience, 20,*
2664–2672.

Weil, A. (1981). The therapeutic value of coca in contemporary medicine. *Journal of Ethnopharmacology, 3,* 367–376.

Weiss, A., Inoue-Murayama, M., Hong, K.-W., Inoue, E., Udono, S., Ochiai,
T., . . . King, J. E. (2009). Assessing chimpanzee personality and subjective
well-being in Japan. *American Journal of Primatology, 71,* 283–292.

Weiss, A., King, J. E., & Figueredo, A. J. (2000). The heritability of personality
factors in chimpanzees (*Pan troglodytes*). *Behavior Genetics, 30,* 213–221.

Weiss, A., King, J. E., & Hopkins, W. D. (2007). A cross-setting study of chimpanzee (*Pan troglodytes*) personality structure and development: Zoological

parks and Yerkes National Primate Research Center. *American Journal of Primatology, 69,* 1264–1277.

Weiss, A., King, J. E., & Perkins, L. (2006). Personality and subjective well-being in orangutans (*Pongo pygmaeus* and *Pongo abelii*). *Journal of Personality and Social Psychology, 90,* 501–511.

Weissman, J., Naidu, S., & Bjornsson, H. T. (2014). Abnormalities of the DNA methylation mark and its machinery: An emerging cause of neurologic dysfunction. *Seminars in Neurology, 34,* 249–257.

Whitaker, R. (2010). *Anatomy of an epidemic.* New York, NY: Crown.

Widiger, T. A., Costa, P. T., Jr., & McCrae, R. R. (2013). Diagnosis of personality disorder using the five-factor model and the proposed *DSM-V*. In T. A. Widiger & P. T Costa Jr. (Eds.), *Personality disorders and the five-factor model of personality* (3rd ed., pp. 285–310). Washington, DC: American Psychological Association.

Wigger, A., Loerscher, P., Weissenbacher, P., Holsboer, F., & Landgraf, R. (2001). Cross-fostering and cross-breeding of HAB and LAB rats: A genetic rat model of anxiety. *Behavior Genetics, 31,* 371–382.

Will, C. C., Aird, F., & Redei, E. E. (2003). Selectively bred Wistar-Kyoto rats: an animal model of depression and hyper-responsiveness to antidepressants. *Molecular Psychiatry, 8,* 925–932.

Wilsson, E., & Sundgren, P. (1998). Behaviour test for eight-week old puppies— Heritabilities of tested behaviour traits and its correspondence to later behaviour. *Applied Animal Behaviour Science, 58,* 151–162.

Wohr, M., & Schwarting, R. K. (2007). Ultrasonic communication in rats: Can playback of 50-kHz calls induce approach behavior? *PLoS One, 2,* 1–12.

Wong, M. Y. L., Munday, P. L., Buston, P. M., & Jones, G. P. (2008). Monogamy when there is potential for polygyny: Tests of multiple hypotheses in a group-living fish. *Behavioral Ecology, 19,* 353–361.

Wright, J. S., & Panksepp, J. (2009). An evolutionary framework to understand foraging, wanting, and desire: The neuropsychology of the SEEKING System. *Neuropsychoanalysis, 14,* 5–39.

Yerkes, R. M. (1925). *Almost human.* New York, NY: Century.

Yovell, Y., Bar, G., Mashiah, M., Baruch, Y., Briskman, I., Asherov, J., . . . Panksepp, J. (2016). Ultra-low-dose buprenorphine as a time-limited treatment for severe suicidal ideation: A randomized controlled trial. *American Journal of Psychiatry, 173,* 491–498.

Zuckerman, M., & Cloninger, C. R. (1996). Relationships between Cloninger's, Zuckerman's, and Eysenck's dimensions of personality. *Personality and Individual Differences, 21,* 283–285.

Notes

1. We use the terms *BrainMind* and *MindBrain* interchangeably, depending on the intended emphasis. They are capitalized without a space to convey a monistic view of the brain (based on Spinoza's dual-aspect monism) as a unified experience-generating organ, in contrast to the mind-body dualism associated with René Descartes that has traditionally hindered scientific thinking. We also sometimes use *brain-mind*.
2. Some scholars believe that many of the patients that Kraepelin diagnosed actually had developed brain damage as a result of the flu pandemic; although the pandemic killed many individuals, many survivors had a permanent form of dementia, which was eventually named postencephalitic lethargica.
3. Modern genetic theory had not yet been established, and like Darwin, McDougall still accepted the Lamarckian theory of biological evolution. Lamarckian transmission held that needed characteristics acquired by individuals through effort and practice could be passed on to their offspring. For example, giraffes acquired long necks by continually stretching to reach leaves high in the trees. The kernel of truth in this statement is currently being cashed out in the newly emergent (and powerful) field of epigenetics (see Chapter 15).
4. Colin DeYoung did not report an honesty-humility aspect when he subdivided Conscientiousness, in contrast to Michael Ashton's factor analytic work reviewed in Chapter 8. Such differences continue to highlight the difficulties of identifying personality universals when working from a factor-analytic top-down perspective.
5. Indeed, Scott was instrumental in attracting Jaak Panksepp to BGSU in the hope of adding a neurobiological dimension to the ongoing research, and Ken Davis was one of Scott's graduate students who eventually finished his dissertation with Panksepp after Scott retired in 1980. Panksepp was hired in part to eventually take over the canine research lab, to integrate the dog work with cross-species emotional perspectives. As fate would have it, the National Institutes of Health had internally decided to cease funding the lab upon Scott's retirement, and Panksepp's many attempts to obtain funding for social-brain-behavioral studies in dogs and other animals at BGSU never succeeded. The resistance was also due partly to the fact that Panksepp's research aimed to understand human emotional feelings by studying evolutionarily homologous processes in animal models, as a model for primal human emotional feelings—science politics in the United States, because of

behavioristic "never-mind" traditions, has often been biased against the study of emotions in animals.

6. In 2011, IBM's Watson computer developed by by an IBM research team led by principal investigator David Ferrucci competed on the television game show *Jeopardy* winning the first place prize of $1 million.

7. Although the original target for this Walt Kelly humor was human pollution, it seems applicable to the human condition in general and the surprising conditions we often create for ourselves.

8. In this quote Cloninger cited Comings et al. (2000) and Gillespie, Cloninger, Heath, and Martin (2003); in the next one he cites Cloniger (2004) and Gillespie et al. (2003).

9. The study was initially begun at Northeast Ohio Medical University at Akron before being interrupted by powerful anti-opioid interests fearing the potential of buprenorphine abuse. Fortunately, new backers of the study were obtained in Israel where the work was finally completed.

Index

In this index, *f* denotes figure, *t* denotes table, and *n* denotes note.

NBH. *See* Nested BrainMind Hierarchy (NBH)

negative emotions, compounding effects of, 181–82

Negative Valence, 188, 189

neocortex
about, 143, 238, 245
personality and damage to, 249
regulation between subcortical brain structures and, 227–28, 231, 254
See also anterior cingulate gyrus (ACC); orbitofrontal cortex (OFC); premotor cortex; top-down approaches to personality

NEO-PI. *See* Neuroticism Extraversion Openness Personality Inventory (NEO- PI)

Nested BrainMind Hierarchy (NBH), 76–78, 77*f*, 83–84, 167, 269–74
See also primary emotions; secondary emotions; tertiary emotions

neuromodulators. *See* dopamine; norepinephrine; serotonin

neuroplasticity, 80–81, 237–38

Neuroticism, 87, 96, 194–95
See also FEAR/Anxiety

neuroticism, 71, 234–36

Neuroticism Extraversion Openness Personality Inventory (NEO-PI), 69–70, 162, 176, 235

Nirenberg, Marshall, 215

nominal fallacy, 63–64

norepinephrine, 200, 254

Norman, Warren, 162, 175, 176

Normansell, Larry, 30

Northoff, Georg, 251

Novelty Seeking, 199–201, 206
See also SEEKING/Enthusiasm

nurturance. *See* CARE/Nurturance

Odbert, Henry, 161, 174, 186–88, 191

OFC. *See* orbitofrontal cortex (OFC)

Olds, James, 102–3, 278

Openness/Intellect, 87, 96

Openness to Experience, 31, 92

opioid blockers, 108, 113, 125

opioids, 113, 134, 253, 261–62, 278, 316*n*9
See also brain opioids

optimistic, 62, 64, 120

orangutan behavior and temperament, 41, 43, 45, 93

orbitofrontal cortex (OFC), 230, 237, 239

On the Origin of Species (Darwin), 37

oxytocin genes, 222

PAG. *See* periaqueductal gray (PAG)

Palmer, R., 119

panic attacks, 181–82

PANIC/Sadness
about, 17, 19, 20, 22, 144
in animals, 41, 107, 134–36
autism and, 278
BAS versus BIS, 198
bipolar disorder categorization and, 258–59
Darwin on, 43–44
insecure attachment and, 119
McDougall versus Panksepp on, 60
suicidal ideation and, 254
See also depression; predator simulations; suicidal ideation